2020

What the Future Holds

Vernon Coleman

Boring Bit For Lawyers

These days, most books include disclaimers in which the authors apologetically warn readers that they should not rely on any information their books contain, and nor should they follow any of the advice they may find within. The predictions in the second part of this book are merely opinions which were originally intended for my own personal use and which are now aired in public purely as entertainment. I certainly do not recommend that any reader makes any decisions of any kind based on any of the absurd ramblings in this book.

Disclaimers invariably go on to insist that readers who rely on anything in the book they are reading do so at their own risk. These warnings are included because the world is now full of lawyers and litigants who, under the often misguided impression that there might be money to be made, will leap at every opportunity to gouge lolly out of anyone who can be blamed for fate's little tricks. And so, as author and publisher, I feel that I must follow fashion and warn readers that if they act on any of the facts in this book, or decide to follow any of the advice, they do so entirely at their own risk. I advise readers to treat facts with disdain. I recommend that advice and opinions should be disregarded or treated with great suspicion. Any reader who believes the facts in this book, or follows advice the book contains, does so entirely at their own risk. Moreover, I would also like to make it clear that books can be dangerous objects and should not be dropped, thrown or otherwise projected into areas where people or delicate objects might be damaged. In other words, dear reader, drop this book onto your toes and you're on your own.

To Donna Antoinette,

You hold the other end of my dreams.

Always on my mind. Always in my heart.

Note

When it was originally published in 2010 this book was intended to be a look into the future. It was called 2020 and subtitled `Tomorrow's Secrets: Social, Political and Financial Forecasts for the Coming Decade'.

Naturally, I filled the book with a series of predictions.

In 2019, nine years after publication, and with a year to go, I picked up a copy of the book to see how well I had done.

I was relieved to see that a number of the forecasts have come true, in part or in whole, and many of the rest are on the way to coming true.

It seemed to me that in view of this the book still had value. You can see for yourself just how many of the remaining predictions are likely to come true in the next year or two. And by looking back at what was happening in 2010 you can see how our present world was formed and how our future years are likely to be shaped.

.

Contents List

Part One: The World In Which We Live

The UK is broken in every conceivable way. Thirteen year sof Labour misrule have been more than unlucky for Britain. The UK is now officially the most statist, centralist country in Europe. The nation where modern democracy was born has become just one small part of a fascist regime. Freedom, independence and rights that took centuries to acquire, and which involved the shedding of much blood, have been given away within little more than a decade by people acting without authority or permission. There has, curiously, been little more than a few peeps of protest. The governments of Blair and Brown have destroyed the moral, fabric and economy of the country. They have paid to give away our independence to a fascist Eurostate and they have created a divided, unhappily multicultural state of bullies, scroungers and greedy bastards. (I'd really like to know who voted for Labour in the 2010 elections. Having proved themselves incapable of thought or sense or they should be barred from voting ever again.) Browns egregious incompetence will result in genuine pain and distress for millions of good, hard working people who have done nothing wrong: screwed by the bankers at the top and the scroungers at bottom. A third of the country works for the government, a third works hard and a third consists of scroungers and chisellers on benefits. The system is now designed to reward the first group and the third group and to punish the middle group. (People receiving benefits may receive a refund of their expenses if they have to go to hospital. On other hand, people working for a living, who may end up with less money in their pockets than the folk on benefits, have to pay their own travel costs. The words `absurd' and `unfair' are irresistible.)

Anyone who says that the UK is not stuffed should know that England is currently knocking down 400,000 perfectly good houses in the north of England because the Government decided that to do so would increase the value of the remaining stock while councils pay for pole dancing classes for children but tell old people that there is no money for meals on wheels. In the years since Labour came into power in 1997, the number of hospitals and clinics in Britain has fallen by 580. We have 2,380 fewer schools than we had when Blair entered Downing Street in triumph. We have 7,500 fewer post offices, 196 fewer libraries, 150 fewer swimming pools, 1,310 fewer public lavatories. Blair and Brown have, however, given us some extra facilities. There are 1,270 more bookmakers than there were in 1997 and 1,060 more supermarkets. There are also 276 more lapdancing clubs. And they have, of course, given us more administrators and managers. In 1997 the NHS each hospital manager had 12 hospital beds to look after. Now there is one hospital manager for every four hospital beds. And the bureaucrats are better paid. In 1997 there were just 3,300 council workers earning more than £50,000 a year. By 2010 there were 38,000 council workers taking home in excess of £50,000 a year.

We have a society in which banks lend money to people who cannot afford to pay it back (and whom the banks knew would never be able to afford to pay it back) and, as a result, the banks then go bust and then start taking houses off people who are struggling to pay and then the banks are lumbered with vast amounts of real estate that no one can buy because the banks won't lend any money and so the houses stays empty and the people sleep in the street. We have a society which positively encouraged greed and risk taking. In the 1970s and 1980s finance companies (banks and hedge funds) grew much faster than the economy. In the 1980s, finance companies earned around 15% of all American profits. But by 2005, they were earning over 25% of every dollar earned in the country. People who were hired to manage money were skimming 25% off the top!. It is hardly surprising that by the middle of the first decade of the 21st century every young graduate wanted to go into the hedge fund industry. No one wanted to make things any more. Less than 5% of Harvard graduates in America entered the world of finance in the 1960s. By the 2000s over 20% of Harvard graduates were going into the Shylocking business. Things were the same in Britain. Throughout the 1990s and onwards hedge funds grew much faster than the economy. In 2006 a survey of 300 hedge fund professionals found that, on average, they each spent £260,000 on jewellery and £190,000 on watches. Each year.

We live in a world in which our money is wasted in a thousand ways every day. I see in a Welsh newspaper that a glass reinforced plastic hump at one railway station cost £70,000 to install. I would have called the OFT if a builder had wanted more than £2000 to build it but the people who had paid the £70,000 said that it would normally have cost at least £250,000 to build a small glass-reinforced plastic hump on a railway station platform. Inevitably, an application has been made for EU funding so that more humps can be built at the bargain price of £70,000. If I can found out who to contact I shall be attempting to bid for the contract to build the humps.

We live in a world in which politicians display extraordinary levels of self interest and greed, in which morally inverted bent ex ministers sell ministerial access without a blush. Our political representatives seem, almost to a man and woman, unaware that intentions are the basis of all morality.

We live in a world in which nearly 90% of girls aged 13-17 have been in at least one intimate relationship (your chances of finding a 13 year old virgin in Britain today are slim). One in three teenage girls in Britain has suffered sexual abuse from a boyfriend and one in four has experienced violence in a relationship. We live in a world where most children are bastards; literally and possibly figuratively.We live in a world in which every year people vote for, demand and expect more and more benefits and because the number of people receiving benefits is so high politicians can rely on winning office by continuing to hand out benefits. (This is one of the recurring, vicious circle wickednesses of the party political system.) We live in a world in which appeasement encourages aggression and abasement encourages oppression. We live in a world in which teachers tell schoolchildren to do all their research on the internet (which is known to be so unreliable that even experts find it nigh on impossible to do worthwhile research using websites), in which dieticians and nutritionists advise patients to eat meat (which is known to be the main cause of cancer in our society) and in which doctors and nurses recommend vaccination to the parents of small children (even though the evidence suggests that vaccination is neither safe nor effective and may well be a major cause of brain damage). We live in a world where if you have problems with a government department or utility, and you need to ring to complain, you will end up paying extra for your call because you'll have to ring a premium rate telephone number!

We live in a world in which few, if any, of our politicians are the people they wanted to be. We live in a world in which the system, the establishment, guarantees and supports the corrupt. This is true now of all parts of the establishment; the political establishment, the bureaucratic establishment, the medical establishment. They all serve the monster, the State, and damn the collateral damage. (Just think of doctors vaccinating healthy children, whole communities of them, for the sake of the State and ignoring the thousands who, as a result of their actions, are brain damaged. That's collateral damage.)

We live in a world where governments betray each coming generation by pandering to the whims and fancies of today's voters and government dependants. Not since 1979 has the winning political party been supported by more than a third of the total electorate. Even when Blair won in 1997, and had a massive majority in the House of Commons, he went into Downing Street with only a third of the electorate having voted for him. It wasn't always thus but today's parliaments do not represent the people in any way. Political parties can, as I first pointed out some years ago, obtain power simply by relying on government dependants - public sector workers and people living on benefits. It is perfectly possible for a political party to gain power without obtaining a single vote from a taxpayer.

The politicians protect the present and the past against disasters (even and especially of their own making) with bailouts and subsidies. Normal healthy capitalism works by a system of creative destruction. Old, out of date institutions and industries are destroyed by new ones. A badly run company fails and goes bust but its buildings are bought by a new company which is growing and which will hire many of the redundant employees of the failed company. It is the corporate equivalent of Darwin's theory of the survival of the fittest. But Governments today work hard to prevent this natural and healthy process occurring and in order to do so they take over increasing amounts of society until (like the USSR) they implode and everything starts again.

We live in a world which no longer punishes the guilty and therefore no longer discourages their behaviour. Hugely overpaid bankers are bailed out and given vast bonuses and new jobs when they destroy financial institutions. Footballers who are violent on or off the pitch are slapped on the wrist. And teenager hoodlums who cause havoc and threaten and maim are given free CDs and sent on skiing holidays.

We live in a world where the poor get poorer and the rich get richer; the gap between rich and poor has widened throughout Labour's time in government. During the last 13 years the rich got richer, faster than ever, and the poor got poorer, faster than ever. So much for Brown, Blair et al. By introducing student loans the labour party deliberately made it more difficult for children from poorer families to study professions such as medicine which require a long training period and therefore result in accumulation of soul destroying debts.

We live in a world we can't understand anything and we cannot change anything; all we can do is try to predict what they will do next, how it will affect us and how best we can protect ourselves and those close to us. We live in a world where we are denied the truth about wars, global warming, oil supplies, terrorism and everything else of importance. We live in a world in which the principle of putting individual freedom above all else (including collectivist slavery) has long been forgotten. We live in a world where is now pretty well illegal to protest against war (unless you do it very carefully, quietly and politely and preferably alone in your own home) but if you protest against peace no one is likely to bother you very much. We live in a world where war criminals are feted and applauded and regarded as statesmen. We live in a world where public libraries, founded to provide education for all, have more space devoted to DVDs (which can be rented out) than to books (which have to be made available without charge). We live in a world in which the government would undoubtedly suppress books if they weren't aware that doing so would reek a little too much of Nazi Germany.

We live in a world where we sow and they reap. We live in a world where no one cares about anything anymore; where employees hide behind their rules and regulations and where the sensitive are broken by frustration, rage, disappointment and righteous anger. We live in a world where the zombies have taken over and where there is no future; only survival. We live in a world where service and manufacturing values shrink every year. We live in a world where we are constantly under threat from civil servants with too much authority, too much power, and far too little sense of responsibility and no sense of duty.

It as though we have been invaded and occupied by aliens with completely different moral standards and survive because the mass of people have been turned into zombies by crap on television. We live in a corrupt and decadent society where hard working young people in their 30s still can't afford their own home and so are forced to leech off their parents and where millions have pension funds that will give them an income of no more than £1,000 a year when they retire. We live in a world where we denied the truth about wars, global warming, oil supplies, terrorism and everything else of importance.

We live in a world where anger and resentment burn holes in those who still have souls. We live in a world where we all depend on one another more than ever but in which we are encouraged (even forced) to be ever more selfish.

We live in a corrupt and decadent society where young people in their 30s cannot afford their own home and can't afford to save for a pension. We live in a world where the average private pension fund is enough to provide less than £1,000 a year in pension. We live in a world of endless lies and deceit. We live in a world where no one tells the people the truth about wars, global warming, oil supplies or terrorism. We are constantly threatened, made fearful and terrorised by new and often imaginary beasts. We live in a country which has the worst trains, roads, health service, schools in world. And where everything is getting worse. We live in a world full of comfortable homes for drunks, and drug addicts and released prisoners. We live in a world where whole towns are populated almost exclusively by the workshy and the lazy, fakers who parlay a bunion or a bit of backache into a lifetime of satellite television. It is organised, nationalised scrounging. We live in a world where pit bulls pull along tattooed hoodies and where the elderly dare not leave their homes.

We live in a world which is divided into three unequal parts: the scroungers (ones on the sick and the dole)
the bureaucrats (the public sector workers) and the disenfranchised workers who spend their lives working and paying tax but whose needs and hopes and aspirations and ambitions are ignored by politicians who pander to the first two unequal parts of the population. We live in a world which is being run by the dishonest and the greedy for the feckless, the lazy and the greedy. We live in a world where kids are unable to understand the meaning of words such as `honour' and `gratitude' and have a sense of entitlement that would embarrass royal princes. And we know, in the darkest recesses of our hearts, that these are the good times that we will all look back on with fondness. And that is truly scary.

We live in a world where the future will be slow economic growth, permanently high unemployment, higher taxes (open and hidden), increased government regulations (coming from Brussels), lower long term returns for investors, impoverishment of the elderly, rising inflation, slowly rising interest rates, collapsing currency, frequent strikes and a steady rise in crime. We live in a world where cancer rates will continue to increase and where millions of people who love their country no longer love their government.

We live in a world where people who are not inherently bad feel forced to be bad (to cheat, and to ignore the law) by a remorselessly bad government. We live in a world where small girls have as their role model a woman whose sole, original claim to fame was the size of her artificially augmented breasts. Breast enlargement is now, for thousands, a seemingly plausible career plan. We live in a world where people who choose to live on welfare payments receive more money than people who work long, arduous hours at jobs they dislike. We live in a world where, if the government and the multinationals want something and encourage it then you can be sure that it is bad for you. We live in a world where those who tolerate the evil deeds perpetuated by our government in our name shame themselves by their silence.

We no longer live in a world of hope and real ambition. We live in a world dominated by, and run by, small-minded, clock-watching bureaucrats who have strangled entrepreneurs with red tape and a constant stream of invariably pointless, usually counter-productive and sometimes contradictory instructions. We live in a world where those who can say that they have always been honest in their dealings with the government, can also say that the government has always been dishonest in its dealings with them. They have created a world in which it is seen as weak to be well intentioned, honest or sensitive. All they want us to do is to obey, conform and consume. There is an air of desperation in Britain these days. For most of those under 25 having a `good time' seems to involve getting drunk (not drinking, getting drunk), having sex and fighting. The two sexes share these humble ambitions. Maybe this is because they understand that they are living lives of hopelessness and unfairness and injustice and despair. And they have no idea how to escape.

We live in a world where it is becoming increasingly clear that, as I predicted, Britain is going to come out of the crash of 2007-8 in far worse condition than any other country in the world. This is almost entirely due to the efforts of one miserable Scotsman (Gordon Brown). No one in Britain deserves to be serving a long prison sentence more than this sorry excuse for a human being. We live in a world where politicians will always fuck up everything they can fuck up; whenever they are given a choice politicians will choose the solution that is better for them personally, whatever the consequences for their country.

We live in a world that is more communistic than the USSR ever was. Around 50% of our GDP is spent by the politicians and the civil servants. And yet the USSR proved that collective planning in particular and collectivism in general don't work. Are our politicians too busy fiddling their expenses to read newspapers as well as history books? I suspect not. I think they're still wallowing in the fact that statism benefits just one group of people: the statist rules, the people who control the nation's purse's strings, the people with authority with no responsibility, the people with rights but no responsibilities. And, for the sort of people who become politicians in our party system, those are irresistible attractions.

We live in a world where many of the people on disability scooters use them not because they are disabled but because they are either just fat or lazy. We live in a world where people take little interest in big questions such as liberty and democracy (and their absence) because they are overwhelmed by problems of daily existence; battling so many rules and so much legislation that they have no time to see, or fight for, the big picture. (Do you think this is an accident?)

We live in a world in which people demand rights but aren't prepared to do anything for them; a world in which the government deliberately takes money from savers and the prudent and gives it to the greedy and wasteful. When I was in my early 20s I wrote an article drawing attention to the separation of responsibility and authority. But now there is something else: rights and obligations have parted too.

We live in a world in which schoolchildren are taught to shoot guns, in which McDonalds, the hamburger chain, is being allowed to give A levels gherkin slicing and how to put a greasy cheeseburger into a plastic box and in which a woman is arrested for using threatening behaviour to youths who were damaging a war memorial.

We live in a world in which seemingly intelligent and definitely well-to-do people seem willing to trade their freedom for prosperity and comfort. People have disengaged from politics. They (probably rightly) don't believe they can change anything so they don't try; they don't even try to save themselves. The mass of people put up with being pushed around and bullied at airports, they allow the local council to look through their rubbish, to check that it has been properly sorted, they allow eavesdropping, they allow unknown watchers to observe our every public move. The government has given itself apparently unending rights and authorities and has lumbered us with all the responsibilities, duties and obligations. Much of what has happened in the last decade or so has happened quietly. How many people know, for example, that Her Majesty's Revenue and Customs (the tax man to you and I) is now legally entitled to intercept and bug letters, phone calls and emails?

According to the politicians the average voter wants cheap petrol, cheap food, low taxes, little work (preferably none at all), generous pensions, lots of laws and regulations, free education, constant wars, a multicultural society, no national identity or culture, generous, unlimited benefits for everyone, free health care, authoritarian policemen who shoot innocent citizens and get away with it, no privacy, lots of cameras everyone and no freedom or democracy. That's what they must think we want because that is the world they have given us and that is the world they insist we accept. (There is a widespread belief that people are entitled to free education. This is a nonsense. If people are to be entitled to free education why aren't they entitled to free food?)

We're in a long term depression (not just a simple recession). Our economy is going to stagnate. When the inflation kicks in the result will be something very nasty known as `stagflation. Gordon Brown's solution to the problems he bequeathed us will, I believe, lead to a prolonged depression, far, far deeper than it should have been. We have massive debts, a damaged currency, and unnecessary overregulated citizens (the regulations destroy and discourage entrepreneurs).

By the time Gordon Brown called an election in 2010 the Government was borrowing £1 for every £4 it spent. There is no way that growth is going to pay for that sort of overspend. The British has to cut back on its spending (by at least £1 in each £4) and pay the interest on the nation's enormous, seemingly endless debts, and pay off the debts, and pay the constantly rising bill for civil service pensioners and find the money to pay for expensive, environmentally-friendly energy sources (to replace the old fashioned power stations the Government agreed to close down) and continue to fight a war in Afghanistan and continue to pay billions of pounds every year to the European Union in membership fees.

The next ten years are going to be bleaker than anyone can remember. Even citizens old enough to remember the days of rationing which followed the Second World War are going to be shocked. The over-cossetted millions who have grown accustomed to the State satisfying their every need, and having an apparently endlessly deep pocket, are going to have to face a very painful reality. The hard-working tax paying few who have paid for the Labour Party's decade of exuberance are going to find themselves paying vastly more tax for vastly reduced services.

In the wonderful modern world created by Brown, our governments rely upon the banks to buy their debt but the banks are bust and so the government has to lend them the money they need to buy the debt. Living in Britain today is like living in a fantasy world created by a sadist with a black sense of humour.

For Brown to claim that he helped protect the nation against economic chaos was absurd. It would have been like Hitler claiming that without him we would all be speaking Polish - confusing, self praising gibberish. Brown's philosophy was that if you say something enough (even if it is a downright lie or complete gibberish) people will eventually believe it. He says he saved us from the world crisis. He saved us from the world crisis. He saved the world from the crisis. Dour Scot. Have cape. Will travel. Unfortunately, the financial crisis made tens of millions unemployed and in China alone 20 million lost their jobs; inevitably millions were driven into poverty, losing their homes. The Scottish crusader proved more than slightly fallible.

The falling currency will exacerbate the problems caused by rising energy prices. We have a bloated and effectively bankrupt banking sector (still too big to be allowed to fail) and that will create endless financial crises which will be exacerbated by crafty traders who are driven only by the search for the next billion bucks. We have an increasingly unstable country, broken by multiculturalism and political correctness. All this was created by our two war criminals, Blair and Brown, and their special chums the Americans. Brown deliberately made it worse as he delayed an election in order to increase his chances of retaining his chauffeur driven car and central London home.

The economy is like the human body in that sometimes you have to let the bad out of the system. You have to allow the pus to come out of an abscess because if you don't the problem will just get worse. The government tried to deal with the problems created by the banks without removing the poison.

Nearly everyone except bankers, politicians, senior civil servants, those on long term social security of various kinds, (and, of course, EU employees) is going to be a lot poorer in five and ten years time than they are now. We need politicians who display leadership, wisdom, imagination, and common sense and a sense of social justice. Instead we have half wits whose main qualities are prejudice, rank stupidity and self serving greed.

We live in a world run by public servants who have all decided they know what is best for us and aren't going to bother us with the details, whether they are politicians and foreign office civil servants signing away our rights with another EU treaty or BBC bosses spending our money by paying huge sums to entertainers who couldn't get half the money anywhere else. Under Labour the number of front-line public sector staff (the ones who do the work) rose by about 10%. But the spending on managers in the NHS and other departments doubled. The number of local council staff earning £50,000 or more rocketed from 3,300 to 38,000. (In the economy as a whole the number of high paid workers rose by a factor of three.)

We have bankrupt banks, pot hole ridden roads, policemen who appear in public as often as Father Christmas, doctors who are too self-important (and too rich) to do emergency home visits and who use premium rate telephone numbers so that patients who call for help have to pay a premium, hospitals where patients are a bloody nuisance. There is, I fear, a better than evens chance that we are heading for a hyperinflationary Great Depression. There is a real possibility that we, as a nation, will lose our AAA rating, that the value of our currency will slump still further, that interest rates will soar and that strikes and rioting will disrupt every aspect of our lives. Browns boom was a private debt financed spending spree, sustained by a housing boom and a government with a spending problem, getting rid of every penny it took in ever rising taxes and much that it hadn't taken. For example, UK households were, in mid March 2010, in debt to energy suppliers. Around 5.5 million households owed £728 million to the energy suppliers. That's a lot of debt.

Brown, the Naked Chancellor, was the most imprudent guardian of the nation's finances ever given office. His economic models were the dotcom bubble and the housing bubble. His legacy: generations of debt, poverty and misery. Britain will do worse than other countries because their politicians care about their countries enough to be selfish in their favour ours don't. The sense of loyalty to Britain or England is non existent among British politicians. Scottish politicians are patriotic to a fault. And so are Welsh politicians. But there is no one fighting for England. Our politicians deny, lie and spin so much that the truth is lost and no one has any idea what is going on. The government's targets have created a web of false accounting so all the figures they use are bent.

Brown and his successor, Darling, consistently argued that everything that had gone wrong in Britain was a result of problems elsewhere in the world - notably in America.

This wasn't true, of course.

Thanks to Brown's economic policies Britain has been in steep decline for years. Unwilling to make the difficult choices (the ones requiring character and, above all, courage) and to force the country to accept some short and medium term self-sacrifice (something that would, of course, have meant that they would have had to accept some popularity, and, it would, therefore have involved an element of self-sacrifice) the Labour Government simply threw taxpayers money around in their attempts to keep people employed. And when they ran out of money they just turned on the printing presses and made some more. They did nothing to improve the economy. They made no fundamental changes.

The `cash for clunkers' scheme which was introduced, at huge expense, benefited foreign car companies (the Labour party had presumably forgotten that the British car industry is defunct). Sales came from inventory so few jobs were saved (the fall off in sales will come in 2010 and 2011 because people were simply buying early to get the money back). The scheme took down second hand car prices, removed low end vehicles from the market (they had to be physically destroyed even though driveable) thereby causing enormous waste and making cars too expensive for really poor people. So the scheme damaged the environment, hurt car owners and the poor, benefitted foreign car companies and cost taxpayers hundreds of millions. Only a Government could screw up so completely and then be proud of it.

By 2010 the country was in such a dire state that it was patently clear that an election win would be a poisoned chalice. The historical evidence shows that once a state consumes more than 40% of GDP, growth will stagnate. For years, the only bit of Britain that has been growing is the bit that creates rules and regulations (or, more accurately, imports them from the European Union). By May 2010, Brown's Government was borrowing a pound for every four pounds it spent. If Gordon Brown ever, ever uses the word `prudent' again I will personally sue him under the Trades Descriptions Act.

The UK's level of borrowing in 2010 and the increase in borrowing between 2007 and 2010 are the highest as a share of national income in the G20 (the group of 20 leading economies in the world). We are the worst in the world. Moreover, the forecast level of public sector debt in the UK is increasing faster now and in the officially predicted future than anywhere other than Japan. The politicians who had created this mess (and who exhibited vast quantities of hubris) seemed to find humility beyond them. They also seemed quite unaware of the size of the problem. A Labour minister called Ed Balls was talking about making education cuts of £500 million by 2013. He might as well have talked about changing to a cheaper paperclip supplier. Not the figures mean anything much. The government's ability to forecast the direction of the economy is dismal. And without being able to predict the future to some degree it is obviously impossible to plan or make useful decisions.

If one man can be truly said to be responsible for the massive misery, loss of wealth and unemployment that has enveloped England since 2007 that man is the miserable, Scottish nationalist Gordon Brown. The mess Britain is now in is Gordon Brown's fault. It's a mess that is going to last for years and cause enormous misery and pain. It's a mess that will result in millions of people lining up for dole money and hundreds of thousands being thrown out of their homes. And it's a mess that was entirely predictable.

I know it was predictable because I predicted it.

Gordon Brown, darling of the left wing and the Daily Mail, is a moron. And here's a scary thought: Gordon Brown was, for three years, in charge of nuclear weapons. I wouldn't put him in charge of a bow and arrow - even if the arrow had a suction cup on the end. Having wrecked one country, the haggis-brained Scot who betrayed his party's promise and signed the Lisbon Treaty without a referendum, wandered the world hunting for opportunities to pose as a statesman; to pose, moreover, as our saviour, our Churchill, the man who will rescue the world from financial doom.

Brown is no statesman, no Churchill and no saviour. The dour Scot has, for over a decade, displayed mammoth quantities of ignorance and prejudice and done his damnedest to destroy our society with applied Soviet-quality social engineering. It is easy to feel sorry for him now that he's gone. But no shows much pity for Hitler these days, do they? And it is possible to argue that Brown did more long term damage to Britain than even Hitler managed.

Not many people know just how much damage Brown did (and is still doing) because far too many journalists are gutless wimps. We live in a society where the truth is solidly and determinedly suppressed. Even the magazine Private Eye, once regarded as daring but now as adventurous as your local Parish magazine, has banned advertisements for my book `Gordon Is A Moron'.

The truth, you see, is far too dangerous to share.

Brown has screwed Britain in general and England in particular. His performance target culture has destroyed public services; polluting and corrupting our world. Here's an example. In Manchester during the snow of January 2010 policemen logged snowball throwing (without injury or damage) as `serious violent crime' - thus ranking it alongside murder and rape. Presumably, they could then announce to the world that they solved these crimes and dealt with them. Stamped them out.

As a chancellor Brown was so imprudent that we have one of the worst budget deficits in the world. Pakistan and Iceland might be worse but it's a close run thing. He has squeezed the poor so hard the pips squeak. His means testing programme is just another example of practical fascism. He sold off the nation's gold at rock bottom prices and cost us billions. He has strangled the economy with red tape. He is the architect of Britain's housing crisis. He has created a society of scroungers dependent upon the state. He destroyed the pensions of millions of hard-working men and women. He has destroyed what was left of the traditional doctor-patient relationship and is to blame for the dumbing-down of school examinations. He has wrecked the police and...I could go on and on. The gulf between the haves and the havenotverymuches is now wider than ever. Instead of pulling up the lower classes in both uk and usa, the middle classes have been pushed down to create a huge disempowered under class of workers enslaved for the glory and enrichment of the bankers, the politicians and the quango drones. The finance industry is supposed to help British companies and individuals to grow. It doesn't. It fails at what it does. The bosses have become an industry of their own; their purpose is now simply to make money for themselves. Britain's relatively small number of highest paid bankers have for years now taken home nearly one third of the UK's total wage bill. Small customers (eg the holders of PIBS with Bradford and Bingley) were the ones who got shafted. Big American bondholders were protected. It was the Labour way. Look after the big American investors and screw the small ones because they don't matter. A country has to have exports to survive. When did you last see Made in England on anything? We had a finance industry. That pretty well went. We had some oil. But we used that. We had a car industry but the unions finished that off. We act as a middle man for the drug companies but they send their big profits elsewhere. Our companies, unable to adapt to a changing world, and hamstrung by red tape and hundreds of thousands of niggling new laws (so many that not even the lawyers can keep up) have been destroyed by the globalisation our leaders cherish so dearly. The nation that once led the world (and ruled a quarter of it) has been impoverished by small minded, craven men anxious only to find new ways to fiddle their expenses and improve their pensions. (This is, indeed, a recurring theme in the world of public service. Senior civil servants spend their best years doing nothing but feather their own nests and, as a result, the jobs they are paid so well to do are left undone.)

In the world Brown and Blair created savers are treated with disdain. Under our present system, prudence is neither valued nor appreciated. If you spend all your money on alcohol, drugs and gambling the state will look after you. If you work hard and save some of your earnings, the Government will tax you to the death (and beyond) but will deny you help when you need it. There are many people in England who do nothing but watch television who are paid considerably more than people who work long hours at arduous employment. This is wrong, bizarre irrational, and unfair and it leads to resentment and injustice. It also encourages large section sof the population to regard improvidence as the only rational course of action.

Thousands of people who borrowed far more money than they could afford were in 2009 let off interest completely, while people who had saved and been prudent were punished by receiving no interest. They were actually losing money because inflation was still several above zero. There were even some commentators and politicians calling for banks to charge savers interest on their deposit accounts. The idea behind this cruel and thoroughly stupid notion was that savers would spend their money if they were having to pay to keep it in the bank. I was brought up to believe that saving was good and arch hypocrite Brown always seemed to favour prudence; he was certainly always talking about it. But his policies were unrelentingly in favour of borrowers and spenders because their debts were wiped out by inflation. Borrowing huge amounts to buy big houses gave huge leveraged profits. For house buyers it was the home version of investment bank profits. Leveraging produced profits.

The sensible way out of the economic mess would have been to encourage savings by raising interest rates. Did they do this? No. Raising interest rates would have discouraged speculation, asset bubbles and credit card debt and it would have encouraged saving. These would have been good things. But they would have been unpopular with the vote controlling minority and so no political party would do it. Modern politicians have no ambitions other than to acquire power; they know that power leads to wealth.

The finance industry does not create products that improve the lives of customers or the efficiency or wealth of the nation (by accident or design). Instead, and uniquely, the finance industry creates new products which are only of benefit to its own members. Liar loans and usurious credit card fees make huge amounts of money for their creators and are quickly copied by other banks. These things are popular only with bankers and are bad for everyone else. No other business does so much stuff that is utterly, completely selfish. Banks also help governments lie and cheat and cover up financial messes. It was absurdly dangerous for Britain to allow itself to become dependent upon the financial industry.

Brown got the nation dependent on the banks, introduced his own version of socialised capitalism to bail them out when they went bust, and then, for quick political reasons, introduced taxes and rules which will result in the best of the bankers buggering off. He introduced special taxes on the banks. There were always two problem with these taxes. First, UK taxpayers now own half the banks. Second, the banks will pass the costs on to customers and shareholders. It will be taxpayers, small shareholders and pensioners who will suffer; not the bankers. Once again Brown's policies allowed people to avoid responsibility. And that, it seems to me, was one of the Labour Party's great faults: they pushed through policies which allowed everyone to avoid personal responsibility. The bankers were bailed out, and didn't have to take any responsibility for their incompetence. Public employees were given a working structure which enabled them to avoid personal responsibility. And increasing numbers of people were given state hand outs and allowed to avoid responsibility for their own lives. Even when Blair was Prime Minister it was Brown who was creating the policies that did the damage. Blair did the grinning. Brown did the really destructive work.

The booms and busts are getting worse. As Karl Marx predicted they will cause our ruin.

The list of damage Brown has done is seemingly endless. He is a political hoodie, a state-sized vandal. His greatest achievement, however, was undoubtedly to turn a prosperous nation into one teetering on the edge of bankruptcy.

Today, the economic mess is far worse than the government admits. Never before has a UK government borrowed more in peacetime than Brown did in 2009. Never before has a government had to borrow £1 for every £4 it spends. The government has lied a good deal about the size of the debt, of course. Misleading statistics and self-congratulatory nonsense about `growth' and the `end of recession' encouraged people to believe that the worst was over.

The era of free money, with the stuff falling out of trees and into a select few of Gordon and Tony's very best friends, is over. Now we have to pay the bills for the good times most of us didn't actually enjoy. In 2010/11 the government will have to borrow £6,000 on behalf of every household in the country (including all the ones with no savings and no income other than what the State gives them). Before the next election the Government will borrow £25,000 on behalf of every household (once again, including all the ones with no savings and n income other than what the State gives them). Bailing out the bankrupt Scottish banks will cost English taxpayers at least £500 billion - and probably much more. Reversing the rise in debt caused by Brown's reckless profligacy will take the UK generations. Only 30 years of tight budgets, and considerable inflation, helped get rid of the debt we had accumulated after the Second World War. We now owe more than ever before. Oh, and on top of all our other shared debts, together we owe an estimated £770 billion in pensions to public sector workers and £56 billion in debt to infrastructure projects built under Brown's wretched private finance initiative. The idea that people like our current bunch of wasters and no-hopers could possibly steer our way out of this sewage is laughable.   The Great British Pound (aka sterling) will remain in decline for some time and as interest rates rise so the cost of meeting the massive interest payments on our national debt will rocket. Thanks to Gordon Brown, Britain is the weakest western economy. (Technically, America is probably more bankrupt than Britain. But America has the world's reserve currency and Britain has a currency which will increasingly be seen as something of an embarrassment.)

Most of it is the fault of one man: Gordon Brown. The head of the US Federal Reserve as reported that Gordon Brown's decision to strip the Bank of England of its supervisory role caused major problems for the British economy and that the UK was poorly prepared to deal with the crisis because of decisions made by brown when he was chancellor. Brown used to describe social security and debt interest as social and economic failure. If he ever really believed that then just how he now has the nerve to crawl out of bed in the morning is beyond me.

But Brown has now retired to backbench comfort and the loving arms of his no doubt grateful Scots, leaving England and the English to pick up the tab for his 13 year profligacy, his seemingly endless state aided party.

In order to begin to pay off the debt before we lose our AAA rating and the currency finally disappears around the U bend we have to cut £4,000 to £6,000 a year per household off public sector spending. A year. Every year. And that should just stop the debt getting too much bigger at too fast a rate. Things are that bad.

The politicians (most of whom have never run a business, met a payroll or made any money except through politics) will talk about cuts in tax credits and limited public sector pay restraints and a few redundancies but none of that will make a damn of difference. They talk about saving money by cutting waste (just before the election the Labour Government admitted, without even the merest hint of a blush, that they had been wasting £11 billion a year for the last 13 years and so could save a bit by cutting back some of the waste). And they talk about economic growth as if all that needs is a few days of sunshine and an occasional light shower. The Tories talked about making cuts which would have no effect on the quality of public services (thereby confirming that vast amounts of money have been wasted on a regular basis).

But the truth is that none of this will be enough. Not building any new ships won't be enough. Making soldiers buy their own bullets won't be enough. Growth is going to be miserable because we have a manufacturing industry that would just about keep the Isle of Wight alive, we have a population which is getting older and older by the minute and we have a nation weighed down with scroungers who believe that the state owes them a living.

The UK is no longer a world leader in manufacturing or technology and so we have a bleak future. Coming generations are going to be very poor in their old age. (When will young people realise just what sort of prospects they have? They will, I suspect, be very pissed off when they finally understand just how bad things are.) Brown's policies closed factories which made cars, ships, planes and machinery and got the staff working as highly paid and entirely unnecessary hospital bureaucrats, nappy managers and nail varnish technicians. The Keynsian theory, spend, spend spend and pump money into the economy, is fine as far as it goes but the spending has to be effective. The money has to be spent either on improving the infrastructure or on creating productive jobs where workmen make things, earn money and then spend it on other things that people have made. The money has to be spent encouraging small businesses. Instead, Brown's government did the opposite. They messed around with taxes and national insurance and introduced a ton of absurd new regulations. And they spent vast amounts of public money on hiring more nappy folding experts. They did everything they could to screw the country.

In their determination to protect their greedy pals the Labour Government, elitist capitalism lovers, have betrayed the people who trusted them and put them in power.

Borrowing money to pay off existing debts is the modern way to deal with financial problems (it was the route favoured by the Greeks) but it doesn't solve anything. And if a nation doesn't grow faster than the interest rate on its debts the end will be nasty.

The Budget of march 2010, high point of the plan to rescue the nation from the mess they'd got it into was a plan to save £8 billion through efficiencies (£8 billion would not of course begin to touch the size of the deficit which is better measured in hundreds of billions or possibly even trillions, but it sounds a lot). This splendid sum included a proposed £555 million to be saved by reducing sickness absences among NHS workers. How do they do that? How do they work out to such a precise figure how much they can save by encouraging NHS employees not to fall ill? And how, indeed, do they stop NHS employees falling ill? And if they can do it in 2011 why didn't they do it in 2009? And is it actually saving the nation money (and reducing the debt) or is it merely improving the service (by reducing the number of absent staff)? There is a difference. And how come they have suddenly found £8 billion they can save by being more efficient? Why were they so wasteful (and inefficient) that they have been wasting £8 billion a year. None of these questions were answered or, indeed, asked by anyone else.

The nation is now spending more money on debt interest than on education. This outrageous state of affairs which, thanks to Gordon Brown and his greedy Scottish banker friends, will continue for years to come. According to the budget the government will accumulate more debt between 2008 and 2012 than in the entire history of British governments until Brown left the treasury. No one (not even Hitler) has done more to damage Britain and the British way of life than Gordon Brown. Even the smiling, inept Blair only started illegal wars. It was Brown, left to manage the economy, who did the real damage.

The government has to borrow vast amounts of money from other countries (specifically the Chinese and the Arabs and anyone else who actually has money to invest). The problem is that British government gilts (which are effectively IOUs handed out by the Government with a promise to repay with interest) are proving to be poor investments. And there is a real chance that the people buying them will stop. That's what happened to Iceland and Greece, for example. When that happens the government's only option will be to increase interest rates in order to attract money. And when we pay a greater rate of interest on our official IOUs then interest rates go up for everyone. Just imagine what that will do to the job market. And the housing market. (Some commentators claim that Britain's position is not as bad as that of Greece. That's not at all clear. Some of the figures suggest that Britain's position is far worse than that of Greece. Our biggest advantage is that our national loans tend to be longer term than those of Greece. This is good because we have longer to sort things out before we find ourselves having to find new lenders. But it is bad because if growth is not as good as expected then we will be in very serious trouble. And, as a member of the euro, Greece could turn to other European countries for help. Germany, France et al had a vested, personal interest in protecting Greece, partly because they share a currency, and it would be embarrassing and inconvenient to see part of it collapse and partly because if Greece defaults on its loans it will be French and German banks which will go bust. No other EU country will lift a finger to help Britain. We will be thrown straight into the unyielding arms of the always unsympathetic American run IMF.)

The awful truths are as endless as they are dispiriting.
A quarter of Britain's workforce is on the government payroll and half of all government spending goes on wages for civil servants. The like-it-or-not, inevitable cuts are, therefore, predictable.

The UK is borrowing more than £50 a week for every person in the country. Every week. And it's rising. And it's being used to help pay the interest on our debts so it's going to go on and on. Who the hell is going to pay it all back? We are in a worse state than any other country in the world (with the possible exception of America, which has the world's reserve currency and can get other countries to pay its bills by buying its currency and which also has a good amount of commodities.)

British public and private debt (according to figures in the FT) is now 449 % of GDP which makes us the worst country in the world other than possibly japan which is, everyone knows, so bust that for years the banks have been paying people to borrow money. So where is all this going to take us? We have three options, politicians will lead us wisely and firmly and there will be belt tightening in a big, big way. A lot of excess public spending will have to be cut. There will need to be a large number of redundancies among civil servants (probably measuring a million or more) and the ones left will have to take pay cuts. The silliness that is civil service pensions will have to stop. Taxes will have to go up. Quite a lot. And services will be poor for a decade or two. That's the easy, light, option. And you know as well as I do that it isn't going to happen. That leaves...inflation. Or default. What no politicians mentioned in the run up to the May 2010 election was that the current fiscal crisis could lead to severe sterling weakness, a collapse in the price of government bonds, an increase in interest rates and a deep, deep economic depression. The Labour party deserved to lose the 2010 election. The Tories didn't deserve to win it. The Liberal Democrats didn't deserve to be in it. I seriously doubt if any of them wanted to win it. It was a delight that all three major parties lost the election. (It was surely the first time in history that a general election was held and not just did no one win, but everyone lost.)

Politicians have forecast that there will be `more self-service by the public, with lessons being learned from the retail sector'. So expect to find yourself helping the nurse to tie your bandage or handing the doctor the forceps.

And still the Government constantly introduces interfering policies which they say will help business instead of doing the one thing that would really help: reduce red tape, unnecessary burdensome regulations and leave entrepreneurs some freedom to get on with what they do best. In 1997 the new Labour Government promised that there would be `no more tax and spend'. Did they ever mean that? They've done more of both than any government in history. One of the first acts of the new Conservative Liberal Coalition was to announce plans (formulated by the EU) to give workers the right to decide to work part-time. Only bureaucrats and politicians who had never done a proper day's work (and certainly never run a business) would propose such an absurd nonsense.

The politicians will, of course, try to blame the civil servants. And in a way they have a point. Between 1999 and 2007 the average error in forecasts for borrowing one year ahead was £8.3 billion and for two years ahead it was £11 billion. The 2008 budget under-predicted deficits in the following two years by around £180 billion. Maybe it would be better if the civil servants at the Treasury moved to the Met Office and the civil servants at the Met Office moved to the Treasury. Then they would at least all have a decent excuse for their incompetence. But none of this is much of an excuse. Politicians should know that most senior civil servants are incompetent fools who invariably progress beyond their level of competence. They should know too that economics is no more a science than astrology or iridology.

Economists are terrible diagnosticians and terrible prognosticators and terrible at choosing the correct treatment. If they were doctors their patients would all be dead and they would be struck off the medical register. Economists working outside the government aren't any better than the ones working within. Economists (many employed by the big banks it has to be said) all agreed that the government should bail out the banks that had gone bust. In reality it would have made more sense to let them go bust and to introduce a new rule that banks that dealt with real life customers could not go gambling with the customers' money. It would, incidentally, have also been better to let countries such as Greece go bankrupt. The EU and the IMF didn't want to do that, however, because if Greece had gone bust it would have been French and German banks which would have paid the price. The bailout of Greece wasn't done to protect the Greeks but to protect the banks. Once again taxpayers' money was used to protect bankers who had made reckless loans. (If you or I lend money and don't get it back then we lose out. If banks lend money they are bailed out by us. The banks, it seems, are more important than anything else on the planet.)

The only other times when governments have spent as much of the nation's money as now were during the two Great Wars of the 20th century. And immediately after both wars the percentage of government spending halved within five years of the end of the war (though it was still higher than it had been before the war).

The situation at the moment is that government spending, as a percentage of GDP, is now much greater than it ever reached during the First World War and almost as much as it was during the second world war. And it is not going to fall as it did in the late 1940s and early 1950s.

Brown and co, not understanding anything, have interrupted a normal business cycle by bailing out losers, socialising risk taking and transferring money from the cautious and the successful to reckless failures. Pensioners are having to miss meals in order to ensure that millionaire bankers, who caused the problem by messing with real estate derivatives they didn't understand, don't have to miss their bonuses. And that, remember, is exactly what is happening. It would have been so much better for the people, the citizens, the voters, for the banks which failed to have been allowed to bust. (Just as it would have been better for the world at large for the countries which had overspent to have been allowed to go bust and then rebuild themselves slowly and to relearn the Micawber Principles of financial solidity.)

The government will, inevitably, rely on growth to help pay off the huge debts Brown accumulated while he was pretending to be in charge. If the growth doesn't come as expected (which it won't) the size of the debt will rise, the problems created by compound interest will kick in as the cost of borrowing increases and taxes will have to rise, thereby damaging the economy still further.

A sensible government would slash public spending and encourage private sector growth. It is the only logical way to pay off Brown's debts.

But right up until the last minute Brown's Government was doing everything wrong. In the final quarter of 2009, the private sector employed 61,000 fewer people. But in that same quarter, the Government hired an addition 7,000 civil servants.

And the cost of the civil servants is extraordinarily high. The average total pay (including bonuses) was £451 per week in the private sector in 2009. But the average total pay (including bonuses) in the public sector was £462 per week. Private sector pay has been frozen or rising very slowly for months, but public sector pay has been rising at 3.7% - that's above inflation.

To make things worse the figures show that while private sector productivity has risen 20% in the last few years, public sector productivity has fallen 3%. So, while they were getting huge pay rises, public sector workers were working less.

Brown created an overpaid public sector army which largely sat on its collective fat bum and leeched off a shrinking private sector. Over half of the economy now consists of the public sector (it actually makes up 52% of the economy). And that's before we start discussing the cost of providing inflation proof, index-linked pensions out of taxpayers' money for all those public sector employees. Or the cost of meeting another commitment the Coalition Government has made. The Conservatives and the Liberal Democrats are determined to raise our aid to rich, foreign countries such as China and India by a staggering £4 billion a year. We are within a whisker of bankruptcy and our politicians still want to give our money away so that they can look good when they swan off to international conferences. (The absurdities of our generosity are never-ending. The Reserve Bank of India to which Britain recently gave much aid money, as though it was some hard-up developing country, is reported to have $254 billion in foreign exchange reserves. Since Britain has huge debts that means that India is about a trillion quid richer than Britain. In a sensible, logical world we would be applying to India for developed country aid.)

It is hardly surprising that of 18 countries in the world with AAA rating, Britain is only one `on watch'. The only one that the credit rating agencies are genuinely concerned about. And you can't blame them. We owe tons of money. Our currency is going to go down, inflation and interest rates will go up, unemployment will soar and house prices (the source of so much apparent wealth) will fall.

The UK is now in such a mess, and has such vast debts, that we can only look on fondly at those European countries which have sound economies and decent balance sheets. Germany and Austria are obviously far better fixed than Britain. But even Brown must wince a little when he looks at the figures and realises that countries such as Poland, Latvia, Slovenia, Lithuania, Slovakia, Czech Republic, Romania, Bulgaria and Estonia are in a much stronger economic position than Britain. And we can only dream that one day we will once again be as strong as Cyprus and Malta. One of Browns golden rules was `only to borrow for capital investment and not for day to day spending'. If all goes well, and everything goes to plan, and the economy booms, and there aren't any more problems, the UK will manage this in 2017-18. But it will be then have failed to keep the golden rule for every single year between 2001-2 and 2017-8.

In the midst of the financial carnage caused by a decade of greed and debt Brown tried to persuade us that our only way to escape from our indebtedness was to spend. To buy more digital cameras, flat screen television sets, DVDs, vacuous ghost written celebrity autobiographies. And so, incredibly, unbelievably, people did as they were told.

And now we are in a mess. And it is going to get much, much worse. Perverse incentives mean the survival of the weakest and destruction of the fittest (individuals and companies and banks).

The politicians take from the working prudent who tend to vote for what they genuinely believe will be best for the country, and give that money to the lazy and feckless and greedy because their votes can be bought by simply promising not to cut benefits or the number of public sector workers.

Brown doesn't like England. He's even signed the Scottish Claim of Right which states: `We...do hereby declare and pledge that in all our actions and deliberations (the) interests (of the Scottish people) shall be paramount.'

When the world economy imploded, Britain was already in a weak state; new businesses were being stifled by unreasonable rules and employment legislation and ambitious citizens were leaving the country as fast as they could sell their homes and leave, having realised, with considerable regret, that in modern Britain the phrase `it makes no sense' is no longer a reason for something not to happen. Most remained loyal to their country but recognised that a country and its government are two separate entities and that when the government becomes corrupt and toxic the wisest move must be to distance oneself in order to survive.

The New Gestapo (an ever expanding group which consists of everyone working for central or local government, any transport entity, any bank and the helpline belonging to any international corporation, though it has to be remembered that most members of the New Gestapo stop being New Gestapo the minute they leave work and head for the home when they become, like the rest of us, victims of the New Gestapo) now control every moment of our lives.

By the time the economic crisis was well under way it was clear that Britain was, of all the countries in the world, probably the most poorly placed to cope. Brown's policies had made the country vulnerable.

Britain needs savings and investment in business. But Brown has done just about everything possible to discourage savings and investment. Why bother saving when your money is going to earn you nothing and, as a result of inflation, simply deteriorate in value? Why bother saving when, if you spend all your money the state will look after you?

The only growth area has, for years, been the public sector. And now that the state has to cut back (in order to try and clear some of the debts) the public sector is going to lose jobs and shrink. Britain is in serious, serious trouble. The currency is going to collapse, interest rates will have to rise, inflation will increase, unemployment will go up, up and up and everything is going to get worse. The worst of the financial crisis is ahead of us, the social and political consequences are only just beginning.

There will be strikes galore and a noticeable decline in public services and the services provided by all large companies as they struggle to cope with increased costs, reduced profits and ever increasing red tape from the EU. The banking and political fuckups will lead to rioting and strikes and chaos and revolution. Everywhere we look there will be vagrants and tramps. Shanty towns will appear in Britain for the first time, built, I suspect, in multi storey car parks. Squatters will move into deserted stores and warehouses.

We used to live in a country where people looked out for one another, where doors could be left unlocked in the daytime (burglars only came out at night), children played in the street and society was built on shared values, real hopes and

Today, we live in a world dominated by a centralised authority. Our freedom is disappearing bit by bit, so slowly that no one really notices that it's going. It's like being eaten by ants. Governments talk incessantly about freedom of speech and democracy but whenever a free voice appears they become hysterical and do all they can to suppress it. Temporary security legislation is always permanent; it is never repealed. Those who think we live in a free country should know that in recent weeks a man was arrested for discussing religion in his own home and an Englishman was sent to prison for being rude about the Scots.

We live in a world which is changing and deteriorating (the two words can be used as synonyms these days) every day. In a town near where I have a home there used to be a street which contained a book shop, a bread shop, a greengrocers, a baker's shop (bread and buns baked in the ovens behind the shop, a model shop, a good junk shop, a shop offering alterations to clothes, an old fashioned jewellers and a toy shop. We patronised them all. Today the same street contains two tattoo shops, a body piercing parlour and two nail parlours (run by college `graduates' with government grants - the parlours close every six months and are replaced by more of the same). The rest are charity shops. That's not progress.

We live in a world where whatever justice we had has been turned upside down and buried too deep to see. Here are some stories I spotted on the same day.

1. A 78 year old man suffering from Alzheimer's rebuked a yob for urinating in public (outside a supermarket). The 22 year old picked up the old man and hurled him to the ground. (The old man then died 13 days later.) After throwing the old man to the ground the yob and a pal strolled into the supermarket to steal alcohol and then stepped over the pensioner as they left with their haul. The murderer was given two years in jail. (Probably for stealing the alcohol from the supermarket).

2. An animal rights activist was jailed for four years for trying to intimidate companies to stop dealing with a firm which experiments on animals. He pleaded guilty to conspiring to interfere with a contractual relationship. The activist apologised and said he wouldn't do it again but was sent to prison for four years.

3. A professional footballer who stamped on the head of another footballer received a mild rebuke.

4. An old couple who were so under siege by neighbourhood hoodies that they did not dare leave their home paid to have their groceries delivered from a local supermarket. (They had telephoned the police for help but nothing had happened.) By mistake the supermarket delivered an extra pot of yoghurt worth 79 pence. The couple rang the supermarket to report

the mistake. They were told to take the yoghurt into the store. They didn't because they didn't dare leave their home. The police were called by the supermarket and the old couple were arrested for stealing and receiving stolen goods.

We now live in a world where spontaneity and recklessness are banned; everything has to be organised and planned so that the appropriate permission can be obtained. If you want to sing Happy Birthday in a local pub you have to obtain a licence from your local council and a copyright release from the American who copyrighted the song. If you want a spontaneous street party to celebrate a Royal wedding you need to apply nine months in advance, obtain permission in triplicate and pay a huge fee to the council. A nation which sends tanks to Heathrow to prevent terrorists hijacking aeroplanes and which confiscates nail files from 85 year old women and takes bottles of baby's milk from young mothers has truly lost its way.

If Hitler had won the Second World War we would now be living in a pan European state dominated by Germany and run by an army of state employed bureaucrats. There would be a million laws controlling the citizens who would be kept in a constant state of fear and uncertainty. Democracy would, at best, be superficial and all real decisions would be made by a small group of unelected commissioners and eurocrats. Corruption would be rife. There is, of course, no difference between Hitler's dream and what we have now. We may think we won the Second World War but somewhere, amidst the crackling flames, the little Austrian Jew is laughing.

Just about the only thing we can rely on these days is that the people in charge will screw everything up: for heaven's sake they can't even run an election efficiently. The truth is that the politicians will do the wrong thing for the country and the right thing for themselves. Power destroys those who do not have it and today's politicians are a new breed of professionals who have no experience of real life; who live in their own aloof, isolated, chauffeur driven, expense account world; who care only for themselves and their own interests. They are driven by expediency and self-interest and remote, in all senses, from those they are paid to serve and represent. They seemingly have no sense of right or wrong. When found out cheating on their expenses they profess dismay that they should be considered dishonest. It was, they all claim, an honest mistake. (Though the mistakes are, you will have noted, always in their favour.) They offer to pay back the money they've stolen as though that makes everything all right and seem genuinely puzzled when members of the public say it doesn't. They happily suppress the truth about their misdeeds in the obvious belief that a crime doesn't count if it isn't found out. Professional politicians have lost the trust of the public because they are, as a breed, crooks who no longer respect the public's wishes, or even acknowledge them (or, possibly, are allowed to acknowledge what those worries are). If one of the Big Three political parties had announced in its manifesto its intention to withdraw Britain from the EU and from Afghanistan it would have won the election by the biggest landslide in British political history.

Politicians, so dependent on their jobs for their personal wealth, so rarely do the `right' thing. They so rarely resign when resignation is the honourable course. To see the truth in this we only have to look at Gordon Brown squatting in Downing Street after being rejected by the British people. Unwanted, unloved, unwelcome but still he refused to resign. He was not ever, I guess, the honest sort of man likely to resign with the dignity shown by John Major. Mind you, the Conservatives ought to have been embarrassed by their showing at the election. If the Tories had been any good at all they would have won every seat at the last election simply by turning up.

There is one excellent way to forecast what is going to happen next. Ask yourself what the politicians will regard as best for them and their party. That is what they will do. They will claim to be doing what is best for the country. They will claim to have the country's interests at heart. But all modern politicians are the same: their every action is selfish. Understanding and accepting this isn't cynicism, it is practical (and knowing it is how things work these days is an essential aspect of self-preservation). Look at what happened in the aftermath of the May 2010 election which all the three big parties lost resoundingly. The Tory party began by flirting with the Liberal Democrats. At first they offered a kiss and then a feel. When the Liberal Democrats threatened to go off with the Labour Party the Tories offered to let the Liberals screw them as long as they used a condom. The Labour Party then trumped this by offering full sex, oral sex and anal sex. `Anything you like,' was their desperate cry.

All three parties were prepared to stuff the electorate and the country as long as they got what THEY wanted.

The sight of Cameron and Clegg (surely the most dangerous man in Britain) dancing around one another as they talked of coalition and partnership was equally nauseating. The sight of the Liberal Democrats using the nation's precarious position as a sneaky opportunity to put its own party policies first - ahead of the nation's interests - was, to say the least, one of the low points of political life for decades. (If there is any justice left in Britain, the Liberal Democrats will be utterly humiliated and expunged from public life for a century at least, at the next election for promoting and preferring self-interest so blatantly.) The Conservatives were out negotiated by the Labour Party (which offered all sorts of goodies and then effectively withdrew them once the Tories had been tricked into upping their offer). Members of the Conservative-Liberal coalition talked incessantly about acting in the national interest. Both leaders (who had a few months earlier been taking full advantage of the MPs expenses - the nauseatingly sanctimonious Clegg, for example, had claimed for a new kitchen, £5,857 worth of decorating, curtains, curtain rails and repairs to a garage door, a £2.49 cake pan and £4.99 worth of cushions as well as international phone calls, the cost of which he later paid back having, like just about all MPs, made a `mistake' with his accounting) claimed to be now thinking of the country. Clegg, like other MPs, was probably aware of Leo Trotsky's remark that: `Nobody who has wealth to distribute ever omits himself.' But if they had really cared for the country, if they really wanted to act in the national interest rather than in their own interests and the interests of their parties, they would have joined together as soon as it was clear that the nation had rejected them all in order to deal with the nation's two huge problems. `Economic stability is the basis of any partnership,' was the content of a joint statement prepared after two days of talk, as though `economic instability' had ever been under serious consideration. I really cannot convince myself that these two, the Sarah Palins of European politics, will really have the strength of mind or the political courage to deal with our serious economic problems. (I was about to ask if either Cameron or Clegg would be anyone's politician of choice to lead the country in time of war. And then I remembered that we are at war. And then I remembered Churchill, the life-hardened colossus and I wanted to weep. Clegg and Cameron are merely another two in a lengthening line of British war criminals.)

First, the terrible economic mess, bequeathed by the awful Brown and his equally awful Government and second the fact that we were at war. British soldiers were fighting in Afghanistan in a war hardly anyone in the country, or Parliament or the army understands and yet the politicians were squabbling and fighting for their party's favourite policies - and doing in secrecy, behind closed doors, as though the public had no right to know how their country was being carved up. All other issues should have been put on one side to deal with these two big issues. And decent politicians who genuinely cared would have done just that. These people, who should have been sorting out the nation's problems, locked themselves away to wheel and deal for their benefits and their parties' benefits. It was such a perfect example of how the party system has destroyed our country. Once a government has been formed there is no real debate because the parties in power know that whatever happens they will win important votes - simply by threatening or bribing individual MPs. (`Vote with us and you will be awarded an important sounding ministerial position and a chauffeur driven car. Vote against us and you will be thrown out of the party and lose your seat.')

Modern politicians do what they do arrogantly; but they will do it badly. It is, after all, the government that runs the NHS, the Royal Mail and HMRC: without a doubt the three most inefficient, incompetent organisations in the world. Am I the only person who was astonished that none of the big three parties, awash with advisors and consultants and counsellors, had a strategy plan for post election consequences. If they did it was of the `Oh shit, what do we do now?' variety. These are the people now running the country. Cameron should have decided to form a minority government, drawn detailed attention to the mess left by Brown, got thrown out when the other parties turned sulky, gone to the country for a proper mandate, blamed the other parties for the new election, and probably won easily.

Politicians lie so much I don't even think they know they are doing it - or understand just how offensive the rest of us find it. After Gordon Brown called a woman a `bigot' for daring to ask about immigration (thinking he would not be heard by the idiot voters) he grovelled endlessly in an attempt to repair the damage he had done to his career and his party (that one incident lost Labour the election and finished Brown's career because it showed how far removed he was from the electorate's fears and feelings). It was, it seemed to me, the only moment Brown had talked honestly in the whole election campaign - and, because he was accidently overheard, he felt he had to apologise for it. Says it all, really, doesn't it? Politicians do not expect the voters to ask questions - particularly tricky ones. If one asks questions then no one has to provide any answers. They have created a world in which it is seen as weak to be well intentioned, honest or sensitive. All they want us to do is to obey, conform and consume. They frighten us with things that aren't happening and aren't going to happen. A few years ago I coined the phrase `intellectual terrorism' to describe this. (If you aren't terrified then you probably don't know what is going on.)The honest, the decent, the sensitive now go through life expecting to be ignored, treated unfairly, bullied, abused, accused, suspected and mistreated. In these things they are rarely disappointed.

Modern politicians aren't just crooked they are also extraordinarily inept. The idea of banana eating David Milliband ever becoming prime minister is truly scary. Arrogance and ineptness are not usually regarded as qualities which make a man suitable for high office. We have, in recent years, had some of the worst ever ministers. Was Milliband the worst foreign secretary ever? I suspect so. Blunkett was certainly the worst ever home secretary (though Straw gave him a run for his money), Blair and Brown take the prize as joint worst ever prime ministers and Brown is without a doubt the worst Chancellor of the Exchequer the nation has ever seen. Prescott was just a joke. The Labour party since 1997 can claim a clean sweep of the awards. I cannot think of any Labour minister who would be capable of running a shoeshine stand.

I hesitate to say this because I know it makes me sound like Johnny-marching-out-of-step, but the establishment is now so deeply corrupt that it is wrong about almost everything. The establishment is wrong about genetic engineering, global warming, the EU, the war in Afghanistan, the absence of a coming energy crisis, the usefulness of vaccination, vivisection and health screening.

Every piece of evidence shows that if you increase taxes on income then people won't work as hard and, consequently, tax revenue will fall. Logic supports this view. Similarly, the evidence shows that if you increase taxes on the things people buy (especially luxuries) they will spend less and save more. In 2008 and 2009 the UK desperately needed people to work harder and spend less. Everyone in the world with a brain agreed with this. (Gordon might or might not have also agreed with it.) So, what did the Government do? They increased taxes, reduced VAT and helped people who had bought houses they couldn't afford by reducing interest rates. Naturally, this had the added effect of discouraging people from saving. In other words, the Government did exactly the opposite of what any sane and sensible group of people should have done. It was no great surprise to anyone (other than the Government) when their policies made things considerably worse than they had been.

The government have punished the innocent and let the guilty go free. New regulations were needed. And so they arrived thick and fast. Pension funds were to be more tightly controlled. There would be a clamp down on people with offshore investments. Governments started buying stolen bank records so that they could spy on investors. But banks? Well there was a lot of talk but very little real action against the banks - the organisations whose greedy employees had caused the situation in the first place. It was easier to punish the innocent and to let the guilty go scot-free. That is the modern way.

Here are twelve reasons why Britain is stuffed:

1. The Government will always do the wrong thing.

2. The unions, now far too strong, will practise their own version of irresponsible protectionism - disrupting and destroying the lives of others in the process. Their actions will prevent an economic recovery.

3. There are too many civil servants. They are too highly paid and they have become accustomed to an easy life. Their unions will resist the changes which are necessary.

4. Civil service pensions (often paid to people retiring in their 50s) are unsustainable and place an unbearable burden on those working in the private sector (whose own pensions have been devastated by politicians).

5. Banks are still taking risks with other people's money.

6. There is virtually no manufacturing industry left.

7. The infrastructure is crumbling. (Transport, education, health facilities and so on.)

8. Energy supplies are running out.

9. We are in the EU and, as a result, overladen with bureaucrats and, thanks to our governments, gold plated EU regulations.

10. We have a world in which people demand rights but aren't prepared to do anything for them; a world in which the government deliberately takes money from savers and the prudent and gives it to the greedy and wasteful. When I was in my early 20s I wrote an article drawing attention to the separation of responsibility and authority. But now there is something else: rights and obligations have parted too. Authority and responsibility have long been separated. So too have rights and obligations. Too many people who are capable of work live on benefits paid by the state - and expect this to continue.

11. Absurd immigration policies have led to overcrowding and a stressed infrastructure. Politicians ignore the fact that we are at war with the people

we are encouraging to immigrate. The result of the government's multicultural policies will be racism.

12. The party political system ensures that people who do not work (or who work for the government) decide who rules the country. Proposed changes to the voting system will make this worse. I am not against change but I am against change without purpose.

As if all that was not enough we are also tied (in much of the world's eyes) to America, the world's most hated nation.

Our politicians downplay real risks and exaggerate small ones to suit their purposes. They ignore the big causes of cancer but get us all terrified about diseases which are of relatively small importance. They impose harsh new regulations about a problem (climate change) which the scientists can't prove exists.

Truth is now such a rarity in our world that major public decisions (including so-called democratic elections) are invariably taken on the basis of perception, rather than reality. In essence this means that perception has become reality. It is nothing new to say that all history is biased because of the often self-serving prejudices of those who write it. The same event can be interpreted in any number of different ways. But what is new now is the fact that the present is being reported and influenced according to the deliberately guided perceptions of the electorate. And if our understanding and appreciation of the present is being altered in this way then our actions will be changed and the future changed too.

True history is what we remember & what influences our lives (perception becomes reality). It may or may not be true in reality in terms of facts but facts in themselves are of far less significance than myths. Perception is more important than reality, and so paintings may be inaccurate but we accept the image. Truth & facts are ultimately of far less significance than widely appreciated myths, images & perceived truths. A widely believed falsehood is more powerful & relevant than a little known truth

There are people who think Blair was a good prime minister, Brown was a good chancellor, vaccination helps prevent illness and we invaded Iraq was to find and destroy the country's weapons of mass destruction. (Anyone who believes one or more of those should have a multiple lobotomy because their brain is entirely without purpose.) In the May 2010, millions of people voted for the Labour Party; the first government run by truly evil people: Blair and Brown: our first war criminals: our Hitler and Mussolini.

We live in a world where everyone knows that the system is broken, and that this will eventually lead to some sort of revolution. In the meanwhile it leads to frustration and feeling of injustice. The reforms the government introduced would have not prevented the last crisis and will not prevent the next one; they merely rewarded the guilty and punished the innocent in order to disguise the fact that the system is broken. Brown's legacy is that the innocent, and the poor, are punished and the guilty receive support and free corporate welfare.

The only way to mend our society is for mass production has to end; for design for obsolescence to end and for the `throw away' society has to end. The truth is that recycling won't solve any of our problems. Windmills are for Don Quixote. But the politicians do not see truths: they see only cheque books and chauffeur driven cars and free holidays.

We live in a world where the future will bring us a bigger, more intrusive government (despite all talk of reducing it), slower growth (making it difficult or impossible for the country to pay off its debts), more regulations (making life increasing difficult for private citizens and small businesses, but doing nothing to curb the greed of corporate bosses and bankers) and diminishing corporate profits (resulting in weaker pension funds). It is not a cheery future. All we can do is ensure that we prepare ourselves for what is to come, and to know how best we can ensure that we and our loved ones survive.

I occasionally receive letters accusing me of being too rude about our leaders. They think I should be `nicer' about them.

Well, bugger niceness. I'm too angry for niceness. There's too much happened to be nice. It's too late to be nice. These low life scheming bastards have stolen our freedom, our reputations, our history and our money and our future and being nice isn't going to get any of it back. There is a common misconception that when the financial crisis hit, money was somehow lost. It wasn't. No one went around burning tenners. The money that disappeared from the system went into the pockets of the bankers. The billions that Britain now owes bought mansions, and yachts and aeroplanes and vintage motor cars and jewels and plastic surgery and divorces for American bankers from disgusting companies such as Goldman Sachs. Blair, Brown and the other devious pirates who have betrayed us into cultural, political and financial slavery will not be influenced by niceness. They see niceness as weakness. Well, I'm not going to be weak and lie down. Other people can if they like. But I'm not. Modern politicians are, on the whole, offensive, crooked, egocentric, narcissistic and hypocritical. They are composed of gristle and tripe. They are soulless and deprived of spirit. I loathe people who say we should respect and understand them because they are doing a difficult job. I despise compromise. I have contempt for people who work for the government and who say `It's not my fault, I'm just doing my job' because they are the people who would operate the gas chambers for a good salary and a guaranteed index linked non contributory pension.

I am angry. Angry at the Americans. Angry at the Israelis. Angry at the bureaucrats of the EU. Angry at the politicians who lie. And angry at the people who don't see what is happening and wouldn't care even if they did see. Actually, I am most angry about the fact that I don't have time to be angry because of all the crap which invades my life. The brand new toaster which is too narrow to take a slice of bread. Angry at the council and the police who refuse to do anything about the neighbours who regularly put one of their (many) cars directly across our driveway. Angry at people who still travel to America. Angry at people who want freebies. Angry at the Blairs and their bloody holidays, houses and million pound a year jobs. Angry at the fact that bookshops, music shops and decent junk shops have all disappeared from our streets to be replaced by charity shops, estate agents and `gift' shops selling fridge magnets, fairy statues, personalised pens and scented candles. Bloody scented candles. Angry at the people who, because of the web, assume that everything should be free. Angry at Google (one of the nastiest firms on the planet) which wants to steal my work and publish it free of charge on their damned website so that they sell advertising space on my back. Angry at the fact that I wrote this list without hesitation. Angry that I so bloody angry that I can feel my blood pressure rising. Angry at useless bloody hospitals. Angry at shops which have queues which mean that I now have to wait twenty minutes to buy a newspaper. Angry at so called civil servants. We live in a world in which there is, on the one hand, independence, responsibility and self respect while on the other there is dependence, collectivism, welfare and an all powerful state. We all have to choose.

We've been betrayed by the political parties but not enough people care, or have the strength or level of desperation to do anything. It is not yet time for the revolution. The Government has failed us and will continue to fail us. We cannot yet get rid of them. So we have to adapt to survive. We live in a hostile and alien world; a world which seems, increasingly often, to be just a little too much for the sensitive, the caring and the thoughtful. It isn't yet time for the revolution (though it will come). Meanwhile, we must `read' the future in order to enable ourselves to survive. This book is my survival plan.

Our future world is now out of hands. Most of us are disenfranchised. Effective voter power is non existent. We do not live in a democracy. We have no control over our lives. We cannot change things because the nation is run by people who do not do what we want them to do. (If the nation was run as the people required it to be run we would not be in the European Union and we would not be at war.) If we all march through the streets we will be arrested. All that is left is for us to learn how to survive.

This book is not about politics but about life as a whole. The world is such a mess that no amount of intellectual effort is going to repair the damage. The only advantage to be gained from spending any effort studying the chaos is personal and financial in that it is possible to survive more comfortably if we know what is coming.

Looking after ourselves must, for the time being, be our sole salvation. If we choose not to leave the country, but to stay here, then we must learn how to deal with the vicissitudes which lie ahead. Look after ourselves, and our families, must now be our primary objective. Harsh and rugged days are ahead and we need to rope ourselves together. It is, for now, all that we can do. This book was researched and written for myself. It is offered as a guide. All we can do is try to predict what they will do next, how it will affect us and how best we can protect ourselves and those close to us.

Back in 2007 I forecast the economic crash, the recession (and what I believe still will be a depression), the rise in the oil price, the collapse of sterling, and hyperinflation. In the earlier part of the decade I predicted trouble for the euro and, indeed, the European Union. There have been dozens of other predictions. Of them all only the prediction about hyperinflation is yet to be proved true. And I'm still backing that one. I was never convinced by the argument that we would have a long period of deflation (a theory favoured by many commentators). Hyperinflation will come because it is, for them, the most painless way for governments to get rid of their debts.

Making predictions is like tightrope walking. Some of the predictions in my previous books were dismissed as far fetched. But they turned out to be true. Similarly my numerous medical predictions were dismissed and yet proved in time to be entirely accurate - sometimes ten or twenty years ahead of their time.

Originally, the predictions in this book were made for my own benefit: to help me make investment judgements. But I decided to turn the predictions into a book in order to make them available to readers who have been loyal over the years. You may think that some of my predictions seem unlikely. But just ask yourself how likely you thought it would be that Lloyds Bank and Royal Bank of Scotland would both be government controlled?

In previous books I have predicted many things which have already come true. While writing this book I found that things were happening so fast that some predictions were coming true, or obviously about to come true, within months or weeks of my writing them - and had to be deleted from the text.

I have written a number of books on politics in recent years. The predictions I made in such books as `Why Everything Is Going To Get Worse' and `What Happens Next?' have come true.

Many readers have been kind enough to write and say that the books made sense. But not one of my books on politics has been reviewed in a national newspaper or magazine (up until the age of around

26 my books were reviewed widely - it was then realised that I was rather too dangerous and so my books were banned).

Despite this, for a long time I believed, or at least hoped, that it was possible to change things for the better. Sadly, I now no longer believe that is possible. My book Bloodless Revolution was my last attempt to really make a noticeable difference and although many readers were enthusiastic and helpful the lack of publicity meant that the book quickly died.

I have, therefore, spent six months studying the economy and deciding what I can do to protect myself and Donna Antoinette. I have decided to share my conclusions with those among my regular readers who are interested. I believe that the information this book contains is valuable and so in order to limit the circulation this book will not be offered to outsiders who are not already readers of my books, it will not be advertised, it will not be officially sold on the internet or in my website, it will not be sold in bookshops, it will not be reprinted and it will offered to my regular readers only once. No review copies will be sent out.

Once you have an idea about what will happen you make a judgement about how the future might affect you, and, if you can't change things (which you probably can't) how you can best survive the changes. These are my dispatches from the front line in the fight against fascism; these are things no one else will tell you. And this is the book that will help you survive until the revolution comes. I don't think we can save the country. All we can do is save ourselves. That's what this book is for. It is a combination of forecasts for the prudent, hard -working and independent minded. It is, in short, food for thought, written for the `middle half': the people who work hard but who are disenfranchised, unrepresented, squeezed, used and abused and forgotten by the law-makers.

I do not advise you to make any plans or investments according to my predictions. i am not an authorised adviser and am not licensed to do anything other than prescribe drugs and chop bits out of people. I'm not a registered investment adviser and I don't run an authorised bank. I don't work for, and never have worked for, Halifax Bank Of Scotland (HBOS), Royal Bank of Scotland, Northern Rock, Lloyds Bank, Barclays or Bradford and Bingley. So, you can trust me. No, sorry, seriously, what I mean to say is that because I'm not employed by a bankrupt, failing or discredited financial institution, or registered as an investment adviser with a bunch of overpaid regulators who have failed utterly to protect investors, I can't give investment advice in this book. (You can, however, obtain financial advice from many of the institutions which would have gone bankrupt if they hadn't been bailed out with taxpayers' money.)

So, since I don't fancy a £250,000 fine and nine months sharing a cell with Tony Blair (who, if there is any justice in the world will soon be banged up for war crimes) I'm not going to give you any financial advice whatsoever.

The basic principle behind my thoughts is that the government will always do the worst for the economy, because what is bad for us is nearly always good for the politicians. That isn't cynicism. It's self protection. No professional financial advisers makes that assumption and that is, I suggest, why so many of them have succeeded in losing huge amounts of money for their clients during the last decade or two. Those who are innocent enough to believe that politicians will keep doing the right thing will fail.

To write this book I spent six months studying the economy, trying to see the big picture and deciding what I can do to protect myself and my family.

There won't be a revolution for some time. People aren't ready for one yet. They aren't ready for a revolution because they aren't suffering enough. Most people the reassurances they constantly hear. Most people think the worst is over. Most people think that they can carry on spending more than they earn. And there are, of course, whole legions of people who don't care a damn (or dare to speak up) about anything - as enquiring as molluscs.

And even the people who are getting fed up, and who believe that our society is broken, will be kept too busy making ends meet (and sorting their rubbish into five separate plastic containers every week) to go out onto the streets.

After all, the Government has given itself a lot of laws to help it deal with public dissent. Wander onto the streets with a friend and two placards and you will be photographed, probably beaten up and, eventually, undoubtedly arrested. The authorities can charge you with any one of a vast number of offenses (including conspiracy and terrorism).

But there will come a time, before 2020, when people have had enough.

And then there will be a revolution.

It will be a proper revolution led not by the unemployed but, as all the best revolutions are, by the middle classes. And the people who lead the revolution will be mostly over 50. Citizens under 50 are too ill educated to know when things are wrong and too complacent to do anything about and too cowardly to stick their heads above the parapet when there is a real revolution to be fought.

We need collective action to change society. It is not going to come through the government. Why should it? So it has to come from the people. And the only way it can happen is through some sort of revolution. I tried to trigger a peaceful revolution through my book `Bloodless Revolution' but, although many readers helped by distributing copies we just didn't hit the critical level of readership needed to change voting patterns. So it failed.

Revolutionary violence in South Africa was acceptable because it was politically correct. Mandela, the most famous and successful terrorist of the 20th century, is still revered by the fascists as some sort of god-like figure.

Nothing will happen in the UK for a good long while, because people are too busy dealing with the rubbish in their lives (literally as well as figuratively). But the main problem is that people don't know the truth. The media won't and don't tell people the real facts, or allow the publication of the inescapable conclusions. My books get no reviews, and advertisements for them are banned.

Britain was once a proud nation; marked by tolerance, courage and a sense of humour not matched anywhere else. The British were a proud people; proud of their history and their culture and their national achievements. Most of it Britain was the country which gave the world the concepts of fairness and decency.

All that is gone.

The British have had their self-confidence destroyed and their faith in human nature badly scarred. Political correctness, unlimited immigration and multiculturalism (the devil's work) have destroyed the very fabric of the country. There is no faith in politicians, no faith in justice, no faith in anything: just despair and a suspicion that only a revolution can change things. The country is, more than ever before, ripe for the growth and development of extreme ideologies. And they will come. Someone has to give the people a sense of purpose, a feeling of hope, an idea of a future better than the present; someone has to support and lead a dispirited population. Anarchy is the only sensible credo for a thinking person to follow at the moment. The fact that it is impossible to say this out loud is proof that it is true.

People should be screaming in the streets. After all, we have politicians most of us wouldn't trust to cut the lawn or fetch the groceries. They are systematically, partly deliberately and partly through incompetence and it doesn't really matter much which, destroying our country and doing their damned best to make us ashamed of our world. The bankers and corporate crooks are stealing millions in unearned bonuses and golden hellos and golden goodbyes and private planes and heaven knows what else. We can't make a decent road or a building that looks good or stands up. An amazing number of ordinary people care little about any of this. Fiction has to make sense to be believable but modern life is often a mystery of confusion and distortions. Many people hear what they want to hear. Some hear what they want to believe. Only a few hear the truth.

The revolution, when it finally comes, will come through the breaking of the parties. In the aftermath of my book Bloodless Revolution there were, I am delighted to say, more independent candidates at the 2010 election than there have been for many years. (The deposit candidates have to pay in order to stand has risen dramatically in recent years in a deliberate and grossly undemocratic attempt to stop independent candidates standing.)

For a peaceful revolution to work the party system must be overthrown. (The planned changes to the voting system, being promoted by the Liberal Democrats, will strengthen the position of the parties and weaken the position of the independents.)

Politicians will never take brave steps or tackle big issues because the party machines are controlled by lobbyists and big corporations or unions (because that is where the parties gets their money from). And so, for example, they ignore real ways to tackle the health of the country and mess around at the edge of the NHS, doing nothing whatsoever that is original, logical or based on science.

The bloodless revolution will come when the outrage rises.

The young don't care at the moment. But they will eventually because things are going to get worse. The young will be the ones to revolt because their expectations are high and their disappointment will be massive. They won't be able to use their gadgets and they won't know how to live without them. Unemployed, bored, cold, hungry - today's spoilt brats will eventually realise that they have nothing to lose. And that's when there will be a revolution.

Meanwhile, inspired by a mixture of rage, frustration, despair, injustice and disappointment I wrote this book to tide myself over the uncomfortable waiting period. I offer the following social, political and financial forecasts for the coming decade to you in that spirit of despair and hope and in the hope that they will help you survive at home in the foreign country we now inhabit. Keep this book handy and tick off the predictions as they come true.

Part Two

Social, Political and Financial Forecasts For The Coming Decade

1. Our Society Will Continue To Discriminate Against The Elderly

The only -ism that no one cares about is ageism. It is, indeed, official government policy to ignore the needs of the elderly. Doctors and nurses are told to let old people die - and to withhold treatment which might save their lives. Nursing home staff have even been given the right to sedate elderly patients without their knowledge.

How old is old? Anything over 60 is now officially old, though in a growing number of hospitals the cut off age for resuscitation is 55.

We live in a politically correct world but the elderly don't count - particularly if they are white and English. Report after report after report shows elderly patients being left in pain, in soiled bed clothes. Elderly patients in hospital are ignored by staff and left to starve to death, denied even water if they cannot get out of bed and fetch it themselves. Old people are a burden which the government cannot afford and so the politicians will continue to authorise whatever methods are necessary to ensure that the number of burdensome old people is kept to a minimum.

The chances of the elderly continuing to get an ever-increasingly raw deal in our society: 100%.

2. Allergies Will Become Increasingly Common

The incidence of allergy problems (asthma, hay fever, eczema etc) has been rising at an astonishing rate for some years. These disorders (and many others like them) will continue to become more common.

There are several reasons for this.

First, people are more aware of these problems than they used to be. Magazines, television programmes and websites encourage people to look out for problems. And, once spotted, problems tend to be taken seriously and reported to a doctor without delay.

Second, when a doctor sees a patient who is wheezing she is likely to diagnose asthma. And once the diagnosis has been made it tends to be permanent. The patient (who may well have wheezed once simply because he or she inhaled a seasonal irritant) will be given a prescription for an inhaler containing a powerful drug, a series of appointments and a branding as an asthma patient. Doctors and nurses are far more likely to diagnose allergy conditions than they ever were. This is partly because parents want a diagnosis (and are not happy to be sent away with reassurance) and partly because drug companies encourage doctors to diagnose chronic medical conditions which will require long term medication. A child who wheezes once is likely to be labelled as asthmatic and likely to retain that label for life.

The incidence of allergy disorders is probably higher than it ever has been for the simple reason that there are far more drugs and chemicals around in our environment. Most households are crammed with chemicals which cause allergies. Foods contain chemicals which cause allergies. And most children are now given vast numbers of vaccines in early childhood.

Allergy problems are going to continue to increase for many years to come.

The chances of allergies being commoner in 2020 than they are now: 100%.

3. Allotment Gardening Is Going To Become Fashionable

As food becomes increasingly expensive (and driving to the shops to collect it becomes impossible because of high fuel prices) so more and more people will discover the joy of allotment gardening.

The delights of being able to grow your own food, save money and know that what you are eating is fresher, healthier and better for you will combine with the joy of spending time gardening to make vegetable gardening a national obsession. Enthusiasts will point out that digging the allotment, and cycling to and from home, will provide all the exercise an individual needs - without having to spend a fortune on a gym membership.

The many millions who do not have a large enough garden to grow their own food will take up all the available council allotments and eventually farmers with land close to a town or even a suburban housing estate will start dividing up their land and renting it out.

The chances of allotment gardening becoming fashionable: 90%.

4. Alcohol Will Be Banned In Pubs?

Now that smoking has been banned in public places (including public houses) it makes sense to wonder what will be next for the ban.

The obvious target would be meat - the major cause of cancer in our diets and the biggest cause of cancer now that tobacco smoking is becoming a minority activity.

But the authorities won't ban (or even warn about) meat eating for the simple reason that any such ban would have to come from the European Union and the French farmers would never allow such a ban to be considered let alone brought into place. There are, quite simply, too many people prepared to fight a ban on meat for it to be considered let alone introduced.

That leaves alcohol.

It is not difficult to argue that alcohol should be controlled in the same way that tobacco is now controlled. There is no doubt that health problems caused by alcohol are almost as big a problem (and almost as expensive for society) as problems caused by tobacco. And, of course, alcohol tends to cause far more social problems than tobacco. Smokers don't tend to become violent, or run amok, when they've smoked half a packet too many. The other problem is that whereas smokers tend to die fairly quickly after developing cancer, alcoholics can go on for years - and become a huge burden on the state.

The first step from the EU will be stern warnings about alcohol drinking (with warnings printed on all bottles and cans of alcohol). But the next step will undoubtedly be a ban on drinking in public places - such as restaurants, bars and public houses.

The alcohol industry's opposition to such a ban will be fierce. But the hugely wealthy tobacco industry fought a long, hard battle against the introduction of warnings and controls on smoking - and it lost.

It will be a year or two before drinking alcohol in public places is banned. But I'm betting that the European Union will ensure that it comes. I certainly wouldn't risk investing in any industry which makes its money selling alcohol.

The chances of alcohol being banned in pubs: 80%.

5. Attention Spans Will Get Shorter

It started just a few decades ago. I believe that a television station called MTV, which appeared in the 1970s and which was a specialist music channel, was probably the beginning of this phenomenon. Prior to the formation of MTV, television programmes tended to last half an hour or an hour. MTV changed all that. Programmes consisted of very short music videos with fast introductions. And the screen also contained other images - word boxes popping up all over the place and crawler information running along the bottom of the screen. Attention spans suddenly got shorter.

The fall in attention span was started by television in the 1970s. American programmes such as MTV and a very fast action cop show Hill Street Blues debased audience taste and created a demand for superficial, fast moving programmes that raced along on the surface of life without ever delving into anything very deeply.

Magazines and newspapers were the next to change. Magazines which had regularly run articles of 1,500 words (often illustrated with no more than one or two photographs) suddenly started running articles of just a couple of hundred words. Photographs dominated the pages and words became secondary. In the 1970s I used to write for magazines such as Woman and Woman's Own and would often contribute lengthy articles without ever having to worry about how they were to be illustrated. Readers were accustomed to reading long articles.

By the late 1980s everything had changed. Within just a few years attention spans had altered. Readers wanted much shorter articles and they needed everything to be illustrated with photographs, graphs, drawings and other highly coloured images.

Women's magazines which had once carried 1,500 word articles illustrated by one or perhaps two photographs or drawings suddenly started printing much shorter pieces and much more pictures. Everything declined in quality and worth. The internet finished expedited the decline and today we have Twitter, the ultimate in selfishness, self obsession and superficiality; the medium for the me-me-me society. In fiction originality and creativity are not wanted. In non fiction questioning exposes are rarer than warm, sunny days in January. Today, there are websites such as Twitter where messages have to be compressed into just a sentence or two. And as the messages have got shorter so they have become increasingly trite, shallow and inconsequential. Websites such as You Tube have encouraged web users to expect politicians and others to cram their messages into a minute (or two at the most).

The result is that today's teenagers find it difficult to concentrate on anything that requires their real attention. The few books they read are littered with photographs and cartoons (in the same way that books designed for six or seven year olds were illustrated a generation or so ago). The films they watch contain little in the way of plot or character development but rely on a series of poorly connected scenic anecdotes. (The apparently entirely plotless Pirates of the Caribbean series of films illustrate this perfectly.)

The next generation will find Twitter far too wordy for their taste.

The chances of attention spans getting shorter: 100%.

6. There Will Be An Increase In The Incidence Of Autism

Autism is a very convenient label but it is used to describe patients with two very different problems

First, it is used as a label to describe patients who have severe brain damage. These patients are, I believe, invariably suffering from vaccine damage. Many of these patients developed their so called autistic symptoms within hours or days of being given a vaccination. It is, however, much cheaper for the government, the medical profession and the pharmaceutical industry to describe such patients as `autistic' rather than as `vaccine damaged'.

Second, the word `autism' is used to describe individuals who have social or behavioural problems. It is far more acceptable for parents to be able to say that their child is `autistic' than for them to have to tell friends and neighbours that he is `badly behaved' or has `social problems'.

It is clear, therefore, that the incidence of autism will continue to increase dramatically in the coming years. The government, the drug company controlled medical establishment and the autism-industry all claim that there is no link between vaccination and autism. It is, they say, just a strange coincidence that the incidence of autism has risen at almost precisely the same rate as the increase in the number of vaccines being given and the total number of vaccinations children receive. Just a coincidence. And it is just another coincidence that all the people who claim that the obvious link doesn't exist happen to have a vested interest in it not existing.

The chances of the incidence of autism increasing: 100%.

7. Commodity Prices Will Soar

China, India and other Asian economies are growing fast. So are countries such as Brazil and Russia. They all need stuff with which to make buildings and things. They need commodities. They also need lots more food because the people who live in those countries no longer want to live on the breadline. They want good food and they want lots of it.

The result is that countries which are `lucky', such as Australia and Canada, will do very well because they are rich in commodities. And countries which are poor in commodities, and which are reduced to scratching around for a few barrels of oil or a few shovelfuls of coal, are going to do badly.

We're near the top of the list of countries which are going to do badly.

What a pity it is that we didn't stick with the Commonwealth, and build up our relationships with Canada and Australia. We would by now be so much better off than we are as a result of our disastrous membership of the unremittingly evil European Union.

Chances of commodity prices being much higher in 2020 than they are now (even allowing for inflation): 100%

8. Our Freedom Will Continue To Disappear

The government, the secret intelligence service, the police are all paid to protect the rights and freedoms of people like you and I, the freedom to write what we like and say what we like. The deal is that we can say and write what we like as long as we don't physically interfere with one another or with property of one another. If we say something unfair, unreasonable we can be sued in the civil courts. That's the deal.

We employ the authorities to protect our freedom to be, do, say and write what we want. That is their purpose, their only real purpose. The provision of an infrastructure (roads and so on are tacked on responsibilities which have, in any case, been largely contracted out and sold to private industries).

But they have forgotten all that; ignored it; pushed it aside in the name of their new, improved version of `freedom'; a new brand that gives them, and only them, all the rights and all the freedoms and gives us only responsibilities; responsibilities to the state, responsibilities to the government, responsibilities to the European Union, responsibilities to the local authorities, responsibilities to obey and behave and to do as we are told.

The people we pay to look after us have taken away our basic human rights in order to protect them. It's like having a lovely, freshly baked loaf and putting it into a safe so that it doesn't get eaten. Meanwhile you starve to death.

The authorities, the people we employ to look after us, have done the job of the (quite possibly non existent) terrorists. What other country can you think of that had tight, vigorously enforced legislation, a very powerful and out of control police force, and a controlled and regulated media?

Try the Soviet Union.

And then there's us.

Inmates of the European Union.

It is now illegal to sit in a private room and talk to other people about vivisection for example. People who talk about animal rights are officially classified as terrorists. Sitting in an audience listening to someone talk about vivisection is now just as much a crime and standing up reading out the names of British soldiers who have been killed in Iraq. Holding the wrong sort of opinions is a criminal offence. Say the wrong things about the holocaust and you can be put in prison. Try saying you don't think gays should be able to adopt. Try writing a letter to the BBC arguing that we have enough immigrants in Britain. Try suggesting (in public) that most street crime is caused by black youths. Try criticising the Scots and you'll end up in prison if `they' hear you. It is illegal to have a viewpoint? It is if the viewpoint is considered unacceptable. Where will they stop? Which of your views are they going to make illegal next? Scientific evidence is legally suppressed. Books are very effectively banned. How long will it be before membership of disliked political parties is made illegal? Liberty means allowing dissent - even if the dissent is annoying and the dissenters obviously barking. Thinking for yourself, relying on yourself; these are unwanted traits.

Anyone who questions the official EU/Government/Establishment line is likely to be oppressed and suppressed. Proper discussion and debate about big issues is strictly verboten on the BBC or in other mainstream media, whether print or broadcast. When did you last see, hear or read an open, honest discussion about the values (and otherwise) of the European Union, genetic engineering, AIDS, global warming, vaccination, vivisection or any other contentious issue? You may think you hear something that is fair and open but it ain't, because people with views the EU/Government/Establishment don't like simply won't be heard. You get to hear two lots of people with the same viewpoint discussing the issue in a cosy, cosy way. Uncomfortable truths are not wanted on screen, thank you very much for offering and please don't bother us again.

The EU, and our own puppet government, loathe freedom. And they no longer bother to hide their loathing. As the months go by, so they will become increasingly contemptuous of those who disapprove and disagree.

Chances of our freedom continuing to disappear by 2020: 100%.

9. Our Infrastructure Is Going To Continue To Deteriorate

Britain's infrastructure, already the worst in Europe because Labour have spent all our money on staff not stuff, will get worse. Projects to repair, improve or build new roads, bridges, schools and hospitals will be abandoned. (So, don't invest in companies which make their money on public sector projects. They are due for a hard time.) The only exception will be EU mandated projects, such as those absurdly expensive, dangerous and over-engineered concrete barriers that are being erected on motorways everywhere (and which seem to me to be designed to throw errant cars back into the traffic, rather than holding them safely in position).

In May 2009 a survey of 2376 European travellers showed that London is Europe's dirtiest and most expensive city and has the worst cuisine and also has the most tourist traps and has the worst dressed locals. What a surprise that was. We want safe clean towns and cities and decent public transport. We get Prime Ministers who spend their time and our money waging wars against people who have never done us any harm.

It is clear that our roads will never be as good as they once were. Motorists pay taxes to use the roads and pay again with tyre and suspension damage and cracked and chipped windscreens and paintwork as stones are thrown up from crumbling roads. We pay our taxes so that the government can provide us with a safe and efficient infrastructure. But they don't spend our money on that. They spend it on quangos and wars and consultants and image makers and parties. That's why everything is so crap (from sewers to hospitals).They endanger lives (and homes) by allowing building on flood plains but doing nothing about the sewers - which now have even more waste to carry away. They close the public lavatories. Have you noticed how crafty they are about that? They allow the lavatories to fall into total disrepair. They never clean them. Then they say they are a health and safety threat and so they close them. Why don't councils do what the French do? Either set up `pay as you go' self-cleaning loos or rent out the convenience to a woman who charges a fee and cleans the cubicle after each use. It works and it actually makes money. The French have always had too many civil servants. But at least some of their public sector workers actually do something and, as a result, they have the best infrastructure in the world. I find it embarrassing and slightly unbelievable to have to admit this but we have more paper-shufflers than even the French. And the French don't mind allowing the public sector and the private sector to mix to everyone's advantage. In Britain the only people who benefit are the crooks and the tricksters.

The authorities repair our roads so badly that they constantly need repairing. They're now selling the bridges and roads that with built with our taxes to foreign companies so that we can be charged a fee to use our own infrastructure. Our rail network is in constant disarray with engineering works interrupting virtually every journey. In Japan, for the last 25 years all rail repairs have been done at night between midnight and 6 am. According to the managing director of the Central Japan Railway, the company did repairs during the day once - in the 1980s - and there was such an outcry it has never happened again. Why do we put up with the way we are treated? The government is digging up streets to lay cable television which no one wants (and which isn't needed) but doing nothing about archaic water and sewage systems which were brilliant when the Victorians put them in but which are now well past their `use-by' date.

The Department of Transport has admitted that more than 900,000 people are injured in accidents on Britain's roads each year. That's four times the number according to the official figures used by the police and the government. The reason is that our roads are much more dangerous than we've been told and the absurd reliance on speed cameras has made no difference. The number of people injured in accidents is soaring with 220,000 serious road traffic accident casualties a year now. That is eight times the number in the data issued by the police (who do, of course, have a vested interest in claiming that injuries are going down and that their speed cameras are having a useful effect). The discrepancy may be caused by the fact that policemen don't have quite the same view of `serious' as doctors. And, of course, these days many people don't bother to report accidents to the police (just as they don't report burglaries, muggings, sex offenses and so on).

Even allowing for the very real suspicion that road traffic injuries are rising because more and more people are claiming compensation as a source of income (as times get harder) the evidence suggests that our roads are becoming increasingly dangerous. There are many reasons for this. Pot holes don't help. Nor do stupid speed limits which push drivers into going faster than is safe when the limit is lifted.

Still, there's one thing I can guarantee.

The trains are not going to be late as often in the future.

How do I know this?

They used to deal with persistent late trains by changing the time table. Journeys which used to take an hour took an hour and ten minutes so that trains would not be late.

But they've got a better system now.

The words `on time' have been redefined and will presumably continue to be redefined until all trains arrive on time (ie the same day). At the moment a train is on time officially if it arrives within ten minutes of its supposed time. They're going to stretch that. A train will arrive on time if they arrive `within 60 minutes of their expected time'.

I never fail to be impressed by the way the government uses targets in a imaginative way to improve our infrastructure and our world.

For us the answer must be equally imaginative.

Expect less and less of the infrastructure the government provides and you will be less disappointed by the result.

Chances of our infrastructure continuing to deteriorate: 100%.

10. It Will Become Increasingly Difficult To Buy Insurance At Reasonable Cost (and increasingly difficult to persuade insurance companies to pay out for genuine claims)

Big insurance companies are already reporting that they are seeing far more fraudulent claims. The economic crisis means that vast numbers of people are using their insurance company as a bank and making claims for injuries or lost property that are, to be polite, of questionable probity.

Not surprisingly, the insurance companies (already suffering at the hands of the new army of ambulance chasing lawyers now wrecking British businesses, hospitals and councils) are treating all claims as potentially fraudulent, and will doubtless make it more difficult for honest policy holders to make claims.

On top of this understandable scepticism I suspect that insurance companies will often find new and devious ways to avoid paying out, either by introducing fine print exclusions or by finding other excuses not to get out their cheque books. The people will suffer most will, of course, be honest holders of car and house insurance. They will have to put up with the suspicions of cynical insurance companies and they will have to fight hard to make their claims. If they receive any money they will doubtless find that their policy premium will be raised quite dramatically.

On the other hand, the crooks, the cheats and the fraudsters will always find a way to ensure that their claims are paid. And since many don't have jobs they have all the time in the world to cope with the insurance company bureaucracy.

The answer?

We don't bother buying insurance except it's for something potentially very expensive. We take out public liability insurance (so that if our chimney crashes onto a car parked nearby we are covered). But we don't take out insurance to cover us in case our bicycles are stolen. We use locks, try not to leave them unattended and are prepared to pay the cost of replacing them if they are stolen.

Chances of it becoming more difficult (and expensive) to obtain insurance: 100%.

Chances of it becoming more difficult to persuade insurance companies to pay for genuine claims: 80%.

11. House Prices Are Going Nowhere (except down)

For years, the system encouraged high house prices and large loans. There were huge incentives to borrow money and low starter rates meant that buyers could leverage up and dramatically increase their profits. Imagine. You have nothing and no job. You borrow £300,000 and buy a big house. You sell it in five years for £600,000. You've doubled your money with a massive tax free gain. The massive housing boom of the early 21st century was the first time people in Britain have really been offered free money. No one seemed to notice that there is something curiously wrong (not to say self-deluding) about buying a property entirely with someone else's money and then convincing yourself that you have bought your own home.

The banks played along with this because they wanted the fees and the interest on the big loans. How could anyone lose? House prices would always rise. It was the tulip bulb game. Everyone wanted prices to keep rising. The government made money out of taxes (such as stamp duty) and rising prices made people feel rich. Many re-mortgaged and spent the money on cars, second homes, huge television sets. And all this helped keep the economy growing and made Brown look like a genius.   Much the same thing was happening in America and American bankers, not content with merely making millions, hit on a new wheeze - securitisation. They mixed all the mortgages up into a big mess and sold portions to gullible bankers in other countries (such as the UK). The ratings agencies, who were being paid by the banks, said these new products were all wonderful AAA investments. No one much cared because everyone, politicians, banks, rating agencies and buyers all assumed house prices would only go up because that's what they wanted to believe. Right at the bottom of this teetering tower of financial jiggery pokery lay absurd examples of reckless lending. A couple of strawberry pickers with a joint gross income of $600 a week each were allowed to buy a $720,000 house and given a mortgage with monthly payments of $5,378.

The UK's economy was destroyed by Gordon Brown with a little help from his rich pals in the banking trade. But the trigger was the collapse of the house price bubble in America which led to the collapse of a lot of complex financial derivatives which were built the idea of mixing up and re-selling large mortgages sold to people who couldn't afford them.

And that particular problem isn't over yet.

American house prices are still falling and the market there is loaded with unsold houses and if the prices continue to fall (the average price in Feb 2010 for a house in Detroit was down to $10,000) there will be a second serious attack of the heeby jeebies among banks and bankers will again be screaming for help (in the shape of lorry loads of free taxpayer cash).

And the bubble in the UK was always much, much bigger (and more dangerous) than the American bubble. The British index of house prices rose, in real terms, from 100 in 1890 to 110 by the end of 20th century. In other words, house prices only just beat inflation. Then, by 2006, after just six more years, the index had rocketed to 199. That is an award winning bubble.

In 2009 Brown announced that there would be no more 100% mortgages. He might as well have announced that there would be no more steam engines. There were no 100% mortgages. He should have made his brave announcement in 2003. It might have done some good then.

But, helped along by the Government, things just got worse. In January 2010 mortgage rates for new loans were the lowest in recorded history. So, the country was in trouble because of all the debt. And the banks, some of which are bankrupt and owned by taxpayers, were lending money at the lowest ever rates.

By May 2010 house prices in the UK were, much to the bewilderment of people just about everywhere else on the planet, still absurdly high. They had, indeed, actually continued to rise during the crisis because the government interfered with the normal, healthy process (most notably by lowering interest rates and thereby transferring money from savers to spenders but also by providing greedy people who had borrowed too much with taxpayer funded support).

The government even used taxpayers' money to compulsorily purchase 400,000 perfectly sound and well-built Victorian homes in the north of England in order to increase the value of the houses left remaining. (One official excuse was that old houses are expensive to adapt to modern environmental regulations.) Many of the demolished houses are now simply derelict plots that no one wants to build on. And even if new homes are built who builds houses these days as good as Victorian and Edwardian did? How many will last 150 years? Even councils often charge more to rent out old houses because they are better made and make better homes. The majority of houses built today are so poorly built that they are unlikely to last more than 30 years. (A fact which makes a nonsense of the fact that house prices keep going up, instead of, like second hand cars, losing value as the years go by.)

In the run up to the 2010 May election Brown's Government was proud of the fact that house prices hadn't fallen but this was rather like saying the drunk has stayed drunk because we have kept giving him booze. The house price bubble was kept up because the Labour party (in a desperate attempt to influence people and win votes) kept pumping in air and sticking on patches whenever there seemed to be any chance of a collapse.

In truth, the rise in prices which took place in 2009 and the first half of 2010, a rise which looked like a bounce or recovery, was due solely to the fact that there was very little property on the market and so there were more buyers than sellers. When there are more buyers than sellers, the price always rises. There was little property on the market because the Government was keeping interest rates low to help to protect people who had bought houses they couldn't afford.   The problem is that the support, in all its various forms, has to stop eventually and the longer it all goes on for the more painful the hangover is going to be. Naturally, by the time the Brown stuff hits the fan, Britain's worst ever chancellor and prime minister, world-class hypocrite and war criminal, hopes to be enjoying some of the hugely profitable perks enjoyed by his predecessor.

When house values eventually fall (which they will) and more and more people struggle with negative equity there will doubtless be a flood of repossessions, with many people simply choosing to go bankrupt rather than be hounded by banks trying to get their money back. In early March 2010 the Greek government had to pay 6.25% to borrow £4.5 billion. If the British government has to pay anything like that mortgage rates will go to 10-15% and millions of people will lose their homes.

House prices are nowhere near their long term average. On the contrary, they are still in a bubble. When prices of anything go into a bubble and the bubble finally bursts, prices go into decline and fall below the long term average. My guess? House prices have another 30% to fall.

And they could go further than that. The coalition government's rise in capital gains tax may well trigger thousands of sales by second home owners and buy to let owners. And banks which still carry thousands of bad debts on their books, and which have been reluctant to evict house `owners' because every time they do so they crystallise a loss, will do so when prices start to fall.

By the time inflation is taken into account I would be very surprised if anyone made much money out of house prices in the next decade. If a house price is the same in 2020 as it is now (and I think that's probably the best people can hope for) then the owner will have lost money because of inflation. If house prices do soar before then it will be because inflation has also soared.

House prices may or may not crash (I think that there has to be a crash) but my certainty is that they won't be much, if any, higher in 2020 than they are today (less if you count inflation). The falling currency will mean that expensive houses in London will be cheap for foreigners. But will rich foreigners want to live in a broken society with constant strikes, rioting in the streets, high taxes and more and more rules?

Chances of a house price crash before 2020: 80%

Chances of inflation adjusted house prices being notably higher in 2020 than they are now: 30%

12. The Economically Inactive Mass Will Grow

By March 2010 the number of people who were described as `economically inactive' in the UK had risen to a record 8.16 million. This figure relates only to adults who might reasonably be expected to be working; it does not include children or the elderly. The number of people not working was rising fast and likely to rise faster. If you add in the number of civil servants, quango employees, BBC staff, nail technicians and other entirely useless parasites the total number of `economically inactive' people in the UK is probably in excess of 20 million. The few remaining carry the weight of the nation's economy (and prospects) on their shoulders.

In the April 2009 budget the Chancellor guaranteed that all under 25's who had been out of work for a year or more would be promised a job or training. (The jobs would, of course, be within the NHS - soon to overtake the Chinese army as the biggest employer in the world.)

A television reporter interviewed a healthy looking man as he left a job centre and asked him about the Chancellor's promise. `Well, he said, after considering the promise for a few moments, `they would have to offer me some incentive'.

`How about we don't give you any more money if you don't get a job, you lazy bastard? I screamed at the television screen.

The one certainty is that unemployment is going to soar. But the government will of course fiddle the unemployment figures. There will be training schemes that don't train anyone for anything. There will be more opportunities for people suffering from `stress' or `a bad back' to settle into a life of disability payments. There will be shorter working weeks and part time contracts so that people seem to be working but are, in reality, only half working.

Many years ago I wrote a short story entitled The Office (It was published in Argosy magazine). The story was about a man who was preparing himself for his big day. And his big day was his one day of employment. His life was divided into three parts: the part during which he prepared himself for his day's work, his day at the office and the rest of his life when he remembered that one day of glorious work.

Maybe we're not close to that yet.

But the story doesn't seem as far fetched now as it did when I wrote it.

Chances of the jobless increasing by 2020: 100%.

13. Litigation Is Going To Soar

Solicitors pay £600 to £800 to buy cases from the claims management companies which advertise on television. You know the sort of thing. A half-witted actor falls off a ladder which has one leg shorter than the other, grimaces a lot and then pulls his telephone out of his pocket and rings for advice on whether to sue the person who owns the pavement, the company who built the ladder, the person who owns the ladder, the shoe manufacturer who sold him his shoes, the shop where he bought his shoes, his granny who didn't tell him to be careful with ladders or all of the above. The smarmy solicitor who handled the case will use his share of the loot to buy another home in the Bahamas. Fourteen small companies will go bankrupt as a result of the litigation and 528 honest, hard-working souls will lose their jobs. The half-wit who fell off the ladder will spend two years giving evidence and will, in the end, receive a cheque for £19.45. He will be one of the new unemployed.

This sort of rather sad and destructive litigation (which, in the end, benefits only the damned lawyers) will increase as more and more people find themselves struggling to pay their mortgage, taxes and petrol bills.

Suing the council, the hospital, the doctor and the company you work for will become a common way of making ends meet.

Insurance premiums will continue to rocket.

Let's just hope some people sue their lawyers too.

Chances of litigation soaring: 100%.

14. Metrication Will Taking Over

Distances and weights should still be described in imperial measurements. The mile and the pound are still the official British way to measure things. But, the Lisbon Treaty will change everything. And various arms of the establishment (such as the BBC) will make sure that imperial measurements are completely replaced by metric measurements. Another piece of our history will be lost. (And probably lost for ever. When the EU collapses we will probably be left with metrication as a permanent memory of the European misadventure.)

It would, of course, make complete commercial sense for us to continue using imperial measurements. The Americans use them and they provide a pretty big trading market.

But we won't.

The signs are all around us.

New road signs are being erected without mileage distances on them. The dear old finger posts (a few of which still remain in rural areas) always had a figure in miles after the name of each village or town. But an increasing number of road signs carry no numbers. They daren't put the numbers on in kilometres just yet. But they won't put them on in miles.

Just about every time a BBC presenter talks about a distance or a weight he or she will give the details in metric measurements. I can't remember the last time I heard a proper British imperial measurement mentioned on the BBC. Even those parts of the media which aren't official government mouthpieces use metric measurements rather than imperial ones. Whatever happened to our culture and heritage? I'll answer my own question. They're being washed away in waves of fascist inspired multiculturalism.

We drove not long ago behind lorry being used to transport stuff to M&S stores. On the back of the vehicle there was a notice. Here is what it said: `This vehicle is limited to 85 kph to save on fuel consumption and carbon emissions'.

Two things.

First, I thought that speed limits were imposed by governments in order to help reduce serious accidents. I didn't realise they were imposed by Marks and Spencer in another daft plan to save the planet.

Second, and most important, speed limits in Britain are still officially measured in miles per hour. When stores which provide underwear for the British middle classes start measuring in kilometres we really are losing the plot.

Bloody metrication gets everywhere these days.

You can't even buy a dozen roses any more.

Every florist I know sells them in tens, just to make sure that the EU stays happy.

It's going to get worse.

Within a year or two they'll start putting distances in kilometres on the road signs.

Chances of metrication taking over, and imperial measurements disappearing: 90%.

15. We Are Going To Have To Drive On The Right

When the EU decides that the time is right they will tell us that we have to drive on the right. After all the EU is now one country. And you can't have people in one part of a country driving on the left and in another part of it driving on the right.

Car manufacturers are keen on this because it will save them making `left-hand' and `right-hand' versions of their motor cars. The financial savings will be enormous. Lorry drivers from the continent of Europe will find things much easier too.

The cost of converting Britain's road system will be enormous but the EU will not help with this. Government vehicles (police cars, ministerial limousines etc) will all be converted to left hand drive. Independent motorists will have to struggle on with the steering wheel on the wrong side of the car, though I have no doubt that right hand drive motor cars will be made illegal within a year or two of the changeover.

How likely is this to happen?

It will happen. The only question is `When?'

Chances of our having to drive on the right by 2020: 80%.

16. The Drug Addiction Problem Will Continue To Soar.

Friends of ours live in the centre of a small provincial English town. Grand Victorian houses detached and semi detached. The police called round one day recently. There were around a dozen of them, some sort of special task force. `A girl was raped near here a few nights ago,' said one of the policemen. `We're looking for a knife that was used in the attack. Do you mind if we search your garden?'

`Of course not,' replied our friend. `But watch out for needles and syringes.'

The policeman looked at him.

`I haven't cleared the garden out for a week,' explained our friend, apologetically. `The drug addicts throw them over the wall.'

And that's England today.

Another friend who lives near to a drug addiction treatment centre tells that her life has become unbearable. Addicts stand around much of the night injecting, drinking and shouting on their mobile phones.

Some years ago the Government made the war on drugs one of its priorities. It is now clear that the drugs have won a resounding victory. The Government's own figures show that the amounts of Class A drugs (such as heroin and cocaine) which are seized are plummeting. There are such huge quantities of drugs now available on Britain's streets that the price of drugs such as heroin, cocaine and cannabis have all been falling since Labour took office.

Naturally, the Government claims that it is winning this war. It has even produced figures which show that the police are seizing more drugs than ever before. Naturally, the figures are misleading. (As they always are with the Labour Government.). The Government's selected figures refer to the number of seizures made by customs and police. But the police and customs have managed to push up the total number of seizures by targeting the easy marks - the dopeheads with a tiny stash in their pocket or handbag.

The real evidence shows conclusively that Britain is fast becoming Europe's drug heaven. It's been a long, long time since dangerous drugs were as cheap as they are now.

And the Labour Government's policies ensure that this trend is set to continue for the foreseeable future. Drug addiction is a rapidly growing problem in Britain. As I have been arguing for twenty years decriminalisation is the only real answer. But no politician has the courage to go down that route. And so drug addiction will continue to rise. And thefts, muggings and street violence by drug addicts will continue to rise too. There are two million people in prison in the USA and half of them are there on drug related charges. Legalising drugs would cut the American prison population in half and prevent terrorists financing their arms purchases through growing opium (eg in Afghanistan). But American politicians as gutless as British politicians.

The whole problem will continue to get bigger (and cost ever more money) because millions of people who can't (or don't want to) find employment find it far more rewarding to be a drug addict than an unemployed labourer. Being a drug addict provides a `get out of work free' card. Being a drug addict means that the police have to treat you with kid gloves. being a drug addict means that you will always have somewhere to go and be treated as `special'. Being a drug addict means that you will be the recipient of vast amounts of public money - above and beyond that which is paid out to all run of the mill work-shy shirkers.

And so, as the number of young people who are unemployed, rises inexorably so the number of drug addicts will also rise. The crimes they commit will rise. The suffering of the innocent will increase. The cost to an already bankrupt and broken society will soar.

The government spends a fortune looking after drug addicts (and a smaller but significant fortune on looking after alcoholics who remain in denial). Huge chunks of the nation's increasingly sparse budget is spent on providing resources for addicts.

And yet people with very real problems (which are not of their own making) are often refused help.

To give a simple example.

I know a lonely, not very bright man who turned up at a drop in centre in a large town. He was looking for a cup of tea and some companionship. But because he wasn't an addict of some kind he was thrown out onto the street.

In modern Britain you have to be the right sort of needy if you've going to get help. You have to be a member of a socially recognised group if you want support.

If you are a drug addict (or any kind), an alcoholic or an AIDS patient then you will do well. You will be constantly surrounded by social workers who are desperate to help you and give you money.

But if you are simply struggling to survive in a cruel, harsh, bureaucratic world, you are on your own.

As more and more people hit problems the resentment at the resources offered to addicts will grow and grow. Addicts enjoy one on one care and vast fortunes are spent on them. Huge armies of social workers are employed to look after them. And yet far more deserving members of the community (carers struggling to look after disabled or elderly relatives spring to mind) are ruthlessly denied help and support.

The industry caring for drug addicts is based on two false premises. First, it is based on the theory that addiction to drugs such as heroin and cocaine is hard to kick. This is a well sustained myth. The truth, as I was the first to point out some years ago in books such as Life Without Tranquillisers and Addicts and Addictions, is that addiction to some prescription tranquillisers and sleeping tablets is far harder to kick than addiction to heroin and cocaine. Compared to Valium and Ativan, drugs such as heroin and cocaine are about as addictive Smarties. As I showed decades ago in books such as Addicts and Addictions and Life Without Tranquillisers, the hard scientific evidence shows conclusively that it is far harder to give up benzodiazepine tranquillisers than it is to give up heroin or cocaine. And yet virtually no public money is spent helping benzodiazepine addicts? Good heavens, it is harder to give up cigarettes or alcohol than it is to give up heroin or cocaine. Second, the drug addiction industry believes that the people it assists really need help and will benefit from it. The truth is that they won't benefit from it because if you give loads of special attention to whingeing, self-obsessed, weak, vain individuals then you will make them more, not less, self-obsessed. By encouraging them to concentrate all their energy and effort onto a not very significant addiction (and praising them when they make a modest effort to reform) social workers are actually making the problem far, far worse. Courts which take a soft line on drug addicts ('If you were not a drug addict I would send you to prison for beating up the old lady and stealing her purse. Instead you must visit a clinic where you will be treated like a very fragile and special person and made to feel important and told that your sins are not your fault.')

There is, of course, a moral hazard here. People who have use heroin or cocaine have chosen to do so. The fact that they then steal in order to buy the drugs they want doesn't mean that we should feel sorry for them or help them more than we help people who are in trouble for no fault of their own. People who use heroin and cocaine choose to do so. They choose to steal in order to keep buying their drugs of choice.

My prediction is that politicians, together with the lobbyists who have a massive and expensive drug-addiction industry to support, will continue to remain hooked on the policy of over treating drug addicts. Drug addicts, and the industry which has grown up around them, are a powerful money-hungry lobby.

Chances of the drug addiction problem continuing to soar: 90%.

17. Our Energy Sources Will Run Out

Our energy is running out fast. Prices are going to soar. There are going to be shortages. People will die of cold. Schools, factories, offices and shops will close for several days a week because, without central heating, they won't be allowed to open.

I've been predicting all this for years. In February 2010 OFGEM, the energy regulator, finally agreed and warned that mainland Britain could face power shortages in coming years (starting in 2015 and 2016). OFGEM also warned that prices will rise considerably. Energy bills are already twice as high, and rising faster in the UK than anywhere else in the world. It is clear that gas, oil and coal prices are going to go through the roof.

In recognition of this fact the UK Government responded by announcing plans to start storing gas in huge caverns under the Irish Sea. They were, they said, doing this in order to provide some protection in case Russia decides to raise gas prices or divert supplies (something it has done in the past). The caverns, it was announced, would be ready by 2014 - just a year or so before the energy crisis is due. If we get lots of men digging these right now they can be ready by 2014 if all goes perfectly. Preparing these caves will cost a large fortune and it is worth remembering that motorway works which are advertised as lasting 12 weeks usually seem to last twice as long and cost ten times as much. Digging out caverns under the Irish Sea and preparing them as gas storage areas might hit the odd snag.

Our reliance on foreign energy and foreign energy suppliers is a real problem. It didn't matter so much when they were just allowing foreigners to buy our car industry. That meant that the jobs and the profits would be someone else's but hey what the hell the workers weren't usually keen to work anyway. But the British Government has allowed us to become reliant on Russian oil and gas (we get what they don't need). they've allowed our water industry to be sold to the French (whose main interest is, naturally, making a profit rather than preserving a reliable supply of clean drinking water). And they have allowed our nuclear industry to be bought by foreigners. So when the uranium is running out and the nuclear industry is struggling to find stuff to buy which country's nuclear industry is going to be last in line?

Britain desperately needs nuclear power stations. But successive governments have refused to acknowledge this and now it is too late. Politicians have talked, and promised and delayed. At the moment official government policy is that the private sector must take on the big risks of constructing a power station, operating one and coping with variations in energy prices. Nowhere in the world have nuclear power stations been built on this basis.

To make things worse, the Labour Government has made Britain one of the very few countries in the world that is committed to a legally binding carbon efficiency target. The Labour party has committed us to closing down our existing power stations but, apart from allowing private companies to build a few rather pathetic windmills, has done bugger all to deal with the coming energy problem. (We are closing down our coal fired power stations to please the EU's absurd climate change regulations. Britain is the only country in the EU dependent on coal power stations.)

If things go according to plan new designs for two British reactors (which the country can't afford to build and can't afford not to build) should be approved by June 2011. Or ready for approval by then. Or there will be a meeting to discuss a revised date by then. Or perhaps not. It then probably take a decade to build the darned things.

Just to add to our problems, the Labour Government signed us up to the European Union's Renewable Energy Directive, an ambitious scheme which is much more demanding than any other target in the world, which requires signatories to obtain 15% of their energy to be generated from wind, solar or tidal generation facilities by 2020. And, of course, Brown and Blair gold-plated this (as they usually did with anything coming from the EU) and signed us up to a Renewable Energy Strategy which requires us to cut emissions by 18% from 2008 levels by 2020 and to cut them by 80% from 1990 levels by 2050.

To meet the targets for the generation of renewable energy the UK requires a sevenfold increase in the amount of electricity we generate by wind and other renewable sources. (That is far more than any other EU member state.) We start from a poor position. Even India has four times as much wind generation capacity as the UK.

There are, of course, a few snags with all this.

First, there is the cost. Replacing obsolete power generating plants is expensive. If you plan to reduce carbon emissions it becomes much more expensive and difficult. And if you insist that some of the energy is obtained from renewable sources then the build becomes even more difficult and far, far more expensive. In order to incorporate the amount of wind power the Government has signed us up for, power prices will have to rise by 39% - according to the Government. If the Government's estimate is wrong the rise in the cost could be much higher. Much higher. Much, much higher. American consumers will not have to face these massive costs because America hasn't signed up for any of this wind-solar-tide nonsense.

The Government has at least started its wind farm construction. Fifteen miles off the south-east coast of England poles are planted in up to 100 foot of water. Turbines will reach as high as 400 feet above the sea. Its difficult and dangerous work and will eventually result in the construction of 140 turbines. The Government needs more to be built if it is to satisfy its targets. The cost? Oh, an estimated £100 billion or so. It could be higher, of course. Much higher. Much, much higher. Early in

2010 the government handed out nine areas of North Sea waters to build 32 gigawatts of generating capacity. That's the equivalence of 30 small power stations and the Government announced with pride that these wind farms could generate a quarter of the UK's demand for electricity.

But its phooey.

The 32 gigawatts is the theoretical maximum. Wind farms operate far below their operational capacity. After all, they rely on wind if they are going to work, and there isn't always any. Plus the salt water tends to corrode the equipment. The truth is that the massive, and hugely expensive wind farms the Government is planning will be doing very well if they manage to produce 10 gigawatts of power. And that is a third of a quarter of the UK's demand for electricity which is one twelfth.

There are other problems.

The biggest planned wind farm will be built on the Dogger Bank which just happens to be 100 miles off the coast of Northern England. It will be difficult and very expensive to build a wind farm 100 miles out at sea. And difficult and very expensive to bring the electricity back to land.

The £100 billion estimated build cost of the new 32 gigawatt facilities will cost £1,650 for every man, woman and child. This, you will recall, at a time when we already have to find even more than that each year to service the interest on the debts Gordon Brown built up on our behalf.

The government claims with great glee that the UK is a world leader in wind microgeneration. By this they mean those entirely pointless little generators that greenies and politicians stick on the sides sof their houses to show how much they care. in reality of course they are entirely useless. Under normal conditions they barely provide enough electricity to power the computer the owner uses to update his blogs and tweets describing his green credentials - and certainly don't provide enough electricity to cover the energy used in making the machinery. When the weather blows hard the little generator will go round so quickly it may tear down the house wall to which it is attached. So, what the government is boasting is that we lead the world in entirely pointless technology that makes the user look good but serves no practical purpose.

The bottom line is that solar and wind energy are fine as long as the people who advocate them don't mind only playing with their electricity devouring computers when it is sunny or windy.

Meanwhile, here are some tips. Be prepared for electricity, gas, oil and petrol shortages. Remember that gas central heating doesn't work without an electricity supply. Try to make sure that you have as many sources of energy (including heat) as possible. My advice would be to make sure that you have a home which includes a log fire or a log burning stove of some kind.

Keep a supply of logs and candles in stock. And buy a bicycle for each member of the family.

The chances of the energy running out by 2020: 90%.

18. Globalisation Will Continue To Destroy The World

The notion that there are any benefits at all from globalisation is a myth of gargantuan proportions and those who work hard to perpetuate it are probably descendants of the tricksters who sold the Eiffel Tower three times to gullible Americans. The truth is that we have much for which we can blame globalisation. And nothing much that we can thank it for. The only people who really benefit from globalisation are the executives of large American corporations (and, to a lesser extent, their shareholders). Anyone who tells you different is a double dealing good for nothing lowlife who is probably a lawyer and should be (and probably is) in politics, enjoying a fat retainer from one or more of the large American corporations.

The unfashionable truth is that globalisation has hit the poor and the middle classes particularly hard for it is they who have paid for the huge profits enjoyed by the uber-rich; the financiers who have enjoyed the massive profits to be made out of investing in businesses built on Asian slave and child labour. Why employ a man or woman in England, Scotland or Wales when you can get a child in Asia to do the same work for a tiny fraction of the price - and without any of the restrictions brought in by the European Union and so slavishly obeyed by British politicians? Globalisation may have given us cheap television sets but there has been quite a price to pay.

All over Britain there are now economic microclimates where local industries, built up since the Industrial Revolution, have been devastated and destroyed.

The gap between the poor and the rich has risen faster in the last decade than ever before; widened by the never fading enthusiasm for globalisation. Only in America is there a bigger gap between poor and rich than there now is in Britain. The Labour Government's policies (and in particular their slavish worship of the finance industry, the bankers and the hedge fund managers) have ensured that the gap in Britain is considerably wider than it is anywhere else in Europe.

Things are, of course, going to continue to get much, much worse. Globalisation has given banking crooks carte blanche to rip off people in other countries. Agriculture and manufacturing been destroyed by globalisation. Now service industries being destroyed by globalisation. Only the already rich bankers benefit. Poor people and working people everywhere have suffered, do suffer and will suffer: their lives ruined by globalisation.

Chances of globalisation continuing to destroy the world: 100%.

19. Home-Working Will Increase (for several reasons)

Many companies can no longer afford to buy or rent property. The cost of fuel (and train tickets) makes commuting incredibly expensive. And increasing transport strikes, affecting trains and petrol supplies, mean that it makes sense to work at home. New technology makes it just as easy for a clerk, telephone operator or accountant to work at home as in an office.

Some people will find it pleasant.

Many will find it lonely and extremely difficult. They will drink and smoke and take drugs in order to deal with the problems of working by themselves.

Chances of home-working increasing: 80%.

20. More NHS Charges Will Be Introduced

Desperate not to make obvious cuts but to bring in more money the government will probably introduce hotel charges for English patients needing to stay in hospital and fees for English patients who visit a GP. Patients living on benefits won't be charged these fees, of course. And nor will patients in Scotland or Wales who will be protected from the charges. The result will be that the burden will hit hardest on those who are struggling to survive on a low, earned income. And pensioners, on fixed incomes, will suffer too.

Chances of NHS charges being introduced: 90%.

21. Our Manufacturing Industry Is Dying

One of Britain's fundamental problems is that our fake prosperity was built on three things.

First, our relatively high employment figures, and apparently successful society was built substantially upon a constantly growing public sector which kept employing people at high salaries (and paying them big bonuses) and kept hiring companies to build new office blocks in which to house the public sector employees. Public sector employees are never part of a nation's growth. They are a cost; a drain on resources.

Second, millions of people felt wealthy because the value of their home kept rising. Constantly rising house prices made people feel rich and enabled them to a constant source of real money. By borrowing more against their house or flat they had more money to spend on television sets, cars and boats.

Third, our economy was built upon a big, profitable financial sector which is now weak and discredited and is likely to be subject to all sorts of new rules and regulations from the EU and the IMF. The real problem with the financial sector was that, instead of being shared out, the profits were kept by a very small number of people. A few bankers and hedge fund managers got very, very rich and paid hardly any tax on their profits.

Now that these three sources of apparent wealth are disappearing we are left with nothing because under the Labour Governments of the last thirteen years our manufacturing industry has all but disappeared.

We don't actually make much anymore in Britain. British manufacturing lost 1.7 million jobs (people making things) during Brown's decade. Most of the people who lost their jobs went to work for the government as highly paid consultants teaching people how to blow their noses or make sandwiches.

We buy tons of stuff made in other countries.

But not much stuff has `Made in England' stamped on its bottom any more. (We would, in any case, have to be satisfied with `Made in EC'.)

The importance of manufacturing to the economy declined more rapidly under Labour Governments since 1997 than just about any other era. The big winners under Labour were, inevitably, public sector workers, estate agents and bankers. Since 1997 there has been a massive growth in the number of people employed by councils and quangos and a massive fall in the number of people employed by companies making things. Manufacturing accounted for more than 20% of the economy in 1997 when Labour came to power. (Incidentally, at that time the new Labour Government of the toxic war criminal Blair criticised the fact that the country had too small and too narrow an industrial base.

But, by 2007, after just ten years of Labour, manufacturing accounted for just over 12% of the economy. And it is still falling (as I write it is 11%).

The Labour Government has successfully halved the role of manufacturing in the British economy. Civil servants don't make things, nor do they create wealth for the nation. They are, on the contrary, a constant drain on our resources. Bankers, lawyers, hedge fund managers, estate agents and all the rest of them are also a drain. They don't make a damned thing between them.

Labour party politicians, having no experience of real industry and no understanding of basic economic truths, simply don't understand that employing more public administrators costs the country money and doesn't bring in any money. A country's wealth is built upon what it sells abroad. Unlike Australia and Canada, Britain does not have a huge store of commodities which it can sell to the rest of the world. And so Britain has find other things it can sell to a hungry world - such as motor cars, television sets, films, telephones, technology, experience, know-how and so on.

A household would not survive long if everyone in it spent all their time finding new ways to regulate the servants. (`You must polish the silver with the rag in your right hand. Two people must be available to supervise when floors are being cleaned.') And spent none of its time bring money into the house.

And yet that is precisely what Britain is doing. The Labour party has created a nation where enterprise, justice and fairness have all succumbed to the heavy hand of state regulation.

According to figures in the Financial Times in December 2009, no successful nation anywhere in the world has less than 15% of its GDP produced by manufacturing industry. Britain, let me remind you, has just 11% of its GDP produced by manufacturing industry. And that figure is falling fast.

And things aren't going to get any better.

Companies in Asia are now making cars that will cost £2,500 each and computers that will cost £100 each. Companies in India are beginning to outsource some work back to America because the strong rupee has made American labour cheaper than Indian labour (but not cheaper than British labour).

The fastest growing occupations in Britain are those which involve people who are paid to talk to us about our problems, people paid to make us look more attractive and people paid to conserve the environment.

Colleges are churning out vast quantities of nail technicians, hairdressers, beauticians and psychologists but there has in recent years been a dramatic fall in jobs in manufacturing industries. Quangos, charities and trade bodies and unions are growth industries. Public sector jobs are growing. But none of these jobs create wealth - they all suck it up. There are now 482,979 educational assistants paid for with public money. That's an increase in 91% over the last eight years. The number of legal associate professionals (such as legal assistants and data protection officers) has risen by 109% to 51,250.

Even in those growth areas employers admit that they are having to hire people who are incompetent. Employers report that in 2009 they had 1.7 million employees who were not fully proficient in their jobs (it was 1.3 million in 2005). The country's first audit of national skills showed that the UK's growth in highly skilled jobs has been one of the lowest in the Organisation for Economic Cooperation and Development since 2001. That spells disaster for the future.

To make things worse, it was reported in May 2010 that some manufacturing companies were managing to make money only by selling their machinery to foreign companies. And that, of course, is the equivalent of the ship's captain ordering the crew to chop up the ship to keep the boilers fed. There really is no future in it.

On the 12th April 2010 it was announced with some pride that an oil price rise would affect Britain less than other countries around the world. Politicians seemed to think that this was a wonderful thing.

But I'll tell you the real reason why oil price rises affect Britain less than they affect other countries.

It's because the UK has so little manufacturing industry left. It is factories which use oil. But Britain has hardly got any of those. So we don't use much oil.

And the politicians think that is a good thing.

It's scary.

Honestly, it's truly scary.

What are the chances of Britain's manufacturing industry regaining its strength and starting to boom?

Nil.

There is no chance whatsoever.

Our blind allegiance to the EU and its rules and regulations means that we are doomed.

Chances of our manufacturing industry continuing to die: 100%.

22. Local Authorities Are Going To Face Hard Times. (Services will deteriorate dramatically. Some councils will go bankrupt and be unable to pay their debts.)

At the end of March 2009 it was revealed by the Audit Commission that 127 local authorities had nearly £1billion on deposit when the Icelandic banks went bust. Most worryingly, however, seven local authorities were branded `negligent' in failing to heed the warning signs and continuing to deposit money in Icelandic banks days before their collapse in 2008. The seven put £32.8 million into banks after September 30th - the date when the rating agencies severely marked down the credit worthiness of the banks. In one case a council put in a deposit that exceeded the local authority's investment limit for a single institution. Did any of the idiots responsible get punished for their gross incompetence? Is John Prescott a genius? Incidentally, the Audit Commission said that there was no evidence that the sums at risk (approximately a billion quid) would produce service cuts or council tax rises. So, what that really means is that the councils had overcharged local taxpayers by at least a billion.)

All over the world local authorities have been investing local taxpayers' money in structured products which they didn't understand. Convinced by snake oil salesmen in sharp suits that they could make trillions by investing their funds in some super sophisticated derivative they handed over the money and waited for the bonanza. Sadly, there has been no bonanza. Local authorities in America, France, Germany and elsewhere have huge debts (and will probably go bust) because local finance `experts' who didn't even understand how stupid and inexperienced they were, and who had never handled anything bigger than their own mortgage, were foolish enough to hand over untold millions of other people's money to salesmen they hardly knew. Some even leveraged their investments and took on massive debts.

Local councils have to stop wasting money. Every spring, all over the country, absurd road works spring up. I have for years called the month of March `National Kerb Month'. Unnecessary road works are done simply to get rid of money - so that next year's roads budget will not be cut. Roundabouts are altered, pavements are widened, road signs are ripped out and replaced and kerbs are dug up and put back. Miles and miles of perfectly good kerb stones are ripped out, thrown out and replaced. In how many other departments does this go on where it isn't quite as obvious?

And local councils have to stop paying their employees such absurd salaries. In 2009 there were now 1,000 town hall executives in England who were paid more than £100,000 a year. That's a 20% rise on 2008. There were 182 people in local authorities being paid more than Cabinet ministers. (And yet some of these were the people who put nearly a billion pounds of taxpayers hard earned money into Icelandic banks that were about to go bust.) The argument, as always, is that you have to pay such huge salaries to get the best people. It's the same argument that was used to support the huge salaries paid to bankers. And the response is the same. First, we are clearly not getting the `best' people. Second, all these people would do the work for half the money because there is nothing else they are equipped to do.

Chances of local authorities facing really hard times in the coming decade: 100%.

23. The Number Of Laws Which Rule Our Lives Will Continue To Increase Dramatically

We do not live in a democracy and anyone who believes we do really needs medical attention. The truth is that they make the laws (and the rules about how they make the laws) but then they revise them, fine tune them, add to them and drive fleets of limousines through them when it suits them (or their friends). But for us the laws are barbed wire, concrete gun emplacements and a shoot to kill policy. The laws they make are not to protect us (as they should be) but to oppress us, harass us and control us.

And thus it will continue until such time as the revolution comes.

There will be many, many new laws. It will be impossible to keep up with what is legal and what is illegal. We now live in a fascist country (the EU) and the fascists always love laws. No one seems to know exactly how many new laws the EU has introduced (and since the number increases daily it is a moving feast) but it is agreed to be well in excess of 100,000. These have, of course, been added to the laws which we already had. And our EU-loving governments have gold-plated many of the EU laws - making them even more stifling than the oppressive EU intended. You should, of course, know them all. It is your duty to yourself, your family and the EU to know and understand them intimately. If you don't then the consequences could be very serious.

We are moving quickly from our old Magna Carta based society in which everything not forbidden is allowed to an EU world in which everything not allowed is forbidden. It's an important difference but most people haven't noticed.

And since, at the same time, the number of things allowed is being reduced on a daily basis (the EU has brought in several hundred thousand new laws in the last few years and no one, not even the lawyers or the judges, know what they all are) so our freedom is being decimated.

There is no law and there is certainly no justice. Now, all we have left is in knowing what is right and what is wrong and being able to differentiate in our hearts and minds between what is wrong and what is right and then living our lives accordingly.

Our society relies on the existence of and respect for reliable, sensible laws. When the laws are distorted and forced into disrepute then society crumbles. Thus it is that the EU, and generations of compliant, treacherous politicians, have destroyed the very basis of our society.

Today our laws are no longer debated and passed by elected representatives sitting in Parliament. Today our laws are created by unelected bureaucrats sitting in expensive offices in distant Brussels who, well, just make them up. There is no debate, no discussion, no argument. The bureaucrats of Brussels simply make up our new laws and the puppets at the House of Commons pass them. This will not go on for much longer, of course. Now that the Treaty of Lisbon has been signed, the EU will, when its ready, get rid of the House of Commons (which has been a sham for years) and simply pass laws directly from Brussels.

Chances of us having far more laws in 2020 than we have now: 100%. (Unless the EU breaks up.)

24. Politicians Will Continue To Defile Our Language

I have, in previous books, often shown how politicians have adapted their own version of Orwell's newspeak language. So, for example, when a British soldier is killed by an American soldier (or the pilot of an American aeroplane) the death is invariably described as a `friendly fire incident'. The aim, of course, is to make the death seem somehow less awful.

Two new examples of Newspeak have come out of the financial crisis. The printing of vast amounts of money, in order to pay off government debts, has been described as `quantitative easing' (a misnomer if ever I heard one) and toxic loans and debts which have been taken over by the Government (so that the banks don't have to worry about them) are known as `legacy assets'.

Politicians will continue to use creative language management in order to disguise what they are doing.

We will all need to be alert if we are to know what is going on around us.

Chances of politicians continuing to defile our language: 100%.

25. Medical Tourism Will Soar

I have, over the years, received many letters from readers telling me that they have travelled abroad for medical treatment. Some have found surgeons or physicians providing efficient, effective and simple treatments not available in this country. (I remember, in particular, a reader who wrote to tell me about the surgeon he had found near Paris who cured a nasty affliction called Dupuytren's Contracture with a very simple operation not available in the UK.) Others have gone abroad because they didn't want to wait for years for treatment in Britain and couldn't afford to pay for private care in a British private hospital (where the consultant and `hospital' fees can be obscene).

The sad truth is that medical care in Britain's NHS was never better than it was in the 1960s and 1970s, and private medical care in Britain is today barely as good as NHS care was then. The quality of care and service provided by both the NHS and the private medical sector have collapsed in recent years.

In contrast to this decline, the quality of medical care in foreign countries has soared. New hospitals built in India and Thailand, for example, now attract an enormous number of international patients. The facilities are second to none, the surgeons and physicians and nurses are all well-trained to international standards and the prices are far lower than the prices in the UK.

And so I believe that an increasing number of patients will become `medical tourists'; travelling thousands of miles in order to receive medical treatment. After all, one of the great indictments of the health care provided in Britain is that many immigrants now go back home if they need medical care. The `free' medical care available in British hospitals is considered so poor (and the risk of catching a serious and possibly fatal infectious disease such a huge one) that they would rather go back to Turkey or Poland (or wherever) and be treated there.

Medical tourism is one of the great growth industries of the future. It won't be long before there are consulting doctors in British towns and cities offering advice on where to go for what operation. And travel agents will abandon taking tourists to Spain for a fortnight and instead offer trips to Thailand for hip replacement surgery.

Chances of more Britons going abroad for medical treatment: 90%.

26. The Official Theft Of Houses Will Accelerate

Councils are using powers given them by John Prescott which entitle them to grab `empty' properties. The law allows councils to take possession of any property that has been empty for more than six months and councils are taking houses from the elderly and the sick and the estates of the recently deceased (where the estate hasn't been able to sell the property). Councils have taken homes from people who were simply away looking after relatives or who had gone into residential accommodation. The law entitles councils to let the houses they take to council tenants and although they are supposed to deduct only costs before passing the rent to the owner this is obviously a cheap and effective way for councils to cut their building and property management costs.

Chances of councils continuing to take advantage of this profitable form of legalised theft: 90%.

27. Vaccination Will Become Compulsory

The government will try to reduce the size (and cost of the NHS) because they have to save so much money to avoid national bankruptcy that not even the NHS will be immune to cuts. But the cuts won't be enough. And so, the government's advisers will suggest that it might help to cut costs if the nation became healthier. And that will, of course, mean more laws. It will mean compulsory all sorts of things. It may mean that people who are overweight and who refuse to lose weight may be punished in some way (possibly by being denied treatment or benefits) or fined. But my best bet is that the government will introduce a compulsory vaccination programme. The drug companies and the doctors (both of whom will make vast amounts of money out of a compulsory vaccination programme) will recommend that all children be vaccinated whether or not their parents approve. Those parents who refuse to have their children vaccinated will have them taken away from them. As Dr Ron Paul, American Presidential candidate, has pointed out: `When we give government the power to make medical decisions for us, we, in essence, accept that the state owns our bodies.'

When a reader asked me how likely I thought it was that childhood vaccination would become compulsory (as they already are in some parts of the world, with children whose parents refuse being taken away from them and put into care) I pointed out that some GPs are already refusing to have patients on their lists if they don't agree to have their vaccinated we are getting close. (GPs are, of course, taking purely commercial decisions. If the percentage of patients on their lists that haven't been vaccinated gets too high then the GPs lose out on one of their cash bonuses.)

Despite the dangers and inefficiencies known to be associated with it, vaccination will become compulsory. The hazards and inadequacies will be ignored. It will not be the first time. Compulsory vaccination was introduced in Britain in the mid 19th century and in 1871 Public Vaccinators were appointed.

In Britain, recommendations relating to vaccines are made by the Joint Committee on Vaccination and Immunisation which is made up of a variety of people. I would be very surprised if, at any one time, the committee did not include members who had financial links to drug companies or were or are receiving grants from drug companies making vaccines. I have been researching vaccination and drug hazards for over 40 years and I have never yet found an official committee which did not include individuals with drug company links. (I have on numerous occasions found committees which were composed entirely of individuals who had financial links with drug companies.)

Up until 2009, the JCVI made recommendations. But then the Labour Government created a Statutory Instrument amending the Public Health (Control of Diseases) Act 1984 which states that recommendations of the JCVI will in future receive the full support of the Secretary of State for Health. They will, therefore, become law.

Will the JCVI make vaccination compulsory? Well, the better question would probably be: `When will the JCVI make vaccination compulsory?' because there are already many senior members of the medical establishment who want vaccination to be compulsory. You will not be convulsed with shock when I tell you that drug companies which make vaccines would not be averse to their products being made compulsory. I understand that. I would like my books to be made compulsory reading.

And guess what, Britain isn't the only country in Europe which is heading for compulsory vaccination. The French, for example, have also started talking about mass vaccination programmes. I have absolutely no doubt that compulsory vaccination is EU policy. And since the EU always gets what it wants, compulsory vaccination will come to be.

One local authority in England has already created secret vaccination centres, stating that it is doing so under `special powers granted to HM Government under the Civil Contingencies Act 2004'.

And another NHS Trust has recently sent out letters inviting people to attend for vaccination. The letter states: `It is important that you attend this session. If you are unable to attend, you will need to go to one of the later sessions listed overleaf.'

That sounds to me very much as though the NHS Trust already

regards vaccination as compulsory. And a good many doctors would heartily approve. Senior doctors recently suggested not only that vaccination should be compulsory but that children who were not vaccinated should not be allowed into school. Social workers would doubtless be quick (and eager) to take children away from parents who opposed vaccination.

Why will vaccination become compulsory?

Simple.

Politicians have been persuaded that vaccinating the population at large helps save money. The theory is that if you vaccinate 1,000,000 children against, say, whooping cough and as a result you prevent 1,000 children getting the disease then the country will avoid the cost of 1,000 parents staying at home for a week or so to look after their child. If one child is permanently brain damaged that is bad luck on the child and his or her parents but, as long as the state can avoid financial responsibility by denying that there is any link between vaccination and brain damage, then it is ahead of the game. In reality, the evidence shows that even this cold-blooded, steel-hearted philosophy is faulty. The problem is that vaccines are so ineffective and so dangerous that instead of being an advantage to society as a whole they are a costly disadvantage.

Drug companies tighten the screw on politicians by threatening to move their industry abroad, to some more congenial environment, if their suggestions are not heeded. Drug companies are almost as good at threatening people as they are at bribing them. They hire strong, efficient lobbyists who might not actually wander around with briefcases stuffed full of notes but they might as well do.

So why are drug companies so keen to promote vaccination programmes? Why have politicians been persuaded that vaccinating the population benefits the many at the expense of the few?

That's simply because the drug companies make huge amounts of money out of selling vaccines. And they have fiddled the evidence, and denied or suppressed the inconvenient truths, in order to promote their point of view.

The global vaccine market reached $21 billion in 2010 and is growing at rate of 16.5%. The whole business of vaccinating people is so hugely profitable (largely because it is something that doesn't rely on finding a large number of sick people but also because it is something that can be done on a regular basis) that drug companies, having almost saturated the `vaccinating-children' market moving are moving heavily into adult vaccines. There is, for example, a vaccine planned to prevent atherosclerosis. I suspect that doctors will claim that this will enable people to keep eating a bad diet and yet avoid heart attacks.

The drug industry is made up of nasty companies run by nasty, ruthless people who care nothing whatsoever for people but who care a great deal for money. In many previous books of mine I have exposed the nasty behaviour of the drug industry which likes to describe itself as `ethical' but which is, in my view, rather more contemptible than the Columbian drug barons who sell cocaine but who do not exhibit such nauseating quantities of hypocrisy.

Those who promote vaccines often claim that vaccination programmes have reduced illness, prevented millions of deaths and are the main reason why the average life expectation has risen.

These are all barefaced lies.

The whole vaccination story is one of the great modern scandals of our time. The entire medical profession (at least the part of it in general practice) has been bribed by the drug industry, working through the government and using taxpayers' money. In my first book The Medicine Men (1975) I wrote that doctors who did what the drug industry told them to do could hardly describe themselves as belonging to a profession. Even I did not then imagine just how easy it would be to bribe and buy an entire profession.

The few doctors who do stand up and say something, and who dare to point out that vaccination programmes are a hazard and do more harm than good, will quickly be silenced. They are discredited and scorned and their work is not published.   There are other dangers too. My books are never reviewed these days. Most national newspapers and magazines ban all advertisements for my books. Planned interviews are invariably cancelled before they take place. In the last ten years I have twice been investigated at length by HMRC (on both occasions they ended up by giving me money because I had paid too much tax.)

The truth is that doctors, whether working as hospital consultants, GPs or public health officials, know very little about vaccination. Most simply follow the establishment line, never question what they are told by the drug industry and dismiss all critics of vaccination as dangerous lunatics.

Doctors give five vaccines to babies with developing immune systems. They start dumping the damned stuff into babies when they are two months old, for heaven's sake. And yet there is no evidence that vaccines are safe in the long-term. No research is done to check this. The establishment puts the onus on the doubters to find the evidence, knowing that is pretty well impossible. In the USA a huge medical practice of paediatricians with 30,000 child patients do not vaccinate their patients at all. Guess how many patients with autism they have? If you guessed `none' you guessed right.

The truth is that the evidence clearly shows that vaccination programmes have not done the things they are credited with but have done most of the things they are blamed for. The decline in disease, the reduction in infant mortality rates and the increase in average life expectation are all due to improved living conditions. Cleaner water, efficient methods of removing sewage, fresher food, less poverty and less overcrowding are the real reasons why these improvements have taken place. Anyone who doubts this has only to look at graphs showing mortality rates and life expectation rates alongside graphs showing when vaccines were introduced. The graphs show clearly that the improvements took place before vaccines were introduced.

Why don't doctors say anything?

Sadly, that is because the medical profession has been bought. GPs lost their final scrap of integrity on the day when they agreed to take money if they managed to vaccinate enough patients. That sort of conveyor belt, bonus ridden philosophy is better suited to the manufacture of motor car parts than the practise of medicine.

Many GPs deny this but the truth is that GPs receive huge bonus payments if they vaccinate enough patients. Every vaccination they give (or authorise) is another nice noise in the cash register. Epidemics produce a bonus bonus. In the autumn of 2009 GPs (paid on average £106,000 a year) were demanding £7.51 to give each swine flu vaccination. That meant that each GP would earn £27,000 from giving vaccinations against swine flu. (And most would tell their practice nurse to give the vaccination, so they wouldn't have to do anything themselves. A practice clerk would fill in the claim forms. So that's £27,000 for doing absolutely nothing at all.) With 33,000 GPs in the country, giving the swine flu jabs would cost the country just under £900 million.

The enormous and rich vaccine industry has bought the medical profession, lock stock and syringe barrel. GPs, once members of a proud and distinguished profession which gave us such medical giants as Joseph Lister, have been reduced to snivelling, whining needle-men for the drug industry; hand-maidens to an industry which cares nothing for people but everything for profits. In my first book, The Medicine Men, I wrote that a profession which exists to do the bidding of an industry is no longer a profession. Doctors have lost their way. The drug industry has done it cleverly, of course. GPs receive massive bonus payments for vaccinating patients not from the drug industry directly but from the Government. A GP who jabs enough patients gets a thumping great wodge of cash. A GP who is questioning and discerning will be punished. And so the vast majority of GPs, no longer professionals, do as they are damned well told. Most know nothing about the dangers of the damned vaccines they so happily jab into patients' arms. Most don't even do the dirty work themselves. It's far more profitable to get a nurse to do it. Or someone pretending to be a nurse. And the government will provide these subsidiary hand maidens to do the work. And the government will provide propaganda witches to chase the patients and the parents who don't turn up to be jabbed. They're called health visitors. Question the whole damned sordid business and these ill-educated propagandists (who know nothing about the risks of the toxic mixtures they are promoting) will accuse you of being a flat-earther or hating your child or whatever.

Most doctors working for the NHS long ago lost any sense of right or wrong. They long ago lost the passions and beliefs and yearnings that (hopefully) took them into medicine. Today, the lives of the vast majority of practising doctors are driven by a potent and destructive (and distinctly patient-unfriendly) mixture of ambition and greed and denial. There are very few doctors in practice today who want to save the world, or even change it very much. Their aims are selfish and personal. A bigger house, a faster car, shorting working hours and longer holidays.

The number of health problems (varying from autism to severe brain damage) caused by vaccines will soar. The link between vaccinations and illness will continue to be as strenuously denied as was the link between smoking and lung cancer.

Chances of vaccinations becoming compulsory: 90%.

28. Sterling Is Going To Go Down (a lot)

The recent massive fall in sterling (when measured against the dollar and the euro) has been a great help to the nation's few remaining exporters. It has made their products far more attractive to foreign buyers.

But the fall in sterling also makes imports more expensive and since our imports include oil and food and other commodities and most of the manufactured things we use (stuff like cars, television sets, wine, building materials, toys and clothes) this can be quite a problem.

Indeed, the fall in the currency has already pushed up inflation. This has apparently surprised the government and the financial establishment though to be honest it always seemed pretty obviously going to happen.

And of course if inflation goes up too much then interest rates will have to rise in an attempt to slow things down. And that isn't something the politicians want to do because if interest rates go up businesses and home buyers will suffer and the country will slide back deeper into the depression we never got out of when the people in the expensive suits said we had. (The Government claimed just before the election that we had come out of recession. Their evidence for this was a collection of pretty ropey figures showing that the economy was beginning to move in a positive direction. But when I looked at the figures behind the figures I found that the good news seemed to involve the government in general and the NHS in particular suddenly hiring more people. Loads more people. Private companies, both big and small, were `letting people go'.

The government was hiring as fast as the forms could be completed. If that's evidence for the end of a recession I'm a panda.)

The bottom line is that the country is buggered.

We have virtually no manufacturing industry. Our finance industry (the banks and the hedge funds and the private equity companies) are disgraced and in debt up to the top of their yacht masts. And foreigners would rather hold the Australian dollar or the Canadian loonie than the Great British Pound.

Our country's massive debts, and the by no means impossible chance that the nation will go bankrupt, mean that sterling's decline is likely to continue for years to come.

There will, of course, be ups and downs.

Currencies never move smoothly in one direction.

But if I was living in Spain or New Zealand or America or China or Australia and relying on an income in sterling to help buy me food, I would be trying to find some way to ensure that I would not be sitting cross legged on the pavement with a hat between my legs and a small sign on a piece of cardboard reading `British. Please give money for food.' hung around my neck.

The pound will go down and keep going down because if it isn't by now it will soon be the short end of the carry trade (in other words people will borrow sterling to invest in currencies which are stronger) and that will push it down.

Another problem is that sterling risks losing its AAA rating and even the risk (as much as the reality) will push down sterling.

Britain's debts are so bad and the political system so corrupt and incompetent that sterling has an exceedingly poor future.

Chances of sterling declining in value against other currencies: 90%.

29. Public Sector Strikes Will Increase

During the next few years public sector workers have to start paying for the gravy and jam they've been dining on for the last decade or so. Naturally, being public sector workers, unaccustomed to having to tighten their belts, and accustomed to regarding themselves as above all rules and regulations, they will not like it when public sector jobs are cut, when wages are frozen or cut, when benefits are top sliced, when pensions are tightened. They've had greedy good times but will, I have no doubt, be woefully unwilling to accept their share of the pain their greed has helped to cause. Public sector strikes will be common as government employees realise that they are also going to have to help pay the price for the crisis their very employment helped create. The unions destroyed much of British industry. (We used to be a world leader in car manufacturing. Now the Germans own Rolls Royce and Bentley.) Next, perhaps, the unions will destroy what little remains of Britain.

As a result we are going to be bullied by merciless, overbearing, obstructive public sector trades unions, whose officials and members believe that they, and they are alone, are entitled to sail through the coming years of national hardship without suffering any change in their financial circumstances unless it is for the better.

People working for the government will find it difficult to accept that their standard of living must fall. They have grown fat and flabby and they expect to live rich, bloated lives. Those who work for the private sector understand a little better that times can be good and bad. And the self-employed know this better than anyone. But civil servants (and, thanks to Brown and Blair, they now make up a massive part of our society) have no idea what the future will involve and do not yet understand that they too will have to feel a little pain. People working for organisations which used to be run by the Government (such as British Airways and British Telecom, British Railways and British Gas) have the same problem: many of them still think they live in a world where work is something you do to while away a few minutes between tea breaks. British Airways is pretty well a pension fund that runs a damned near bankrupt airline and the sight, in 2010, of cabin staff destroying the holiday hopes, and business plans, of thousands of Britons in order to preserve a way of working that went out of fashion when spats were still the new thing was, to say the least, embarrassing.

Civil servants and the people working for these companies which used to be government run, won't like it the cuts that are inevitable if the country is to avoid bankruptcy. Since their selfishness and sense of self importance runs deep they won't like it one little bit.

The result is that there are going to be a lot more strikes and walk outs and disruptions and inconveniences. Most of these will, as usual, be organised by, for and on behalf of public service employees who have enjoyed high salaries, massive pensions, huge benefits and small workloads for a long time and who will become increasingly upset when they are forced to work harder and for less money. Bureaucracies never implode peacefully and there will be trials and tribulations as politicians and civil servants are shuffled off into the sunset.

The strikes will, of course, mostly be called for times when they will cause most pain and discomfort to the general public. This inevitably means that transport workers, keen to cause their neighbours as much pain as possible, will call strikes on bank holidays in order to ensure that the television news is dominated by pictures of unhappy families sleeping on the floor in overcrowded airports; their long looked-forward to holiday in the sun turned by the pitiless greed of the union bosses into an insanitary disaster. Union bosses at state-owned enterprises such as Royal Mail, immune to the vagaries of the real world, and with love or care for their country, or understanding of the very real financial predicament the politicians and bankers have put us in, will continue to use their muscle to bully and extort and destroy.

Of course it won't only be public sector workers who go on strike. Some private sector workers will strike too - particularly the ones working for companies which used to be state owned. For example, the people who hand out plastic trays of plastic food on British Airways went on strike because the airline bosses were trying to keep the company alive and to cut back on absurd over-manning practices which made the airline economically unsound. The irresponsible bastards who run Unite, a massive public service union, make the wankers who destroyed British Leyland look like responsible citizens. The new government will have to introduce tough fiscal policies in order to try and protect the currency. Unfortunately, the unions will respond by calling strikes and strikes will slow the recovery (which is going to be pretty slow anyway) and will result in the collapse of sterling being heightened. I suspect that we may soon see the first general strikes for many a decade. Most of the people involved will be greedy, selfish, stupid public sector workers. The private sector's attempts to grow will be destroyed by the strikes.

Here's a safe prediction: the Unite union will become about as popular as a black rat with fleas and while BA staff and postmen were told not to wear their uniforms when out in public (because of their unpopularity) Unite staff will, at the smart dinner parties they undoubtedly attend, pretend to be tax collectors or estate agents rather than admit to working for Unite.

There will be cutbacks and, in Britain more than anywhere else, there will be idiotic, destructive strikes which will create great inconvenience, deepen the depression, weaken the country and create more unemployment with the result that there will be more cutbacks, higher taxes and more strikes. The people striking will, almost exclusively, be people working for government run bodies or companies which used to be owned and run by the government and which still have civil-servant mentality and old fashioned, no longer affordable civil-servant style pensions.

Chances of there being more strikes: 100%.

30. Britain Will Continue To Be Run For People Who Don't Pay Taxes

Only 60% to 70% of the population vote at general elections. As the public become increasingly disenchanted with politicians (and accustomed to the fact that to them the words `promise' and `lie' are interchangeable) so this figure is likely to fall ever lower. To win an election a political party needs only about a third of the vote. The other two thirds of the votes are divided between the other two main parties and the many small parties which now exist.

So, to win an election, a political party needs only 20% to 25% of the nation's votes.

And this means that a political party can get into power in the UK by obtaining the votes only of people who pay no taxes.

That's how the Labour Party stayed in power for 12 years. At the May 2010 election, the Labour Party got very little support in southern England but it got massive support in Scotland, Wales and the far North of England. Those are all regions where unemployment is high and where there are many towns which are reliant on public sector jobs for employment.

Think about that. And what it means. The country is being run by and for people who do not pay taxes but who expect their needs and wants to be met by the State.

This bizarre state of affairs is now likely to continue indefinitely.

Chances of country continuing to be run on behalf of people who don't pay taxes: 100%.

31. Quangos Will Keep On Growing (in number and in size)

Instead of closing down quangos, huge amounts of money is spent reorganising them in an attempt to distract critics who realise that most quangos do nothing useful but contribute enormously to the vast repertoire of unnecessary rules and regulations.

In the spring of 2010 the National Audit Office admitted that £1 billion of taxpayers' money had been wasted on 93 Whitehall reorganisations - most of which were `unnecessary'.

Sadly, instead of getting rid of quangos, future governments will merely reorganise them and rename them.

Quango employees aren't civil servants (strictly speaking) but they are paid by taxpayers. There are well over 1,000 quangos now. The Labour Government which came into power in 1997 obviously felt that creating quangos was something it should do to help get rid of surplus public money. And the one thing you can say in favour of quangos is that they do get rid of money very effectively. Over 100 quango employees earn more than £100,000 each. Some earn over £300,000. The cost of Britain's quangos is estimated to be around £60 billion a year (that's £2,550 for every British household) and the number of them is growing annually. They provide a comfortable final resting place for politicians (accustomed to living well on index linked pensions and enjoying chauffeur driven cars) who want a large extra chunk of cash for turning up occasionally and doing very little.

What the hell do they do?

Well, that's a very good question.

Some are just lobbying organisations for regions or particular industries. They do no harm and nothing of importance. Some, however, do massive harm to the nation. The National Institute of Clinical Excellence is a quango which actually has the right to decide which drugs the NHS will pay for. Many have the word `Independent' in front of their name which makes them sound, well, `independent' when, in truth, they are about as independent and impartial as Manchester United Supporters Club or, indeed, the BBC.

Whenever the government isolates a specific problem (teenage pregnancy, obesity or whatever it might be) it creates a quango and hires a lot of expensive bureaucrats to run it. Some of them have a good deal of power; certainly far more than is good for them or for us. Some of them even seem to think they are entitled to make laws or control the way we live our lives. For example, the Equality and Human Rights Commission (yet another bloody quango) says that the British National Party's policies are `indirectly discriminatory' because they require members to pledge to oppose integration if it might affect the unity or maintenance of the `indigenous British'.

Their favourite occupation is organising and funding festivals and conferences where they and employees from other quangos can mix with favoured fee-paid consultants and parade their prejudices. They enjoy expensive wines, gourmet food and applaud one another's hypocrisies. They obtain support for their existence by spending vast sums on entirely pointless (and ineffective) advertising campaigns. They pay full price for magazine advertisements and their leaflets, booklets and specially commissioned books are always printed in the most expensive fashion. (One of the reasons that you won't read much criticism of quangos in the press is that quangos often have huge advertising budgets. At a time when commercial groups are cutting back on their advertising the quango advertising is even more valuable than usual.)

Who are these people on this damned quango?

I would have thought that the vast majority of Britons (and all patriotic ones) would have applauded that particularly aspect of BNP policies.

Many quangos simply duplicate the work of government departments or existing quangos.

The one thing all quangos have in common is that their primary purpose is to ensure their own survival. If you go through a list of all 1100 odd quangos and ask yourself: `Is this organisation necessary, and does it perform a useful function in a transparent and democratic way?' you will find yourself answering `No and No' and nothing else.

Every Prime Minister for decades has promised to get rid of them. But every Prime Minister for decades has added to the number. The thing is that quangos are a very useful way to do something without doing anything (`we've set up a quango and we're awaiting their report') and an almost perfect way to avoid responsibility for the fact that nothing is being done. Quangos are a perfect example of a modern society which has separated authority from responsibility and rights from obligations.

But the big advantage of quangos is that they enable Prime Ministers and their chums to bow to lobbying pressure without being too obvious about it and to find ludicrously well-paid employment for their otherwise unemployable political friends.

Despite the fact that all the decisions that affect us are, thanks to the

Treaty of Lisbon, now made in Brussels, the number of quangos, and their cost, is set to rise for years to come. The one thing we can be certain of is that no quango will ever decide that it does not perform an essential task.

There is nothing you and I can do about it though since you have probably not annoyed the government as much as I have there is, I suppose, a chance that you could wangle yourself a nice well-paid position on a quango.

Britain would be a better, safer, richer, more productive country if all the quangos were closed and all the quango staff forced, after appropriate training, to take up useful employment. But my bet is that although there will much talk about cutting back and getting rid of unnecessary quangos, there will be more quangos (and more quango staff) in 2020 than there are now. The inevitable cuts in public service that are coming to help pay for Brown's debts won't affect the quangos.

Chances of quangos growing in number, power and cost: 90%.

32. Book Publishing Will Hit Hard Times

In a February 2010 copy of Country Life magazine I read a quote from a bookshop owner forecasting that the that the threat from the iPad could, in ten to fifteen years' time, change publishing in the same way that MP3s have changed the music business.

Really.

Ten to fifteen years.

I confess I didn't know whether to cry or to laugh.

The internet, and associated new technology, have already darned near destroyed the music industry. (How many shops are there near your home which sell CDs?) The film industry is fighting for its life as DVD sales collapse. It can take hours to download a DVD from an internet site. But people do it. And pirated copies are absurdly easy to make.

It is much easier to download a book from the internet. And much, much easier to print pirated copies - particularly when a book consists only of text. Online piracy will destroy publishers who rely on selling eBooks.

It won't take ten or fifteen years for computers to destroy the publishing industry. It won't take five years. The damage is already being done. And the problems started long before technology companies started producing e-readers which were able to hold copies of thousands of books, and pick up zillions more from the internet (with little or no money going to the authors or the original publishers).

First to put the boot in were websites such as Amazon which allow `associates' to sell books for a penny (plus the postage). This is undoubtedly a great service for book buyers, and a wonderful way to find rare books. But the ready, and cheap, availability of books in this way has destroyed back list sales. Authors and publishers can no longer rely on their books being in print for years because all the books that have ever been sold stay in the system. Instead of hiding on the shelves of second hand bookshops in Hay on Wye or the Charing Cross Road, waiting to be found by assiduous book hunters, they can be found within seconds and bought just as quickly. Often for pennies. Books sent out for review end up on Amazon or eBay within a day or two of being put into the post. The publisher and the author of a book that might have expected to sell just a thousand or so copies to start with, and to have then remained in print for years and earned a steady income, will now die an early death. A book which might have survived in print for years will now be allowed to go out of print very quickly. The publisher and the author must keep on producing new books if they are to continue to eat. It is hardly surprising that the output of new books is constantly accelerating. And hardly surprising that authors, publishers and small book shops are suffering. The disappearance of the backlist will destroy small publishers and specialist authors. All this, note, was happening long before the arrival of eBooks and those damned reading devices. (One of the most absurd sights of 2009 was that of WH Smith and Waterstones both selling e-book reading devices. It was an extraordinary example of the murder victim loading the gun for his assassin. If publishers, bookshops and authors had united to defend their world then they could have protected themselves effectively.)

Second, the destructive effects of Google (one of the world's three most evil companies) are impossible to overestimate. Google decided some time ago that it was entitled to help itself to the work of thousands of authors from around the world. With scant regard for copyright it started putting books onto the internet. Authors and publishers around the world protested and leapt for lawyers. But Google continues with its evil work. I wonder how Google would like it if I started a company and nicked the name Google for it? Now there's a thought. I think I'll do that. My defence will be that Google doesn't believe in copyright.

Google plans to digitise all the world's 168 million books. Since 2004 the search engine has scanned in about 5 million titles, many of them still under copyright. Google has negotiated a `settlement' with the Authors Guide and the Association of American Publishers which will result in the money which is raised by selling the rights to the Google library being shared between Google and a registry run by publishers' and authors' representatives.

Several European governments (led by France and Germany but not, of course, Britain) are opposing the deal. Publishers, authors and photographers have all begun lawsuits against Google whom I now regard as one of the top two or three most evil companies on the planet. (I would put it alongside Monsanto as one of the two most evil companies in existence.)

Google stands to make a fortune, of course. It can learn a lot about the people who read the books it is scanning into its damned computers. It can (and undoubtedly will) then sell that information to advertisers who want to know who is interested in French history, holidays in the Seychelles or motor racing.

Does Google's plan hinder competition? Is it wrong for one search engine to have control of all the books in the world? Should authors have the right to offer, grant or withhold permission for their books to be taken from them and offered by some American company with dubious morals and a yearning for world domination? Do property rights mean anything anymore? Does a large corporation have the right to help itself to the work of millions of authors (dead and alive) who may or may not have any interest in their work being available on the internet. How much will Google's plans affect the sale of books? How will authors earn a living? Will anyone bother to write books for a living in the future? Will they be able to?

Maybe these are all irrelevant, insignificant questions.

They must be.

I seem to be the only person asking them.

The end result of all this is that bookshops will continue to disappear. And so will publishers (especially the small ones which cannot rely on income from television stations to survive). New book lists will exist almost exclusively of biographies and autobiographies written by and about minor celebrities. The most interesting books, specialist books, books that explore new ideas, adventurous, daring, questioning books will be increasingly expensive. Professional authors who aren't lucky enough to write huge international bestsellers (and there is a huge element of luck involved in writing a big bestseller) will find themselves joining the job queues and trying to supplement their meagre incomes in some other way. As e-book reading devices become cheaper so the death of the entire publishing industry will accelerate.

I am, incidentally, looking at ways to prevent Amazon and other websites selling new copies of my books.

Chances of book publishing, as we know it, coming to an end: 80%.

33. We Will See The Decline And Decline Of The Middle Classes

The government's policies in Germany after First World War led to the betrayal and destruction of the German middle classes, the people who had made Germany so strong. The collapse of the German currency led to poverty to people who had worked hard, saved hard and been prudent all their lives.

The same thing has happened in England. Today's middle classes have been betrayed and are heading for destruction. Is it an accident? A result of a series of cock ups? Or a result of a conspiracy to destroy the middle classes - the people who are always the greatest defenders of freedom and democracy.

The middle classes today are suffering. But it is tomorrow's middle classes which will suffer most.

When they get into their 50s, today's 20 year olds will have four generations to worry about.

Many will still have their children living at home. Their sons and daughters, in their late twenties and early thirties, will still be paying off their student loans and saving for the deposit on their first home. They probably won't even be able to afford to rent somewhere. As their children work long hours in order to make enough money to pay their bills, so mum and dad will be left with the job of babysitting and then with the task of helping with the school fees. They will have to look after their own ageing parents too. Public sector pensions are going to be far less generous than anyone imagines. And private sector pensions are doomed to years of under performance. The state, destroyed by Brown's profligate government, will not be able to look after them. All the promises, so easily made, will be forgotten. Brown himself will be enjoying the luxury of life in a Scottish castle.

When I was a medical student I ran a non profit making nightclub for young people in Birmingham city centre. The club was attacked one night by a gang of marauding youths. The kids with whom I had set up the club fought so hard that it was clear they would have given their lives. The invaders were repulsed. When I asked them why had they fought so hard, one of my club members replied, quite simply, that the club was all they had. They had everything to lose and so they fought with their lives.

Maybe when the middle classes finally realise that they stand to lose everything they will stand up and fight for themselves and the things they hold dear.

Chances of the oppression of the middle classes continuing: 90%.

34. More And More Jobs Will Go Abroad

More and more jobs are going to go abroad. There are 500 million people in India living on under £2 a day. They are just as skilled as most Britons and far more willing to work. And much cheaper to employ. The future is gloomy for people in Britain (and America and much of the rest of Europe) who do not have specific (and adaptable) skills.

Chances of more jobs moving from Britain to Asia: 100%.

35. Genetic Engineering Will Threaten to Destroy The World (as we know it)

The use of genetically modified food is increasing by about 7% a year. Three quarters of the soyabeans grown around the world are now genetically modified as over a quarter of the corn. The Chinese Government has approved GM varieties of rice and corn. Scientists (who have become increasingly partisan in recent years) constantly sneer at those who doubt the safety of genetic engineering and yet they provide no evidence whatsoever that genetic engineered food is safe and will not cause major problems in the future. The people who support the genetic modification of food with such enthusiasm fail to understand that one problem could cause mass starvation and billions of deaths. With the whole world using one genetically modified seed an infection that affected that seed could cause widespread mayhem. Actually, even that isn't scary enough. One big problem with a GM product could destroy the planet as we know it.

And still journalists and politicians (encouraged by bent scientists) continue to promote the interests of companies flogging the damned products.

Genetically modified (GM) crops are foreign substances that have never been part of a normal diet. No one knows what the long term effects of consumption will be. The truth is that Governments are running a huge, uncontrolled clinical trial and are, consequently, putting our health at risk.

I am unaware of any independent study showing that they are safe or nutritious and the fact that they are classed as `food' is merely a consequence of the marketing skills of the people making them and the gullibility and stupidity and greediness of our politicians. The only information that is available suggests that they are unsafe. For example, a report published in the International Journal of Microbiology has verified that animals fed GM corn suffered liver and kidney damage in just three months.

What's the risk of a major GM crisis in the future? I don't know, but my guess is as good as anyone else's. And it's certainly a better guess than that of any of the GM company paid scientists. (I once did a radio debate on GM food with a number of scientists who thought GM food was the greatest invention since the wheel. I asked them all if they had ever received money from making GM seeds or involved in the GM industry. Every single scientist admitted that they had. None of them seemed to think that this affected their judgement or their right to discuss the issue in public. One said `Every scientist in this field has been paid by the GM industry' as though that made it all acceptable. It doesn't make it acceptable.)

The European Union agriculture commissioner has warned that resisting the import of genetically modified products is contributing to the rising cost of raising pigs and chickens and could pose a threat to the meat industry. Poor old meat industry. (The EU always seems to worry most about industry. Fascism always involves a deadly mixture of state and industry.)

There is no evidence to show that genetically modified products are safe. On the contrary many experts believe that they could pose serious, long term problems to human health.

Naturally, our Government ministers support the European Union on this as on all other issues. When Prince Charles criticised genetically modified food, and warned of the potential dangers, the Environment Minister of the day - I don't know his name and I don't really care what it is or what he's doing now - put down his rattle and spoke up. You might imagine that the Environment Minister might be interested in the Environment. Not this one. His response was to claim that it was down to the opponents of genetically modified food to prove that it is unsafe.

This was probably the most stupid thing said by a Minister.

First, how, pray, do you prove that something is unsafe unless you test it?

Second, why should the consumer be forced to pay for the test to prove that something they are told they must accept is safe?

A report published in the international journal of microbiology has verified that genetically modified crops are causing health problems. Animals which were fed GM corn suffered liver and kidney damage within just three months. The simple fact is that GM crops are new and foreign to the human body. Many of them contain inbuilt chemicals - insecticides for example. No one can tell what the long term effects of consumption will be. Anyone who claims that these products are entirely safe is a liar and a fool. What few tests have been done have shown significant disruption of normal body functions and no proper studies have ever shown them safe or nutritious. The burden of proof should be on producers, not on the doubters to prove them unsafe. (It is in any case impossible to prove that something is unsafe, without very expensive research, unless you simply wait until things happen)

The makers of GM seeds say their products will end starvation. In fact their damned products do exactly the opposite: they force people to buy patented versions of seeds that were once widely available. Those who cannot afford the seeds die of hunger. Simple.

And meanwhile we wait to see what happens.

Imagine what will happen when everyone in the world is using the same genetically modified corn seed and that seed is devastated by a bug. There will be no more corn. Think potato blight on a global scale.

In my book `Betrayal of Trust' (published in 1994) I warned of the dangers involved in mixing human and animal genetic material. In my book `Superbody' (published in 1999) I warned again about the danger of superbugs being created by scientists messing around with genetic material.

Is it just remotely possible that `swine flu' was the first indication that someone should have taken notice of my warnings?

I don't know.

Nor do you.

Nor does anyone else.

The chances of there being a major disaster caused by genetic engineering and genetic modification within the next ten years must be frighteningly high

I can't prove genetically modified food is dangerous.

But they can't prove it's safe.

Chances of a major problem being caused by genetic engineering by the end of 2020: 50%

36. Food Is Going To Be Scarce, More Expensive And Less Nutritious

The Americans are burning food to keep their cars going so the global food shortage is going to get worse. The EU approves of, and is a keen supporter of, biofuels too. This obsession with burning food in cars and lorries means that a lot of people will starve to death, but bureaucrats don't want to be the ones to stop people using their cars. So food will become increasingly scarce and expensive.

In order to try and keep up with demand, farmers are encouraged to use genetically modified seeds. There is no evidence to show that these are safe but, hey, what does safety matter when there are big profits to be made? Farmers are also encouraged to use vast amounts of fertiliser and pesticides. Many even use hormones. Millions of animals are given antibiotics because it makes them grow more muscle. Some of the chemicals given to animals are carcinogenic. (That means they cause cancer in the people who eat them.) But no one much cares about that either.

Food in Britain is deteriorating in quality faster than food anywhere else because the food market in Britain is dominated by just four large supermarket chains. In no other country in the world is the provision of food in the hands of such a small number of people. The result is that the big supermarkets have the power to drive down prices and that inevitably forces suppliers (both manufacturers and farmers) to cut costs and provide poorer and poorer quality food. It is partly because of the fact that their margins are constantly being squeezed, that farmers give their animals antibiotics (to make them grow bigger muscles) and use vast quantities of carcinogenic pesticides and insecticides and other nasties on their farms.

It would, of course, help if consumers could understand what they were buying by looking at the labels. But the food companies don't approve of that sort of nonsense. So it doesn't happen. Indeed, anyone who still imagines that the European Union exists to protect individuals should consider this. When in March 2010 efforts were made to introduce colour-coded warnings on food labels they were defeated in a committee vote at the European parliament. Consumer groups, acting on behalf of citizens throughout Europe, had pushed hard for the so-called `traffic light system' because it is acknowledged to be the simplest way to inform Europe's increasingly obese citizens about the real nutritional value of food. Food companies would, if the legislation had gone through, been required to label the front of their packages with red, amber or green icons to denote the amounts of fat, saturated fat, salt and sugar they contain. A trade group representing food companies such s Coca-Cola and Nestle opposed the scheme, arguing that it would hurt them commercially and would demonise foods that contained a good deal of fat. They proposed instead a scheme keeping most nutritional information on the back of packets, in tiny type and far less comprehensible. The EU's environment committee sided with the industry. `We're very pleased with the outcome,' said a spokesperson for the trade group. I bet they were.

The result of all this is that you need a degree in mathematics to know what you're buying. For example, the label on a food item may appear say that it contains 2% fat per so many grams or meat balls or cheese biscuits, but when you look closely you realise that it says that the stuff it contains 2% of your daily allowance per little bit so you can get through a week's daily total fat allowance in the time it takes to turn on the digital television set and wait for it to warm up. (Why do digital televisions take longer to warm up than the old ones with valves?)

And what about the messages they put on food? The best before dates? The use before dates? According to the Food Standards Agency `best before' usually refers to quality rather than safety. Eat it after the date given and the food might not taste as good, might lose flavour or texture, but will still be edible. `Use by dates' appear on foods that go off and even if they look and smell ok could be dangerous. But `use by' doesn't necessarily always mean `eat by' because you can freeze it and maybe use it later. All this confusing, bewildering nonsense is, of course, the reason why the British throw away almost as much of the food they buy as they actually manage to eat. People don't throw away food because they want to, or because they suddenly decide they've changed their minds about it. They throw away food because they are worried that if they eat it they might die or vomit for a week or both.

None of this is going to get any better.

And if the food manufacturers, and their chums at the EU, have anything to do with it, things are probably going to get a good deal worse.

Just to add to the fun, eating out will be increasingly dangerous. This applies whether you have a five course meal for £200 at some overpriced restaurant run by a megalomaniac with a shiny teeth and a TV show or you buy a sandwich. Health and safety regulations and compliance officials will ensure that things will get not-so steadily worse. There's a hardly a sandwich or a salad served in the UK that doesn't come supplied with an extra portion of escherichia coli bacteria. If my princess and I eat out these days we take our own food with us. When restaurants allow customers to bring their own food (as well as their own wine) we'll patronise them.

Britain desperately needs to grow more food. As the oil runs out so it will become increasingly expensive to move food around the planet. And as the Americans use an increasingly high proportion of their food crops as a substitute for oil so the world shortage of food will become increasingly desperate.   In the 13 years of Labour misrule, from 1997 to 2010, agriculture production in the UK declined alarmingly and we now produce only 60% of what we eat. We import the rest at great cost (both to the planet and to ourselves).

Moreover, even though we could perfectly well grow most of them ourselves, we import rapidly increasing quantities of fruit and vegetables from countries where water is in desperately short supply and where the world's water shortage is likely to prove to be a major problem in the future.

Britain needs to start growing more of its own food. And it needs to start doing so now. If we don't (and I very much doubt if we will) then there will be repeated food crises from the year 2015 onwards.

Chances of food becoming scarcer, more expensive, less nutritious and more hazardous for your health: 100%

37. The End Of America Is Nigh

America has enjoyed a short but eventful period as the world's most powerful country. During that period it gave the world (and will, doubtless, be long remembered for) barbed wire, McDonalds, Peyton Place, the Monkees, Star Wars and genetically modified seeds. While at its most powerful America obtained (and deserved) a reputation for doing its best to avoid the wars it should have fought (World War I and II) and starting the wars it should not have fought (the wars in Korea, Vietnam, Iraq (twice) and Afghanistan to name but a few).

Today, the good days are over. America is now in permanent decline and the good days for the fat people with no fashion sense are over.

Why is the USA currently the wealthiest and most powerful nation on earth?

There are three main reasons.

First, America was for much of the twentieth century the world's most significant source of oil. All that `free' energy, available on their doorstep, gave the Americans a huge if temporary advantage. European countries had to import their oil from the other side of the world (from countries such as Indonesia). The Americans could get what they wanted without leaving home. America's store of energy giving oil was so vast that until 1943 it remained a net exporter - using its own oil for domestic purposes and selling excess oil to other countries.

Second, once their own oil started to run out the Americans showed extraordinary ruthlessness in being prepared to take oil from any other country on the planet. American foreign policy has, for decades, been built around the basic principle of stealing oil and other natural resources from other countries. The rate of discovery of new oil wells in the USA peaked in the 1930s and the Americans reached their own `peak oil' in 1970. Since 1970 `home' production of oil has been in steady and steep decline and so, in order to preserve the American way of life (big petrol guzzling motorcars, sprawling suburbs, aeroplanes instead of trains) America had to find oil from elsewhere. To begin with the Americans were fairly civilised about their need for oil. They fed their addiction by buying what they needed and as a result the American balance of trade soon became negative. Like addicts everywhere America was spending more than it was earning. And, like addicts everywhere, America then decided that instead of buying the oil it needed it would just take it. America became a global mugger. America maintained and increased its access to the world's resources through American run organisations such as the World Bank, the World Trade Organisation and the International Monetary Fund. America created treaties such as the North American Free Trade Agreement which said that wherever in the world there are resources they must be available to the highest bidder. In other words America gave itself the right to buy whatever it wanted (at a price it wanted to pay). And so America had decided that if oil was discovered in another country that oil belonged to America just as surely as if it had been discovered in Texas. America decided that it had the right to take out patents on whatever it wanted. American corporations even claimed copyright on the human body and on seeds and plants that had grown for centuries in other countries. Protestors who objected to this approach (known as `globalisation') were vilified as anarchists or terrorists and the media (much of it owned by large American corporations with energy interests) meekly cooperated. America became rich not through hard work but through luck. America remained rich through ruthlessness and through geopolitical plans based on nothing more complicated than theft.

Third, for several decades the American dollar has been the default global currency. After the dollar was divorced from the value of gold the Americans had an opportunity to print money. And the Americans have used this fact ruthlessly to live well at the expense of the rest of the world.

American success has been built not on genius, inventiveness of hard work but on greed and deceit. American wealth was created directly as a result of the two world wars and of abusing their position as holders of the reserve currency. Materialistic Americans have for decades been subsidised by poor countries. A few mega rich, greedy bastards have sucked all the money out of the system, leaving countless millions impoverished.

America has a third of a million troops in 134 different countries around the world. The Americans attempted to starve the people of Iraq. Madeleine Albright said on national television that the deaths of 500,000 Iraqi children was worth `it'. They have funded Israeli expansionism, supported the Saudi Arabian regime. They've never really worked out that if you bully people, and steal from them, then they tend not to like you very much. America's decline will be helped by the fact that it has so many enemies. Around the world no one (except British politicians looking for highly paid employment when they leave office) and Jews relying on American protection for Israel will care about its decline. In fact most nations will enjoy the spectacle. The Americans have so little insight that they think people around the world hate them because they are jealous.

Once the bastion of capitalism, America has become almost as statist as Britain. According to a CNN survey 56% of Americans believe that `the federal government has become so large and powerful, it poses an immediate threat to the rights and freedoms of ordinary citizens.' In 1939 the USA had five million government employees. By 2009 America had around 25 million government employees. Instead of making things, American workers now simply push paper around. And buy their cars and television sets from China. The companies that are left are greedy and unwholesome. Many of the worst companies in the world (think Monsanto, Goldman Sachs, Google and Microsoft) are American.

America's death throes are going to be dangerous and violent: there will be wars, odious examples of protectionism and massive currency problems as the dollar declines. America is in bigger financial trouble than Greece. America is comprised of malcontents who left their native countries (except the native north Americans of course, who have marginally less authority in their own country than the bison) because they were unsuccessful in the countries they left.

One in four black men in America are in prison, have been in prison or are on probation. That's not a country, it's a social swamp; an obscene apology for a nation; a land of overweight, ignorant fools who support Israel, defend Guantanamo Bay, bullies the weak and robs from the poor to give to the rich; it is an unequal land where the rich become obscenely rich, and glory in their undeserved wealth, at the expense of the poor who struggle to stay alive. A survey showed that almost half of all the women in one US city had been raped or subjected to attempted rape at least once in their lives. In Iraq a female America soldier is more likely to be raped by a fellow American soldier than killed by enemy fire.

As I predicted in `What Happens Next?' Obama turned out to be the Son of Blair, the smiling, war mongering, incompetent liar.   Actually, he has turned out to be more like Reagan. Smiling, comforting and reassuring and doesn't have a clue what is going on. He accepted the Nobel peace prize a week after ordering another 30,000 troops into the field - the largest troop surge since the tragedy known as the Vietnam war. He appointed as British ambassador a man who gave £500,000 to his campaign fund.

The Chinese will destroy the USA economically rather than militarily. It will be cheaper than any other way and quicker too. They won't do it yet, of course. They want to sell more fridges and TV sets before they bring America to its knees. But the Americans should be aware that they are on borrowed time.

It is absurd embarrassing and naive that British politicians still regard the Americans as allies. It is even more absurd, embarrassing and naive that many believe that Britain has some sort of special relationship with the USA. If we do have a special relationship it is certainly not one of equals but is more one of a slightly simple minded brother hanging around a richer, better looking and more successful sibling in the hope that a little of his gloss may rub off. The Americans took advantage of two world wars to get rich at Britain's expense. Our honesty and fiscal naivety allied to American greed led directly to America's current position as the dominant world power (a position that will not last long) and Britain's current position as the impoverished relative, struggling gamely to keep up appearances but always having to turn up at the Ball wearing last year's frock and stockings with holes in them.

America tries to run the world, and behaves as if it already does, especially when there is money involved. The special relationship with the UK is a joke. They take what they want. When we had a problem with Argentina recently the Americans offered to mediate. (Oil was involved). When the Americans have problems we fight their wars for them.

How many people know that Lloyds Banking Group paid the

Americans $350 million in a settlement because the Aamericans said that Lloyds had covered up wire transfers between Iran and Sudan. Now, if Lloyds bank has been naughty shouldn't the British Government (and the British taxpayer) be taking the $350 million?

We should stop creeping to America and pretending that we have a `special relationship' with them. It is embarrassing. It was never true. And there is no value in it. Our politicians do it because, like Blair, there's something in it for them. Blair took us into America's oil grabbing war in Iraq and has become a multimillionaire as a result. I can see what America gets out of the `special relationship'
but just what do we get out of it - except soldiers in body bags?

The chances of America being less powerful in 2020 than in 2010: 100%.

38. More Banking Crises Are To Come

Another financial crisis isn't a possibility, it's an inevitability because nothing has changed since before the last one. The ruthless, selfish greed that caused the last crisis (the one that hasn't really got properly started yet) hasn't been suppressed. If bank staff had behaved responsibly and morally there would have been no crisis. But nothing has changed. Bank staff are still overpaid, still helping themselves to indecently huge bonuses and still behaving immorally and irresponsibly; notable only for their greed, stupidity and chicanery. Amazingly, none of the bankers responsible for the nation's mess ended up in gaol. Bank employees who had gambled bank depositors' money on high risk financial derivatives they didn't understand, encouraged people to borrow 125% of the value of a house and allowed liars to self-certificate their earnings which they knew were totally dependent on the housing bubble never bursting, and who had then concealed their trickery from investors, ended up enriched and free while their victims ended up fearful and in penury. Justice hide your head and weep in shame.

Bankers like modern politicians act in their own self interest. it is, after all, the capitalist way. As the crisis unfolded no one admitted that there was anything fundamentally wrong with the system and so afterwards everything carried on as before. The bankers shared out the taxpayers' money they were given so that they did not suffer personally, and the banks remained bankrupt. Investors and low and middle grade employees suffered enormously but the overpaid, under-principled, under-talented and greedy bosses continued to be overpaid, under-principled, under-talented and greedy. And bosses.

When our ancestors thought of `banks' the words that sprang to mind were `integrity, boring and trust'. Today, we think of `risk, gamble, greed, reckless'. Investment bankers roll their own dice but use other people's money. When things went wrong the bankers blamed the borrowers but this wasn't fair. Most of the borrowers who got into trouble were financially illiterate; they were dealing with sums they couldn't really comprehend and they were trusting the bankers. If a doctor prescribes a deadly drug and patients fall ill, do the patients get the blame? No, of course not. It's the same. The bankers were greedy and didn't understand the risks they and their customers were taking. When things went wrong the bankers then ran away from the responsibility.

When a company pollutes a river it is rightly expected to pay to clean up the river. It will also be fined, and responsible directors may be prosecuted and even sent to prison. This is how corporate life works. If you do bad things, which affect the rest of the nation, then you will be punished. But, for the banks, the rules were changed. The banks had screwed up badly. They had done it not through bad luck but through a potent mixture of greed and incompetence. Nevertheless, they were given billions of taxpayers' money. There were no fines and no prosecutions. Rather than being punished the directors were allowed to give themselves huge bonuses. When, belatedly, a special one off tax on bonuses was introduce, the banks passed the tax onto shareholders (which means pensions and small investors). The banks that had made the biggest mistakes were given the most money. it was like lining up speeding motorists and, instead of fining them, giving them bonuses with the ones who had been doing the greatest speed being given the biggest bonus. It wasn't a bit like that. it was exactly like that. The bail out was a waste of public money and it was done to save a few Scottish votes and a few rich pals of the government. It was the first example in our history of corporate welfare. What next? A social services department catering to Russian billionaires having trouble with their yachts?

And so, while monsters like Goldman Sachs are still roaming the planet, there is worse to come. After all, Goldman Sachs cold bloodedly made money out of the mortgage crisis they'd helped create. They helped blow up the housing bubble, cold-bloodedly bet that the bubble would burst and then crowed about the money they were making. They were not so clever, however, that, like the other banks, they didn't need bailing out with taxpayers' money. Goldman Sachs helped cause the crisis through greed and then made money out of the taxpayer funded rescue. What Goldman Sachs did was akin to selling someone a really dangerous old car and then taking out insurance on his life. They got the money for selling the dangerous car and they got paid out when the car crashed (as they knew it would) killing the driver. It is so, so profitable to be utterly ruthless. The philosophy at Goldman Sachs and other similar enterprises, the many homes of Gekko shaped greed, seems to be that no banker should be expected to live on a paltry £10 million a year. You need £100 million a year to live half-decently, and if that means that thousands of hard working folk lose their homes, their jobs and their will to live then so be it. The Shylocks of Goldman Sachs know how to live the ruthless life. Anyone who, in the future, invests in any product sold by Goldman Sachs deserves what they get. Personally, I would rather give my money to Bernie Madoff to look after. (Actually, it's an insult to Shylock's memory to mention him and Goldman Sachs in the same paragraph. Compared to the slimeballs of Goldman Sachs, Shylock was a soft-hearted philanthropist.)

During the pre election campaign of 2010 Brown attacked the moral bankruptcy of Goldman Sachs (therefore managing to take the moral high ground for the first time in many a year). When Gordon Brown can preach to a group of people and sound convincing you know you are dealing with real slime balls. Anyone who works for Goldman Sachs (and any of the other banks which exist to make money at any cost) should be ostracised, treated as kindly and warmly as paedophiles. (It goes without saying that Brown's Government was one of Goldman Sach's employers). The simple truth is that the self styled masters of the universe are horribly light on common sense, responsibility, foresight, planning, integrity or indeed, any virtues whatsoever. To describe them as criminals is to demean the relatively honest souls in striped jerseys and black masks who wander around filling bags labelled Swag with silver. It was, don't forget, Goldman Sachs who dreamt up the Trojan Horse securities which helped Greece hide the truth about its financial position from the EU bean counters.

Generally speaking, investment banks exist to enrich themselves by impoverishing their customers. They do this deliberately, routinely and randomly. There is no sense of right or wrong, no sense of responsibility, no guilt, no humanity. The sole aim is to acquire wealth. They do this by a mixture of overtrading, market manipulation and insider knowledge, which may usually be officially classified as illegal but which does, nevertheless, give the bank an edge.

(The problem is that this sort of dealing has, for years now, been enjoyed by the sort of bank which takes deposits from high street customers. The result has been that the customers' money has been lent to traders betting on the price of cocoa or has, indeed, been used by the bank itself to bet on the price of cocoa. Any regulation which doesn't divide banks into two groups will fail to solve this problem because bankers and traders, although not particularly smart, will always be smarter than the regulators.)

The banks which created the mess were, and are, run by incredibly stupid people who think they are cleverer than they are. Bankers claimed that there was no risk with credit default swaps because there was no chance of the counterparties going bankrupt.

Er, wrong.

Credit default swaps (complex financial instruments which most of the people running the banks didn't understand) were in reality merely bets on whether or not the counterparty would go bankrupt.

So, there had to be a risk. But the bankers didn't just get the risk wrong, they even denied the very existence of the risk. The number of former sports stars who become wealth management advisers and brokers, with no training and within weeks of giving up their sport, shows just how little these people need to know and, therefore, how absurdly overpaid they are. Investment bankers (the ones who play around with pensioners' savings and ruin the boring but necessary banks which clear cheques and keep the ATM machines filled with cash) aren't the brightest, hardworking or most useful members of society. In fact they are in the bottom ten per cent for the first two and the bottom one per cent for third. Why, in the name of everything remotely holy, do they imagine that they are entitled to steal so much money from investors and pensioners?

In the USA, a senate inquiry decided that the top two USA ratings agencies, Moodys and Standard and Poor's, were unduly influenced by investment bankers who paid their fees, and wilfully ignored signs of fraud in the lending industry in the lead up to the financial crisis. On page 83754 of this book you will find a full list of the many and varied ways in which the ratings agencies are now better controlled.

The banks, and other financial service companies, need to slash their costs, reduce their fees and control their greed. But they won't. Even ordinary bank employees have become accustomed to the delights of their greed (the London town house, the country mansion, the helicopter, the private plane, the yacht). Why would they voluntarily give up all these expensive toys?

How much taxpayers money will be needed to bail out the banks?It seems that your guess is as good as anyone else's and almost certainly better than anyone at the Treasury. The Financial Services Authority reckons it could be £140 billion. That works out at around £2,500 per man, woman and child but if you ignore the people who don't pay tax then it is, of course, considerably higher than that. And this is not money that is invested. It is money that we have spent to make sure that Scottish banking jobs weren't lost and to ensure that incompetent quarter-witted bank bosses carried on taking home those huge bonuses they seem to regard as their right. We always have to remember that bankers don't create anything. They don't build businesses or create jobs. Like the Jewish moneylenders that led Shakespeare to write about Shylock, they are just money lenders. And they aren't very good at it.

In addition, banks are allowed to claim interest as a tax deductible expense. Is there no limit to the perks these people get? British home owners long ago (and quite sensibly) lost the right to claim tax relief on their mortgage interest payments. But if a wanker borrows a gazillion quid for some dodgy deals on the derivatives market he gets tax relief on the interest he pays. There's one law for the wankers, you see, and one law for the rest of us.

As a rule bankers show almost as much hubris as politicians but when they were faced with the nemesis of bankruptcy they went running to Mummy Brown who used taxpayers' money to protect them from the release of a necessary catharsis. Money went from taxpayers to the Government and then direct to the idiots who had caused the problem. Brown did this because the two biggest banks which were buggered were Scottish and if he'd let them go bust he and Alistair Darling (both of whose parliamentary seats are in Scotland) would have probably looking for real jobs. If the Government had allowed the Royal Bank of Scotland and HBOS to go bankrupt the nation would have saved a fortune and the greedy Scot Fred Goodwin would have received a pension of around £20,000 instead of £700,000. Goodwin and his idiot chums didn't just make small mistakes. If they had been doctors they would have cut off the wrong legs on just about every possible occasion. They would have amputated arms when asked to syringe wax out of ears and performed colostomies on patients wanting treatment for dandruff. Brown and Darling would, of course, have been embarrassed and in enhanced danger of losing their Scottish parliamentary seats.

RBS had been throwing money around, sponsoring a rugby tournament, a Grand Prix team and even paying £4 million a year to a Scot who last won a Grand Prix when William Pitt the Younger was Prime Minister. Even after the bank had been bailed out the sponsorship deals continued. The value of the Six Nations rugby tournament title sponsorship deal signed by the Royal Bank of Scotland has been estimated at £20 million over four years. Incredibly, the bank announced in 2009 that the sponsorship would be extended until 2013. Many taxpayers undoubtedly enjoy watching rugby. But should taxpayers be paying sponsorship money to a rugby tournament (and, thereby, already well-paid rugby players).

The bankers at the banks which had been bailed out continued to enjoy the good times they'd enjoyed before they lost all our money. In the FT on 7.11.09 a spokesman for the bailed out Lloyds Bank, discussing Christmas parties, describes them as `colleague-related activity'. I presume he thought that made it acceptable that taxpayers should fork out for more canapes and champagne.

The disgraced bosses were rewarded for their incompetence with massive pensions (the most famous being the £32 million pension fund given, on behalf of taxpayers, to Fred Goodwin, the former boss of RBS).

Fred Goodwin and his greedy, half-witted chums (their own identifiable human quality is hubris) have effectively destroyed a year's work done by every hard working taxpayer in the country. And we've given them massive bonuses as a `thank you'. In a fair and just world Sir Fred Goodwin would be wearing a shirt with a number on it or sitting on the pavement in Barnsley selling the Big Issue. Instead we are giving him £560,000 a year until he dies. He left the bank he ran close to bankruptcy and cost every man, woman and child in the UK an estimated £10,000. His efforts led to 20,000 people losing their jobs. Inevitably, when the royal Bank of Scotland started wielding the axe the vast majority of the jobs `lost' were in England, rather than in Scotland.

And just when you think it couldn't get any worse it gets worse. In 2009 RBS was one of the top five currency traders in Europe. In other words a bank owned by taxpayers was still playing the currency markets and, presumably, selling the pound sterling when it felt it could make a buck. In March 2010 Royal Bank of Scotland (the sport supporting taxpayer owned bank) was fined £28 million for sharing price data in breach of competition laws. RBS was fined by another taxpayer owned body - the Office of Fair Trading. (There is something inherently absurd - not to say stupid - about one taxpayer funded body spending taxpayers money on investigating and then fining another taxpayer funded body without any individual having to suffer. And what the hell happened to the £28 million? It should by rights have been handed back to the taxpayers. But I haven't seen my share of it and I bet you haven't seen your share either.)

Plus, the thing that most taxpayers probably find hardest to stomach is the sight and sound of RBS spokesidiots giving opinions on the global and national economy and offering advice to companies, savers, investors and pensioners. How dare anyone working for RBS offer any sort of financial advice? The Royal Bank of Scotland continues to exist as a bank only through the unwitting generosity of English taxpayers. In 2008 the Royal Bank of Scotland had the biggest losses of any bank in the world. How its employees dare speak out in public is beyond my comprehension. The ultimate irony of 2010 was undoubtedly the fact that NatWest bank announced that it was helping schoolchildren to learn to manage their finances properly. NatWest is, remember, a subsidiary of the Royal Bank of Scotland. If there are people at NatWest who know how to manage money they would, perhaps, have done us all a favour if they had held seminars for the staff of the Royal Bank of Scotland.

Things were bad during the Crash of 2007 because reckless bankers and investors and speculators found new and ever more remunerative ways to increase their profits (at great risk) by taking on ever greater debts. Leverage (or borrowing) has always been a good way to get very rich quickly with limited capital and an equally good way to get very poor quickly too. Investors and pensioners were suckered into investing in their projects because they wanted to believe that they too could get rich. The South Sea Bubble, the Florida land boom and the Great Property boom of the early 21st century were all a result of greed and ignorance overcoming common sense. Of course, Brown had created the environment for the boom because he had destroyed pensions so effectively that hard working men and women who could not rely on public sector pensions had little choice but to look elsewhere for somewhere to put their savings. And so people bought houses they couldn't afford, enjoyed lifestyles beyond their means and assumed, for the time being, that they were as rich as they appeared to be. People had great faith, confidence and optimism; they believed that they were destined to be rich and that it was their right. (People who are cautious and suspicious are immune to what Galbraith called `speculative enthusiasms'.)

Financial crises, and crashes, reveal the danger of speculation. And it is customary too for financial crises to expose thieves and swindlers. (John Kenneth Galbraith has pointed out that there is a period of weeks, months and even years before embezzlement is discovered and that during this period the embezzler enjoys his gain but the man who has been embezzled is unaware of it. For that period there is, Galbraith pointed out a net increase in psychic wealth. The thief knows he has money he didn't have and the victim thinks he still has the money that has been stolen from him.)

To watch Brown searching for people to blame and punish for the nation's economic problems and blaming tax havens was akin to Hitler searching for someone to blame for World War II and ending up blaming New Zealand. The world's two most successful tax havens are, of course, London and New York both of which provide secure and confidential home for the ill gotten gains of the world's biggest fraudsters and money launderers. Most money laundering goes on in London and New York. These are the places where stolen money is hidden. These are the favourite places for tax evaders to hide their money. And so the British and the American Governments are desperate to close down offshore havens in order to get rid of the competition. (Money laundering and tax evasion are big business in Britain. For around £500 it is possible to form a company in Britain without providing any identification and to be issued with nominee directors, a company secretary and bearer shares which give complete anonymity.)

One official argument is that those tax havens which charge less tax, or provide superior financial services, have an advantage over other countries. This is deemed to be unfair and is one of the most stupid arguments of all time. If we are going to eliminate unfairness from society then presumably countries which are good at doing other things will be banned from doing them. So, the Germans will be banned from making cars, the Scots will be banned from making whisky and the French will be banned from making wine.

There was a widespread assumption that because the bankers were paying themselves huge sums of money they must be doing great and worthwhile work. They were not, of course, doing great work anymore than members of the Mafia, who also pay themselves vast sums, are doing great and good work.

Trust between, on the one hand, politicians and bankers, and us on the other, has been lost as a result of insider trading, huge undeserved bonuses, predatory lending, credit card schemes designed to (legally) fleece the innocent and financially unguarded, packaged toxic products, Ponzi schemes galore and a thousand Shylocks. And, of course, the fiscal sewage known as the giant vampire squid: Goldman Sachs; the Arthur Daley bank of the banking world. (Incidentally, readers will not be surprised to hear that Goldman Sachs lists war criminal Tony Blair on its payroll. Blair was, for example, paid £300,000 to give one lecture to

Goldman Sachs employees and guests. Involving Britain in America's illegal war has, as I predicted in my books on America (Rogue Nation and Global Bully) certainly been profitable for Blair if not so much fun for the unfortunate soldiers who died so that the loathsome one could stack up brownie points with the Yanks prior to handing over the country to his war criminal pal, Gordon the Moron.)

We have, with their help, created a society built on materialism and without any sense of moral responsibility or social commitment, environmentally unsustainable (forget about that absurd red herring `climate change' and think instead polluted seas, polluted children and a planet ripped apart and raped by greedy corporate bastards) and socially irresponsible. We have, with their help, created a society with no sense of responsibility to individuals and no sense of community. We have created a society overseen by the blood-raw fascism of the European Union, the most evil organisation ever invented, a society which defines itself by its exploitation of the vulneration and the unwary and our scarce and dwindling resources. We have created a society which encouraged these greedy bankers. We have done nothing to control their greed. A banker who was fired turned down 8 million euros as his `fuck off' money. So he sued the bank for more. He was fired and he turned down 8 million euros. That's a big chunk in real money. It wasn't enough. Does that perhaps qualify as greedy? Someone should tear his balls off, fry them and feed them to him. Everywhere you look there are examples of absurd levels of compensation. A banker sued his former employers for a personal fee of £882,000 for helping to raise £18 million. They had good ways of dealing with scrofulous slime balls in olden England. They'd put them on the rack, torture for a few days, tear out their intestines while they were still alive, and then hang them on a gibbet. Now under normal circumstances I would say that was over the top. But for bankers? Maybe we could prolong the torture bit for an extra week or so. Footballers are absurdly overpaid but they have relatively short careers and society punishes them by forcing them to shack up with women who have absolutely no sense of taste and who expose their sexual inadequacies in the Sunday press. Bankers, on the other hand, remain unpunished.

It is absurd that investment bankers get so much money. They aren't brighter than other people. They aren't talented. They don't work harder. They just happen to work with money and be dishonest and have opportunities to help themselves. Like postmen have plenty of rubber bands so investment bankers have plenty of money. It isn't right or good for society. The wastage of rubber bands is a relatively minor problem for society (though probably quite a big one for Royal Mail). But allowing investment bankers to help themselves to handfuls of free money is bad for everyone else.

The banking crisis was the direct responsibility of three groups of people: the bankers themselves (whose greed was matched only by their incompetence), the politicians (by which I mean Gordon Brown and the half-wits who allowed him to destroy the country) and the regulators (who were too busy forcing banks to stockpile photocopies of gas bills and passports to do anything about the real problems).

In my book `What Happens Next?' I argued that banks should be decide whether they wanted to be `ordinary' banks (offering cheque books and current accounts) or `investment' banks, making huge bets on the markets. I argued that `ordinary' banks should be forced to go back to a deposit styled model and that such banks should only lend money they actually have. The fractional reserve banking system (whereby banks keep only a tiny proportion of the assets deposited with them as cash, and look to the central bank to lend them money if they get into trouble) has to end. Investment banks can do whatever the hell they like. But high street banks have to be separate from the nonsenses, and must in future be boring and reliable. Banks which take people's money and which offer cheque books and general banking facilities should not be allowed to speculate. Investment banks can do whatever they like with their own funds but they should know that they are on their own if things go wrong. If they lose money then they sell the yachts. Allowing banks to do both means that banks cannot be allowed to fail. And then simply protects the greedy bastards who are helping themselves to the cream - and forcing their depositors and the nation's taxpayers to take all the risk. Instead of doing this both the British and American Governments (and their appointed regulators) have actually allowed the present system to get worse. Thanks to the politicians the banks into which you put your savings are probably still risking everything on a few huge bets so that a few very rich gamblers can get even richer.

But the obvious simple solution was too honest, too simple, too effective and, most important of all, too unpopular with the bankers for the Government to consider it seriously. Instead they prefer to threaten the banks with masses of new regulations and special taxes on bonuses which everyone (by which I mean bankers, regulators and politicians) knows will merely hurt customers (who will be charged extra fees to cover the taxes) and shareholders and pensioners who will pay their share of the extra taxes out of their already barely visible dividends.

By the beginning of 2009, British banks were in a worse state than they had ever been. (No major British bank failed during the Great Depression of the 1930s but during Brown's Depression the number banks which were failing, or surviving only when taxpayers' money was stuffed into their vaults, exceeded the number which stayed solvent.) The Bank of England said in March 2009 that the banks' losses amounted to well over £2,000,000,000,000. Two thousand billion pounds if I've managed to cram enough noughts in. That's about a year's worth of economic production.

Modern banking systems aren't designed to cope if more than one or two in a 100 savers turn up demanding their money in cash. Banks lend out the money they take in and they don't have it to give back.

In March 2009, the International Monetary Fund announced that Britain had been forced to make the world's biggest down payments to rescue its failing banks. Brown said he was angry about the banking crisis. (Brown, Blair and their Labour colleagues seem unable to admit, or apologise for, their past mistakes. And so they will definitely never learn from them. The man or woman who does not admit their mistakes will be doomed to repeat them time and time again.)

Speculators making money with own money is perfectly fair and proper, though society seems to disapprove. Bankers speculating with other people's money is accepted and supported by government and taxpayers but seems to me to be utterly indefensible.

After the South Sea Bubble the company's managers were held to account. They had not broken the law but were accused of immorally exploiting investors. Up to 95% of their personal wealth was confiscated. The Chancellor of the Exchequer was locked up in the Tower of London. If bankers were vulnerable to retrospective moral hazard the problems might disappear.

But none of the bankers who created the huge problems that engulfed us all were fined or imprisoned. Instead they received huge bonuses and pensions. The people least affected by the banking crash of 2008 were, predictably, the bankers who caused it.Not placing the responsibility for speculative errors on those who made the mistakes (the bankers and home buyers who all took imprudent risks in the hope of great personal gain) but placing it on the shoulders of taxpayers and prudent investors and savers is just plain wrong. It is unfair and unjust and typically Brownian and turned the whole principles of free market capitalism upside down. Home owners who used their houses as eternal piggy banks (increasing their mortgages as their house value grew, and then spending the money on bigger television sets) and bankers who made fortunes out of lending money without care and thought are the only people not to have paid for the financial mess. The bailouts will lead Britain into the gutter. Worse, they leave us morally bankrupt. Short term political expediency has taken over and fair play and individual responsibility have disappeared. Brown and Darling gleefully claimed in 2010 that their actions had been vindicated and that they had done the right thing. Their actions were not vindicated and they did not do the right thing.

The bankers took the lion's share of the profits in the good times but customers, investors and taxpayers were expected to take all the losses when things go badly. That's moral hazard, and nothing has changed. The banks will fail again. If bankers who receive bonuses had unlimited personal liability for their daring, risky financial adventures they would take more care with our money

Greedy bankers, stupid politicians and incompetent regulators caused our economic problems. The bankers are still greedy. The politicians aren't any brighter. And the regulators haven't suddenly become competent. So economic crisis round II isn't a possibility, it's an inevitability.

The chances of more banking crises before 2020: 100%.

39. The Benefits System (Although Unfair) Will Continue Unchanged

I am a fiscal conservative but a social liberal. I believe in looking after people and providing services but in making sure that the money is well spent.

This is not an attitude which is widely held in government.

The benefits system seems to have been created as some sort of giant puzzle. It could not possibly have been designed to work efficiently or fairly or in such a way to help anyone. The Department of Work and Pensions has 14 separate manuals explaining the benefits system and these run to a total of 8,690 pages. I will be very surprised indeed if there is anyone in the entire country who knows the contents of these manuals off by heart. And just in case there is then there is, of course, also there is the wonderfully complex tax credit system, run by HM Treasury. No one understands that either. The only people who really seem to understand the system the people who use it and who regard it as some sort of career path.

The benefits system is mad. The UK government offers teenage girls who are leaving school, but who have no specific skills or qualifications, two clear choices. First, they can try and find a job. It won't be easy. If she manages to land a job as a hairdresser or a teaching assistant she can probably hope to earn no more than £200 a week. (That's the average wage for those jobs). If she is bright and can find a job as a library assistant or a doctor's receptionist then she might manage £300 a week. The alternative is to get pregnant and to stay at home. And, to be honest, it's a much clearer and better paid career path. A teenage girl with one child will receive £207 a week (or she would when I wrote this – it's undoubtedly more now). If she acquires two children she will receive £260 a week. And if she finds herself with three children the state will give her £324 a week. You will not be surprised to hear that there are the best part of 200,000 single girls in Britain today who have three or more children, who live on benefits and who have no other career plans. It is not surprising that six million people in the UK now exist on benefits, many are third generation welfare junkies.

During the 1980s, American state of Wisconsin (a by word in America for left wing, politically correct paternalism) found that it was spending too much on welfare and unemployment benefits. The state introduced a scheme whereby benefits were dependent on claimants attending a training course, taking subsidised employment or doing a community service job. Benefit was restricted to a lifetime total of 60 months and claimants were told that they could spend no more than two years on benefits. There were special exemptions for the genuinely disabled (suffering from real physical or mental problems which made it impossible for them to work). This simple system worked and was later rolled out in other parts of America.

If such a scheme was introduced in Britain there would be a huge outcry from soft-headed do-gooders (none of whom actually do any real work themselves), from people involved who have jobs in the `welfare' business, from welfare claimants (who face the awful prospect of having to get up and go to work in the morning) and from Labour politicians who realise that it is the votes of all these people who keep them in power. As I have been warning for years, the Labour Party got into power by appealing to scroungers. And it has stayed in power by giving them huge amounts of money gouged out of hardworking taxpayers. Tony Blair won his second election by appealing to (and gathering votes from) people who did not pay any taxes at all - and probably never had. It was probably the first time in any nation's history when a government had been elected entirely by, and on behalf of, people living off the government rather than contributing to it.

If we don't do something similar to Wisconsin very soon, it will be too late. It may, indeed, already be too late. My guess is that the chances that the present, unfair (and damaging) benefits system will continue are 70%.

40. Will We See The End Of Cheques?

The EU wants to phase out cheques and cash. Governments and banks keep making loud noises about the end of the former and about limits for the legal use of the latter. But the abolition of cheques has been as exaggerated as Mark Twain's death. Many people (particularly small businesses) prefer paying and being paid by cheque. There is something more substantial, and reliable, about a cheque than there is about a credit card or debit card payment. And, of course, the bank charges are less substantial. Attempts have been made to prevent people paying more than £100 in cash when buying something, or paying for a service, but the limits on the use of cash are so widely ignored that they hardly exist.

 The EU, politicians everywhere, and banks will continue to fight for the end of cheques and cash. They would all much prefer us all to pay for everything with a piece of plastic. There are several reasons for this. First, when we pay by plastic it is easy for them to help themselves to a few percentage points of the transaction. Second, when we pay by plastic we tend to spend more than we should. And this makes it look as though the economy is growing. (It isn't really because the debt still has to be paid.) Third, when we pay by plastic the politicians and the banks and the big stores know where we are, what we are doing and how we are spending our money. Paying by cash (or to a less extent by cheque) helps preserve privacy.

The EU and the banks will win in the end, of course. But those of us who insist on avoiding `plastic' can probably hold them off for quite a few years yet. All we have to do is keep paying by cash as often as we can. As the recession turns into a deep depression there will be very few retailers or service providers who will refuse to accept cash.

The chances of cheques and cash payments being phased out completely by 2020 are less than 20%.

41. Everything Will Get Cheaper And Nastier (and when you complain they always say it's to help save the environment).

I bagged up and put our rubbish tonight. As usual I had to double wrap everything in two black plastic bin liners. The reason? The only bags we can buy are so terribly thin that they rip easily. I complained to the manufacturer and was told that the bags were being made thinner in order to prevent global warming and to save the world. (Readers of my book `What Happens Next?' will know that this is a nonsense.)

When I asked why the bags were also more expensive I was told that the machinery had to be altered and that they were also keen to force people to use less bags by making them more expensive. The spokesidiot I spoke to managed to imply that anyone who wants thicker bin liners must be a psychopathic mass murderer.

The truth is different. The truth, of course, is that the manufacturers are making bags thinner because they are cheaper to produce. This increases their profits.

But the problem is that the bags are now so thin that they rip if you accidentally breathe on them. Heavens, they burst open if a sparrow flaps its wings within a furlong. The result is that we are forced to double wrap our rubbish. This wastes money and wastes time but it's my money and my time so no one cares. But it increases the profits for the manufacturers and retailers producing and selling plastic bags.

And, of course, it means that we use twice as many plastic bin bags.

Chances of everything getting cheaper and nastier: 100%.

42. Don't Bother Complaining About Anything Any More (you'll be wasting your time and energy)

I used to complain about everything I thought was wrong. I used to complain about poor merchandise and poor service. I used to complain if I didn't get what I had paid for. I used to complain about public sector workers who were rude, unhelpful or ignorant.

I've given up complaining.

These days it doesn't do any good.

All systems (particularly those involving government departments and council workers) are designed to protect the staff, whatever happens. If you try making a complaint about a health service worker you will die or go mad before you receive justice or anything remotely resembling an apology.

And a word of warning: many organisations are so wary of complainants that they keep a record of everything you do `wrong' so that if you ever do find cause to complaint they can throw them back at you. So, for example, NHS staff keep a written record of every mildly critical comment you make. Then, if you do try to make a complaint, they will produce their list of evidence to show that you are a long-term complainant and not to be taken seriously.

Chances of complaining being pointless by 2020: 80%.

43. Everything Is Going To Become Infinitely More Complex

When I bought my first iPhone I was horrified to discover that before I could make it work I had to find someone who had access to something called iTunes in order to set it up. When television transmissions were changed from analogue to digital it took us several days of telephone calls and discussions with so-called experts in order to make our television set work again. The whole process seemed designed to be as difficult, as incomprehensible and as time consuming as possible.

Life is constantly become more complicated. Even ordinary responsibilities (the sort of thing we used to do without thinking) are becoming irritatingly time consuming and complicated. We used to put our rubbish out once a week. Men would drive by with a big lorry and pick it up. Today, we have so many different collections that I cannot keep track of which goes out when and which is collected where and which must be in which plastic container and which must not be in which plastic container. Every bank holiday screws up the system still further: the Tuesday collections is taken away the following Monday and the Monday collection is collected on Wednesday. Put out the wrong box on the right day and there's a hefty fine to pay.

Travelling abroad has become a dark nightmare. Passengers have to arrive at airports hours before their flight is due. And then, if there are no strikes or computer failures or clouds of volcanic ash or conveyor belt breakdowns there are confrontations with thuggish guards who inspect shoes and riffle through underwear and open laptops and who do everything without a smile or a polite murmur of `thank you'.

Everything that used to be simple has become complicated. And everything that used to be complicated has become unbearable. And it's all going to get worse.

The only answer is to do everything you can to make your life as simple as possible and to leave room for the sort of complications that used to be unexpected but which must now be regarded as entirely predictable.

Chances of everything become increasingly complex: 100%.

44. The E Bomb Threat

If a nuclear electromagnetic pulse bomb, or E-bomb, was exploded over any modern city it would destroy all communications, computer chips, electric grids, networks and so on. Everything would come to a halt. Lighting wouldn't work. Heating wouldn't work. Factories would stop. Computers wouldn't work. Shop tills would stop working. It would not be possible to pump water or deal with sewage. Petrol pumps wouldn't work. Electronic components in cars, planes, trains and lorries would all stop working. We would be taken back in an instant to the days before electricity. But we would not have the infrastructure to enable us to cope.

The authorities don't like to talk about things like this. You can't prevent this sort of disaster by making travellers hand over their nail files and remove their shoes.

How likely is an e-bomb?

I don't know.

But it's a possibility. There are, undoubtedly, terrorist organisations working on one now.

Chances of an e-bomb are 30%.

45. The Quality Of Education In Britain Will Continue To Deteriorate.

It isn't difficult to see why the quality of education in Britain is deteriorating. Basic subjects are forgotten, new education methods don't work, to make life easier for students and teachers there is an absurd and dangerous emphasis on soft subjects such as media studies, at the expense of subjects such as mathematics. Exams are made easier so that schools can hit their designated targets. Problems are compounded by the fact that in many schools a majority of pupils don't speak English. It may be true that more pupils than ever go to university but it is also a fact that the incidence of illiteracy and innumeracy is higher than ever. Back in 2006 the government was advised that half of all school leavers were effectively unfit to work. The number of school leavers passing examinations rises every year, but the quality of school leavers falls constantly and the incidence of illiteracy and innumeracy rises. The present system preserves and protects bad teachers. A laughably moronic politician recently suggested that students don't need to be taught things in school because they could always find information on the web. I find it truly scary that anyone - let alone a senior politician - should believe such nonsense. The truth, of course, is that basic skills are rarely taught well on the internet and in order to glean information from the internet one needs to be extraordinarily skilled in assessing the value of information.

It is, perhaps, hardly surprising that a recent Learning and Skills Council survey of 1000 adults found that over half couldn't work out what a packet of sausages would cost if it had a third off. I always pay by cash for just about everything I buy and I find these days that I am given the wrong change in about one in three transactions. Shop assistants are either innumerate or they are simply incapable of dealing with real money (as opposed to plastic cards) that even though they have a computerised till that does everything apart from blow their noses for them they still manage to get it wrong. They aren't on the fiddle because they get it wrong in my favour at least half of the time. It is hardly surprising that the children of immigrants from countries such as Poland now go back home to be educated. Good teachers know that in the end all smart people educate themselves and the role of the teacher is to teach the ability and will to learn and to encourage curiosity. Good teachers know that you can't do any of this without some learning by rote and a certain amount of discipline. Teachers and the educational system have tried to disguise their global incompetence by making examinations easier and easier so that more and more students pass them. School discipline has declined since corporal punishment was outlawed in 1986. Since then attacks on pupils and teachers has increased dramatically.

Ask any nineteen years old to multiply five and a half by four without the aid of a calculator or a computer and watch him or her start to sweat. Ask the same teenager to spell diarrhoea and the stress and effort will probably turn the word into reality.

Education started to go downhill when a vast new breed of progressive, politically correct school-teachers took over our primary schools.

Instead of being satisfied with simply teaching children to read, write and do simple sums and then moving on to helping them learn how to learn things for themselves these progressive educators decided to experiment with new and untried forms of teaching.

Children are indoctrinated by teachers who get their information about the world from search engines which are controlled by huge international death industries devoted to killing people, sometimes slowly and sometimes quickly but killing them nevertheless, and the EU, which is controlled by all sorts of very unsavoury people including huge industrial death industries which are devoted to killing people sometimes slowly and sometimes quickly. Considerate, thoughtful, knowledgeable people despair about the prejudiced, bigoted, fascist nonsense taught in schools these days and sold as `environmentally important'. Worse still, many school teachers have been determined to remove any sense of competition from our schools. Tests and examinations have been abandoned because they might upset children who are slow to learn. Objective testing has been largely replaced by various forms of subjective continual assessment. Today, the child who wants to do well at school doesn't have to learn anything; he or she simply has to suck up to teacher. The result is that the child who makes sure that he or she is well liked will do well.

The troublesome, creative, innovative, thoughtful, gifted child who threatens the system or makes the school teacher realise what a loser he or she is will probably struggle in this noxious environment. School sports days have been abandoned because the athletically ungifted might feel downhearted if they leave the playing field without a medal. If there are any sporting events then everyone has to win something.

What dangerous rubbish this all is. Like it or not life is competitive and an education which does not reflect this reality does no one any favours.

It's about time some of our school teachers took a look at the big, nasty world outside their comfortable, cosy, unreal school lives. Life is tough and competitive and guarding children against disappointment does them no favours. If they are going to cope with the real world children need to be encouraged to be ambitious and determined. But that is not the modern way.

All things considered it is hardly surprising that our schools are now in chaos and that school teachers everywhere are moaning that they are frightened of the children who are supposed to be in their care.

It is now commonplace for schoolteachers to complain that they cannot control the children in their classes. Although I do believe that today's children are probably slightly more violent than yesterday's children (we can blame violence on television for this) I don't think that the basic problem lies with the children. And nor do I think we can blame the parents. School teachers are incapable of coping, and children are running riot in our schools, because school teachers have forgotten that teaching requires discipline, that rules are an essential part of growing up and that competition is healthy.

Whenever it is suggested that school teachers be assessed - and that the useless ones be fired - there are mass mumblings and protests in the nation's staff rooms.

`Oh dearie me, no,' they cry. `We couldn't possibly accept that!'

Why the hell not?

Why are school teachers so special that they don't need to be assessed and fired if they can't do their jobs properly?

I think it is time to call a stop to this protective nonsense. There is nothing wrong with our educational system that couldn't be put right by firing a few score thousand incompetent school teachers. We have to get rid of the duds and hire teachers who are prepared to teach.

We are taught to take education seriously. We are told that the quality and extent of our education will shape and govern our lives. We are told that if we work hard at school and at college then we will reap the benefits later.

`Study hard, pass your examinations and you will obtain a better job, earn more money and be able to enjoy a more luxurious lifestyle than those who spurn their educational opportunities.'

How many children hear that each year? It is the standard stuff of school speech days.

What we are told is, to a large extent, true. But there is another truth about education which is even more important and which is never talked about. We are never told the real price that we will have to pay for our years of education. We are never told the spiritual price that society expects us to pay in return for having our lives shaped and improved.

To understand the potential costs to the spirit and the soul it is necessary to understand the purpose of the education society offers us all. We must understand what society stands to gain from the deal we are offered.

Sadly, nothing that society offers ever comes free and an education is certainly no exception. The main reason society offers to educate us all is to prepare us for work. Society doesn't want to educate us so that we become more thoughtful, more creative or wiser individuals. Society doesn't want to broaden our horizons or enhance our sense of vision. Society doesn't want to instill passion in us (that can be troublesome and inconvenient) and it doesn't want us to know how to think for ourselves (that can be costly and disruptive).

What society really wants is obedience.

Our education system encourages people not to think. It encourages them to be prepared for employment (ideally with the government) both in their working patterns and in their thinking patterns. This is why so many people who leave school early, or who never go to university, do so well as entrepreneurs. Society - the social structure which we have created but which has now acquired a strength and a force of its own - values obedience highly and rewards the obedient more than any other group.

Society knows that the obedient will work hard without question. Society knows that the obedient can be relied upon to do work that is dull, repetitive and possibly even dangerous.

Society knows that the obedient are unlikely to be troubled by spiritual or moral fears. Society knows that the obedient will fit neatly into whatever hierarchy may exist and society knows that the obedient will put always loyalty above honesty and integrity. Society will always reward those who are obedient because by doing so it can demonstrate to others the value of obedience!

The obedient are always prepared to do what others tell them to do. The obedient are allowed to climb higher up the ladder. But because they are obedient they always do what they are told - however high they climb. The obedient obey the boss, the politicians, the administrators and the bureaucrats. Millions of men and women are blindly obedient because of the lessons they learned at school. They do work they dislike. They listen to people they despise. They do what they are told without questioning. They are blindly obedient because that is what the educational system taught them to be.

The obedient also become a good and reliable customers. The obedient obey the advertisers and buy things that they don't need. By doing so they help society to evolve and stay strong. The obedient accept shoddy workmanship and unreliability without complaint. They accept new fashions as necessary and they buy new clothes and new cars when society wants them to buy those things - not when they need them. The obedient customer is a passive customer and the passive customer is the best customer.

Think back to your own education and you'll see how important obedience was. With some honourable exceptions most courses which involve a textbook and a teacher, and conclude with an examination, are designed to prevent thought and to encourage obedience.

The educational system prepared us all for a life in a meritocracy where nothing is more meritorious than silent obedience.

If you were a good student then you will have been rewarded. If your education was successful - on society's terms - then you will have been offered choices that marked you for life. Whatever profession you choose to follow society will have taught you to feel special. You will have been encouraged to believe that you are superior to those who do not have your own specific skills. You will have been taught prejudices rather than truths.

You must remember that one aim of a modern education is to harness the minds of the imaginative or potentially disruptive. Such individuals are dangerous to a smooth running society.

Society's schoolteachers - the handmaidens of the system - are prepared and willing to manipulate the minds of the young because that is what society expects them to do in return for their own status in society.

Education, the most fundamental force of all, is designed to help produce a neat and layered world.

The price we pay for our education is a high one. And the more successful our education is in society's terms (and the higher our subsequent position in the meritocracy) the greater the price we must pay.

Your choices - or the choices that society helped you make - will have strictly defined the boundaries of your life. You may be better rewarded (in material terms) than many of those who were less capable of satisfying the system but the price you pay will be high too. The price you pay for educational success is intellectual constraint. You pay for your success with your freedom. You pay for your success with guilt, frustration, dissatisfaction and boredom.

The modern educational system is designed to support the structure of our society but it is also a major force in the development of stress and misery.

If it is true that our schooldays are the happiest days of our lives it is because by the time we leave school freedom is, for most of us, nothing more than a faint memory.

`The best part of every man's education, is that which he gives to himself,' wrote Sir Walter Scott.

Regular, mass market schooling for everyone was originally a by product of the industrial revolution. Prior to the industrial revolution most people lived in villages and hamlets and only a relatively small percentage of the population lived in towns and cities.

The first factories and industrial towns developed in England when industrial machinery such as spinning wheels which had been installed in cottages, barns and village halls were smashed by the Luddites; rebellious workers who believed that the introduction of machinery threatened their livelihoods.

As a direct result of the Luddite activities the machine owners put their replacement equipment into specially built `factories' so that they could be protected against vandalism. Since public transport did not exist this, inevitably, meant that the people who were going to work in those factories had to be housed nearby. In this way the first new, purpose built industrial towns developed.

The first schools were built not to educate or to inform but because unless some provision was made for looking after children factory owners could not employ women as well as men. The development of the first towns had meant that family units had been splintered and it was no longer possible for young parents to turn to their own parents for help and support.

Either by purpose, design or simple good fortune it was quickly discovered that the development of formal schooling had an additional benefit. Employers found that children who got into the habit of attending a school for regular hours during the day adapted more readily to work in a factory. Many of their parents, who had been brought up working as farm labourers, found factory work, hours and discipline difficult to get used to. Children who were accustomed to school work, hours and discipline had no such problems.

Today a formal education is still primarily designed to occupy pupils, to keep them busy and out of mischief and to prepare them for an ordinary working life. Very little of the tedious by rote learning which goes on in schools has any practical purpose. Modern education teaches children to learn the right answers by rote and punishes them when they make mistakes (instead of teaching them to learn from their mistakes).Children are taught algebra, trigonometry and Latin - and then subjected to examinations designed to find out how well they have absorbed the entirely useless material they have been taught, the aim is to not to teach or impart learning but to produce school leavers who will feel comfortable with the standard working ritual of modern life.

Formal education constrains ambition and vision by giving specific achievable, limiting goals, by discouraging original thought and eradicating all last traces of common sense.

Schooling is a disciplinary activity rather than an educational one (although the latest and most fashionable educational methods - those which are designed to educate without work, study, labour or pain - fail even to instil discipline into pupils). Students are certainly not being given information which would enable them to live independent lives. They are being taught to fit into society's demands for them, rather than taught how to think.

Why, after all, would society want to teach young people how to think for themselves? People who can think for themselves are likely to be a nuisance rather than an asset to a closely structured society which depends more on discipline and routine than on innovation or imagination.

Students, at schools, colleges and universities, are trained to do as they are told. Is it is for this reason that rules play such a crucial part in all educational establishments. Learning to obey the rules and do as you are told is a more important part of any educational establishment than learning to create or to question. Most education and training is designed to make sure that people do not maximise or optimise their own skills but that they accept whatever life or fate offers.

The `society' which we have created, which now has a purpose and an agenda of its own, does not want thinking citizens. People who think are likely to threaten the status quo.

And yet there are many citizens in our society who believe (with apparent sincerity) that once their formal education is over they can stop learning. They assume that when they leave school, college or university they do so as educationally complete individuals, and that they can, from that point in their lives onwards, stop expanding, exploring and discovering.

This is no accident.

It is exactly what `society' wants.

When graduating students believe that they no longer need to learn they inevitably become content and stable cogs in society's complex machinery.

The truth, of course, is very different. The truth is that a genuine education, one which encouraged original and creative thinking, would be merely a beginning.

The word `educate' is derived from the word `educo' which means to draw out and develop. Once a child has learned to read and write education should not be about learning and remembering dates and mathematical formulae. An educated man is one who has developed his mind to take advantage of his skills and talents and to get where he wants to be without hurting the innocent. Under our present system it is perfectly possible to be both ignorant and yet well educated.

An ignorant man who has been taught to think can get hold of all the knowledge he needs in order to deal with his ignorance - either from a library or from people who have the knowledge.

But a man who is merely educated, and who may wrongly think he is knowledgeable, will remain in an intellectual rut. The truth is that a modern, formal education is irrelevant to life. How many of the great thinkers of the past do you think were school or college graduates?

All of which explains why so many people do so well without any formal education and why so many modern employers prefer to hire intelligent and enthusiastic staff who do not have any formal (and often stifling) education.

Knowledge is only valuable when it is used. The knowledge you have stored - but which you do not use - is of no value to you or anyone else. Knowledge does not become money unless you do something with it. Knowledge is potential power and potential wealth. But knowledge and wisdom, unlike money, only really show their value when you put them to use. And knowledge and wisdom can, unlike money, be spent more than once. A good formal education should (in theory) show you how to acquire knowledge and how to use knowledge when you have acquired it. Sadly, however, very little modern formal education teaches people where or how to acquire more knowledge for themselves and hardly any formal education is designed to show people how to use what they have learned.

Too many students assume that their education ends when they finish their formal schooling or university or college course. A frightening number of people who regard themselves as `well educated' have never read a non fiction book since qualifying and leaving college. Too many teachers regard education as `acquiring skills and training' - whatever that means. Too many teachers regard education as passing examinations and jumping through hoops. Too many parents and politicians expect the educational system to teach children nothing more than the information they need to get a job - and how to obey the rules. It is a dangerous myth to assume that education is designed to teach knowledge. The education system we have at the moment certainly doesn't do that; and nor, more importantly, does it teach students how to think and learn for themselves. And that, surely, is the most important aim of any teacher.

There are many questions about education that are never asked.

Should the government be allowed to forcibly remove kids from their homes and parental care, and to take them away to force them to undergo training of which their parents might not approve? That's what our education system does.

Should citizens be forced to pay for the education of children who are not their own - thereby subsidising other parents?

Should the education system be used to teach children propaganda? (British schoolchildren are taught about the wonders and alleged advantages of the EU.)

Is it right that standards and content of education are controlled by state?

Is the low quality of modern education a consequence of the fact that education is now run by bureaucrats and politicians?

Would it not be better to allow parents to buy education for their children and to allocate that part of their resources which they consider appropriate?

Statists likes state education because it gives the state authority over children and control over the way they develop. The state does this by pretending that education is a free gift to which all are entitled. But why should we provide free education and not free food? Are not people just as entitled to food as education? It's important to remember that state education was originally designed to provide a creche for kids so that both parents could work.

Chances of the quality of education in Britain continuing to deteriorate: 90%.

46. Estate Agencies Will Disappear From Our High Streets

The internet is going to change the business of selling houses beyond all recognition.

In a decade's time we will look back at the time when our main streets were full of estate agents shops as quite inexplicable. By then the vast majority of houses will be sold on the web. Local papers will have largely died off because the advertising from local agencies will have dried up. And there will be no point in estate agents having shops because buyers will simply key their home requirements into a search engine and be served up a dozen or so suitable properties. Potential buyers will be able to take a video walk through likely houses and details of the house will be accompanied by details of local crime rates, flood risks and so on. This system will bring down the price of houses just as the internet has brought down the price of CDs, DVDs and books.

Chances of estate agencies disappearing from our high streets: 80%.

47. Welcome To Life In The Fifth Reich (for now)

The EU is the organisation Hitler would have given us if he'd lived. But it is doomed.

The EU was always doomed because it was an attempt to force entirely separate countries to fit into one mould. But it couldn't (and will not) work. The Greeks like to sit in cafes or lounge on the beach for 52 weeks a year. The Germans like to work hard and lounge on the beach for two weeks a year. To create a superstate with a universal standard of living by forcing German workers to support Greek loungers was never going to work. (The Greeks didn't mind, but the Germans were bound to become resentful when the Greeks had spent all their `free' money and wanted to more.) The EU will continue to destroy Britain in general and England in particular (though eventually the EU itself will implode). There are few political systems on which chaos and anarchy would be an improvement, but the European Union is definitely one of them. The Greek economy disaster (brought on people lying about their incomes, spending too much and then lying about it afterwards) is only the start of the fun. Romania, Bulgaria and Hungary have also enjoyed spend, spend spend economies (on the basis that if they get into trouble the EU will bail them out, cover their debts and give them plenty of pocket money) and Portugal, Spain and Ireland aren't countries you'd want to lend money to if they came into the pub and asked you for a tenner.

Apart from the Irish most of Europe has not been given the chance to vote for the Lisbon Treaty (which takes away the remains of our rights). And yet every survey available shows that the vast majority of people are vehemently opposed to it and those who have been given the chance to vote have only voted for it after been made to re-vote and bullied and threatened and lied to. That's democracy EU style, welcome to their new world.

No one who understands what democracy really means could possibly claim that the EU is a democratic state. The EU has enormous, unprecedented power over citizens who have no control of power over the people with the power. The EU is obsessed with control; it's the only reason for its existence. And, to make matters worse, the whole damned organisation is intrinsically corrupt and crooked. At the end of 2009, for the 15th year in a row, auditors refused to endorse the spending of large parts of the EU budget. The reason? Nothing much apart from systematic corruption.

The EU is responsible for nearly all the bad things that happen to our country. It is responsible for all the truly stupid things that happen. If something bad happens, and you lose rights or find yourself oppressed in some new and possibly imaginative way, I can pretty well guarantee that the EU is behind it. Its endless armies of crackpot eurocrats create endless lists of barmy regulations and then crooks make sure we implement them. The world full of people who take no risks, no blame, but think up lots of rules to stop other people doing things. Most of these people work for the EU. And there are, of course, no rules for the people who make the rules. They live in a world of rights without obligations and authority without responsibility.

The EU (and our handmaiden government of rubber-stamping political clerks) is changing everything the most fundamental principles upon which our society has been founded.

Traditionally, in Britain, everything has been allowed unless it was specifically forbidden. The Magna Carta gave the English basic human rights that entitled them to live their lives freely and without hindrance.

That is changing.

The EU intends to rewrite the rules so that everything will be forbidden unless it is expressly allowed. They will use anti-terrorism laws to achieve this change.

The EU itself is hardly a democratic organisation. When the proposal for introducing a permanent president of the European Council was first debated at the Convention on the Future of Europe, 47 out of 49 speakers spoke against it. Only the representatives of France and the UK were in favour of a permanent EU president. But Valery Giscard d'Estaing, the convention chairman, and a man who wrote the original Lisbon Treaty and was suspected of rather fancying the job of President himself, declared that with just 47 out of 49 being opposed to the proposal there was clearly a consensus in favour of it. When a British MEP accused the Frenchman of being deaf, Giscard d'Estaing thought for a moment and then declared that he could `perceive when a consensus might emerge in the future'. Democracy, EU style.

The EU has banned mercury from barometers (presumably on the grounds that people might eat them) but not from low energy light bulbs (which the EU has made compulsory and which break rather more often than barometers), dental amalgam (put into people's mouths) and vaccines (injected directly into children's bodies).

Ironically, those who support the EU most enthusiastically are often the same people who complain most vociferously about the closure of local Post Offices or the introduction of daft rules about the collection of rubbish. The EU controls us with fear and rules in the same way that bad school teachers control children.

The EU has for years been handing money from rich countries (notably England and German) to poor countries (Spain and Greece for example). The idea always was that since the EU was to become a single country it should have a single economy and you can't have a country with people in some bits of it are luxuriating in scented candles and widescreen television sets while other bits of it are scratching at the earth with home made hoes. Unfortunately, the recipients of these enforced charitable donations didn't realise just how the money was supposed to be spent. And so, instead of using it to buy scented candles for all the senior civil servants kept the dosh for themselves, giving each other huge pay rises, vast bonuses and massive pensions. They also decided that since the money seemed endless they could retire early and enjoy life on the beaches. The end result we all know. Civil servants who were told that they had to start turning up for work in the afternoons and couldn't have a pay rise went on strike and started burning the banks. If Greece hasn't gone bankrupt by the time you read this then it is because they've been given even more money earned by hard-working citizens. (Incidentally, the EU will use the Greek fiasco for more intrusion, just as they and all individual governments have used the financial mess as an excuse for more intrusion and as they use terrorism and money laundering etc as an excuse for more intrusion.)

The EU was, of course, behind the ludicrous ban on flying which disrupted European air travel in the wake of the Icelandic volcano eruption. (The EU admitted there were scientific flaws in its decision to ground flights but blamed the unnecessary ban on a faulty computer model. As always, when things go wrong with the EU, no human beings were involved and so it was unnecessary to discipline anyone. The flawed computer responsible for the expensive chaos was presumably given a good telling off.) Airlines lost £165 million a day throughout the extended ban on flying and millions of business and leisure travellers had their plans disrupted (though somehow I suspect that EU leaders and employees who wanted to travel found ways to get around the ban). One airline boss who seemed a trifle upset by the ban pointed out that his planes regularly flew over Africa during sandstorms.

In May 2010 a small band of Scottish fisherman won a huge diplomatic victory over the EU. Eurocrats in Brussels had made an egregious mistake, switching data between columns of a table used to set cod fishing quotas and thereby reducing by 10% the number of fishing days allocated to fishing boats in the west of Scotland. Everyone knew that the eurocrats had blundered. But it took three years of protests to (and ultimately by) the EU's ombudsman for the error to be rectified. The EU commission steadfastly refused to admit that anything was wrong.

When asked why the commission had taken so long to rectify an obvious error a spokesperson for the ombudsman replied: `That's exactly what we were asking ourselves.' When asked the same question one of the Scottish fisherman replied: `You don't tell God that he's fallible. The commission doesn't make mistakes.'

The EU describes itself as the friend of the consumer and small investor. In reality it is the opposite. Everything it does impoverishes investors and weakens consumers. Mussolini, the inventor of fascism, would have been enormously proud of the EU. As indeed would Hitler. Hitler would have loved the EU. It is the organisation he would have created if he had won the war. When the wall came down in Berlin most people thought that the East was going to be Westernised. it didn't happen that way. Instead, communism came West to us in the form of the EU statism. (Fascism and communism are the same).

For example, the EU does bugger all about the carcinogens all around us because they are protected by huge industries.

We're all stuffed to the gills with toxic chemicals that the EU doesn't do anything about because they are made by big international companies that no one working for the EU wants to piss off. The EU never likes to annoy the big international death companies (sometimes they kill people slowly, sometimes they kill people quickly but in the end it doesn't matter, they're in business of killing people and making money of it.

There was a time, just a few decades ago, when elected politicians would sit in London and mess up the country. They had little idea what they went on in the rest of the country but they had the one small advantage that they were our representatives. We had elected them. We were responsible for their mistakes. These days, unelected eurocrats mess up the country but they do it in Brussels. We have not elected them or had anything to do with them. We don't know their names, or anything about them. They run our lives from afar. It is the ultimate example of imperial management.

We wonder today at the way the German people kept silent during the rise of the Nazis. But today we have remained just as silent during the rise of the EU. The EU may not be as obviously evil as the Nazis. But the people who run the EU are the same as the people as the people who ran the National Socialist Party that ran Germany before and during the Second World War. The only difference is that they have learned and become cleverer. The aims are identical: control, power and a complete absence of freedom and democracy. In order to meet those aims they spend good chunks of our money persuading children, adults and anyone else it can find that the EU is a wonderful thing. (Fortunately, much of its promotional material is wonderfully inept and is presumably thought up by the usual brand of corporate half-wits who inhabit the EU buildings.

Politicians always back down when they plan to do anything that might hurt the EU. The Czech leader promised faithfully (`over my dead body stuff`) not to sign the Treat of Lisbon. But a few weeks later he signed. Gordon Brown promised a referendum on the Lisbon Treaty but changed his mind and signed the damned thing. David Cameron gave `a cast iron guarantee of a referendum' but changed his mind. The Liberal Democrats had promised a Referendum on Constitutional changes affecting Britain. They reneged on that by instructing MPs to vote against a referendum.  It's always because `circumstances have changed'. I bet they have. The real reason the three political parties reneged on promises to have a referendum was that they knew that any referendum would result in the British people voting against the Treaty and voting against the EU. The politicians couldn't win a pro-EU vote so they abandoned their promises to have one. Before the May 2010 election, Cameron even promised to do something about the Lisbon Treaty if it was ratified (presumably knowing that it would mean leaving the EU) but he then quickly backed down (as all politicians do if they seriously hope to be allowed to enjoy the trappings of power).

When the Irish people were told that they had to vote again on the Lisbon Treaty (stupidly, they got it wrong the first time they tried) the whole of the Irish establishment got behind the `Yes' campaign. Every mainstream party and business was in Yes camp and the Broadcasting Commission of Ireland (which is supposed to ensure impartiality) suspended its rule that both sides of the debate in a national referendum should be given equal airtime. For the first time in history votes weren't counted on election night. They were held, in their boxes, by the government which was telling people how to vote. The ballot boxes weren't all locked. It was a hugely important vote. The EU had to win this one. And, surprise, surprise, they won it.

Such little opposition as is reported arouses great concern among EU enthusiasts. In April 2010 the Financial Times, a slavish devotee of the European Union, seemed peeved when it announced that `almost half' of Britons think that the UK has not benefitted from membership of the EU. Actually, I suspect that a fairer figure would be closer to three quarters - a figure which fairly closely matches the percentage of the population which is literate. The Spanish and the Poles quite like the EU. Gosh, what a surprise. Spain gets £3 billion a year out of the EU. Poland gets £5 billion. Romania and the Czech Republic get another £1 billion. In contrast, Britain pays £6 billion a year for membership of a club which is ruining our country. We are paying handsomely to be oppressed. We are paying to have our freedom taken from us.

The FT argued that politicians have failed to make the case for

Britain's membership of the EU which is, it said, `clearly in the national interest'. And why does the FT think that membership is of benefit to the UK? Here are their reasons: `It gives the UK access to, and influence over, the world's greatest market. It is one of the things that keeps Britain's relationship with the US special. And it amplifies the UK's clout in a world in which power is shifting east.'

That's it.

That's what we get for the billions of pounds we give the EU every year. That's what we get in return for accepting busloads of pointless and enormously damaging red tape. That's what we get for abandoning our sovereignty and our democracy. That's what we get for living in a world ruled by unelected Brussels eurocrats. That's what we get for living in a superstate which has absurd and wasteful policies on agriculture and fishing. That's what we get for living in a superstate which must, as a result of its agricultural policies, bear a huge amount of responsibility for starvation in Africa. That's what we get in return for being forced to accept millions of unwelcome, unwanted and costly immigrants? And so on, and so on.

Let's look at these `advantages' the FT lists.

First, they claim that membership of the EU gives us access to a large market. This is one of the hoariest and stupidest chestnuts to come out of the mouths of europhiles. Do they really believe that Germany is going to refuse to trade with us if we leave the EU? No one but a halfwit would believe that.

Second, they claim that our membership of the EU helps keep our relationship with the US `special'. (It was, as I have described in books such as OFPIS, the USA which wanted us to join the EU in the first place - so that we could tell them what was going on.) Anyone who thinks that we have a `special' relationship with the USA has clearly been smoking something illegal. Our relationship with the USA is one-sided. We support their wars and allow them to do what they like with us and our citizens. In return we are ignored, abused, cheated and ripped off. Our misplaced loyalty to the USA has made us targets for terrorists everywhere. Our appeals to the Americans for help and support are always ignored - unless there is some benefit available for America.

Third, the FT claims that our membership of the EU amplifies our clout in the world. This is absurd. Whether inside or outside the EU, the UK no longer has any real clout in the world. We are struggling to avoid bankruptcy. And does the FT really think that China, India or the USA really take the EU seriously? The EU's new finance minister is a global joke. Britain would have more influence, and receive more respect, if its politicians were more honest and more honourable. Blair and Brown and their army of reprehensible ministers, aides and hangers on have destroyed our reputation globally.

Anyone who dares to criticise the EU, the most fascist organisation in the history of the world, is immediately dismissed as - guess what - a fascist! It is the ultimate in chuzpah. During the 2010 election I heard one leading politician claim that anyone who disapproved of the EU was an antisemitic, homophobic nutter who cared nothing about the environment, the planet or mankind. Every time it mentions the EU favourably the bent-as-a-paperclip BBC should mention that it gets around £130 million a year from the EU.

Today, many of our politicians have close links to the European Union. Nick Clegg, leader of the Liberal Democrats, worked as an EU official from 1994 to 1999 and then worked as an MEP from 1999 to 2004. Since he was born in 1967 this means that he was around 27 years old when he started his EU career and around 37 when he finished it. Nevertheless, despite his youth, he was during that time he was entitled to an estimated £2.52 million in salaries and allowances. He would have been entitled to £195,000 for actually turning up to work and been entitled to £495,000 in travel allowances. A pamphlet Clegg wrote agreed that the system encourages MEPs to find the lowest priced ticket available, charge for the highest class ticket allowed, and pocket the difference. All this means that he could have received around £250,000 a year for ten years (much of it tax free I have no doubt) for being a fairly insignificant cog in the EU wheel. Oh and there will be some nice pension money too. What a surprise it is that Mr Clegg is now such an unbridled enthusiastic supporter of the EU and that he has no time for those of us who question the purpose and aims of the organisation which served him so well. There should be a rule forbidding the two way street between EU and British Government. But there isn't and there won't be, of course. Too many British politicians move backwards and forwards and enjoy the fruits of their relationships with the EU. (If Bin Laden were living in England - which as far as the police know he might well be - Nick Clegg would still, in my opinion, be the most dangerous man in the country.)

During the May 2010 election Clegg (opposing a Tory plan to cut immigration) actually admitted that 80% of our immigration is forced on us by the EU.

The EU wants constant growth to keep income up so that taxes can stay productive. Only way to do this is through immigration (because taxes are already so high that sensible, earning people voluntarily limit their family sizes because they are paying so much to support the large families of the unemployed). Countries such as France and Italy aren't keen on this, and don't allow immigration, so the UK has to take most of Europe's immigrants. (Within a decade Britain and much of the rest of the EU could be Muslim rather than Christian countries.)

The ONLY advantage for Britain which has come through joining the

EU is that for the first time the Inland Revenue can levy income tax on prostitutes. British governments had previously been sensitive to accusations that if they taxed prostitutes they could be accused of living on immoral earnings. But when Britain joined the EU in the 1970s prostitutes could be taxed, thanks to the EU. So, that's it. That's the benefit.

You cannot believe anything you read or hear about the EU. Question everything. Including me. And this book.

But think about this: the people promoting the EU do so for power and money. What do I have to gain?

If I just wanted to sell books and make money I could apply for, and doubtless obtain, a large EU grant. I could, I suspect, arrange for the EU to purchase thousands of copies of such a book to give away.

A book extolling the virtues of the EU would prove enormously profitable without needing to sell a single copy.

On the other hand, this book, written from the heart, will be difficult to sell. Huge publishing groups will refuse to take advertisements for it. Newspapers and broadcasters will refuse to review it or promote it.

Why on earth would I write and publish such a book if the facts weren't true and I didn't believe wholeheartedly in the message?

Most of our new laws come from the EU. They call them `directives' but that's just the posh new word for `law'. (I work on the basis that if they can fine me or send me to prison for disobeying it then it's a law whatever they may call it.) Fascists make the ultimate nannies, constantly allocating fiscal and legal responsibilities to individuals (but keeping all the authority for themselves). They have devised and now control an oppressive state. The EU trade laws are created by people who have never run a business of their own. The result is that every single business in Britain breaks laws every day. The Government now claims that it is illegal to display either national flag on motor car number plates. Anyone who does so can be fined £60. A vehicle carrying a union jack or a cross of St George will fail the MOT test. Drivers are, however, permitted to display the European blue and yellow flag on their number plates. Who, I wonder decided that car number plates should be decorated with an EU flag as a default? They didn't used to put GB plates on number plates. (I recently saw a large car parked outside the Foreign Office in London. There was a sticker on the back window which read: `Love Europe hate the EU'. Europe and the EU are, contrary to the EU's view, two separate entities.

The EU doesn't just oppress its own citizens. The EU has already deployed more than 70,000 soldiers, policemen and other officials on missions in four continents

And the EU has a squad of lawyers who are skilful at accommodating member states which are temporarily embarrassed by laws which are or might be seen to be politically unacceptable. The lawyers will twitch the laws in a way that looks both highly significant and utterly inconsequential. The politicians can then go home and announce that they have forced the EU to accept their requirements when in fact the EU hasn't done a darned thing.

The EU is preparing an uber database with information about EU citizens. People will be locked up for what they might do at some time in the future (remember the film `Minority Report'). The title of this is Project INDECT, it costs millions of pounds (your pounds) and the aim is to collect information and identify anti-social behaviour before it takes place. Individuals identified by the system can then be targeted. I'm not kidding. I never kid about the EU.

During the May 2010 general election both main political parties were competing with one another. One offered that they would make sure that GPs would be available for 12 hours a day. The other tried to up the ante by promising that they would make sure that GPs would be available on Sundays. Neither would be able to do this, of course, because of EU working hours rules. To appease voters the two parties would probably set up a special GP clinic in Sheffield so that patients from all over the country could use that whenever they fell ill.

Much of the absurd health and safety nonsense which affects our lives comes from the European Union (and this explains why most of the health and safety regulations ignore real risks and simply create unnecessary problems).

The EU working directive makes it illegal for anyone to work more than 48 hours a week. (I know why they do it. It's so that we don't think the EU is making our laws. But I hate the fact that they call them directives. They're laws. You can go to prison if you don't obey them. If you can go to prison for not obeying them then they are laws and that's an end to it.) I've been taking what the self employed call a holiday this week and out of curiosity I added up the hours I had spent working. It came to 61, if you don't count the time I spent writing down ideas in the bath or the times I scribbled stuff down in bed. Still, unless the eurocrats read this (or you tell them) they'll never know and I'll be OK.

The weight of a huge, intolerant and committed eurocracy lies behind every order and every form. Every institutional demand, however meaningless and trivial, pointless and wrong-headed in concept, was carved in stone and delivered by truck. There is never room for dissent, discussion or such old-fashioned luxuries as logic and common sense. Politicians never blame the EU because they don't want to look weak (by blaming foreigners for things they are doing) and they sometimes don't know that what they're doing is at the behest of the EU eurocrats. Oh, and they aren't allowed to mention it anyway. I have spoken to long standing councillors who did not even know that they were being forced to bring in unpopular new rubbish collecting measures because of EU legislation. Some thought they were obeying rules thought up in London and one or two actually thought that the rubbish collecting regulations were designed locally by their own rubbish collecting supremo.

Judges from Azerbaijan, Albania and Latvia now sit on the bench at the European Court and decide what happens in Britain. After the Law Lords ruled that a man identified as Al Qaeda's spiritual leader in England could be deported the European Court of Human Rights awarded the man damages against the English taxpayer. Moreover, the European Court now has to hear the man's appeal. This could take years. France, of course, avoids all this problems by simply ignoring any rulings of the European Court or the European Commission which they don't like.

Most European countries apply the rules set in Brussels on a pick and choose basis. If France, Italy or Greece doesn't like a law then they just ignore it. There is just one country which regards every law from Brussels as though it had been brought by Moses and chiselled in stone. That country is, of course, Britain. Indeed, successive British governments have gone further than the EU has demanded. Our political leaders have repeatedly `gold-plated' legislation sent from Brussels in their desperation to please their EU masters (and mistresses).

Very few people understand just how pathetic and incompetent our government has been in its dealing with the European Union. I described the principle of `gold plating' (a process by which the British Government makes EU legislation worse...) in my book The OFPIS File and in `What Happens Next?' I described how the civil servants had made a huge mistake in the way our rubbish is dealt with. But the problems seem to get worse by the day. In January 2009 it emerged that England's poorest regions could lose out on up to £671 million of extra funding from the European Union. (The money is, of course, in reality simple a refund of some of the billions we pay to the EU as our membership fee.) The collapse of sterling boosted the value of euro-denominated EU grants by about a fifth. The EU offered to extend the spending deadline for unused regional aid to enable Britain to take advantage of this windfall. However, Labour Ministers decided that there was insufficient time for the regions to spend the windfall and so they accepted the EU's offer for Scotland and Wales but rejected it for England. And it also became known that the Department for Communities was to be fined £250 million by Brussels for failing to monitor European regional aid properly during the years 1997 and 2006. It seems doubly absurd that such a corrupt and inept organisation as the European Union should be able to fine Britain such a huge sum for failing to keep proper accounts.

Incidentally, everyone in politics always pretends that regionalisation has nothing to do with the EU. The artificial carving up of European nations has had to be done secretly, without revealing the true purpose, and it has not proved popular. In the UK very few people have any idea of the geographical boundaries deciding the arrangement of MEP seats. In France, few voters feel attached to their regions (created in 1986) and in a recent poll less than a third of voters could name their regional president.

Just about everything intrusive and destructive that has happened to Britain in general (and England in particular) has come from the European Union. Nothing good has ever come out of the EU. We pay massive membership fees to be members of a club no sane person would want to join. And the EU uses our money to promote itself to us. We pay to be indoctrinated.

The EU has ensured that there is very little future for entrepreneurs in Europe. The sensible thing for any school leaver today is to get a job as a eurocrat. There is little work to be done but massive benefits: high pay, the best pension in the world, long holidays, no stress, no weekend work, no responsibilities. And lots of power. (Incidentally, although the UK represents 12% of the EU population, and contributes hugely to the EU budget, its citizens make up only 6% of the Commission staff. Britain is now the least well represented country in the Commission, with the possible exception of the new entrant Romania.)

The EU has always been an organisation which exists primarily to provide jobs for the boys (and girls). If you know the right people and say the right things (`The EU is wonderful. The EU is wonderful. The EU is wonderful.') There are plenty of jobs available. All with lovely big salaries, splendid expense accounts and massive, take-it-early gold-plated, inflation linked pensions.

Amazingly, the EU has four presidents (one would be more than enough). There is the President of the European Council, the President of the European Commission, the President of the European Parliament and the Rotating President of the European Union. Naturally, each president is surrounded and supported by an expensive presidential administration. Four presidents. We've living in a fascist superstate which has four bloody presidents.

The new Foreign Minister for the EU will be officially known as the High Representative for Foreign Affairs. Honest. W.S.Gilbert would have laughed so much he would have fallen off his chair. And who will hold this post? Catherine Ashton, aka Lady Ashton, never received a vote from anyone outside the Campaign for Nuclear Disarmament (where she was a treasurer) but is now in charge of representing the continent (state) of Europe to other world powers. She worked in Whitehall doing I know not what. She allegedly trained social workers how to be more politically correct. She was elevated to the House of Lords for I know not what.

In March 2010 the EU announced that it had streamlined the way it recruits eurocrats. (These are the cushiest jobs in the world. Eurocrats count as expatriates, thereby avoiding the horrors of the UK taxman, they can retire early (at 50) on massive pensions (ordinary eurocrats have to try and make do on around £100,000 a year) and they have more perks than a banker.) The new format, boasted a spokesman for the EU, will ensure that candidates will know within five to nine months if they have clinched a job - half the present time.

Only the EU could take 18 months to tell a job applicant if he or she had been successful - and then boast about cutting the waiting time in half.

I couldn't help wondering what the test consists of. What sort of bribe would you take to allow ? What wine would you drink with oysters?

There is no doubt that the EU has become a gravy train for staff and their friends. In February 2010 the President of the European Commission appointed the man who had been his chief of staff for five years to be the EU ambassador to Washington. (Hands up if you didn't know the EU had, or needed, an ambassador to Washington.)

What is the purpose of the EU? I don't believe they want to destroy England out of vindictiveness or racism (though that is, of course, a possibility - some left over hatred from world war II manipulated by very old men or their descendants hiding in south America or some deep dark spot in the black forest), though I have to admit it is a real possibility. They are destroying England (and the fact of the destruction is not at issue, only the cause) because for Hitler's `project' to succeed, individual nations must be crushed and divided up into regions. (As I explained in my book `England Our England' there is no discernible difference between the EU we have and the EU that Hitler planned to create.)

The good news is that the EU and the euro are going to fail. (I first forecast the downfall of both in my book `England Our England'.) Every political career ends in disaster and the same is true of fascist, kleptocratic states.

In 2010, Angela Merkel, asked why Germany should be expected to support Greece when Greek workers retire ten years earlier than their German counterparts. Greek public sector workers have had a wonderful time in recent years. They are paid a fortune and given magnificent perks and pensions. The same question will be asked when Germany is asked to bail out Italy, where workers retire a year earlier than the Greeks and now demand huge salaries which have made their country uncompetitive. In 1995 Italian manufacturers had labour costs that were 60% of Germany's. But between 1995 and 2010, Italian labour costs soared and reached a point 30% higher than Germany's. It is this sort of inequality that will cause chaos within the European Union. The EU will collapse not when Greece defaults on its debts and is thrown out but when the German people decide they have had enough of the EU and Germany, the powerhouse of the euro, leaves. And the German people will decide they've had enough when they eventually realise that they are working harder, and paying more taxes, so that strangers can enjoy luxurious days on the beach. There will be rioting, strikes and much public damage. The German politicians will give in quite quickly.

The euro will collapse, destroyed by the bankruptcies of several nations - Greece, Portugal and possibly Spain. The EU will follow shortly afterwards. By 2020 the EU will have collapsed under the weight of its own laws, eurocracy and inherent corruption. A growing number of people will eventually stir and rise up at the fact that we are ruled by a couple of dozen unelected commissioners.

When Germany leaves the EU the remaining countries will wonder about their roles within the EU. Even the French will question their loyalty to (and the expense of) the European Union. The French loved the EU when it provided their farmers with endless subsidies. They won't be so keen on being members of an organisation which enables `foreigners' to live the good life at their expense.

The EU will implode not because people want it to go (which they do) but through greed and incompetence. The EU has never responded to democratic principles. And in the end its downfall will be inevitable and unavoidable.

Chances of the euro failing by 2020: 50%.

Chances of the EU collapsing by 2020: 30%.

48. The Number Of Britons Being Extradited For Doing Things That Aren't Illegal In Britain Will Increase Dramatically

No country in the world defends its citizens less ferociously against extradition than the United Kingdom. America will always defend its citizens. The American State Department would find reasons steadfastly to refuse extradition for Hitler or the Yorkshire ripper if they could prove that they had been born in Baltimore or Philadelphia.

But thanks to laws introduced by Blair, Brown, Blunkett et al, British citizens cannot rely upon their Government for any protection. If you are British, your country will deny you and refuse to help you. You can be legally extradited to virtually any country in the world. Your rights? Pretty well non existent.The British Government has done deals enabling all the EU countries to take British citizens out of their homes (and their home country) without so much as a murmur of protest. And the British Government has done a one sided deal with America allowing the American Government to help itself to any British citizen whom the Americans might want to put on trial. They don't need to produce any evidence. They just need to want you. Upset the Americans, the Greeks, the Spanish, the Romanians or the Germans (or whoever) and you can look forward to a lengthy spell in a foreign prison.

So, for example, the Americans are using the one sided extradition deal signed by the loathsome Blunkett to grab Briton called Gary McKinnon, a computer hacker accused of entering American military computers. (Surely they should take better of care of their stuff?). When hackers destroyed the server hosting my website the British police traced the hacker to the USA. The FBI refused to cooperate with the British police because the hacker was American and the hackee was British. The hacker, who did a vast amount of expensive damage, was certainly never threatened with extradition. (Interestingly, I discovered that the American military was one of the most frequent visitors to my website.)

The extradition of British citizens, charged with piffling crimes (which are, in many cases not even crimes in the UK) will increase dramatically.

It is no exaggeration to say that no other citizens in the world are as poorly protected as Britons. The biggest growth area for extradition orders will come in the world of the internet. The Americans claim ownership of the world wide web (though it was, of course, an Englishman who invented it) and just about every country in the world is developing its own laws about what can or cannot be said on the internet. The result is that a nerdy internet aficionado sitting in his bedroom in Norwich or Leamington Spa or Walsall can find himself being arrested and flown to Bonn, Washington or Athens at the drop of a warrant through the local police station letterbox. Those wretched individuals who spend their days writing rude messages on blogs and internet chat rooms will soon find that there are more things to worry about than libel actions.

Chances of more Britons being extradited: 100%.

49. Fear Will Increase

The authorities (by which I mean the EU, our Government and their employees) will continue to do everything they can to frighten us. I have, in previous books, discussed in detail the many ways in which governments frighten their citizens. Lenin knew that fear leads to obedience and that people who are frightened usually do as they are told. Modern governments love to scare their citizens. They do it all the time. Some years ago I coined the phrase `intellectual terrorism' to define the act of scaring the population with nonsensical and entirely unsupported scare stories.

So we should expect to be frightened on an almost daily basis. We will subjected to a constant, terrifying diet of news about terrorism, global warming (or, if more appropriate, global cooling again), overpopulation, economic disaster and a vast variety of deadly infections.

The constant exposure to fear will create endemic anxiety and depression which doctors will treat with mind-numbing drugs.

The wise among us will ignore all these warnings and recognise them for what they are.

But, with most of the population drugged into a zombie like state, it will difficult to start a revolution.

Chances of fear increasing: 100%.

50. Greed, Disappointment And Resentment Will Rise

The financial crisis that started in 2007 was created by greed: greedy bankers and greedy home buyers were responsible.

Nothing whatsoever has been done to discourage that greed. In fact, everything that has been done has been done to sustain the greed and protect the greedy.

Giving vast amounts of taxpayers' money to the banks, so that the bankers could continue to receive their absurd bonuses was greed sustaining. Providing taxpayers' money to help people who bought houses they couldn't afford, and should not have bought, was greed sustaining.

The problem is that the country is in deep trouble: far more trouble than most people realise.

And the greed sustaining policies are going to have to change.

The bankers will probably continue to take their huge bonuses. Any penalties imposed on the banks for which they work will be passed on to shareholders and customers. Ordinary citizens will pay for the bankers' greed.

But there is no way that any government can continue to support and protect the greed of the millions who bought property they couldn't afford, and paid prices that were far too high in a market where prices were driven up by greed and a bizarre belief that house prices would always rise and never fall.

Within a very short time people are going to have to start adjusting to a world that is much poorer than they believed.

Most people will earn less, enjoy less security and stability and endure deteriorating public services. They will also have to consume less and pay more taxes.

The greed will turn quickly into disappointment and resentment.

Chances of greed, disappointment and resentment soaring: 100%.

51. Debt, debt And More debt

There has been much talk about the nation's debt. But it isn't the nation which has huge debts. Millions of Britons have also spent far more than they should have done. Here's a scary piece of information: five million Britons regularly - by which I mean every week, every month and every year - spend more than they earn. You don't need to be Einstein to work out that such behaviour can't go on forever and that it is likely to end in tears. It is, after all, the sort of economic behaviour which Gordon Brown practised and which has led to our nation's financial crisis. Never before in our history have so many British people owed so much money to so many lenders.

Much of the debt has been accumulated by people buying houses they could not afford and should not have bought. Other debts are a result of the student loans that the Labour Government introduced. These mean that hundreds of thousands of young people start their lives with huge debts. (The loans were introduced so that the Government could provide more university places at very little expense. They wanted to provide more university places partly so that they could claim that Britain was high up on international education ladders but mainly so that they could shuffle school leavers out of the unemployment queues and thereby fiddle the figures to suggest that Britain was doing well.)

The debts are also a result of some pretty vile loan sharking by the banks (including those which were bailed out by unwilling taxpayers). When banks were paying virtually nothing on deposit accounts the average sort of interest rate charged on credit cards was 1.586%. That's not bad, you might say. But that was the figure per month. Even at simple interest rates (and theirs would be compound) that is a rate of 19% a year. When you compare that to the 0% the bank is were paying to borrow money from the Bank of England and the 0% they were paying depositors there is no doubt that the banks have been Shylocking. It's loan sharking.

It's despicable. It's obscene. It is cruelly, grotesquely irresponsible. And it is, as loan-sharking always is, also hugely profitable. Most disturbing of all is the fact that millions of Britons are now `maxed out' on their credit cards and owe huge sums - on which they are paying vast amounts of interest.

Despite all these huge private debts the government and its advisers have consistently insisted that the economic crisis will be over quicker if people spend more. (That is presumably why they are putting up taxes and reducing the amount of money people have in their wallets and handbags.) The politicians and their economic advisers are all wrong, of course. You don't get out of debt by increasing your spending. You get out of debt by saving. But common sense isn't a quality that one sees often in parliamentary circles these days.

And there are many more debts around that have yet to be sorted out. The years leading up to the crash of 2007 were a fine time for gamblers and financial jugglers. Many hedge funds, property speculators, venture capitalists and private equity managers made fortunes out of borrowing money and using it to buy buildings or companies. While everything was going up, up and away this was a brilliant way to get rich. Even the thick bastards who work in these niche areas of finance could get rich. But now that the party is over there is a price to pay.

For example, the Fitch credit reference agency reports that over £200 billion of European private equity borrowings on which it provides ratings will have to be repaid or refinanced before 2016. That's an average of £30 billion a year; no small sum and coincidentally exactly the same as the eurozone package put together by European countries in order to stop Greece going bankrupt.

Naturally, the problem is even worse in America, where the dickheads are even greedier, and globally there are more than £12 trillion worth of loans due to be paid off by private equity companies over the next six or seven years. That's about £180 billion a year that has to be found from somewhere. Most of the private equity people have spent all their money on yachts and champagne so the banks are probably going to have to whistle (and either take more thumping losses or else take over ownership of empty office blocks and shopping centres that seemed a good idea when they were being built but which are now proving to have more in common with white elephants than cash cows. Another survey showed that one in five shopping centres is at risk of defaulting on their loans. As retailers struggle so the shopping centres will fail. Money is going to continue to be very right for everyone and people wanting to start small manufacturing businesses shouldn't expect to obtain a loan from their bank any time soon.

Chances of debt accumulating (both for the state and for individuals): 100%.

52. More And More People Will Be Fat And Unhealthy

People are getting fatter and will continue to get fatter and unhealthier because the single factor which makes most difference to your health is the food that you eat. And most of the food most people eat is about as good for them as crap. (I speak literally rather than figuratively.)

The British are the fattest in Europe and the Scots are the fattest in Britain. Only the Americans are fatter; though the Australians are waddling up fast on the inside. A horrifying 23% of British women 22.3% of men are clinically obese. That's not pleasantly plump or curvaceous. It isn't even just fat. It's dangerously, grotesquely, American-style, waddling overweight.

Our pavements are dangerous as overweight but otherwise healthy people ride round on their mobility scooters, endangering anyone active enough to walk on their own two feet. (Most of the people riding on mobility scooters could walk about if they just lost some weight.)

Despite the massive amounts of public money being spent on hiring dieticians and nutritionists, things are going to get worse.

First, most of the people being hired know next to nothing about food and nutrition. (They don't even realise that meat is the most carcinogenic food known to man.)

Second, as the nation's economy crumbles so more and more people will buy cheaper and cheaper food. And cheaper food is usually the sort of stuff that makes people fat. The financial crisis will result in more people eating what I regard as `rubbishy' foods. And that will lead to more obesity and more heart disease. (One of the few companies to thrive during the financial meltdown has been McDonalds. I suspect that millions of people have discovered that it is cheaper to collect burgers and fries for all the family than it is to try and cook a wholesome meal with fresh ingredients. My view of the food sold by McDonalds is unprintable.)

So, there are going to be far more fat people in Britain in five years time than there are today.

The only good thing is that maybe not so many of them will be able to afford those damned mobility scooters.

Chances of there being more fat (and unhealthy) individuals in Britain: 100%.

53. There Will Be Fees For Everything

The government is going to introduce fees for everything. So is your local council. Government departments will make increasing use of premium rated advice lines and there will be specific fees for obtaining information about flooding risks and other hazards. The government already plans to charge people who want to make a complaint to the Financial Services Authority about a bank or financial adviser and doctors charge patients who ring for an emergency visit by using premium rate telephone lines.

The charging of a fee for making a complaint about being ripped off by financial crookery is apparently being introduced because the authorities are receiving a large number of complaints from people who've been ripped off. It is obviously cheaper, and more profitable, to charge a fee than it would be to do something to stop innocent citizens having their money stolen by fraudsters.

So, what next?

I don't think there is any public service that is immune to some sort of fee structure.

Will there be a charge to ring 999 and ask for police, fire or ambulance?

Almost certainly.

Chance of the authorities introducing many more fees and licences: 100%.

54. Health And Safety Regulators Will Continue To Introduce More And More Absurd Regulations (but, at the same time, food poisoning and accidents will increase)

Our world is being destroyed by absurd health and safety regulations which are largely thought up by Bureaucrats in Brussels who live in a parallel world where common sense is absent.

When I visit my local Post Office to collect my mail I have to park outside in the street because a few years ago someone was injured in a motor vehicle accident. As a result the Royal Mail now keep the gates shut and all visitors have park half a mile away and risk their lives crossing two busy roads. A health and safety official visiting a leading golf club informed the staff that what he referred to as `the sand pits', which were quite deep, would have to be fenced in to ensure that anyone trespassing on the course at night didn't fall in and hurt themselves.

We have become a nation of over-regulated wimps, constantly looking over our shoulders for men with clip boards and regulated into submission; too frightened to protest. We live in a world in which health and safety bureaucrats create rules not to make the world a safer place but to enhance their own power and status and in so doing end up making the world more dangerous than it was before they started.

Everywhere you look the spoilsports and doom-mongers are busy. Union members at the Trades Union Congress wanted to ban high heels in the workplace for health and safety reasons. When a few flakes of snow fell in January 2010 the nation closed down for days. The rest of Europe laughed as British businesses closed down. Postmen stayed indoors and played cards because the pavements were too dangerous for them to venture out. Workers had to stay at home because thousands of schools had closed (these days headmasters and mistresses close down the moment the first flake of snow hits the ground, spotting an opportunity to use health and safety issues as an excuse to add to their already interminable holidays). Even parents who wanted to go to work couldn't because their child couldn't go to school. Civil servants stayed at home in their millions. Any who bravely made it through the half an inch of snow were given bonuses for their courage and self sacrifice. When power lines went down the repairmen weren't allowed out to mend them because of health and safety rules.

The whole business of `health and safety' is built on a huge network of pseudoscientific myths. Cyclists are told that they must wear helmets at all times (even though there is no evidence that wearing a helmet improves safety and there is some evidence that wearing a helmet might well result in more accidents and more deaths). No one in authority suggests that cycle lanes might be a good idea; even though they would definitely reduce the number of accidents and deaths involving cyclists. The health and safety myth makers simply talk the official talk and stick to whatever the official line might happen to be that week.

Stopping children playing conkers is just one of the many daft health protection laws which are good for the State since they prevent injury and illness. Playing conkers may be fun but it is no value to the State. Indeed, fun never is. The State is opposed to fun as a matter of principle. Throwing snowballs can cause injury and damage. But there is no benefit to the State. In a democratic world human beings would be allowed to decide for themselves whether or not to take the chances involved. But in a fascist country the State takes the decision and outlaws the fun activities.

Health and safety officials insist on absurdly expensive regulations concerning sinks but say nothing about food that sits out in the open to be coughed over and dribbled on. They insist that people preparing food do so in allegedly hygienic surroundings but personal hygiene practices are so poor that the vast majority of meals and sandwiches sold in Britain today are contaminated with e.coli bugs and are unfit for human consumption. When Donna Antoinette and I go out we take our own sandwiches because we know that the people who made them washed their hands before they did so. There are more health and safety rules than ever before and there are whole armies of petty bureaucrats employed to enforce them but neither the rules nor the bureaucrats do anything that is genuinely practical or useful. Point out that allowing dog owners to let their animals foul public parks causes blindness in children and you'll be met with a shrug. One professional told me with a shrug that only 50 children a year go blind this way and so it wasn't considered important enough to do anything about. Really? And how many children are killed or blinded by playing conkers?

The health and safety people always to worry about the wrong things. They spend much of their time worrying about ladders and swimming pools and none of it worrying about fat in food that kills a million times as many people. They do this because it is easier to bully window cleaners and parents who want to teach their kids how to swim (surely a good thing) than it is to bully big companies who can defend themselves with teams of lawyers.

Much health and safety advice seems designed to take away all sense of responsibility. The trouble is that this stops people thinking for themselves. The health and safety people now insist that churches produce complex coloured cards telling people how to leave the building in an emergency. When there is an emergency, of course, people ignore the coloured cards. But we have all stopped thinking for ourselves. The wise thing to do, when entering any building, is to check out where the exits are. In an emergency most people panic unless they are trained not to panic. Even qualified first aiders tend to panic if they don't have some experience or some understanding of what to expect. But instead of encouraging people to be aware of their surroundings and to know the basic principles of self preservation, the health and safety people would rather print another ten million expensive coloured leaflets or cards. It's just a pointless abdication of responsibility in a world where everyone expects someone else to take responsibility for what happens to them.

The real problem, of course, is that the rule-makers and the rule-enforcers don't have any common sense. And there are so many rules to follow that ordinary people no longer bother with common sense. All sense of personal responsibility has been abandoned. Time and time again I see people in food shops and restaurants handling food and then money and then food again. At Paddington Station in London we watched a child pick up an iced bun in a branch of Sainsbury's. He put a finger into the icing and sucked it clean. He then did it again. His mother, who had seen him do this, simply made him put the cake back on the unprotected display basket. In a self-service restaurant I watched in horror as a man with a cold allowed his nose to drop into the uncovered salad displays. We used to eat out at a restaurant in the West Country. But, one day I was just drying my hands in the Gents when the chef came out of a cubicle and left without washing his hands. I followed him out and watched in horror as he went straight into the kitchen. We left and have not eaten out since then. It is, in truth, absurd that chefs and cooks everywhere still prepare food with their bare hands. Television chefs, who as a breed seem to understand little about hygiene or nutrition, use their bare hands all the time. Have they any idea how difficult it is to wash hands so that they are free of infection? Surgeons take several minutes to wash their hands and arms thoroughly. And then they put on rubber gloves. People handling food do so with billions of bugs lurking in their skin creases and under their finger nails. I've written to health and safety people about these problems. They aren't interested.

And so we have to look after ourselves. And use our common sense.

Because things are going to get much, much worse before they get better. If they ever do.

Chances of health and safety regulators continuing to introduce absurd and meaningless regulations: 100%.

55. Our Future Leaders Are Increasingly Likely To Be Psychopaths

Research has shown that top jobs in politics, as indeed in many other walks of life, are frequently successfully held on to by people with psychopathic traits. Throughout history the possession of psychopathic traits has proved a useful passport to high office. Men or women who are unfettered by moral scruples, who are prepared to lie or cheat their way to the top and who will make promises they know they cannot keep have a huge advantage over those held back by notions of decency and fair play.

There is no doubt that leaders who possess psychopathic traits are at an enormous advantage. They have more freedom in their dealings with the public, with those with whom they work and with their potential enemies. They are able to control and manipulate people without any qualms. Psychopaths fake their emotions (which they learn by studying other people) and so suffer very little in circumstances which healthy people would find emotionally difficult. It is not surprising, perhaps, that many people in positions of power (including judges among others) and many people who seem especially pushy are psychopaths. We should not be too surprised at this; after all psychopaths are surprisingly common. (One in every 100 people is a psychopath.)

Here is a list of the traits associated with psychopaths. If you go through it thinking of political figures you will, I suspect, be surprised to see how many people you can identify as psychopaths.

1. Exceptionally selfish
2. Constant liars (and very good at it)
3. Manipulative - socially manipulative
4. Egocentric

5. Callous and indifferent to suffering

6. Grandiose

7. Have a sense of entitlement

8. Lack of personal insight

9. Parasitic - life off others or the state

10. Bullying and abusive

11. Able to trick and con people successfully

12. Superficially charming

13. Apparently strong, calm and confident

14. Unable to experience love or compassion

15. Guilty of random and senseless violence

16. Not anxious and never irrational

17. Anger, rage and frustration are common emotions

18. May appear sincere but invariably insincere

19. Apparently likeable and sane

20. No shame or remorse and doesn't care about the feelings of others

21. Never learns from experience

Now try applying those criteria to the politicians you can think of.

Chances of most of our future leaders being psychopaths: 80%.

56. The Number Of People Leaving The Country Will Soar

Even the most loyal citizens are beginning to think of leaving. In February 2010 75% of Britons said they wanted to leave the country. (I had a terrible suspicion that the 25% who didn't want to go were probably all on benefits). Soon, everyone who can leave the country will do so and since that includes most of the people who contribute to the nation's wealth things will get considerably worse for those who stay behind.

Politicians (particularly Labour politicians) have consistently sneered at Britons leaving the country. `Go!' they say. `We don't need you.'

But the country does need the people who are leaving because the people who are leaving tend to work hard, earn money and pay taxes.

The sneerers always suggest that those leaving are going because they want to live somewhere sunny.

Not true.

Most are leaving because just about everything that can go wrong has gone wrong; British hospitals are irredeemably infected with MRSA, politicians are dishonest and greedy, overbearing gold plating of bureaucracy and red tape has closed long-established honest businesses and forced companies to cut corners. Big companies outsource more and more to foreign lands (thereby speeding up the destruction of Britain), our craven media are a disgrace, our culture is being crushed by multiculturalism, hypocrisy and political correctness (though where one ends and another starts is sometimes difficult to tell), honour is dead, now there are only deals and selfishness. They are leaving because the electricity is about to run out and no one is doing anything about it. They are leaving because they are fed up with the strikes and the selfishness and overbearing demands of public sector workers who contribute nothing but demand everything. They are leaving because crime is rocketing and the police, who have too much power, persecute the innocent and ignore the guilty. They are leaving because they know that the public pensions bill is hanging over the nation like a fiscal sword. They are leaving because private pensions have been decimated by politicians who hate anything not controlled by the state. They are leaving because Britain gold plates absurd EU laws that other countries ignore. They are leaving because Britain's infrastructure is the worst in the western world. They are leaving because Britons are spied upon more than the citizens of any other nation on the planet. They are leaving because the country has been opened up to endless hordes of immigrants who care nothing for the country but simply want free this, free that and free the other. They are leaving because the government has created a culture which encourages laziness and has created a situation in which generations of workshy individuals live better than hard working folk. They are leaving because privacy does not exist in Britain (and is, indeed, frowned upon) and because the government constantly threatens to force everyone to carry identity cards and free citizens don't do that. They are leaving because the streets are full of beggars and illegal immigrants whose culture is very different to theirs and who often make a visit to the shops to buy a loaf of bread a scary and sometimes dangerous journey. They are leaving because the streets are full of alcoholics and drug addicts and because most of the alcoholics and drug addicts are not yet twenty years old and if that is the present what sort of future can there be? They are leaving because the people who come into the country make no effort to become part of the community in which they live but create new, alien communities which exclude the natives. They are leaving because the people who come in are encouraged to force their values, their culture and their laws upon the country they have invaded. They are leaving because the cost of living in Britain is higher than anywhere else in the world. And yet the standard of living keeps going down. They are leaving because they are ashamed of a country which starts wars against people who are no threat to them, and then bombs and kills children with apparent impunity. They are leaving because freedom and democracy are no longer even paid lip service and because politicians have, without their leave, signed away their rights. They are leaving because no one cares about them and they feel like strangers in their own country.

The people who leave aren't abandoning their history or renouncing your nationality; they are going because they care too much about their country to stay and watch its ruin; they are going because only by leaving can they preserve their love. They you are getting out of the clutches of the fascist bureaucrats who have taken over. They are protecting themselves, their health, their families, their freedom and whatever remains of their wealth. They are leaving to preserve their sanity. They are leaving to preserve their strength so that they can fight for your country without being distracted by fighting to survive and without being hampered by waiting for the knock on the door. They are leaving because the time has come when they have to look after themselves and pick somewhere to live where they might be more comfortable.

The people who leave are going to start new lives in a new country where they may, they hope, be treated with respect and decency and compassion and where their basic human rights will be respected.

They are leaving because although it is difficult (and often painful) to leave it is more difficult (and more painful) to stay.

And thus, in time, this becomes a decision we all have to make. When will it be time for you to leave the country?

Chances of a vast increase in the number of people with jobs or money leaving the country by 2020: 100%.

57. The End of Marriage

Marriage is an institution which is the bedrock of our society. It provides stability for both partners and for any children they have. Children whose parents are married are healthier and happier and do better at school.

Families which are solidly built provide their members with support and comfort in difficult and frightening times. For the individual they are good. For a fascist State which wants to keep people alone, frightened and on edge stable families are a bad thing. And so we should not be surprised that the traditional British family has been steadily but deliberately and effectively destroyed by a constant barrage of legislation. Marriage is discouraged because people who are not in solid, secure relationships are easier to frighten and to control. Orwell knew that. No couples were allowed in `1984'.

The Labour Party has used both the tax system and its own appallingly unfair means testing system to help strengthen the power of the state by destroying the institution of marriage.

The Labour Government doesn't want people marrying and being secure. People who feel secure and safe are likely to be independent. And independent individuals are an anathema to a fascist state. So Blair, Brown and the rest of the Labour Party, ever loyal to the needs of the state in general and the European Superstate in particular, did their best to make marriage economically unattractive. The tax system is designed to benefit those who stay single. For example, property gains tax reliefs are much better if a couple stay single - both can claim one property as their home and pay no capital gains tax. The Inland Revenue has targeted couples who have set up small companies together. This has been done in such a blatant way that independent observers have described it as a tax inspired attack on marriage as an institution. Two people who aren't married are allowed to share dividends without the Inland Revenue getting interested. If two people who are married do it then it is tax evasion. If half of a married couple needs institutional care the other must pay for it. If half of an unmarried couple needs institutional care the state will pay. The state gives and gives and gives to unmarried couples, to encourage them, and takes and takes and takes from married couples. Unmarried couples are given all the rights previously bestowed on the married. But they have none of the fiscal responsibilities. It is difficult to argue that homosexuals who commit themselves to long term relationships should not be allowed same rights as heterosexual couples. But why should heterosexuals who refuse to marry be given those rights too? The only possible point of that is to devalue marriage and stability. The whole outrageous attack on marriage has become so potent that Labour's benefit system is totally destroying marriage by rewarding couples if they live apart. Tax credits, introduced by the Britain's worst ever Chancellor, Gordon Brown, were introduced in 1998, favour single parents and discriminate against two-parent families. Evidence produced by the Government's own Office for National Statistics (never published, but leaked) shows that 1.2 million couples in Britain now choose to live apart together. They lie and pretend to be single because the Government's absurd anti-marriage tax credit system means that they will be hugely better off if they do so. The average couple who split up will be £58 a week better off in hand outs. Some couples are more than £200 a week better off if they aren't married. From an economic point of view the system is stupid and indefensible. There is no sound economic reason for it. The Government's system means that it loses tax revenue and has to pay out extra tax benefits and credits. Why would a Government which is desperately short of cash to pay for wars and civil servant pensions behave so stupidly? The only possible explanation is that the Government has a hidden agenda. And the only possible hidden agenda is the destruction of marriage and institution. And the only possible explanation for that is that the Government knows that if they destroy marriage they will strengthen the state. Practical fascism in action: pure, unadulterated fascism. Mussolini, if he were still alive, would be drooling with idiotic delight.

Not surprisingly, the marriage industry is in dire straits. Photographers are going bust faster than ever (and photographers have always gone bust at quite a pace) and dress shops which used to sell wedding gowns now flog prom dresses to teenage girls whose schools have adopted the awful, high pressure American practice of having an annual `prom' where jealousies and vanities can be aired and enjoyed without hindrance.

How long will it be before the concept of the permanent marriage is replaced by an annual, renewable marriage contract? With, of course, an annual licence fee to be paid to the EU.

Chances of the number of people getting married continuing to shrink: 90%.

58. Moral Hazard Has Increased (and will continue to increase)

Prior to the financial crash that started in 2007 I wrote warning about the fact that bankers were being allowed to gamble with investors' money. If the gamble was successful, the banker paid some of the profit to shareholders of the bank and to the investors who had put up the money. If the gamble was unsuccessful, the investors lost their money but the bank's shareholders and the bankers lost nothing. The bankers could only win, they could never lose. It was an absurd situation and it was a perfect example of `moral hazard'.

The financial crisis that started in 2007 has done nothing to change this situation. Indeed, on the contrary, governments in America and the United Kingdom have made things worse. By bailing out the bankers with taxpayers' money the governments let the gamblers off the hook. Even worse, both governments then allowed the bankers to continue to pay themselves the huge bonuses they'd become accustomed to enjoying when their gambles were successful. Brown enjoyed taking credit for this grotesquely unfair policy (it was the basis of his infamous `I saved the world' speech).

The problem is, perhaps, that no one in either government seems to know anything about history. If they did they would be aware that Britain faced a series of financial crises in the first half of the 19th century because the Bank of England promised to buy bills if prices fell below a certain point. This encouraged discount houses to inflate credit. The current situation is almost identical. Brown, and his moronic companions across the Atlantic, has plastered over the problem in a way that will ensure huge problems for the future. Nothing has been altered, nothing has been improved, nothing has been saved.

Moral hazard is not a new problem.

America dealt with it in the 1930s by passing the Glass-Steagall reforms which basically ensured that there were two types of bank: the gun toting, whisky glugging banks which took huge risks and either made huge profits or went bust and the vanilla flavoured home-made cake banks which gave out cheque books, operating savings accounts and lent money to nice couples who wanted to buy a home or start a small business.

In my book `What Happens Next?' I recommended this type of solution. And it is now clear that it was the only sensible solution and that it would have worked. The `remedy' favoured by Brown (and the idiots around the world who, he claims, followed his advice) is no remedy at all.

Brown's legacy has been to leave bankers believing that they cannot lose. They now have a licence to print themselves money and an incentive to carry on cheating their customers, their bondholders and their shareholders. Indeed, they are now allowed to cheat taxpayers too.

Chances of moral hazard increasing and continuing to increase: 70%.

59. The Oil Is Running Out

I have been vilified for the contents of my book Oil Apocalypse. Critics of the peak oil theory (led by politicians and people from the oil producing countries and followed by half-witted folk in denial and freaks who believe that wind and wave power will provide the energy their computers need) have been vitriolic in their abuse. But I have a file stuffed with letters from oil industry experts confirming that everything in Oil Apocalypse is accurate. And I am convinced that the oil is running out and that the price will rise. The evidence strongly supports my contention (just look at the price of petrol at the pump if you doubt me). But the bottom line is that we will find out soon enough who is right. Those who claim that there is plenty of oil out there and that it will be easy enough to find can sit back and make no plans. That's their choice. My choice is to buy oil company shares and make sure that I own a bicycle and have log burning stoves in my home.

Forget all the rubbish about new oil fields being found. Forget about the prospects of using nuclear power to extract untold quantities of oil from the Canadian oil sands.

As I predicted in my book `Oil Apocalypse', the oil is running out.

In 2009 the International Energy Agency warned that a decline in oil investments could lead to another economic crisis in 2013 as oil reserves start to dry up.

Nevertheless, later that year, in November 2009, a whistleblower at the International Energy Agency claimed that the agency had been deliberately underplaying a looming shortage of oil for fear of triggering panic buying. America has been encouraging the I.E.A. to underplay the rate of decline of existing fields while overplaying the chances of finding new reserves. Meanwhile, America was accumulating vast amounts of oil and storing it. They were, of course, also busy grabbing countries which had some oil. (In late May 2010, after a disaster with one of BP's oil drilling rigs, there was much talk among American politicians about banning all drilling off the American coastline. The Americans did not, however, suggest that they might reduce their consumption of oil. And the result will be that oil companies will drill off other coastlines, where the risk of environmental damage may well be considerably higher. American selfishness knows no bounds.)

At about the same time, Total, the French oil group warned politicians that they risked accelerating an oil supply crunch if they enacted environmental policies that deterred investment in oil and gas before enough viable alternatives were available. The company's chief executive, Christophe de Margerie, was quoted as warning that not only the planet would suffer if the UK and other governments failed to enact smart environmental policies. `I hope you have a lot of candles,' said Mr de Margerie.

In April 2010 a Joint Operating Environment report issued by the US Joint Forces Command suggested that the USA could face oil shortages much earlier than many had anticipated. The report speculated that by 2012 surplus oil production capacity will dry up; by 2015, the world could face shortages of nearly 10 million barrels a day; and that by 2030 the world will require production of 118 million barrels of oil per day, but will produce only 100 million barrels of oil a day.

Developed countries now generate almost twice as much output from each barrel of crude as they did in the 1970s. But that's the only bright point. Unconventional sources of fuel, such as the oil sands and biofuels, are environmentally unsound. The first will lead to massive damage to the environment. There will be an increasing number of protests against their use though as the price of oil soars and supply drops, governments will suppress the protests and the companies involved (such As Royal Dutch Shell) will probably do well out of them. The second will lead to massive starvation. Other sources of power, such as wind and wave power, are irrelevant and impractical. Only two things matter. First, we have devised a society which relies upon oil. Second, the oil is running out.

Oil went up 115% in the year from January 2009 and I have no doubt that the price will fluctuate. But I don't believe it is going down to stay down. Every fall in the price will, for me, be another buying opportunity.

The price of petrol is going to keep going up. As our currency declines (either bit by bit or in great leaps and bounds) so the price of the oil we have to import (measured in dollars or, in the future, a basket of currencies) will rise.

The oil price will keep going up. And the shares of companies which find oil will go up with it. Big oil company majors such as BP and Shell are paying big dividends which are well covered. Moreover, the big oil companies are earning much of their money in dollars (and other non-sterling currencies).

As the price of oil goes up, up and away out of sight so we will have to change the way we live. Horse drawn vehicles will become practical again. Barges will be used on our canals to move goods between towns. Houses with chimneys and hearths will become increasingly valuable as people learn that keeping warm with a log fire is preferable to shivering with oil fired central heating that doesn't work.

The coming oil crisis will mean the end of the suburbs and the death of rural villages. People will no longer be able to live miles from shops, schools and work. The cost of travelling 20 miles a day by car will be far too high for most people to consider. Abandoned city centre shops will be converted into living accommodation as more and more people want properties close to the railway station and to the few remaining offices and factories remaining.

The oil is running out. The price of what is left (and not commandeered by the American military) will go up. There will, of course, be protests and (perhaps most stupid of all) conveys of lorry drivers and motorcyclists driving slowly up and down motorways, burning up expensive fuel and achieving absolutely nothing. There will a lot more wars as America and other nations try to commandeer the oil and other strategic commodities that are left.

Nothing anyone does or says will make a damn of difference. The oil is running out. And when something runs out the price goes up. There will many losers (big stores, lorry owners and sales representatives). But there will be winners too. Small local shops (especially when the property is owned by the shopkeeper) will do if they provide a local service. Small arcades of four to five shops will do well. DIY shops will thrive as people decide to save costs and delivery problems by repairing broken appliances. Hiring professional workmen will be made unbelievably tiresome - and expensive - by endless new rules and regulations. Small local fish and chip shops will surely thrive. And people selling logs and log burners and bicycles should do very well. Eventually, horse drawn carts will take stuff to cart boot sales.

Oh, and shareholders in small exploration companies which find oil run the risk of becoming extremely rich.

Chances of the oil running out: 100%.

60. Lots More Old People Will Die Of Starvation And Cold (and not be found for weeks)

The meals on wheels service was formed during Second World War to help people made homeless by the blitz and to assist elderly whose young family members were fighting abroad. It has always been operated by volunteers (I used to drive a meals on wheels van and know just how valuable the service is). It has for years doubled as a neighbourhood watch over the elderly and vulnerable.   Operated   by   WRVS,   which relies on councils to help with the cost, the service charges old people for the meals they get but the idea is that the meals should be affordable.

The system is collapsing.

A 90 year old woman had to live on sandwiches throughout the winter because her local meals on wheels service was cancelled. Another was discharged from hospital on the understanding that she would get meals on wheels. No one bothered to check and so no one knew that the service had been cancelled. Councils are under no legal obligation to provide meals on wheels and so it's one of the first things they cut when times are hard.

The government wasted £150 million on anti swine flu vaccines they were never going to use but can't find food for old people.

The Rotherham council scrapped its meals on wheels service claiming that it was making a loss of £95,000 a year. (I didn't realise public services had to make a profit). They managed, however, to find £125,000 a year to spend on a special kitchen to teach cookery. After Oldham council axed hot meat delivery services a spokesperson said the elderly could eat at the pub or from fast food outlets. (The spokesperson didn't seem to realise that he or she was talking about people who needed meals on wheels because they couldn't leave their homes to go shopping.) Councils all over the country are reducing subsidies where they do carry on with the service and prices of meals vary enormously. In Derbyshire one meal costs £1.40 but in Buckinghamshire a meals on wheel meal costs £5.49. Some councils have cancelled meals on wheels deliveries and replaced em with fortnightly deliveries of frozen microwave meals.

Chances of more elderly people dying of cold and starvation: 100%.

61. The Olympic Games Will Leave Us With Souvenirs We'd Rather Not Have

The Olympic Games are going to be a huge drain on an impoverished nation. Moreover, we can pretty sure that although the games are being held in England little will be done to celebrate England's history or culture. The Millennium celebrations (held in the wretched Dome) showed no respect for or recognition of English - or even British - history. We should have celebrated with English Morris dancers, maypole dancing, English music and English poetry. Instead we had to endure a smorgasbord of international rubbish. I suspect that the Olympics will serve up something similarly disappointing. When Coe, one of the organised of the damned overblown event, was asked for information about the planned Olympic fol de rols he jokingly said that he had ordered 5,000 morris dancers. I missed the joke. It seems to me that 5,000 Morris dancers (if he could have found them) would have been a splendid way to start an English celebration. They are English games. England is paying for them. Did the Chinese do something to celebrate England? Did they buggery. And why should they? They celebrated Chinese culture. The games themselves will be a social disaster. In their attempts to avoid doing anything which might possibly be construed as praising England's culture or heritage the organisers will produce ceremonies which are irrelevant, bland, `ethnic' and meaningless.

One big problem with the Olympic games is, undeniably, the fact that they will leave us with some huge debts. That's inevitable. And, quite probably, an awful lot of expensive buildings which will never be used again. How many athletics meetings will attract 100,000 spectators?

But it is the way the Olympics will affect our lives which will produce more lasting damage.

I can think of two ways in which the politicians and the police will find a way to use the Olympics to their advantage.

First, the Olympic Games are always used as a testing ground for new security technologies. And security technology is an area where Britain already leads the world. I have no doubt that the police will discover, test and introduce countless new ways of spying on us and controlling us as a result of the Olympic Games.

Second, special lanes will be designated for Olympic officials so that they don't get held up in traffic. Just as buses now have priority so, during the Olympics and afterwards, the `important people' (politicians, bureaucrats, policemen and John Prescott) will have special windscreen passes entitling them to use the priority lanes. Special amenity lanes, without speed restrictions, will be made available on autobahns (the roads which we currently call motorways) and other roads for the use of emergency crews, politicians and licensed bureaucrats. Drivers using these lanes will automatically have priority over other road users and will be entitled to ignore road signs and road traffic regulations.

It worked in Moscow and we can expect it in Britain.

Chances of the Olympic Games leaving us with souvenirs we would rather not have: 100%.

62. Pawnbroking Will Be A Growth Industry

The high streets in our towns and cities have already changed. Instead of bookshops and tailors there are now charity shops and discount stores.

The next big retail growth story will be pawnbrokers.

As more and more people struggle to make ends get somewhere close to one another (there is little chance of them actually meeting) so they trundle down to the local pawnbroker's shop with their jewellery, kid's computer games and best clothes, hoping to make enough money to pay for the week's grocery bill.

There will soon be more pawnbrokers than estate agents in our high streets.

Chances of there being more pawnbrokers in 2020 than there are now: 100%.

63. Today, The Customer Is Always Wrong (and that's not going to change)

It started, I believe, with the National Health Service. The complaints system there long ago stopped being run for the benefit of patients. The NHS, and its complaints system, have for years now been run primarily for the benefit of the employees. Patients and relatives are an inconvenient and disruptive nuisance.

This philosophy is spreading rapidly.

For example, employees at Royal Mail, British Telecom, British Gas have no interest in the consumer. Make a complaint, threaten to report them, and they will retort with an insolent sneer, `Do what you like! Bring it on.' You can hear the sneer from several hundred miles away. You can smell the contempt. Protest at the way you've been treated and they simply put the phone down on you. Cocooned in their corporate world, secure in a private-public environment of inflation proof pension and unsackability they have no interest in your concerns, your interests, your fears. Captivated by their own sense of corporate superiority, justice is alien to them. My own experience of these corporate goliaths has led me to deep despair as I struggle to run a small publishing business in what has become increasingly alien territory. My only consolation is the knowledge that when they leave their office and return to the world they too must face a world of sneering indifference. The Royal Mail employee must face the indifference of the British Telecom employee, the British Gas employee, the hospital clerk, the airport. Together they create a world no one wants to live in. And they're not to blame, of course. They're just doing their jobs. They don't make the rules. They just turn the tap and out comes the gas. Not their fault. Don't blame me. Stand up straight and breathe in.

As government departments and large companies fight harder for cash so they will become increasingly ruthless. And so the rights of customers go down, down, down.

Of course, consumers themselves (driven by the same shortage of money) aren't entirely faultless.

Publishing House, which sells my books, often receives packages from customers who return books for a refund or an exchange. The books they return are well thumbed, the pages marked with coffee cup stains and cigarette ash. `You sent this in error,' they claim, when it's painfully obvious that they've read and re-read the volume. And dress shops report that it is increasingly common for their customers to `buy' goods, wear them for a special occasion and return the goods for a refund when they've finished with them. EU law gives customers extraordinary rights and shopkeepers have little choice but to provide the refund. This sort of behaviour can be absorbed by large companies (who are cutting corners in every conceivable way) but small businesses, struggling to cope with red tape and bureaucracy, cannot. The result will be that more and more small shops will go bust.

Chances of the customer being always wrong: 100%.

64. Tuberculosis (aka Consumption) Is Coming Back.

Africans are dying of TB in enormous numbers but they call it AIDS because that's where the money is, and the publicity. The AIDS industry (and it is now an industry) gets all the money and TB is ignored. Then Africans come to Britain. With their tuberculosis. And tuberculosis is going to be a big problem in Britain.

Thanks to the obsession with the imaginary horror of global AIDS, tuberculosis has been totally underestimated. In 2009 nearly 2 million people were killed by tuberculosis and new infections rose to more than 9 million.

People with TB are pouring into the UK and its considered racist to talk about the problem or to test for the disease.

TB lives in the shadow of the wildly exaggerated problem of AIDS. The absurd and irrational (but for a small number of people enormously empowering and profitable) AIDS industry has distracted attention and money away from this, and other, very real problem.

How many thousand Britons will die of tuberculosis in the next ten years?

I have no idea.

Nor has anyone else.

But it's far, far more than you or they thought it would be.

Chances of tuberculosis coming back: 80%.

65. Sex Offences Committed By Children Are Going To Increase

In May 2010 special security precautions had to be taken at the Old Bailey in London where two boys, aged 10 and 11, were on trial for the rape of an 8 year old girl. After much stress and heartache the little girl admitted that she made up the allegation because she had been naughty and was worried that she might not get any sweets. The boys were subsequently found guilty.

Putting aside the question of how effective a 10 year old boy would be as a rapist I find myself wondering just why educationalists cannot see how closely this awful story must be connected with the absurd modern policy of giving sex education lessons to primary school children.

As sex education classes are become a part of our culture so vast numbers of young children will be determined to experiment and to try out the things they have been taught.

Real and imaginary sex crimes committed by young boys will increase dramatically. Thousands of male and female lives will be ruined as a result.

The real villains will be the educationalists who dreamt up the idea of teaching five and six year olds about sex. Sadly, they will probably claim that the answer is not less sex education but more. It's not impossible that pre-school infants and play school inmates will receive sex education along with the finger painting.

Chances of sex offences committed by children increasing: 80%.

66. Taxes Will Rise And Become Increasingly Complex

Taxes will rise and become ever more complicated and unfair and the tax authorities will become increasingly aggressive

Anyone who becomes rich - or even moderately well off - will attract the attention of the tax authorities. This is partly because Britain is going to remain impoverished for generations but also because tax inspectors now get bonuses for every pound they gouge out of taxpayers and it is easier to get money out of rich rather than honest and it is easier to get money out of honest rather than crooked. The state depends on taking money from a diminishing number of people in order to support and subsidise an increasing number of people who are parasitic. And in order to maximise the take the boundaries between evasion and avoidance have been deliberately blurred. Modern taxes are exploitative, protectionism and profiteering. Tax inspectors assume that taxpayers are innocent until proved guilty, rather than the other way round. The modern taxman oozes condescending authority backed by restrained bureaucratic violence. The philosophy is 'we can fuck with your life and it will be a pleasure'.

And the mistakes! When they're not losing confidential records, they're making mistakes. They recently admitted that in one year they had made 24 million tax errors. You will be astonished to hear that by a strange coincidence they were all in favour of government.

We tend to think of the government taking up to 40% of what we earn. but of course it's a lot more than that, because they then take another 17.5% in tax on most things you buy, and much more on fuel (85% of the total) and booze 35%, and there are road taxes, council taxes and stamp duty when you buy a house and national insurance, airport taxes, capital gains tax, taxes on business, taxes on dividends and inheritance tax. None of this would matter very much if the state used this money wisely and provided a secure, effective infrastructure. It does not. More than four in five people now feel they are paying more tax than they were early in the century and three quarters of people resent the level of tax they pay - they don't think they get good value for money.

The fact is that many politicians and civil servants seem to enjoy spending other people's money. And so most taxpayers regard their tax payments as bribes - protection money paid to the government to protect them against physical violence that will otherwise by meted out by the government's agents - and recognise that taxes will never be fair. HMRC has cut our right to reclaim tax back to four years but it can claim back six years or indeed indefinitely. The tax authorities are now legally entitled to intercept, bug letters phone calls and emails. There is no sense of responsibility and as little sense of fairness as there are signs of competence.

It is clearly absurd that individuals who have worked hard all their lives, and paid tax on their earnings, their savings and their investments, should have their money taxed again when they die. But inherited money is taxed for two reasons. First, it is an opportunity for the State to benefit without too much in the way of complaint (the person whose money is being taxed is dead, and the recipients are likely to be in mourning and too distressed to object). Second, inherited money gives freedom to individuals who need to be kept working hard. If the State didn't take a big chunk out of an inheritance too many people would stop work early.

The poll tax, the fairest tax of the 20th century, was withdrawn by a cowardly Conservative government after a tiny number of moaning, unwashed layabouts complained at the prospect of having to pay their way. There is now a vast gulf between the interest rate the HMRC pays if they hold your money (around 0 to 0.5%) and the rate they demand if you are late paying them (3 per cent if you're lucky). That used to be called loan sharking and i find it difficult to understand why HMRC has the authority to go into the loan sharking industry.

Today we have a system which allows the authorities to change tax laws retrospectively. MPs complained about retrospective laws being introduced in relation to their expenses. But the government has been doing that to us over tax for years. (Just imagine how many bureaucrats I would have on my back if I sold books to readers and shops and then, six months or six years later, sent invoices and said that I changed the price upwards). Investors who used a tax -avoidance scheme on the Isle of Man used it for seven years and HMRC, which knew about the scheme, did nothing. Then when the law was changed HMRC pounced and demanded back tax for investing in a scheme which was entirely legal and proper when they'd invested in it. In April 2010 it was announced that HMRC was investigating GPs travel expenses and would be looking back over 20 years of tax records for individual GPs. (Officially, taxpayers are supposed to keep records for six years. This policy appears to have been changed unilaterally and without parliamentary approval and HMRC officials now seem to have given themselves the right to expect taxpayers to keep records indefinitely.) According to one expert firm of accountants it wasn't clear whether or not HMRC would, or would not, be applying its new way of looking at the regulations retrospectively. In other words, no one knew (or no one was saying) whether or not HMRC was going to apply an apparently new piece of legislation over the last one, six or twenty years. In May 2010 the new coalition government announced that it was going to raise capital gains tax. But they would not say whether the rise would take place half way through a tax year (causing chaos), in April 2011 (the sensible option) or would be backdated to April 2010 (forcing people who had made investment decisions on the basis of one tax rate to pay tax at another rate). Whatever they do will undoubtedly affect small investors far more than private equity operators or hedge fund tricksters. The new, raised tax will simply punish, yet again, the hard working and the prudent (who have, of course, already paid tax on the money they have invested and who will be forced to trade even harder - to the benefit of banks and stockbrokers - to try and beat inflation).

The Government seems increasingly willing to back date changes and indeed these days it seems fair to say that people are taxed not on the basis of what the law says but what HMRC thinks the law ought to say (whether it does or not).There is no way that such a system could possibly be regarded as just or reasonable. It used to be said that ignorance was no defence. These days innocence is not much of a defence either. How long do we have to wait for someone who is really rich to sue a government which has introduced retrospective tax legislation? How fair can it possibly be for a government to allow a citizen to make an investment decision thinking that the law is X and to then change the law to Y and tax him accordingly. It is, quite simply, fraud. But then governments are accustomed to fraud; they have been running Ponzi schemes (described as pension programmes) for decades. Moreover, the tax authorities now happily buy stolen information if they think it will help them raise more tax. If you or I deal in stolen information we will end up in prison. But it is, it seems, perfectly acceptable for the government to deal in stolen information.

Capital gains taxes bring in very little money (less even than the taxes on wine or beer). Indeed, as applied to small investors, the capital gains tax is a vindictive tax in that the cost of policing it, and collecting the money, is greater than the money that is raised. It is a political tax. The sole purpose of this tax is to enable the state to punish honest people for making money. How strange then that the first act of the Conservative-Liberal Democrat coalition was to announce that capital gains tax would be increased dramatically. (This will push capital gains tax in the UK far above similar taxes elsewhere in Europe and there may be some protests from the EU where eurocrats want taxes to be uniform across the members units.) If the UK government does manage to push through legislation raising capital gains tax to the sort of levels some politicians were talking about before the May 2010 election any chance of economic growth will be strangled before birth.

Under old rules HMRC could ask banks and estate agents for information about their customers in order to help pursue tax evaders but under a new document titled `Modernising powers, deterrents and safeguards' HMRC proposes that all businesses be required to disclose information on people who trade with them. HMRC intends to build a data base of unprecedented power and size about UK citizens and businesses. The government will be able to check the bank details, purchases etc of every individual in the country. Companies which fail to comply will of course be heavily fined.

Our society now values luck above talent or hard work. The quickest way to show business success is not through hard work, years of experience and the willingness to hone your natural talents, but through appearing on a television talent show where prettified mediocrity and a lack of controversy will take you to the top, above anyone with real talents. If you win the lottery the loot will be tax free. But if you work hard and save what you have left after the taxman has taken his cut, then the interest on your savings will be taxed again.

If you have an offshore account for any reason - and there are a thousand valid reasons for having an account outside the country - then you will be investigated by the government and regarded as a criminal until proved otherwise. HMRC has already demanded that 300 banks hand over details of customers with offshore accounts. If banks don't hand over information then the government will buy what it needs from thieves. You may simply have a foreign account because you have a second home in Spain. But you will be regarded as a crook until you prove otherwise. And yet when a researcher made 47 attempts to create anonymous offshore bank companies complete with bank accounts he found that the efforts were successful in 17 cases. In the UK the researcher was able to set up a company with bearer shares and a bank account, without providing any identification whatsoever. Countries such as Liechtenstein and Panama observed strict due diligence. Britain is an easy target for fraudsters.

The most absurd aspect of our tax system is the relief that corporate raiders receive for borrowing. It was without a doubt the ability of investment bankers, venture capitalists and private equity sharks to claim tax relief on the interest paid when borrowing money which encouraged absurd levels of leverage and risk. Why bother to use your own money when you can borrow vast amounts more (and therefore dramatically increase your potential profits) and then claim much of the cost of the borrowing against tax? It was this absurdity which gave adventurers and carpet baggers a huge advantage over more sensible entrepreneurs.

According to National Audit Office, in 2008/2009 more than four out of 10 telephone calls from taxpayers and benefit claimants to the HMRC went unanswered - a total of 44 million calls simply rang out, ignored, as millions of taxpayers struggled to cope with ever complex rules. Those who do have their calls answered had to wait almost four minutes in peak hours (private sector businesses are expected to answer 90% of calls within 10 seconds - if they don't then they are in trouble). Call centre staff spent only 38% of their time dealing with customers or doing follow up work (compared with 60% in private sector). What they did for 62% of the time isn't record but they presumably spent some of it playing cards, surfing the internet or going to the lavatory. Even when they do advice it is possibly worthless and misleading (or at least that is what I was told a senior HMRC official).

A survey of HMRC staff showed that 30% had no idea that HMRC's role was to `administer the UK's tax and customs systems'. Heaven knows what the hell they think they're paid for.

A good friend who runs a small business and is like everyone else struggling to keep his head above the stormy seas of the recession our Government has arranged for us, requested a copy of an HMRC CD Rom for employers, supposedly containing essential software to help him do the Inland Revenue's work for it. The CD came but when my friend slipped it into his computer he found it didn't work. Further investigation showed that the CD contained fairy tales, read aloud in German. I now have a vast collection of absurd stories illustrating incompetence and plain stupidity shown by Her Majesty's tax inspectors. If these idiots had to work for a living most of them would starve to death.

The government (and its many highly pensioned advisers) don't even understand the consequences of what they do. For example, they don't seem to understand that it is multinational conglomerates, and not poorer workers, who benefit from tax credits. Ghazala Azmat of the Univeristat Pompeu Fabra in Barcelona has estimated that one third of working tax credits paid to male workers actually benefit employers who pay lower wages than they would otherwise pay. The taxpayers are, therefore, subsidising the conglomerates. Then there was Alistair Darling's payroll tax on large bank bonuses. Darling obviously believed that the special tax would deter banks from paying large bonuses. It didn't, of course. The bankers simply paid the large bonuses to themselves, as planned, and the banks paid the extra tax. So, it was shareholders (which means small investors and pensioners) who ended up paying the tax. And finally there was that crazy rise in national insurance payments (national insurance is, of course, just another tax) which the Labour Government announced in the spring of 2010. The government wanted to tax employers but the effect was to lead to lower wages. Employers, many of whom were struggling to survive, merely passed the tax on to their workers.

We live in a crazy world which seems to be run for the benefit of crooked, greedy bankers who steal and, politicians who cheat taxpayers in every conceivable way (and some which are inconceivable except to those with their moral values stitched in upside down). The one thing the government should do is to stop companies obtaining tax relief on interest on loans. It was this tax relief which leads directly reckless leveraging and buying up companies and absurd takeovers and wild, destructive expansions. But politicians won't touch these operations. To do would be to upset their chums in the city.

We need a tax system that looks logical and planned and thought out and that is fair. We aren't going to get one.

The Americans, under Reagan, proved that cutting taxes increases government revenue. If you tax people too much they stop working, they take long holidays or they put much or most of their energy into finding ways to avoid paying tax. No one in Britain seems away of this. And so taxes will go up and up as the government foolishly attempts to repay its huge debts by grabbing more money from an increasingly exhausted electorate.

There will be plenty of new taxes. Anything they can tax they will tax. VAT must inevitably rise to 20% (and perhaps even higher) and be imposed on a wider range of goods, including many which have traditionally been exempt.

I can envisage taxes on school certificates and degree certificates, a tax on using shopping centres and more taxes on car parks. The UK Government will doubtless introduce global tax to catch all the rich exiles. (The Americans already force exiled Americans to pay American tax.) This will result in millions of Britons living in Spain, France, Australia etc to pay British tax and to then try and claim back the taxes paid from the government of the country where they are living. Every time the government plans a new tax it will prepare the way by judicious leaking. The trick will always be the same. They will encourage journalists to suggest that there will be a new tax on walking shoes to cover the cost of repairing pavements. While the uproar over this continues they will announced that the new tax only covers boots. There will be huge relief at this and people who would have been outraged at a tax on boots will accept the new tax without any further complaint. (The tax, now safely introduced, will be widened to cover shoes in a future budget.)

Future Governments will need vast amounts of money just to pay the interest on the debt bequeathed by Gordon Brown. It won't be possible to pay the interest (let alone the debt) simply by making cuts in services. It will be necessary to raise taxes. A lot.

Chances of taxes rising and becoming more complex: 100%.

67. Car Boot Sales And Markets Will Boom

As more people search for bargains, and more people look for ways to turn `things' into cash, there will be an increase in the number of car boot sales and second hand markets. Charities will probably suffer as they receive fewer books, tapes and clothes.

I strongly suspect that before long someone will set up a national organisation to arrange car boot sales, and similar enterprises.

Then local councils will demand huge licensing fees and, perhaps, a cut of the action. Some may even ban private sales so that they can promote their own sale sites more effectively - and more profitably.

Chances of car boot sales and markets booming: 80%.

68. The Popularity of Avatars Will Increase Dramatically

Computer games offering individuals the chance to live an on line imaginary life as an entirely imaginary character in an imaginary computer generated world will become increasingly common. More and more desperate and unhappy people will spend their money buying imaginary on line homes and imaginary on line luxuries. A good number will impoverish themselves and will live in poor real-life circumstances so that they can enjoy their on line imaginary worlds. Many will escape more or less full time to their virtual worlds; sitting in front of a screen pretending to be a character living in a computer world. They will return to the real world only infrequently to perform simple basic functions such as eating and collecting their disability money from the government.

The chances of avatars becoming more popular: 100%.

69. Free Banking Will End

Banking was never free, of course. The people who paid bank charges (because they took out a mortgage or had an overdraft) paid for the free banking for the people who didn't use the bank's facilities other than holding an account.

However, the extra taxes the government is planning (ostensibly as a punishment but in reality as just another way to raise money) will mean that anyone with a bank account will have to pay for it directly.

There will be a charge for having an account, and probably a small supplementary charge for every transaction. There will be no interest paid on current accounts in credit.

And so, the bankers will lose not one penny but ordinary citizens will pay the extra taxes.

(And if these fees don't pay the taxes, the loss will be born by shareholders. Whatever happens, I can guarantee that the bankers who caused the economic crisis will not lose a penny.)

The chances of free banking ending: 100%.

70. The Future Belongs To China

The past was Britain's but the future is China's. America was merely a historical interlude; a light but noisy operetta between two great operas.

During the next ten years (by 2020) around 500 million Chinese citizens will move from villages into cities. That's the greatest urban migration ever recorded. The equivalent of almost twice the population of America will want city accommodation. The Chinese have been the world's busiest builders and have bought a lot of cement, oil, iron and copper. They're going to buy a lot more. China is now the world's technology leader and the world's most efficient producer. It makes the best products at the lowest prices. (When the Chinese make poorly made rubbish it is usually because they have been told to cut costs and corners and turn out poorly made rubbish.)

As people in developing countries become richer so they want to buy more fashionable items. As they acquire money to spend, so they acquire the desire to spend it on the things we've spent our money on. The Americans have been burning up vast quantities of oil for years (and consuming huge amounts of the world's commodities). They've paid for everything they've bought by printing dollars. The Chinese have worked hard and now they own America and most of its dollars. But now the Chinese want fast cars and burgers. And they are going to have them. A recent survey showed that people in China, Russia and Latin America are desperately keen to buy products labelled Chanel, Christian Dior, Versace, Prada, Louis Vuitton, Giorgio Armani, Calvin Klein and Yves St Laurent. Most important of all, however, when income goes up people start demanding a Western style diet - and that means more meat and dairy products. Hundreds of millions of people in China, India, Brazil and many other emerging economies are now rich enough to buy meat. And they want meat. But cattle have to be fed huge amounts of corn so someone's going to have to go hungry. The Africans are first in line for that duty. Europeans and Americans will be next.

American senators, most of whom have probably never been further West than Las Vegas or further East than New York, make a lot of rude noises about China. They should shut up. American politicians occasionally make noises about `bombing the shit out of them little yellow devils'. This is bullying bluster; always conducted by people a long way from any action. They should definitely forget that one. A war between the USA and China would last about twenty minutes and the USA, a flabby, bully of a nation, would come such a very poor second that they'd be lucky to get even a bronze medal. The truth is that China now owns America (I speak literally not figuratively). And, as well as owning America, the Chinese have a big and superbly equipped army. If the Americans ever grew balls big enough to start a war with China they would regret it rather quickly and those brash and noisy American politicians would be tucked away in their private nuclear bomb shelters long before their shirt collars needed restarching.

Of course, the Americans aren't going to start a war with China. Not even the Americans are that stupid. But they probably will continue to find things to moan about. The prize for hypocrisy goes to Business Week, an American magazine devoted to the business world (particularly the American bit of it) which devoted a cover and an editorial to `The Counterfeit Catastrophe'. The magazine reported that am American politician had blasted the Chinese on a visit to Beijing, demanding that they step up efforts to police intellectual-property violations.

Do the Americans really know nothing of history? Was it not America which refused to acknowledge the idea of copyright back in the 19th century. Is it not America which now wanders the world picking up seeds that have been used for generations, patenting them and then charging poor people a small fortune to buy them? Is not America for ever stealing oil? Heavens, they even try to steal British history whenever they think they can get away with it. In their war films British heroism always seems to become American heroism. Read Charles Dickens on the subject of the Americans and copyright. Business Week complained `From the Barbary pirates to the rum runners of Prohibition to today's email spammers every period has its distinctive form of economic criminal: people who flout or break the rules of commerce for their own benefit. Such problems can't be eliminated, but a successful society keeps them under control. By that measure, the era of globalisation may be facing one of its biggest challenges. The astonishing expansion of manufacturing capabilities in less developed countries notably China, has raised incomes and boosted trade around the world but the same production and distribution also have created a frightening phenomenon: an ever-rising flood of counterfeits and fakes coming onto world markets.' The editorial boomed: `If China starts lowering its tolerance for piracy, that will be a sign that it starting to see itself as a major economic power, not a poor nation.'

When a nation stoops to such hypocritical depths, and exhibits such an extent of self-denial and self-righteousness, you just know that it is in deep, deep trouble.

Maybe even the Americans know that their fifteen minutes is over. Even they must soon realise that the future belongs to China.

Chances of the future belonging to China: 100%.

71. The Incidence Of Breast Cancer in China Will Soar

In medicine, as in most things in life, the best way to find a solution is to find the cause. In medicine one of the best ways to do that is through epidemiology - simply looking, watching, thinking and learning. Sadly, since medicine is run by the drug industry modern doctors aren't keen on any of that old fashioned stuff: it tends to throw up uncomfortable truths.

One of the most uncomfortable truths is the fact that breast cancer is a largely avoidable disease. It can usually be prevented. Why is it, then, so common? And why is it getting commoner?

Breast cancer is a major problem because governments, the medical profession and charities ignore the evidence. Why do they do that? Because the evidence is commercially inconvenient.

Most women who die of breast cancer die so that a huge industry can continue to make vast amounts of money.

And the industry is the meat industry: a huge multi billion pound industry involving farmers, abattoir owners, butchers, food companies, supermarkets.

How do I know that the incidence of breast cancer in China is about to soar?

Simple.

Now that they are richer, the Chinese people are dramatically increasing their intake of meat.

And when the same thing happened in Japan a few years ago the result was a dramatic increase in the incidence of breast cancer in Japanese women.

The ones who stuck to a low-meat traditional Japanese diet were far less likely to develop breast cancer when compared to the ones who changed to a high-meat American style diet.

Why does meat cause so much more cancer today than ever before?

That's simple.

The meat sold today is very fatty and it is full of carcinogens because farmers who sell fatty animals get more money for them and because farmers use carcinogenic chemicals on their farms.

It is these two facts which explain why the incidence of cancer always rises when populations start eating more meat.

But why is the incidence of breast cancer particularly likely to rise?

The answer to that is simple too.

When animals eat toxic substances, chemicals which are carcinogenic for example, which have been sprayed on the grass they eat or put into the food they eat, the chemicals are stored in their fatty tissues. The fattier the animal is the more carcinogens it will have stored in its body. And, when it is killed and eaten, those carcinogens will be consumed by the person eating the meat. And, as with animals, the carcinogens will tend to gravitate to, and be stored in, the fatty tissues.

Breasts contain a good deal of fat. There is remarkably little actual breast tissue in a breast. Most of the breast is fat. And the bigger the breast the more fat there is likely to be. This is why breast cancer is commoner among older women. They tend to have more fat on their bodies in general and bigger and fattier breasts in particular. Poorer people tend to eat fattier meat. That's why poor people tend to get more cancer than rich people.

I first pointed all this out in an early (and now out of print) book of mine called `Power Over Cancer'. No one has ever disputed my conclusions. However, instead of discouraging women from eating meat, doctors prefer to remove healthy breasts from women considered genetically susceptible to breast cancer in order to prevent them getting breast cancer. Barbarism.

China will be the next country to notice an `unexplained' increase in the incidence of breast cancer. (There will, of course, also be a dramatic increase in many other types of cancer.)

The Chinese could prevent the cancer explosion. But I fear they won't.

Chances of breast cancer (and other cancers) increasing in China: 100%.

72. The Chinese Currency Will Replace The Dollar As The World's Most Important Currency

The Chinese currency, the renminbi, will replace the American dollar as the world's basic and most stable reserve currency, value store and medium of exchange for commodities such as oil and gold. America's huge debts will lead to the ruin of the dollar. The euro, once widely mooted as the dollar's replacement, has about as much of a future as Gordon Brown.

Chances of the Chinese currency replacing the American dollar as the world's most important currency: 90%.

73. The End Of The Chinese Property Boom

The price of property in China soared in 2009, with rises of 50% to 60% in Shanghai and Beijing. The Chinese have started running property programmes on TV. Residential prices in China are, in relation to income, the highest in the world. (Britain comes a close second and is way out on its own among Western countries.)

What does this matter?

It matters because it was the bursting of the property bubble in America and Europe which led to the financial crash of 2007 and onwards.

If the property bubble in China bursts the Chinese will have their own recession and their own depression.

And the Chinese economy has been the only part of the world economy that has kept the world ticking over since 2007. If China hits trouble, the rest of the world will be in dire straits. (Another problem facing the rest of the world is the growing restlessness and dissatisfaction of an increasing enlightened Chinese population. China recently had its first industrial strikes. As the Chinese workers demand higher wages and better condition so the cost of the goods they produce will rise - resulting in inflation around the rest of the world.)

Chances of Chinese Property bubble bursting before 2010: 60%.

74. English Nationalism Will Rise

Within the UK nationalism has traditionally been most potent in Scotland and Wales but in recent years there has been a clear rise in English nationalism. There are several reasons for this and for the feeling that

England would be stronger, richer and happier as a separate nation. A growing number of English born citizens are aware that much of the abuse and determination to destroy England comes from people (such as the Scots) who have been financially supported by the English for generations.

First, there is increased anger at the racist attitudes of many Scots. Many Englishmen and women are angered that whereas Scottish (and Welsh) nationalists tend to be regarded as proud patriots, English nationalists are dismissed as racists and bigots. Discrimination against the English has become curiously fashionable. `There is no such thing as English,' seems to be a common, though completely false, belief. Moreover, if someone from Scotland does well they are always described as being Scottish whereas if someone from England does well they are invariably described in the media as being British unless they have done something bad.

Second, there is a growing awareness that European Union regionalisation policies will lead to the destruction of England as a country and its replacement by a series of colourless, characterless regions.

Third, there is great resentment in England at the way that English taxpayers are increasingly being expected to subsidise the Scots. How much resentment is going to build among English students as they struggle to pay off the huge debts they have incurred as a result of the Government's student loan scheme? And how much is that resentment going to be fuelled by the knowledge that students from Scotland, who have studied alongside them at English universities, can start life with no debts whatsoever because their bills have been paid by English taxpayers? How much resentment is going to build up when the English realise just how freely the Scottish `government' has been with English money. Lowly state functionaries are paid more than responsible professionals in the rest of the UK. State spending in Scotland is now at 54.7% of GDP. That is the highest in the world and 20% higher per capita than in England, which is funding the `government's generosity. (English taxpayers pay £1.32 each a year to pay for the Scottish parliament's operating expenses.) Give Scotland independence and power to raise its own taxes and see how generous the `government' is allowed to be. The cuts in public services which will affect the country in the coming years will undoubtedly affect England more than Scotland. Public spending will be better protected in Scotland once cuts are made and Scotland will suffer less than England in coming years. Politicians in Britain promised to protect Scotland and though political promises are generally worthless those made to Scotland always seem to be kept. This unfairness is particularly absurd since it was the failure of two Scottish banks which was largely responsible for Britain's economic mess and it was Gordon Brown's determination to protect Scotland (and his constituency) from the consequences of those banking failures that led to his government saving the two banks with taxpayers' money. The result is that England will have to pay back Scotland's debts. Meanwhile, the Scots continue to waste money at an extraordinary rate - and on the most extraordinary nonsenses. The Scottish parliaments website has been rewritten in Scots dialect which is, presumably, now classified as yet another language. The Scottish Executive says that the translation is necessary to prevent discrimination. A total of £800,000 is being spent on making the Scottish parliament's website available in 14 'languages'. Here's the new intro in Scottish dialect: `Walcome tae the Scottish pailament wabsite. The Scottish pailament is here for tae represent aw Scotlan's folk.' I didn't make it up. Honest. Fourth, there is also some anger and resentment at the way that Scottish MPs are still allowed to vote on issues which affect only England while the English have no say on how English money is spent in Scotland. There is a growing clamour for an English Parliament. (This cannot and will not happen as long as the UK is part of the European Union because the EU's official policy is to see England broken up into regions.)

Finally, there is also growing resentment at the fact that many leading politicians in the House of Commons (including the last two Prime Ministers) are Scottish. The fact that the Scottish dominated Labour Party has done enormous damage to the British economy, and that English taxpayers are now being expected to pay for the damage that has been done, has not gone unnoticed.

In Victorian England (a time now sneered at) a quarter of the world's population lived under English rule. England was the wealthiest nation on earth. Things which bore the stamp `Made in England' were built to last and the label was accepted worldwide as a mark of excellence. Today, England has been reduced to penury and even possible bankruptcy.

England has a great past, but I'm not sure it has much of a present. And it certainly doesn't have much of a future.

When pub landlords in Norwich applied for a licence for an extra hours drinking on St George's Day they were told to go away and find evidence that this was a day worthy of special celebration - even though the magistrates had happily granted drinking extensions for St Patrick's Day and the Chinese New Year.

To proclaim your Englishness is to risk an accusation of racism or an accusation of being a Little Englander (has anyone ever heard a proud Scot described as a Little Scotlander?).

Actually those who use the term Little Englander are invariably woefully ignorant and unaware that the term dates from the Boer War and refers to people who were, at the time, opposed to the British Empire and anti-Imperialist, and wanted the English to stop taking over the world.

Such folk were regarded as unpatriotic. Today, ignorant pro EU fascists use the term as one of abuse; it is usually applied to those who are aware that removing England from maps and history books is an essential part of the EU project and who don't want England to disappear and be converted into nine EU regions. The implication is that the person at the receiving end of the abuse is overly patriotic.

Enough.

Chances of English nationalism rising: 80%.

75. Guest Workers Will Be Offered Associate Citizenship

At some point in the next ten years, politicians in Britain will gain much popularity by suggesting that immigrants should be offered what will, in effect, be Associate Citizenship.

This is something other countries have done with considerable success.

For example, Switzerland has two grades of citizen.

There are, on the one hand, the citizens with full membership of the state. They work, pay taxes and vote. They are, if you like, the nation's owners. Then there are the guest workers. They can work in Switzerland but on quite different terms. They pay a flat 10% of their earnings in tax but in return for this low and simple level of taxation they have to realise that they are not entitled to receive any benefits - no social security payments and no pensions. And they aren't entitled to vote.

The European Union will not, of course, allow such a system to exist in Britain.

But the chances are high that someone will suggest it.

And the proposal will prove embarrassingly popular.

Chances of Britain introducing an `associate citizenship' programme:

30%.

76. The Truth Will Continue To Be Suppressed (even though we have access to more information than ever before)

Information is increasing at a rate of 60% per annum. Experts can no longer keep up with everything in their own speciality. The priority is to discriminate, assess, select, interpret and pass judgement. Most of the information is distracting, irrelevant and deliberately misleading but most people have no training, aptitude or skill in differentiating between the good, the bad the bent. The invention of text messages and email has resulted in a veritable daily storm of information.

Information is the only real currency but the politicians, the large media companies and the internet have, between them, devalued it. The message has been devalued by the medium. There is no honest, reliable, questioning newspaper or news magazine in Britain. Television and radio offer only entertainment and are, at best, useful only because they enable us to see what people are being told. On the whole, the web offers only prejudice and propaganda. (Keep an eye on magazine covers, though. When they promote a new investment theme it is usually time to sell and get out. This is, in my experience, particularly true of the Economist, Fortune magazine and Business Week.)

If you are to understand what is really going on you need to distil, to get rid of the rubbish, and to produce wise conclusions based on the important facts. That's easier said than done because most of the stuff that `they' call news isn't news at all. It is propaganda. Journalists have, sadly, become little more than part of the establishment's propaganda machinery. A recently commissioned study showed that 60% of domestic `news' in the quality press consists wholly or mainly of news agency or PR copy. Much of what appears in newspapers is little more than churnalism (defined as `the rapid repackaging of largely unchecked second-hand material'). Experts on TV are usually (nearly always) paid for by someone with a vested interest in the subject. The advice they give is, therefore, worthless. Too many modern journalists (including some of the best-paid, most well-known and highly placed) enjoy close personal relationships with leading political figures. A journalist who publishes material given to him by political `friends' is a propagandist not a journalist. Most of what appears in the press, or on the television or radio, is placed there by lobbyists and press agents. It is hardly surprising that this material is designed to fit the requirements of the individuals and organisations concerned. As far as television is concerned news is usually what they've got pictures of.

I find it alarming that so many people pick up newspapers, or turn on the television, expecting to read or watch the real news. We were told that Iraq had weapons of mass destruction. The media unquestioningly reported politicians' lies. We were told that we were invading Iraq to `free' the people of that country. We weren't told that British troops were being sent to war so that America could grab the oil. Readers of national newspapers, and viewers of mainstream television programmes have never been told the truth about the European Union. On the day of the first Irish vote about the EU's Treaty of Lisbon the story of the vote was the 9th item on the ITV 10 pm news. It was the last item, just before the sport and the details of Wayne Rooney's wedding (if they had had photos of the wedding they would have doubtless put it above the EU vote). I didn't bother to look for details of the vote on the BBC.

We have never been told the truth about peak oil.

Modern journalists will happily attack small time crooks (or, indeed, innocent people who don't have the money to start a libel action) but they are invariably reluctant to tackle large institutions, international companies, government departments or professions. They are also very reluctant to question established dogma, particularly if it is well supported by wealthy commercial interests.

Moreover, modern journalism is often appallingly sloppy. Out of curiosity, I checked five different television stations after a recent coach crash. Although police, fire and ambulance had given pretty precise figures of people taken to hospital the five TV stations reported, with great precision but no real interest in the truth, that 30,40,50,60 and 70 people had been injured. (Those were the figures they reported). No one knew whether the coach was from abroad or not although a glance at the number plate would have told them the truth.

Like it or not, we now live in a world dominated by deceit and incompetence; a world where the medium is far more important than the message and the perception widely considered to be of more importance than the meaning. The media generally (or, in the case of the BBC, exclusively) support the Government and the Establishment.

But Government figures (for everything from unemployment to crime) are about utterly unreliable. When mistakes are made the appropriate department may, if pushed, issue a correction. It is one thing for politicians to lie (no one expects anything else of them) but it is outrageous for the Government to deliberately denies us accurate information. It is even more outrageous for Government employees to use our money provide us with false and misleading information about things which affect us.

As a result no one with more than half a brain believes even the denials any more. Politicians lie because it works - and they've taught us all that denial and lies are productive and profitable. Corruption and compromise are the watchwords for modern politicians and are the foundation upon which our new coalition government will be built.

The problem today isn't collecting information. We are up to our necks in the stuff. The problem lies in analysing, interpreting and understanding the vast acres of information that is available. And, most important of all, being able to differentiate between information which is objective, accurate and valuable and information which is none of those things - though it may well appear to be so.

We are all overwhelmed with information and it is increasingly difficult for any one individual to keep up with what is happening in the world. Acquiring and assessing information is made infinitely more difficult by the fact that none of the major sources of information we use can be trusted. I do not know of a single mainstream newspaper or magazine or television station or radio station which can be trusted to tell the truth or anything close to the truth. Everyone in the mainstream media spins, spins and spins again. The BBC is utterly useless as a source of news and information. Finding trustworthy information on the internet is like panning for gold.

And even when you do manage to find something which just might be the truth, you know that within seconds it will be out of date. Acquiring up to date accurate information is like building a formula one racing car. You are always going to be fighting a losing battle. Something else will always be happening. Financial commentators who talk about an `efficient market' (in which there can be no surprises because every piece of information is available to everyone and therefore already in the price) are living in cloud cuckoo land.

In the future companies will continue to lie and spin and cover up the truth. The tobacco companies knew that cigarettes caused cancer but for years they denied the truth. The drug companies know that vaccines are potentially dangerous and they know that animal experiments are commercially useful but of no scientific value. But they constantly suppress these inconvenient truths.

Chances of the truth continuing to be suppressed: 100%.

77. The Police Will Acquire More Power (And Use It)

My 87 year old father parked his car (quite legally) and went into a hotel to have lunch. While he was enjoying his meal the manager tottered over and told him that the police wanted to speak to him. My father abandoned his meal and struggled down the steps to the roadside. Another motorist had nudged his car while parking. There was no damage to either car. My father's car was parked perfectly legally. The police were in the vicinity only because they had been called to another minor traffic accident. My father confirmed that there was no damage and was eventually allowed to go back into the hotel to finish his (by now cold and ruined) luncheon. A couple of weeks later he received a letter from someone in the local `collisions department' of the constabulary informing him that the police had given themselves six months to decide whether or not to take legal action as a result of his collision. At the time of the offence, remember, he was sitting in a hotel eating his lunch while his car was parked outside. And, remember, there was no damage done to the vehicle and neither he nor anyone else had complained. He received further warnings about this non existent incident and was, as a conscientious, law-abiding citizen unnerved by them. He knew he had done absolutely nothing wrong. But the police were, nevertheless, warning him about some unspecified legal action.

A 71 year old widow who prodded a 17 year old hoodie who had been throwing stones at her window found herself charged with assault. When the hoodie threw stones at her windows she pursued the stone thrower to tell him off. When she caught up with him (the fact that she was able to do so says more than we would like to know about the health and fitness of the current generation) she `addressed him frankly' and prodded him in the chest with a finger. The police were called and instead of arresting the stone thrower they arrested the old lady and bundled her into the back of a police van. She was eventually ordered to pay £50 costs and given a conditional discharge.

The police misuse powers given them under anti-terror legislation. They question photographers who have taken entirely innocent pictures of tourist destinations and landmarks. The police have even taken it upon themselves to delete photographs taken on digital cameras.

In my experience, this sort of quiet bullying goes on all the time and the middle classes (especially the elderly) are most likely to be the victims. They are an easy target. They don't complain much. And if they do complain no one cares.

Everything the police do seems designed to isolate them still further from the communities they are paid to protect. It is difficult to avoid the conclusion that people don't join the police force because they want to serve or protect the community, but because they get a badge, possibly a gun, a lot of power and the legal right to bully and harass people who aren't police officers. They also get the right to break the law with impunity. As in all fascist states the police are employed to harass and frighten law abiding citizens. And, boy, do they enjoy it. And they even dress in a way designed to intimidate. For example, the police seem to have taken to wearing riot gear while wandering around country town centres. This is absurd. It frightens people unnecessarily and damages yet further the already fragile relationship between the police and the public - their employers. On the rare occasions when we do see policemen strutting on our streets they are dressed up in flak jackets. Moreover, policemen constantly demand to be allowed to wander around armed with pistols or taser guns. At least one chief constable wants his policemen to wear baseball caps instead of helmets. He presumably thinks that baseball caps will make them look more American, more paramilitary, and get rid of that old fashioned `Dixon of Dock Green' image that the police seem to find offensive but which the public still prefer.

Every day I pick out bizarre and terrifying new facts about our modern police. At a demonstration recently the police confiscated a bar of soap and a pensioner's walking stick. Both were deemed to be `dangerous'. In a third of all cases, violence not classified as a crime by the police, who are trying to improve the figures in order to please the Government. The police refused to take any interest in a mugging because the victim was white and Christian and they were too busy. How can a crime be worse because the perpetrator has racist motives? What does the race or religion of the victim affect the way a crime is treated? This is political correctness and multiculturalism gone mad. And it is, of course, the arrogance and incompetence of the police which results in motorways and other major highways being left closed for unnecessarily lengthy periods, at great cost to the nation's economy (in terms of fuel wasted) and the health of the nation (in terms of the toxic fuel residues pumped out into the air as cars queue or struggle along at 15 mph.)

The police have for years relied upon, and taken cruel advantage of, the fact that courts, juries and a good chunk of the general public has always believed that policemen always tell the truth and certainly never, ever lie on oath. As people have found out that this is not true public perceptions have changed. But judges, divorced from reality and protected from the horrors of the real world by chauffeurs, servants and a constant police presence wherever they go, still believe that a policeman's word can always be trusted. Sadly, no one in England has grown up until they recognise that the police routinely lie in court. They are, as a breed, inveterate and accomplished liars and perjurers.

It has long been said that the people who become police officers are the same sort of people who become criminals. It's luck and circumstances which decides who becomes which but these days the money policemen receive is vastly superior to the sort of income that can be expected by ordinary criminals. (A 49 year old policeman retired early in disgrace and received a pension in excess of £110,000 a year for life.)

What is most alarming is that there are still citizens around who insist on defending the police whatever they do. An innocent newspaper seller was hit and pushed by the police as he walked home at the end of the G20 fiasco in London. The man fell, got up, fell again and died of a heart attack. The unprovoked attack by the police was originally hushed up (as police brutality invariably is) but a passer by had filmed the incident and so the truth came out. (It is hardly surprising that it is now illegal to film policemen doing anything.)

Subsequently, the following letter from a Scotsman was published in the Daily Telegraph:

`Sir

It is clear from the footage that this man was displaying a less than helpful attitude towards the police. The police wanted him to move on, but he made no great effort to get out of the way. The fact that his hands were in his pockets was a clear sign of defiance. He knew where he was and what he was doing; he was baiting the police and therefore courting a shove in the back.'

`This is not to say, of course, that he was a member of the `violent mob'. He died, and that is tragic, but it was not the fault of the police. How many of us would really expect someone to die from a heart attack after a firm - I would not say violent - shove in the back? We should be congratulating the police for having done a very good job under very difficult circumstances, not trying to prosecute them.'

It is people like this who help to create a fascist state and who are, indeed, responsible for the end of democracy and freedom.

The problems are exacerbated by the fact that the Labour Government's mind-bogglingly stupid red tape and targets culture mean that when the police arrest someone they have to fill in 128 bits of paper. Just 1 in 58 policemen are patrolling the streets they are paid to protect. The rest are doing paperwork. The Labour Government publicly guaranteed that the police spent 80% of their time on the streets. This was just another lie. The fact is that there are 143,000 policemen in Britain and of those only 2,400 are out and about at any one time. Indeed, only 81,877 ever go out into the outside the world. The other 60,000 plus are presumably too important to be expected to do anything except sip coffee and attend meetings. Most of the hours policemen do work are spent sitting in cars on motorway bridges or standing by the roadside holding those absurdly inefficient speed camera gadgets designed to fine motorists who have the gall to leave their homes and go off to work. (The persecution of speeding motorists will decline as politicians realise that society cannot afford to take driving licences away from hard-working taxpayers, nor can it afford to lose the tax they pay on the petrol they buy.)

Sadly, the relationship between the public and the police will deteriorate still further in the coming years. As the new, all reaching State gives them ever more power, and expects to be protected against all insurrections (whether physical, mental or spiritual), so the police will become increasingly arrogant and increasingly superior and distant.

One of the first actions of the coalition government which took office after the May 2010 election was to announce a plan to introduce locally elected police commissioners. This step towards freedom and accountability was immediately opposed by many senior policemen who argued that such a policy could lead to the British National Party setting policy for local police forces. There were no overt complaints that appointed chief constables might be ousted; just a moan that allowing the public to choose their own police chiefs might lead to a sudden outbreak of democracy.

Chances of the police acquiring greater powers (and using them): 100%.

78. Protectionism Is On The Way

In 2009 the leaders of the G20 countries committed their countries to eschew protectionism. But within months of that firm commitment 17 of the 20 countries of them went ahead and did it anyway. Naturally, the Americans were at the head of the queue. They boldly introduced massive `Buy American' policies.

As the world's economy struggles, so tariffs, trade barriers and other examples of protectionism will become commonplace.

Britain will suffer enormously as a result.

Chances of protectionism increasing: 100%.

79. The Royal Family Has Failed Us And Will Continue To Betray Us

It makes me sad to have to write this but I believe it to be true: Queen

Elizabeth has failed in her duty and has betrayed the nation. I suspect that the Royal family will continue to betray us and continue to fail to do the right thing.

After the May 2010 election the Queen was protected from the political squabbling (and that was right) but she has constantly failed to protect us in the way we have a right to have expected her to fight.

Our ancestors fought hard for the rights provided by the Magna Carta. They fought hard for us to have the right to be tried by a jury of our peers. They fought for the right to silence and for habeas corpus. Many of them gave their lives to protect us from bullying and power hungry leaders. The leading member of the royal family is head of our state, our army and our judiciary for a reason. They are supposed to protect us against politicians who want to abuse their powers, who want to take our rights and want to use our power against us.

Queen Elizabeth failed miserably in this important task. She always did the hand waving stuff with great charm and dignity. But being queen is more than hand waving and accepting posies. In the last few years of the 20th century, and the first few of the 21st century, Elizabeth II allowed the politicians to acquire frightening powers and to sign away our rights and freedom to a foreign power - the unelected EU commissioners and eurocrats. During that time the Queen allowed Ministers, the civil service and the courts to be pushed aside as though they were irrelevances. She allowed Blair and Brown to take unto themselves absurd amounts of power and patronage. By the year 2010, Gordon brown had an army of several thousand ministers, advisers and quango leaders (many enjoying chauffeurs, official cars and huge salaries and pensions) dependent upon his patronage.

Queen Elizabeth allowed our country to adopt a presidential form of government. The May 2010 election was fought between Brown, Cameron and Clegg. It wasn't even fought between parties. Other countries have constitutions which protect them against abuse by their leaders. We don't have a constitution. We rely upon our monarch to do the work of a constitution. We rely upon our monarch to keep the politicians in check and to remind them that their task is to protect us from the executive and to represent us not bully us.

Queen Elizabeth has been a complete failure in that important task. We needed a monarch who would stand up for us and tell the politicians that they could not ignore our rights and their responsibilities.

As I have written several times before Queen Elizabeth II has, in comparison with her famous namesake, been a miserable, lily livered failure; too craven to defend her subjects or her country. She has betrayed us all.

The Monarch has a right and a duty to advise, counsel and warn her Government. But, sadly, Queen Elizabeth II has said and done nothing to stop what is happening to her country. Despite receiving many letters from her subjects explaining how they believe they have been tricked and lied to by politicians the Queen seems amazingly happy with the fact that England is about to disappear.

Here is the standard reply sent out by the Queen to those who write and complain about the rise of the EU and the disappearance of England. Since the reply is a `standard' rather than a personal letter (indeed, it is more of a statement than a letter) I do not feel that it is wrong to republish it here.

`The Queen has received your recent letter on membership of the European Union and a possible referendum on the proposed EU Constitutional Treaty. As Her Majesty receives many letters on this subject, it is not possible to send an individual reply to every one.'

`The Queen appreciates the thoughtfulness sof correspondents who take the time to write and give her their views. |Her Majesty follows, with interest, developments in the European Union and recognises that the United Kingdom's membership of the European Union is governed by treaties that were freely entered into, following all normal constitutional procedures.'

`Her Majesty does have prerogative and statutory powers. However, policy on the United Kingdom's membership of the European Union is entirely a matter for The Queen's Ministers. As such, Her Majesty's own powers are exercised, by convention, on and in accordance with advice from those Ministers. As part of this important constitutional convention it is customary for Her Majesty to grant Royal Assent to Bills duly passed by Government.'

`A copy of your letter is being forwarded to the Foreign and Commonwealth Office for the Attention of the Secretary of State for Foreign and Commonwealth Affairs.'

`By providing my Ministers with a full list of those who write to me to complain about the EU I can help ensure that when the new Constitution has been ratified armed members of Europol will come round to your house and drag you off to a maximum security re-education facility in Poland.'

OK I admit it. I made up the last paragraph. The rest is real.

How sad it is to have to report that it seems to me that the English people have been betrayed by Parliament, by Government and by their Monarch, Queen Elizabeth the Last.

I've always rather liked the Queen.

There used to be an old Act of Parliament which entitled her subjects to wander into Buckingham Palace to sign the visitors' book. When I was a kid I used to go there whenever I was in London. I'd totter up to the policeman on the gate, tell him I wanted to sign the visitors' book and saunter through, across the gravel. The tourists admiring the guardsmen (this was in the days when they were on the outside of the railings) would stare in awe. I mention this merely to show that I'm no anti-Royalist.

But I have to say that our Queen has let us all down rather badly. I've no doubt that she has been advised that it isn't her place to disagree with her Ministers. But, in my view, she's been badly advised. The Queen will, I suspect, greatly regret her decision one day. But it will by then be too late.

Compare the rather weedy way our Queen has responded to today's very real threat to our nation's independence and sovereignty and compare it with her namesake's response.

The piece below is the speech Elizabeth I made when addressing her troops who were, at the time, awaiting the arrival of the Spanish Armada in 1588. I think you'll agree that Elizabeth I showed a rather more feisty determination to defend her country than her namesake has exhibited.

`My loving people, we have been persuaded by some that are careful of our safety to take heed how we commit ourselves to armed multitudes for fear of treachery, but I assure you I do not desire to live to distrust my faithful and loving people. Let tyrants fear; I have always so behaved myself under God, I have placed my chiefest strength and safeguard in the loyal hearts and goodwill of my subjects. And therefore I am come amongst you, as you see, at this time not for my recreation and disport, but being resolved in the midst and heat of battle to live and die amongst you all. To lay down for God, my kingdom and for my people, my honour and my blood even in the dust. I know I have the body of a weak and feeble woman, but I have the heart and stomach of a King and a King of England too and think it foul scorn that Parma or Spain or any Prince of

Europe should dare to invade the borders of my realm; to which, rather than any dishonour shall grow by me, I myself will take up arms, I myself will be your General, Judge and Rewarder of every one of your virtues in the field. I know already for your forwardness you have deserved rewards and crowns; and we do assure you, on the word of a Prince, they shall be duly paid you.'

I see no sign that any other members of the royal family will serve us any better. Could William and Harry, both paid as members of the armed forc
es, have done more to fight for their nation? I think so. English kings and princes have always been prepared to fight for their country and, if necessary, to shed blood for it. What makes this miserable pair so special?

My sad conclusion is that our royal family will continue to betray us and avoid their responsibilities. Like the politicians and bureaucrats they will, however, no doubt enjoy their rights and privileges.

The chances of the royal family continuing to betray us: 100%.

80. Although Already Appalling The Service Provided By The Royal Mail Is Going To Continue To Deteriorate

The evidence for the fact that things aren't what they used to be is all around us. Nothing illustrates modern inefficiency, incompetence and poor service better than the Royal Mail. It is scary to realise that these are tomorrow's good old days.

In the bad old days our postman used to deliver the mail twice a day. The first mail arrived before 9.00 am and the second mail arrived at lunchtime. In the really bad really old days the mail invariably arrived at its destination within a day.

Then they split the mail into two - first class and second class.

After this happened it was still possible to get next day delivery with an ordinary letter for first class mail nearly always arrived the next day. (To begin with, so did most second class mail too).

And mail was collected from post boxes seven days a week. Few homes in Britain were more than a short walk away from a red post box, either standing on a street corner or fixed into a wall or onto a fence post.

Of course, in the 19th century, things were much better.

In the years shortly after Rowland Hill invented the post office and Trollope invented the post box there were at least four daily postal deliveries in most provincial towns in Britain and as many as seven a day in London.

`As a young married woman in the 1890s the author's grandmother would see her husband off to his town office each morning, glance at the daily newspapers and then take her dog for a short walk. Into the pillar box at the end of the road she would drop a postcard to her butcher, telling him the cuts of meat she needed for dinner that evening. Within an hour or so the postman would empty the pillar box, and the postcard would be sorted and delivered by the midday post. Early in the afternoon the butcher's body would bring the meat, in good time for the cook to prepare it for the evening meal.'

(Taken from Picture Postcards by C.W.Hill)

Today, thanks to the combined efforts of the European Union and the unions, the Royal Mail has taken incompetence and inefficiency to amazing new heights. England, the home of the postal service, where the first stamp was printed and stuck, now has a postal service that even the Italians would find embarrassing.

Today, we get our mail once a day if we are lucky. It arrives at about lunchtime, though it is quite common not to receive any mail for two or three days at a time not because there isn't any mail but because the postman can't be bothered to deliver it. Collections have been cut and don't occur at all on Sundays. Post boxes are disappearing faster than snowmen during a thaw and postmen struggle around because their bags are full of junk mail that no one wants and everyone has to throw away.

The EU is now running our Post Office from afar (they are planning a pan-European service) and like everything the EU touches it is doomed.

Post offices are pretty terrible too. For some time they have been best known for their queues. And the queues are going to get worse, far worse now that the Government (obeying EU rules) has closed many small post offices.

There were over 19,000 post offices when Labour came to power in 1997. By 2008 that number had shrunk to 16,500 and another 3,000 were due to close. And yet politicians seemed surprised that people were having to queue for hours to buy stamps and post parcels at the post offices that were left.

The incompetence of Post Office staff doesn't help of course. In one recent survey almost a third of post office staff were found to be giving customers the wrong proof of postage. Others were giving poor or inadequate advice about which postal method to use.

The amount of time we all waste in waiting will rise in shops, in offices, in banks and in Government and Council offices. EU employment laws have reduced staffing levels in shops. And Government and council offices have become pension fund managers rather than serving the public - their priority is (like that of the NHS) now merely to ensure that staff members are well looked after, rather than to serve the public.

How long before it is possible to hire someone to stand in a queue for you when you want to post a parcel? How long before groups of unemployed people hang around outside banks and newsagents and offer to stand in the queue for you?

Meanwhile, be prepared to find other ways to move important documents around the country.

Chances of the service provided by the Royal Mail continuing to deteriorate: 100%.

81. We Will Need Several Hundred Thousand More Nurses

The world needs nurses more than ever. But nurses have decided that they don't want to nurse. They want to be quasi-doctors. They are too important to feed patients, change them, bathe them, make sure that take their medicines and don't get bed sores. Modern nurses want to be in meetings. They want to acquire diplomas. They want degrees and respect and power and money. But they're conscious enough of the indispensability of the caring role that they refuse to allow auxiliaries to touch patients. `They can't feed patients,' they cry in horror. `They aren't trained to do things like that.' As if you need years of training to know how to hold a spoon, fill it with food and pop into the patient's mouth when it opens.

Modern nurses wont feed patients, bathe them, lift them (we don't lift patients, say nurses indignantly) or do anything except talk about them. Heavens, how they talk. Eat and talk. Talk and eat.

They don't want to have to wear uniforms which mark them out as nurses. They want to wear skirts and jumpers and discreet name badges and to sit on plastic chairs at long tables eating bourbon biscuits and drinking tea while they discuss new ways to manage holiday rotas and master new software. New nurses don't nurse, they meet.

So, the world, which needs more nurses than anything else, needs other people to do the nursing: thousands and thousands of them. People who will make beds, carry bedpans, feed patients and, generally, nurse. Nurses who don't want to sit in offices discussing patients but who actually want to be on the wards looking after them.

Since nurses own the title `nurse' the people who actually care for patients will have to be called something else.

We could call them caregivers.

Or, in an empire variation on the spirit of modern multiculturalism, we could call them ayahs.

Chances of there being a desperate shortage of nurses: 90%.

82. Prescription Charges Will Rise For Patients In England

Patients in Scotland and Wales obtain their prescription drugs without charge. There is no prescription fee to be paid.

But patients in England have to pay a hefty sum if they fall ill and need to take a prescription drug.

Surprisingly, politicians did actually try to amend this unfairness and enable patients in England to receive free prescription drugs.

But the plan was (and is) opposed by GPs who feared that such a scheme might mean that they had to work harder. Their fear was that patients who would go the chemist and buy something with which to treat themselves would turn up in their surgery and expect a free prescription.

I find it appalling that GPs should be so mean and so desperate to maximise their income and minimise their workload that they would oppose a scheme that would make life fairer and slightly easier for their patients.

Modern GPs are greedy; they run businesses not practices.

Let us not forget that until they were banned from doing it many used 0845 telephone numbers so that they could even earn more money when patients rang up to book up an appointment or to ask for emergency assistance. These days I often feel ashamed to be a doctor.

I have no doubt that the popularity of GPs will continue to decline.

Chances of prescription charges rising for patients in England: 70%.

83. Public Transport Will Deteriorate But Become More Expensive

Public transport services (trains and buses) have been deteriorating for years. Ever since the half-witted Beeching was allowed to close down rail lines and stations on the grounds that not enough people in bowler hats were using them, the train network has been shrinking. Privatisation merely made train tickets more expensive and complicated to buy. (I recently spent 50 minutes at a railway station trying to buy two return train tickets. I knew where I was going from and where I was going to. The journey required no changes. I knew the times of the trains I wanted to travel on. I knew the coach number and even the seat numbers I wanted. It could not have been easier. But the clerk took 50 minutes to key in the information and print out the tickets. In my experience this was by no means unusual. Indeed, I have, on occasion had to leave a railway booking office without tickets because the clerk has, quite simply, been unable to operate the computer successfully.)

Privatising bus services had much the same effect, of course. These days there are many areas of the country where people are marooned in their homes unless they have a motor car or are vigorous enough to ride a bicycle for several miles. Villages and even towns are provided with bus services which are totally impractical. For example, I know of one village where there is a once a week service to the nearby town. The bus that is used for the outward journey is the same bus that is used for the return journey and so passengers have approximately five minutes to conduct whatever business they might have in town. Not surprisingly, the bus service is barely used and the company providing it has announced that the service will soon cease.)

While services have been deteriorating the cost of using them has increased dramatically - and far faster than the rate of inflation. Even cheap tickets are far more expensive than they were just a year or two ago (and you usually have to know that they are available if you want to buy them).

All this is bad enough.

But the rising price of oil means that the need for public transport will soon be rising. Private motorists will simply not be able to afford to use their cars on a daily basis: they will have to use expensive and badly run trains and buses. This will, of course, mean that services will become overcrowded and dirty and even more unpleasant than they are at present.

Other countries subsidise their public transport and, recognising that it is far more economical (and better for the environment) to move people about in buses and trains than in private motor cars they ensure that citizens are provided with an excellent public transport system.

Britain, which had the first railways and first bus services in the world, now has the worst public transport system anywhere in the western world.

Did British governments not realise that petrol was going to become more expensive? Or did they deliberately encourage people to use a system which provides the State with vast amounts of money? The tax on petrol is so high that British motorists pay more for their fuel than motorists anywhere else in the world.

Whatever the answers might be to these questions, the end result is the same: Britain has an inadequate, poorly run and extraordinarily expensive public transport system. And, as petrol prices rise and the pressure on an inadequate public transport system increases so the problems with it will increase. The public will complain and transport workers will go on strike with even greater frequency.

None of this will help a nation which has a broken economy.

The chances of public transport becoming more expensive but providing a poorer service: 100%.

84. Electoral Reform Will Damage Our Democracy

The May 2010 election result will be used as a reason for introducing electoral reform - together with a transferable voting system. This has, for some years, been one of the main demands of the EU super friendly party, the Liberal Democrats.

It may take a while to force through but the transferable voting system will be introduced in Britain. The new system will, you may not be surprised to hear, mean that Britain's parliamentary voting system matches the type of voting system used across the European Union. It will mean that the parties have virtually total control of the nation and that those who choose not to vote for one of the big parties will not be represented (at the May 2010 election around 10% of the population chose to vote for independent candidates but were entirely unrepresented in Parliament). The sort of electoral reform demanded by the Liberal Democrats will ensure that our hopes of democracy recede further into the distance because once it becomes law no independent individuals will ever again be elected to represent the community. Voters who want political reform will be tricked into thinking that proportional representation will give them what they want. But, in reality, proportional representation will give total, complete, permanent power to the political parties. And, within the EU, that will soon mean that it will give total, complete, permanent power to the European Union and its unelected eurocrats. There will be no more independent politicians and no politicians who dare to stand up to bullying whips. The change will give total power to the party system and, ultimately, to the Fascist EU Superstate. I do hope that the half witted nincompoops who pushed for electoral reform enjoy the future they're creating for us all. The rest of us certainly won't. Britain needed political reform but all that was really needed was a reduction in the number of constituencies and some changes made to constituency borders so that elected MPs represented similarly sized groups of voters. This would have ensured that voters could continue to vote for and elect their own political representative.

Voting for MEPs is, of course, already organised on EU lines, using a scheme which involves the big parties producing lists of favoured candidates. The public just get to vote for parties, not people.

Naturally, the more complicated voting system we're eventually going to get will be introduced with the aid of computerised voting. Electors will be entitled to express their preference for an EU approved political party by clicking on their keyboard. It will be possible to vote by email and by text. The authorities will like this. Voting computers are even easier to fiddle than postal voting.

Finally, I fear that the established parties (for which one can safely substitute the interchangeable phrases `the European Union' or `the establishment') will do their best to stop independent candidates standing for office. They will do this by increasing the size of the deposits which candidates have to pay before they are allowed to stand. The dreams I had when I wrote `Bloodless Revolution' (my campaign book against the power of the political parties) will, by then, have been thoroughly and finally shattered.

Chances of electoral reform damaging our democracy still further: 100%.

85. Voting Will Become Compulsory

The main political parties are become more and more alike. Today, the three big parties are virtually indistinguishable. Their policies vary very slightly, and the personalities which represent the parties are different, but for practical purposes the parties are interchangeable. You can could transfer a leading politician from the Labour Party to the Conservative Party and let him continue to say the same things and you would not know that he had switched parties (unless, of course, he was rude about the party he had left and obsequious about the leader of the party he had joined).

The big thing the parties all have in common is, of course, their support for, and allegiance to, the European Union. And the existence of the EU makes the existence of the political parties irrelevant. The House of Commons no longer has power over the United Kingdom. The real power has all passed to the unelected bureaucrats working in Brussels.

It will soon be illegal for any political party to question the authority and purpose of the European Union. The legislation for this has already been passed. We will soon only be allowed to vote for EU approved politicians.

And since the parties are becoming more and more alike, and their policies interchangeable, legislation will soon be introduced to make voting compulsory. This will enable the EU to claim that our democracy is stronger is ever. (It will, of course, be another way for the authorities to keep an eye on us all, and to make sure that they know where we are and what we are doing.)

In reality, of course, voting has been meaningless for some years. The party system and the power of the European Union has made voting a mere nod in the direction of parliamentary democracy.

Chances of voting becoming compulsory: 90%.

86. Will The GP System Be Abolished?

There is a real possibility that NHS general practice as we know it might well be abolished.

General practice has already changed enormously in the last few years. EU rules about the number of hours anyone can work have made it impossible for the government to run a 24 hour a day service. Until we leave the EU it will never be possible to go back to the old system whereby GPs were available for their patients 24 hours a day, 365 days a year. (I believe that it would, however, be possible for private doctors, working outside the NHS, to offer such a service. I have explained this elsewhere in this book. No British government is going to expect its employees to be on call (and being on call is now officially counted as 'working' even if you don't actually do anything except sleep and watch TV) 24 hours a day for weeks but it is difficult for a government to prevent genuinely self-employed individuals from working long hours if they choose to do so.

Despite the fact that GPs now provide a much poorer service than ever before (most now work the same sort of hours as a local authority administrator) the GP service is enormously expensive. Clever contract negotiations mean that the average GP now earns around £120,000 a year and can make huge additional sums if he meets various `targets', such as vaccinating enough of his patients. (Many GPs even had the gall to introduce premium rate telephone numbers so that patients calling for help had to pay the sort of fees paid by callers to telephone sex lines. It was only in April 2010 that the NHS announced that the contract with GPs would be changed to prevent doctors robbing their patients in this wicked way. How appalling that it was left to NHS bureaucrats to protect patients from this thieving.) GPs have recently doubled their income and halved their workload. Whoever managed their latest contract negotiations should be negotiating for England in the next Olympics. Getting rid of GPs would save the government vast amounts of money.

Although the political parties regard the NHS as a `sacred cow' which must be protected from money saving cuts, the GP service is in a peculiar position. Although they are paid by the government, GPs are self employed and do, therefore, work outside the NHS. (Just how and why GPs have managed to retain their advantageous position as self employed contractors has long been a mystery; most people with a single employer are forced by HMRC to be treated as employed. But maybe the government was being crafty in allowing GPs this perk. With GPs officially regarded self employed they can be cut out of the NHS without the NHS being officially affected. It's the sort of trickery politicians love.)

The government is already introducing a number of schemes which could enable them to make the current general practitioner service irrelevant and, in official terms, unnecessary.

First, there are lots of little health service centres popping up all over the place. Ostensibly, these are designed to cater for people who aren't registered with a GP. But it is easy to see that these centres could be used to replace the cumbersome and expensive GP service. It would also get rid of a troublesome group of self employed people who don't fit neatly into the NHS bureaucracy.

Second, the Government is giving nurses increasing powers to prescribe drugs and to perform surgical procedures. It would be possible to staff the health service centres largely with nurses. These are, of course, much cheaper to hire than doctors. And with all the people working in these centres hired as full time employees the costs in terms of extra payments and incentives would disappear. There would be far less administration, lower salaries and, in the fullness of time, a reduction in pension payments.

Third, there is the absurd NHS telephone line which enables sick people to ring up in emergencies and obtain clinical advice from someone who isn't medically qualified, who doesn't know them and who can't see them or examine them. I have, for decades, steadfastly refused to offer telephone advice to strangers. I have always thought it irresponsible and potentially dangerous. I still believe it to be both. The people who run the NHS believe in this system but I suspect they do so because it saves a lot of money and will make it possible to get rid of GPs.

Chances of GPs being abolished: 60%.

87. Private GP Practices Will Spring Up All Over Britain (but especially in England)

The failure of the quality of general practice cover provided by the NHS (and the virtual absence of out of hours cover) will mean that there will be a rise in demand for private GPs all over the country.

Qualified GPs, working alone or groups of two or three, will set up private practices and work from home, completely outside the NHS. They will offer patients a simple and old-fashioned service.

There are several ways that a private GP service might work.

A GP might charge a set annual fee of, say, £200 per person to provide medical cover for 24 hours a day, 365 days a year. The cost of prescription drugs would, of course, be on top of that. Such a service would enable a GP to have a list of 500 patients and provide an excellent service. (NHS GPs look after 2,000 to 3,000 patients each so a private GP with a list of just 500 patients would be able to provide an excellent service and earn £100,000 a year.) GPs working this way would, of course, have to spend very little time on administration and no time at all dealing with NHS bureaucrats. GPs who worked alone would arrange for other local doctors to provide cover during their holidays.

Alternatively, a GP might charge a lower basic `membership' fee but charge an additional fee for each surgery consultation, home visit and night visit.

I suspect that quite a number of patients would be prepared to pay for such a service. The NHS would be left to provide a very basic GP service for patients who could not afford private care - just as the NHS dental service now provides a very basic dental service for patients who cannot afford private dental treatment.

Chances of private GP practices springing up throughout England: 80%.

88. Queues In Shops Are Going To Get Longer

Queues in shops have been travelling far more slowly since the   staff stopped putting things in plastic bags as they enter the details into their till.

Today, the customer has to wait for the goods to be scanned and then wait for the shop assistant to announce the total. The customer then gets out a purse or wallet, removes a credit card and pays for the goods. Only then do they start to put the things they have bought into their shopping bag. The whole process takes much longer than it used to.

Shops display sanctimonious signs explaining that they have stopped using plastic bags in order to save the planet. If they do provide plastic bags they charge for them.

This is, of course, hypocritical nonsense. The shops still package their products in vast quantities of unnecessary plastic. And, as I showed in my book What Happens Next?, shops would be using more plastic bags if they really cared about the planet and wanted to stop the non existent threat of global warming.

The truth is simpler.

Plastic bags cost money.

Shops no longer provide them for one reason only: to save money and increase their profits.

Meanwhile, queues get ever longer and as customers stop using cash and turn to using debit and credit cards when they buy a packet of sweets or a newspaper so the queues will get longer still.

Chances of shop queues getting longer: 90%.

89. Offshore Regulations Will Become More Onerous

When the heads of other nations met in London they spent a day considering the world's financial problems and decided that they would clamp down on offshore tax havens and introduce more regulations and more legislation. They claimed that they were doing this to prevent another financial crash.

But the world's financial crisis was not caused by, or even contributed to by, offshore tax havens. The bankers who did dangerous, reckless things with other people's money (and who created the crisis) did so in London and New York.

And here's an irony. The two cities which provide secret banking facilities for the greatest number of tax evaders and money launderers are London and New York. Though in Britain you have to be foreign to take advantage of the facilities available. No other country comes close to Britain or America when it comes to hiding money from the authorities or its rightful owners.

The truth is that governments are clamping down on people who have money offshore not because they think that such accounts are being used to bring down the economies of major nations but because they are worried that some individuals might not be paying their taxes in full.

In their determination to catch these people (who will, of course, move their money somewhere else long before they are caught) the authorities will make life exceedingly difficult for Britons who have holiday homes abroad - and bank accounts to help them pay their local utility bills and property taxes.

As always it will be the innocent who will suffer.

And suffer they will.

The chances of offshore regulations becoming ever more onerous: 100%.

90. The Hazards Associated With Microwave Ovens Will Become Clear

I have been warning about the potential hazards associated with microwave ovens for a quarter of a century. I have, predictably, been sneered at, scorned and derided for this view. (There is a section dealing with microwave ovens, and the risks which I believe may be associated with them, in my book Food for Thought.)

The manufacturers of microwave ovens claim that their devices have adequate shielding to protect people from possible radiation harm when the device is in operation.

But a reader conducted a simple experiment to test this claim. He put his mobile phone in his microwave oven and closed the door. To his astonishment his mobile phone did not lose reception.

Some shielding.

We don't have a microwave oven.

Lots of people do.

Do microwave ovens cause cancer? Is the food cooked in them safe to eat?

I don't know.

As far as I have been able to find no one has ever done any tests to answer these simple questions.

But at some point in the next decade it will become clear that microwave ovens are dangerous.

There will then be a call for them to be replaced.

They will doubtless be replaced by something that seems safer (but which has not yet been tested).

Chances of the hazards of using microwave ovens becoming clear by 2020: 70%.

91. The Lobbyists Now Control the EU, Which Controls Our Government

The Government is run for, and controlled by, special interest groups and their lobbyists. The arms industry, the food industry, the drug industry, the oil industry - they all have a say in what happens and they have a very big say in what happens in areas that affect their industry.

For example, it is absolutely no secret among those who study these things that the NHS is run for the drug industry - and not for the patients it purports to serve. (It is, for example, for the benefit of the drug industry that GPs are bribed to give vaccinations to their patients. Vaccinations are not given to help people but to boost drug company profits. And the politicians, working on behalf of the drug industry, have devised a very effective way to bribe doctors to give vaccinations.) American President Eisenhower warned of the dangers of the industrial-military complex. He was right to be worried. But the system is far more rancid than ever he feared it might become.

Large corporations, equipped with battalions of lawyers and lobbyists, use the system to help themselves to vast amounts of public money in the form of grants and subsidises. (Some of it comes direct from the Government but most comes from the European Union.) Politically savvy businesses, usually international and huge, hire lobbyists to ensure that they receive the biggest subsidies or that the Government gives them a monopoly or that the Government or the European Union cripple their competitors with oppressive new legislation. Businessmen who rely on state intervention at home also want state intervention abroad - and so the empire becomes imperial in power if not in inches and feet and the principle of collectivist welfare is put high above individual self interest.

When the Government hands out money to particular groups it

makes every company it touches less efficient; it slows the economy; it encourages deceit. The people who benefit most from Government schemes are the politically influential; the lobbyists, the commentators and the politicians themselves. It is hardly surprising that the poor have suffered hugely under the Labour, statist Government. The rich and influential have got richer and more powerful as they have grabbed money and privileges provided by unwilling taxpayers. The weakest and the most vulnerable have suffered, along with the hardest working and the most honest. The Labour Government has, more than any other Government in our history, encouraged dishonesty and deceit. You can't hear anything in Westminster these days for the sound of hobby horses braying and chortling.

Sometimes the lobbyists have to be admired. They are so brilliantly effective that it is impossible not to admire them. Where do you think the rules and regulations about car MOTs came from? Ask yourself who benefits? Motorists? No chance. MOTs don't make cars safer. They just make it compulsory for people to have their cars serviced; and to buy new parts for them. MOTs help push old cars off the roads and force people to buy new ones. (This isn't a good thing as far as global warming is concerned but the bureaucrats know damned well that the global warming scam is just that - a scam.) New industry based rules are coming in all the time. How long before we have to have our home boiler serviced and licensed if it is more than three years old? The rules are introduced by bureaucrats in Brussels, but with the guidance of corporate and trade lobbyists. And, oh how they guide.

In April 2009 it was revealed that in a 15 page handbook European Commission officials had been given tips on how to evade Freedom of Information rules. They were told to keep two sets of documents, a `whitened' text for public release and a `separate' classified version. And you thought it was just dodgy car dealers and restaurant owners who kept two sets of books.

Officials have also been advised: `Don't refer to the great lunch you have had with an industry representative privately.'

Good to know that the idiots running the EU are so stupid that they have to be taught how to be corrupt.

The lobbyists are in charge so that the EU bureaucracy and the multinationals can work together for their mutual benefit.

That's practical, pure fascism in real action.

Enjoy it.

Chances of the lobbyists having even more power in 2020: 100%.

92.   The Incidence Of Brain Cancer Will Increase And Will Be Linked With Mobile Phones

I bought my first mobile phone in the mid 1980s and have owned quite a variety of these devices since then. I have, however, been warning of the possible dangers of mobile phones for almost as long.

I first realised that there could be a problem when I noticed that if I used my phone for more than ten minutes or so I started to get a burning sensation in and around the ear against which I was holding the phone. I wrote about this potential problem many times during the 1980s and 1990s (there is a summary of some of my early thoughts in my book `Superbody') but my fears were laughed off my most commentators, most journalists and virtually the entire mobile phone industry.

I believe that there will soon be evidence that mobile phones cause brain tumours. I think the first signs may well be an increase in the number of people showing serious behavioural problems - becoming exceptionally and unpredictably violent, for example. There may well be an increase in the number of serial killers.

I have been calling for research into the dangers associated with mobile phones for decades but few decent studies have been done. Surprisingly, the phone companies don't seem keen to find out just how dangerous their devices might be. However, in September 2008 a study did confirm that the risk of brain cancer is dramatically increased in people who start using mobile phones before the age of 20.

At some time in the next decade it will at last become obvious that there is a powerful link between mobile phones and brain cancer.

Sadly, it will be too late for the many thousands of people who will die because they were bought mobile phones when they were young.

Chances of the incidence of brain cancer increasing (and being linked with the use of mobile phones - particularly among the young): 90%.

93. Will The Internet Continue To Wreak Havoc On Our World?

The internet has destroyed thousands of jobs. It has certainly not been a benefit to mankind. So far the internet seems to me to be little more than a cesspool of bigotry, libel and pornography; a market place for thieves, tricksters, failures and exhibitionists; a noticeboard for those driven by hatred and envy and a dark world populated by the half witted, the ineffectual and by people who believe that all copyright is theft but who will happily sell their unwanted books for a penny each and make a few pence by overcharging for the postage and packing. The web is a major cause of the mess the world is in; the most overrated invention since the hula hoop. The only people making money out of it, apart from conmen, pornographers and identity thieves, are people selling programmes explaining how to make money out of running a website. The web is occupied by socially and mentally retarded geeks who live on social security, who regard property as theft (unless it's their property) and who think they are revolutionaries because they never bathe.

The Web has killed whole industries and contributed massively to unemployment, poverty, misery, abuse and theft but, unlike the Industrial Revolution, has done nothing whatsoever to improve the quality of our lives by taking over backbreaking physical labour or mind numbingly repetitive tasks. Show me someone who has benefited from the World Wide Web and I will show you 1,000 whose lives have been considerably diminished. Propaganda means that it is almost impossible to obtain accurate, reliable information from the web unless you are already an expert in the subject you are researching and I firmly believe that the world would be a better, happier and richer place if the World Wide Web had never been invented and the computer confined to doing sums.

The internet is changing the world by de-aggregating content of papers and albums (turning into articles and tracks, and books into chapters). Not many people make money out of selling content online though many have tried. The whole thing does, however, give us something to smile about. Attempts to force internet providers to block sites carrying pirated music and films etc were opposed by internet and telecom companies because they `threaten freedom of speech and the open internet'. The people defending the internet have no understanding of the word `irony'.

Because of the internet record publishing has been destroyed. many types of retail are dead or dying (there aren't many record shops, music shops and art shops left and bookshops are disappearing from our high streets at a phenomenal rate). video rental stores have more or less gone. Town centres are struggling to survive as the twin threats of the supermarkets (and their satellite stores) and the internet destroy shopping centres and leave behind a depressing mixture of empty shops, charity shops and nail parlours where beauty college students use government grants to delay unemployment for six months or, if they are frugal, a year. In technical terms it may be progress. But is it progress that we want? And if we don't want it, is it still progress?

Within the next few years big internet sites, such as Google, will enter more and more areas. For example, as I write there is talk that Google will launch an online property site - enabling estate agents to list properties for free and to show pictures taken by Google and to show positions on its maps. Such a development will of course destroy property websites and prove to be the final straw that destroys local newspapers (which are already struggling to survive under the twin attacks from the internet and local councils producing free newspapers to promote themselves and to oppose criticism.

The internet likes to pretend that its free and green. It is neither. To use the internet you need electricity. More of it than you would imagine. And although there are many people using the internet who boast that they never buy things such as books, films, movies, games, news (but prefer to steal them from sites which make this possible) there are many more who discover the hard way just how expensive using the internet can be. One man recently received a £15,000 telephone bill as a result of his son's internet usage. A family on a Mediterranean cruise got home and found that while they'd been enjoying the sites and the sunshine their iPhones had spent £3,200 automatically checking for emails.

The internet seems certain to destroy much of the world we now. Most alarming of all it is now widely used by teachers who encourage their pupils to rely on search engines instead of text books. The truth is that the internet is dominated by people selling things and ideas and it is extremely difficult to be sure that the information you glean from websites is accurate and unbiased. As a research tool the internet is pretty useless - and certainly far less useful than a half-decent library.

Here's a sideways thought for you. Will the internet die because it is too slow and boring for the next generation? What will take its place? Some form of holographic or telepathic communication? I am comforted by this thought that the internet might not self-destruct. Who knows what new technologies are around the corner? Will the number of websites available continues to grow (and the number of people using each one shrinks) or will the internet be one of those fashionable Parisian restaurants that is, one year, the `only' place to eat and then, the following year, deserted.

One can, and must, live in hope.

One thing is certain.

Our technological future will be devised by people who aren't yet at school and who will regard computers and websites as boring and clunky as we regard dot matrix printers. I suspect that, in order to avoid confusion and save time, information will be controlled and selected for us. Maybe Google (or some other search engine) will do a deal with a future government to provide us with the answers to our questions. They could sell such a system to the mass of people on the grounds that it would make life easier for them.

Chances of the internet continuing to destroy the world we know: 80%.

Chances of the internet not surviving in the form we know it (but becoming smaller and weaker): 20%.

I don't work for, and never have worked for bankrupt, failing or discredited institutions such as Halifax Bank Of Scotland (HBOS), Royal Bank of Scotland, Northern Rock, Lloyds Bank, Barclays or Bradford and Bingley. Nor am I registered as an investment adviser with the Financial Services Authority (Government appointed regulators who are paid to ensure that investors are protected from failing banks). I cannot, therefore, give investment advice.

The notes which follow are intended as an aide-memoire for my own use; a sort of route-map for the next few years. I include them simply out of academic interest. You should not regard any of the following thoughts as advice or recommendations.

Here are some of the things I have learned about investing.

First, economists and politicians get things wrong so often that as an investor it is safest to invest on the basis that everything they predict won't happen and everything they do will fail. Governments and the financial markets will screw up far worse than seemed possible. And they will do it for longer, too. Whatever problems the future holds for the world, governments everywhere will mess up everything that can be messed up and they will make everything worse. It is safe to rely on the stupidity and incompetence and dishonesty of politicians. They will not do sensible things (however simple) to correct substantial threats to the economy but can relied upon to lie, cheat and make things worse.

Never, never, never invest on the basis of a politician's promise. Politicians talk a great deal about improving infrastructure, and they boast about improving spending on health care and education. Ignore them.

Politicians' promises are easily abandoned. Companies which adapt their plans to fit in with potentially profitable opportunities which might result from political changes are taking huge chances. Don't invest in a company which will supposedly benefit from any government decision. Politicians love encouraging companies to spend money on their behalf but they never, ever do anything to help private sector companies make money. Companies don't vote and even politicians know that. Successful investing is all about having an edge. Professionals spend zillions on special software, analysis of accounts and lengthy discussions with board members of companies they're investigating. My edge is simpler, cheaper and more reliable and can be summarised in one sentence. I believe all modern politicians (anywhere in the world) will always do the wrong thing; they will make decisions not for the benefit of their country for the benefit of themselves. It is possible to run a successful investment strategy based on the belief that everything the government does will be badly planned and incompetently executed. Once you recognise the truth of that adage then investing becomes a lot simpler and a good deal more profitable. Professional investors often get things wrong because they trust the government to do the right thing for the right reasons. I don't. Politicians have betrayed every promise, every faith, every moral issue, everything they were thought to stand for. Only the reckless trust politicians. This is, I believe, the most important single thing I have learned about investing. Markets have not yet realised this because the financial analysts whose interpretations influence the markets have not realised that politicians will not do the right thing to protect the country whose people pay their wages and expenses unless what they choose to do is also the right thing for them. The markets tend to practise microeconomics rather than macroeconomics: they react to tiny bits of news and are, therefore, extremely volatile. This combination of gullibility and short term thinking mean that it can take the markets a long time to realise what is going to happen to the pound or to interest rates in the long term. It is I believe a secret of successful investing that one should assume that everyone in a position of authority (politicians, bankers, editors etc) is a fool and a liar, utterly devoid of common sense and quite incapable of seeing the woods for the trees. Bankers and investment advisers will always act exclusively in their own interests and never in the interests of their customers or clients because they always think short term and are incurably greedy. We all need a macroeconomic understanding so that we can make judgements on Greece, the euro, the dollar and gold. The important truth is that everything that can be fucked up will be fucked up. Investments should be made according to this assumption. It works well.

Second, investors are today often forced into becoming traders. When I first started investing I liked to `buy and hold'. I liked this philosophy because it kept the dealing costs to a minimum and because it took up less time. But `buying and holding' can be a dangerous game these days. Passive investing is no longer a rational option.

Third, I believe that successful investing depends on understanding the tide of human events. I also believe that sorting out the ebb and flow of human events is best done by reading; I find this quicker and more effective than wasting time going out to social events and talking to opinionated idiots. I don't use the television or the radio as a source of news. Lectures, conferences, and dinner parties are a waste of time. I believe it is possible to obtain information much more readily, more cheaply and with less wasted effort by reading, understand and thinking. I read research reports, annual reports, investment magazines, news magazines and newsletters. But mostly I read books. I read a lot of books because book authors tend to be more independent, more creative and more reliable than journalists or newsletter writers.

Fourth, I look for industries which will in my view do well. And then I buy a mixture of the best and worst companies in that industry. I hope that the best companies will give me a reliable dividend and a decent profit. And I hope that one or two of the wobbly companies will survive, thrive and make ten times the original stake.

Fifth, I don't trust professional investment managers to look after my money. What an indictment it is of investment managers that they all have to put on their advertisements `Past performance is no guarantee or indicator of future performance.' I wonder how many cars Ford would sell if their dealers had to put that sort of slogan on all their dashboards. I don't invest in funds put together by banks. Vast numbers of investors seem more anxious to lose money than to make it. On the same day that Morgan Stanley warned investors that its real estate fund Msref VI could lose as much as $5.4 billion, it was also reported that the same bank had raised more than $6 billion for its next fund, Msref VII. It is perfectly true that you can't predict future results from past results but, hey, I think I might have been reluctant to give a bank money to invest in a specific area when it had done so appallingly so recently in precisely the same area of investment.   Professional investors, the men and women running pension and investment funds, are more interested in looking after the interests of their chums in the city than in protecting small investors. They need to do more to protect the interests of their private investors. At the moment these people seem more concerned with protecting the interests of bankers, brokers and company directors. If pension and fund managers were held personally responsible when their funds lost money because of trickery, corruption and fancy dealing their minds would be concentrated effectively on their duties. Fund managers should be pressuring company executives to start paying dividends again. In recent years company bosses have discovered that they can boost their own salaries and bonuses by using corporate profits to buy back shares. This pushes up the share price and enables them to gain enormously from options and bonuses. Ordinary, private investors are the losers. Companies should be forced to use profits to provide reasonable dividends. Don't overestimate the intelligence of the investment professionals. For example, the so-called `credit-crunch' which devastated the financial markets (and the share prices of banks) in 2007 and 2008 affected Britain because so many leading bankers behaved like idiots and bought packages of mortgage debt without, apparently, having asked fairly fundamental questions about the security of the assets they were buying. The people who lent huge amounts of money who had no chance of ever paying it back were reckless. But it was the hubris of bankers (many of whom had become bosses of big banks only after their building society had become a bank but who had assumed the salaries and arrogance of investment bankers) which led directly to serious losses for investors and real problems for millions. The collapse of Long Term Capital Management (LTCM) in 1998 proved that clever people with lots of computers are not very good at managing, or even keeping, money. LTCM was run by people who had big brains and Nobel prizes. It was supposed to be the Titanic of investment funds. But, like the Titanic, it ran into serious trouble. Hubris led LTCM onto the iceberg of the Russian Government defaulting on sovereign debt. If the American Government hadn't bailed LTCM out (or, rather, strong-armed investment banks to take over its disastrous positions) LTCM would have gone bankrupt with disastrous results.

I was staggered to discover that at the height of the investment management boom, some managers were charging performance fees of up to 50% (I'd thought 20% was the maximum). Moreover, some managers were claiming their performance fee if the investments they were managing outperformed market indices. This meant that investors were paying a fee if their fund fell in value but not as much as the chosen index. Not many investors were delighted to be paying a performance fee for losing money. A study of wealth managers and hedge fund managers showed that many have last money over 5 year periods and the ones that didn't lose money had mostly made less than 5% profit over 5 years. That is, of course, far less than inflation. These managers are terrible at what they do. Their only real skill is, it seems to me, in devising new ways to increase their own personal earnings. They are very good at that.

Sixth, the most important skill for any investor is, in my view, the ability to differentiate between relevant and irrelevant news. To be successful it is essential to be able to dismiss investment or geopolitical `noise' and to focus on crucial bits and pieces of information. It is, of course, also essential to be able to interpret the information you have selected and to use the information to help you draw conclusions. I believe in backing my own judgement. To do this you have to believe that no one knows better than you do what is happening to the economy or the nation or the world. Mix a little common sense (that rarest of all commodities) in with your judgement and the chances are that your guesses will be better educated, and more accurate, than anyone else's.

Seventh, I don't buy shares in companies run by women or where women have a predominant position on the board. I believe women make less effective managers than me. Maybe this is because once a month they are irrational and therefore less effective. Maybe it is because they are nastier and try too hard, thereby alienating staff and customers.

Eighth, don't expect compensation if banks or finance companies steal or lose your money. The only time I ever received compensation was when, after being cheated by the investment trust community and failed by the government's regulator I received a modest amount of compensation for losses made by investment trusts running Zero Dividend Preference shares. The Government, having screwed up, finally arranged for me to receive a relatively modest amount of compensation. And then they then duly charged top rate tax on it. No one gives a toss about private investors. Investors have been treated like garbage ever since Shriti Vadera, a Treasury adviser and one of Gordon's many little friends, is reputed to have announced, as the government prepared to push Railtrack into administration in 2001 that `the grannies lose their blouses...it's the American investors we have to worry about'. That about sums it up. Brown and his cohort regarded investors and private shareholders, and people who try to look after their money, as `grannies' whose interests can be safely ignored. And so investors in such apparently safe institutions as Northern Rock and Bradford Bingley suddenly found that their savings were worthless. Even investors who had money into Bradford and Bingley permanent interest bearing shares (widely reputed to be the safe and sensible way of saving for the especially prudent) found that they had little or nothing left to share for their prudence. The government doesn't give a damn about grannies losing their blouses. The government has, indeed, shown that it despises people who save, people who work hard, save diligently and invest cautiously. Anyone who does these things but isn't mega rich can be treated without respect. Of course, if you're a mega rich banker you will be looked after and your bonus will be paid by the taxpayers - the very poor sods who have lost their investments because of your stupidity, recklessness and greed. These are bad times to be a sensible and cautious investor.

Ninth, lobbyists now control scientists, media and politicians. The public will learn no truths about issues such as climate change, aids, vaccination and vivisection. Policies will vary not according to the emergence of scientific truths but according to the power of the various lobbying forces. Do not, therefore, make any investments according to anything scientists say. Don't take any notice of anything written by journalists who write about money. Most of them are impoverished and, therefore, quite likely to write what they are told to write rather than to offer any original insights. One well known money writer told readers of one magazine he wrote for to buy gold and the readers of another magazine that he had no faith in gold. The articles appeared in the same week.

Tenth, don't bother with schemes which offer tax advantages. So, for example, I don't bother with putting money into an ISA. ISAs have cheated savers of billions. They were created by Gordon Brown and are now a £3 billion a year rip off that enable the banks to pluck in huge amounts of money with the promise of tax relief but to make outrageous profits by paying derisory rates of interest and charging huge fees. They do the old tricks of paying a good rate to begin with and then reducing the rate paid after a few months and making it difficult to move the money. Around 15 million people have ISAs but i wonder how many take advantage of the much more useful £10,000 a year free capital gain (no tax). The tax benefits with ISAs are more than offset by a very poor rate of interest (much less than inflation), high charges and deliberately confusing information. ISAs are splendid for banks, which make a good deal of money out of them. ISAs are always heavily promoted in the appropriate season but there is one other big problem. If you make a loss you can't put it against capital gains. By far best is to make sure you use your annual capital gains allowance. Most people who bother with high cost ISAs don't use their capital gains allowance. That is because most money journalists are crap and too poor to know how to invest wisely. They are, on the other hand, always eager to promote ISAs, the purveyors of which buy vast amounts of advertising in newspapers and magazines.

Eleventh, remember: the best way to beat the market is to make geopolitical and geoeconomic predictions and then invest accordingly. Most investors (and most investment advisers) do not yet do this. This may be because they can't or because they prefer to look at the trees rather than study the woods. In my experience, it always pays to look out for new trends and big themes. Anyone who realised that China would be a booming country a few years before the boom started would have been well placed to make a lot of money (as long as they had sold before China stumbled). Investors who were aware of the problem of peak oil were well placed to take advantage of the rise in oil prices. When global warming and peak oil became `trendy' fears many people started looking at alternative forms of energy as an investment possibility. Sadly, many investments in alternative energy proved disappointing because although the theory was fine the companies often had no realistic chance of making a profit. In some cases there was no real demand for their products. In other cases the products simply weren't terribly good. During the better part of the 20th century the increase in the value of the stock market was largely due to earnings growth. As companies became more efficient and devised new and better ways of doing things so they managed to increase productivity. In many countries and many industries employees actually found themselves working harder and working longer hours than their predecessors.

Will this earnings growth continue throughout the 21st century?

Fund managers at investment companies clearly believe so but I don't.

I believe that the problems caused by peak oil must have a dramatic effect on corporate profitability. In the medium and long term our society will change enormously - and permanently but even in the short term there will be significant changes.

Twelfth, within Britain Government dependent industries will not do well. Financial commentators claim that in a recession it is safe to invest money in companies which rely on Government patronage. In theory this makes sense. In a well run country the government would endeavour to limit the depth of the recession by spending money on building roads, schools and hospitals. But Britain is not (and has not been) a well run country. The country is darned near bankrupt. The Government may want to spend loads of money on repairing old bits of infrastructure, and building new bits. But it simply doesn't have the money. The next decade is, I fear, going to be fairly gloomy (and steadily become gloomier) for companies which rely entirely on Government patronage.

Thirteenth,, I have for a long time had a suspicion that the price of gold may soar. If you don't know what the world is going to look like in five, ten or twenty years' time (and you have a nasty feeling that you are not going to like it) then buy gold. When, shortly after he became Chancellor, Gordon Brown was selling Britain's gold reserves (and losing a fortune for the nation) I was busy buying some of the stuff he was selling. (Brown sold gold at the cheapest price it had been for ages. It's never been back to that price.) It seemed to me then not that gold was particularly cheap but that Brown's economic policies would lead to disaster.

Fourteenth, the price of agriculture crops will rise, rise and rise again.

Fifteenth, I think it's a good idea to buy shares in large, international companies which make most of their money outside the UK and make most of their money in a currency (any currency) other than sterling. I'm investing in companies which have overseas exposure and earn their money in dollars or Swiss francs or yen or anything that isn't sterling.

Sixteenth, gilts pay, say, 3%. But if interest rates go up to 12% (which I fear they will) then gilts will have to pay at least 9%. But for gilts to pay 9% instead of 3% they will have to go down to around 30% of their current value. Pension fund companies which have stocked up on government gilts, thinking them to be the safest form of investment, will be devastated.

Seventeenth, interest rates will soar and inflation will rocket. Index linked gilts (which provide some protection against inflation) are the best variety to buy.

Eighteenth, at some point share prices will rise again. The Great Bull Market of the last quarter of the twentieth century may well turn out to be the last big bull market for some years. The world is facing a number of huge problems and although there will undoubtedly be some good times ahead it seems likely that the future for investors will be much harder work than the recent past. The immediate past has belonged to those who lived beyond their means and who borrowed as much as they could to invest in stocks and property. The future (short term, medium term and possibly even longer term) may well belong to those who live within their means, save as much as they can, borrow little or none at all and invest what they save carefully and with thought. But probably not before a lot of people have lost a lot more money. By the beginning of 2009 it was possible to buy shares in many large, well funded, solid, international companies that were paying considerably more in dividends than could be obtained by investing in Government gilts. This has hardly ever happened for decades. For the last twenty years, for example gilts have been paying twice as much `interest' as shares. If the companies are solid, and their earnings stable, then the dividend income should help me survive.

The bear market began in 2000, or even in 1997. The rises since then have been bear market rallies. We could be in a secular bear market which started in 1997 and may well last until 2017. On polling day in 1997 the FTSE closed at 4445.01. What is it today? If it is lower then share investors have, after over a decade of a Labour Government, lost money on their investments.

It is, I fear, going to be a decade or more before the stock market makes a real recovery. It may be longer than that. We are in a big bear market. And it is going to last. And last. And last. The UK is now the weakest industrialised nation on earth. The good news is that I think there will still be ways to make money out of the market. These are going to depend on investing in companies which deal in currencies outside the GBP and which sell products outside the UK. It is going to be possible to make money out of oil and commodities. But I don't think I will do terribly well trying to make money out of retail consumers or British banks.

The important thing is that British shares never reached the absurd level that Japanese shares reached in the early 1990s. At that time analysts and bankers clubbed together to talk of it being different this time. Some of them were probably stupid enough to believe it. Most just went along with the nonsense for the commission they were making. The Japanese market was selling on a p/e of around 80. Madness. It's important that British shares didn't rise to such absurd heights because, even in the midst of the coming depression, they will not have to so far to fall.

By the end of 2008 some British shares were quite cheap. The companies which were going to survive were cheap. Some, such as the big oil companies were paying big, well covered dividends and seemed a bargain.

And once inflation starts to roar which (thanks to Gordon) it will, share prices will probably be one of the easiest ways for ordinary mortals to stay slightly ahead of the game. Massive inflation isn't far ahead. Interest rates are low, oil prices are going to go up again. And the pound is falling fast. How fast and how far can inflation rise? I don't know. But I suspect that people will at some time be considering themselves fortunate to tie themselves into loans charging 15% interest.

The market as a whole is going nowhere for a while. Up and down and sideways for a decade or two. Instability is the new stability. The aim for many investors, as with businesses, is now simply to survive. It seems to me that the investments which will do best will be the big companies which have safe, well covered dividends. By the start of 2009 many large companies were paying relatively huge, safe dividends and it wasn't difficult to put together a portfolio of shares paying sustainable dividends much greater than the return on gilts or bank deposits. Continue buying shares in companies which have a global income (in currencies other than sterling).

Nineteenth, the most important skill for any investor is, in my view, the ability to differentiate between relevant and irrelevant news. To be successful it is essential to be able to dismiss investment or geopolitical `noise' and to focus on crucial bits and pieces of information. It is, of course, also essential to be able to interpret the information you have selected and to use the information to help you draw conclusions.

Twentieth, if you spot a investment bandwagon you've missed it. If other people are climbing on then you should be climbing off.

Twenty first, markets are neither efficient nor logical. There was never much logic to the financial markets. Today, there is none whatsoever. Markets have always been influenced by two emotions: fear and greed. This has never been the case more than it is now. Stock markets are always assumed to be efficient. And they are also assumed to be ahead of the game. But they are neither. Stock markets are ruled by emotions.

Twenty second, back your own judgement. No one knows better than you do what is happening to the economy or the nation or the world. Mix a little common sense (that rarest of all commodities) in with your judgement and the chances are that your guesses will be better educated, and more accurate, than anyone else's.

Twenty third, banks are going to be weak for years. The new version of Lloyds Bank will probably be safe. (Surely, the Government won't dare let it go bust?) But it's probably wise to avoid leaving too much money on deposit in any bank. It seems to me that buying shares in large, well funded companies is now safer than leaving money in the bank. And the dividends paid by large companies (such as the big oil companies) are considerably greater than the interest paid on deposit accounts.

Twenty fourth, residential property prices are going to keep falling. Eventually, there will come a time when retail and commercial property will be a good investment. But that point won't come for a few years. When the rental income on property reaches 10-15% after tax, all expenses and inflation then good, well-positioned, property will be worth buying. As long as it can be bought with cash.

Twenty fifth, in the coming years investment advice will become increasingly worthless. If you read all the advice provided by investment professionals you will end up exceedingly confused. They contradict one another all the time.

If you were to ask 100 doctors how to treat appendicitis there would be differences but there would be significant similarities too. If you were to ask 100 lawyers a specific legal question you would get largely similar replies. There would be variations but not massive, diametrically opposed viewpoints.

The existence of these huge variations among investment professionals shows that investing is not a science. Read as much as you can, and keep your wits about you, and you can beat the professionals. But be aware that too much information can ruin your life and damage your prowess as an investor.

I suspect (but cannot prove) that investors who ignore the majority of financial news do better than those who read everything they can find about their investments. Much information (and most comment) is meaningless at best and misleading at worst. Nor do I recommend the guidance offered by those describing themselves as investment advisers or mortgage brokers. It is possible to obtain an investment management diploma after just five days of study (though there are comprehensive courses which require seven days of study). It takes longer than that to become a `trained' beautician.

How often should you check your investments? Once a week is good. If you use the internet to keep an eye on your investments on a daily basis you will soon be checking share prices every hour. And, apart from destroying your life, this will almost certainly result in over-trading. And over-trading will damage your results.

I had a BlackBerry device once. I thought it would be a good idea to be able to keep up with investment news and share prices. I signed up to receive one or two daily e-mails and to receive details of breaking news. Within a month or so the little red light on the BlackBerry was blinking nearly all the time. I was overwhelmed with news about commodities, mines, currencies and stock markets. Every time a politician breathed out I heard about it. I was constantly worrying about the significance of the latest bits and pieces of news. Would a flooded mine in Canada affect the price of mines in South Africa? What effect would a leadership contest in Australia have upon my investments? In the end the BlackBerry stopped working (actually it started hiding my e-mails so perhaps even the device itself was overwhelmed). At first I tried to mend it. I spent hours talking to people who (as is increasingly the way these days) promised much but delivered nothing. I tried to buy a replacement but found that my complete lack of a credit rating made this a tricky operation. And then, without a

BlackBerry I rediscovered my life. I felt much better within days.

As a source of reliable, accurate information the internet is a joke; inaccurate, prejudiced, bigoted, controlled by commercial interests and mad bloggers busy grinding axes. Newspaper and magazine articles on money tend to be driven by the advertisements around them. If the marketing experts for banks and investment houses which are selling unit trusts believe that they can sell new funds offering shares investing in China then that's what the advertisements will be about. And that's what the features will be about too. The chances of you finding balanced, general, basic advice on money in a newspaper or magazine are approximately nil. It scares me half to death to know that an increasing number of schoolteachers are training their students to rely on the internet as a research tool.

There are just two reasons for reading the self-styled financial experts who write in newspapers and magazines.

One is for amusement. One week they're advocating putting all your money into uranium mining stocks. Then, the following week they've taken a sudden fancy to Japanese equities. The next week they recommend staying in cash. Then it's property. The week after that it's gold. No doubt about it. Gold. Then it's high yield FTSE 100 shares. Then it's Brazil. And then it's farmland in Argentina. They're always full of enthusiasm for whatever has taken their fancy that week. They always recommend that you put everything you can find into that week's selection and they have all the statistics and quotes to support the week's enthusiastic offering. No matter that the dealing costs would destroy any portfolio within a year.

The other reason for reading what the journalists are recommending is so that you can keep up with what other investors are reading. If your aim is to try and understand why markets move the way they do then, and to try to be aware which way the mass of investors are likely to move next, you need to know what the so-called experts are recommending. As with analysts you could probably do quite well selling when they sell buy and buying when they say sell - though you would have to pick and choose your moments if you didn't want the costs to decimate your portfolio.

The bottom line is that large parts of the media have a negative correlation with reality.

Financial magazines are often full of systems for picking shares. Most of these systems rely on using tricks which are based on what has happened in the past. So, you might be told to buy shares which have done really badly in the last twelve months. This share picking ideas do work for a while. Sadly, however, what has happened in the past tells you very little about what will happen in the future and things tend to change rather quickly. In particular, investors themselves change the rules. If investors all buy shares which did badly in the previous twelve months then the prices of those shares will go up far too high. Markets evolve and so no fixed strategy or formula will succeed for long. From time to time (every day, it sometimes seems) a professional investor or newsletter writer will come up with a fool-proof way to beat the market. All you have to do is pick a portfolio shares that satisfy certain very specific criteria. Surprisingly, the professional investor or newsletter writer will often be prepared to let you share their method if you give them a chunk of your money (either to invest or as a subscription to their newsletter). Such schemes usually have a short life. Even if the scheme does give investors an advantage the advantage will invariably disappear when too many investors use it.

And by the time the scheme is described in newspapers and magazines it will usually be well past its sell by date. But not to worry; the next issue of the newspaper or magazine will contain exclusive details of yet another foolproof investing technique.

I no longer believe anything I read in the financial press. Half of it is probably reliable. Half of it is certainly misleading. When billionaires give me their unsolicited advice I feel (fairly but not reliably) safe in assuming that they are doing so because they want me (and others) to buy what they are selling or to sell what they are buying.

Since it is impossible for me to tell which half of the information is reliable and which half is misleading I must assume that it is all rubbish.

Before deciding how to invest, or what is going to happen, I try to put myself in the politicians' places. And then I try to decide what they will do to benefit themselves.

I always assume the government will do the worst for the economy, because that is nearly always the best for the politicians. Most commentators are innocent enough to believe that politicians will keep doing the right thing. But they won't. I always assume they will do the bad thing, the wrong thing.

Twenty sixth, although there are many people (including a good number of professional investment advisers) who believe it to be true, I believe it is a nonsense that shares are a good long term investment in real, inflated adjusted terms. British equity prices reached peaks in 1906, 1936, 1968 and 1999 but between those years there were some very long, deep troughs. (American shares followed a similar pattern. Maybe each generation discovers an enthusiasm for shares and then loses it as they get older and more experienced.) I have believed for several years that it is, I fear, going to be a decade or more before the stock market makes a real recovery. It may be longer than that. We are in a big bear market. And it is going to last. And last. And last. The UK is now the weakest industrialised nation on earth.

In the spring of 2010 the FTSE 100 was 5700. That's almost exactly what it was when Labour got to power in 1997. Thirteen wasted years without growth or profit. (During that time the chief executives of large companies had annual pay rises that work out at around 9%. The hired hands were making 9% every year while their company owners were losing money.) Long term investors who put their money into a big index fund would, in ten years, have turned £100 into £77, despite a massive rise in 2009.

The bear market began in 2000, or even in 1997. The rises since then have been bear market rallies. We could be in a secular bear market which started in 1997 and may well last until 2017. On polling day in 1997 the FTSE closed at 4445.01. What is it today? If it is lower then share investors have, after over a decade of a Labour Government, lost money on their investments.

By the end of 2008 equity investors who had been in the market for 40 years had made nothing in real terms (though they had their dividends the value of these had been eaten up by inflation). In 1974, equities were trading at around a third of their value at the end of the 19th century. Investors who bought shares in Japanese companies in 1989 now have investments worth 25% of what they paid. The `noughties' produced average real negative returns (even if dividend income is included) for both British and American share investors.

All this is worrying stuff. And I suspect that investors in equity markets are about to experience another decade of disappointment.

However, the enthusiasm of investors for equities (fuelled to a certain extent by low interest rates) has pushed share prices back from the bottom they explored when the financial crash first began to cause problems and banks first started to go bust. Many investors have put their money into unit trust funds, into index linked funds (designed to match the movements of the market) and into exchange traded funds.

The problem is that I really don't think that equities have much of a big future for the general investor. There are several reasons for my pessimism. First, the number of people now reaching retirement is rising in relation to the number of people who have money to invest. People approaching retirement are selling their shares and either taking their money out of the market or putting it into cash or gilts or bonds for safety. (Sadly, putting money into gilts or bonds for safety is an oxymoronic activity. I suspect this may not be wise since I have a strong suspicion that government gilt yields are likely to rise steadily through the next decade (as interest rates go up). If this happens then investing in gilts (other than index linked, inflation `proofed' gilts) will be a good way to get rid of capital.) The relatively few young people who have assets rather than debts have probably been put off the equity markets by what they've seen happen during the last decade or so. In addition, most young people with active brain tissue have lost faith in pension funds - which somehow manage to be both overregulated and to charge absurdly high fees. And, remember, most people under 35 have very little money to invest in equities. Most will have mortgages, student loans and credit card debts to worry about. They will not be inheriting vast sums from their parents because their parents' money will have gone on nursing home fees. Future generations will have far less money to save and so there is going to be far less money available for investment and for buying shares and gilts. All this means that share prices aren't going to go up much and that the government, just when it has a huge deficit, is going to have difficulty selling gilts.

There's another problem too. Thanks to new legislation (if you can't guess where it's coming from then you haven't been paying attention) pension funds are being forced to move away from risky investments (and equities still count as risky) and to put prospective pensioners' money into bonds and bond funds. In the UK pension funds and life assurers have run down their share of the UK equity market to a tad over 25%. Sovereign funds, set up by other nations, such as China, are I fear not going to be excited by the prospects of investing in shares in British companies (they are likely to lose money as sterling continues to decline).

The bottom line is that I suspect that share valuations are likely to be extremely volatile in the years ahead. Political factors, the oil price and currency swings are all going to have a dramatic effect on prices. The end result is probably going to be that most share valuations will, when inflation is taken into account, be lower in 2020 than they are now.

There will, of course, be some exceptions.

I remain enthusiastic about oil companies, for example. I suspect that as the oil price rises so there will be money to be made out of investing in oil exploration companies (though the dangers of the sort of problems experienced by BP in 2010 have to be borne in mind).

The market as a whole is going nowhere for a while. Up and down and sideways for a decade or two. Instability is the new stability. The aim for many investors, as with businesses, is now simply to survive. It seems to me that the investments which will do best will be the big companies which have safe, well covered dividends. By the start of 2009 many large companies were paying relatively huge, safe dividends and it wasn't difficult to put together a portfolio of shares paying sustainable dividends much greater than the return on gilts or bank deposits. Continue buying shares in companies which have a global income (in currencies other than sterling).

It is possible to purchase equities which produce a fairly safe and solid dividend of around 6% before tax. Even with rising interest rates that may be a reward worth grasping and holding onto.

The finance industry will, of course, continue to produce an almost endless series of original ways to invest. Their retrospective computer models will show that their new schemes cannot to lose.

I won't be investing in any of them. Financial derivatives were never a good idea. If I am ever tempted to invest in any of them I burn a ten pound note. I find that this brings me to my senses pretty quickly. It is often said that stock markets represent everything, everybody knows, hopes, believes and anticipates. That is right. But the trouble is that the markets never get the balance right. And it is only the balance that really matters. It is the individuals who can judge the balance who can beat the market.

The economy is going to struggle for the next decade. This is particularly true for the UK which will, thanks to Gordon Brown, be a disaster area for generations to come. The rise and rise of the internet will continue to do serious damage to a whole range of industries. I can't see stock markets being much higher in 2020 than they are in 2010, though there will doubtless be many ups and downs. Investing in broadly based unit trusts, index linked funds and exchange traded funds which track the markets will, I suspect, be a disappointing business. Residential property is going to be a disastrous investment for some years to come and the crash which the Labour Party worked hard to delay prior to the 2010 election will eventually wreck many retirement plans. Commercial property will be unexciting too with retail property doing worst as the internet and the high oil price continue to change the way people shop, as rising unemployment and improving saving rates mean that people have less money to spend on non essentials. I believe that all commodities are getting scarcer and all fiat currencies are vulnerable. Bearing in mind that I see little point in working hard to make dozens of small investment decisions I must prefer to make one or two macroeconomic decisions to make large, general investment allocations accordingly. I am, therefore, investing in a few specific areas:

a) large, international companies which make their money around the world and which pay large and reliable dividends. Big oil companies BP and Shell are both paying around 6% in dividends and I can see no reason why they shouldn't continue to do so. If inflation takes off, and sterling dives, then oil companies should do well.

b) large, international mining companies which dig metals out of the ground.

b) small companies which are exploring for oil

c) gold and silver. But if you allow a bank to look after your gold or silver coins or bars for you beware! One of the world's most reputable banks, Morgan Stanley, was sued for charging customers for the storage of gold. Customers complained that the bank didn't actually hold any of the gold it said it was keeping. The bank paid a fairly huge sum in compensation but the case never got to court.)

d) small companies which are mining for gold

e) emerging markets. Countries which were struggling just a few years ago now far more money than the UK. India and Brazil, for example, have hundreds of billions of dollar reserves.

f) food and water companies. The market for cars, aeroplanes and television sets may fall or rise. The market for food and water will rise.

g) invest in the two strongest nations in terms of low public debt and lots of resource wealth - Canada and Australia. Oh, if only we had kept the Commonwealth...

h) index linked gilts which are inflation protected bonds. The only fear about these is that the government has acquired a nasty habit of making retrospective changes to the tax rules. So if hyperinflation does develop will the government stick by its promise to cover the inflation? or would it take away the protection by changing the rules and altering the terms of the coupon (the interest paid) and the redemption payments. This is now a serious problem.

There are two major truths we should all know. The first is that it is not true that markets are efficient. They are not. The second basic rule is that the government (and all its departments) will always be inefficient and will always do the wrong thing; whenever there is a choice they will make the one which serves them best.

Don't forget: the government will always fuck up. You can rely on it.

Chance of the majority of investors making money (after inflation) between 2010 and 2020: 20%.

95. We'll All Be Drug Addicts (when they put more drugs in the drinking water)

It is nearly 40 years since I first pointed out that our drinking water is contaminated with the residues of prescription drugs. Tranquillisers, anti-depressants, contraceptive pills and many other drugs aren't entirely metabolised in the human body. The residues, excreted by the body, are still active pharmaceutical products. The authorities are well aware of this problem, but they do nothing about it. They do nothing because no one yet knows how to remove pharmaceutical residues from drinking water. You can't filter out these chemicals in the same way that you can filter out spiders, mice and dead dogs.

Indeed, rather than make an effort to remove drugs from our drinking water, the authorities have for years been enthusiastically adding drugs to drinking water.

The one drug that is commonly added is fluoride. The theory is that by adding fluoride to drinking water, teeth will become stronger and will require less repair work. The aim is to cut the cost of providing dental care for citizens. The potential side effects (which I have outlined in books such as Food for Thought and Superbody) are ignored and dismissed as irrelevant though in fact, of course, they should not be ignored and are certainly not irrelevant. The infringement of human rights (by forcing citizens to accept potentially hazardous drug therapy they might not want) is considered irrelevant and, as the economic situation continues to worsen, the enthusiasm for fluoridation will rise. The fact that citizens could be taught to protect their own teeth by brushing regularly, by avoiding too many sugary foods and by using a fluoride toothpaste is ignored.

The enthusiasm of politicians for adding fluoride to drinking water (and therefore saving money on providing dental care) is matched only by the enthusiasm of a small group of scientists for adding other chemicals. The two most popular suggestions are tranquillisers and oral contraceptives. The theory is that a tranquillised population will cause far less trouble than an untranquillised one, while putting oral contraceptives in the water will prevent pregnancies and keep rampant males under control.

Do not laugh at these seemingly absurd proposals. The people who made them are deadly serious.

And if they can persuade politicians that putting fluoride into the water is a safe and proper thing to do, they can certainly persuade them that adding tranquillisers and contraceptives is a similarly wise choice.

Chances of more drugs being put into our drinking water: 80%.

96. The Incidence Of Disability Will Rise (and rise so much that the word will become meaningless).

According to pressure groups there are now 11.5 million disabled people in the UK. How come? Well, officially a woman with a heavy shopping bag counts as disabled because she might have difficulty moving about. And people with mild dyslexia are also officially disabled.

This is madness.

The sanctimonious, politically correct lunatics who think they are campaigning on behalf of the disabled are, in reality, making life worse for them. (Though they may, of course, be making life better for themselves. The greater the number of disabled people there are the more money the lunatics can claim for looking after them and campaigning on their behalf.)

I know of shops and post offices which have been closed because of `limited access'. What this means that since there is a high step that cannot be removed but which is an obstacle to people in wheel chairs then no one can use the shop and it must be closed. This is EU inspired spite.

By wilfully exaggerating the number of disabled people in the country these lunatics are demeaning the genuinely disabled and weakening people who could quite easily live perfectly normal lives. What, pray, is the point of deliberately encouraging people to feel dependent and disabled when they aren't?

According to official figures 1 in 5 Britons are now officially disabled. This is bad for the healthy (encouraging many to feel disabled when they really aren't) and bad for the genuinely disabled too.

The only people who benefit are those running charities and quangos representing the quasi-disabled and those who want to use their quasi-disablement as an excuse to claim benefits and avoid work.

And it's going to get worse.

Chances of disability becoming more common: 100%.

97. The Incidence Of Cancer Will Continue To Rise

If you ask 1,000 doctors to name the commonest cause of cancer in Britain I doubt if more than a handful would know the right answer. It is, therefore, hardly surprising that the incidence of cancer is rising rapidly and is going to continue to rise.   The main cause of cancer in Britain today is not the smoking of cigarettes but the eating of meat. I have repeatedly published evidence proving conclusively that meat is a major cause of cancer. (There is, for example, extensive, detailed evidence proving the link between meat and cancer in my book `Food for Thought'. The indisputable scientific evidence linking meat and cancer is just as good as the evidence linking cigarettes and cancer.) But the evidence has been successfully suppressed for fear of upsetting the meat industry. When I published information on the dangers of eating meat in newspaper articles and in books such Power Over Cancer and Food for Thought I was reprimanded by the Press Complaints Commission and the equally absurd Advertising Standards Authority. My only crime? Telling the truth. Ads for Food for thought have been banned by almost all British publications. (The editor of Private Eye banned an ad for the book because it might upset people.) Most chefs, dieticians, nutritionists know nothing about food. That wouldn't matter if they kept their thoughts to themselves, and didn't offer food or advice to other people, but chefs who appear on television frequently promote meat eating and sometimes sneer at vegetarianism. The evidence linking meat to cancer is so solid that anyone who recommends the cooking and eating of meat (or who cooks and provides meat dishes) should be charged with attempted murder. Hospitals which serve meat to patients are presumably trying to kill them off.

Political decision makers and media brouhaha managers don't take much notice of scientific evidence these days. Their campaigns and preachings, warnings and regulations, are a result of commercial and political expediency rather than a consequence of scientific study or any appraisal of the available evidence. And so, we have politicians and journalists making a great deal of noise about issues that don't real matter and exaggerating issues which are of political, rather than real, significance, and ignoring or distorting the evidence relating to issues which are of tremendous importance to us all. So, politicians talk endlessly about global warming (a non existent problem), but totally ignore the real and proven link between meat eating and cancer. It is worth noting, however, that one big insurance company has just started offering a 6% discount on life insurance for vegetarians. The principle clearly being that vegetarians live longer and are less likely to die early. I think its probably fair to say that insurance companies don't offer discounts without actuarial evidence to back up their judgement.

At one point the Government planned to publish evidence showing the danger. But, they changed their minds when pressured by the meat industry. Advertisements for my books about meat have been widely banned. And, meanwhile, the incidence of cancers involving organs such as the breast, prostate and bowel will continue to grow. Today, the government actually and actively promotes meat eating. The state encourages meat eating because it sustains a huge tax paying industry. The fact that eating meat causes cancer is of little or no concern to the state, as long as the cancers it causes largely kill people quickly and affect the elderly more than the young. (It isn't only the British government which suppresses the truth about cancer. The diagnosis of cancer of lung was officially forbidden in France for years because the Government held the monopoly on the selling of tobacco.) Cancer charities do and say nothing because they are frightened of upsetting the government and the food industry.

Why does meat cause so much cancer these days? Simple. The meat sold today is very fatty and it is full of carcinogens because farmers who sell fatty animals get more money for them and because farmers use carcinogenic chemicals on their farms.

At some point in the next decade the link between meat and cancer will, at last, be officially acknowledged.

The industry will of course continue to fight the truth - just as the tobacco industry fought the truth about the link between tobacco and cancer - and will still be fighting the truth in 2020. It will hire doctors, scientists and others to lie on its behalf.

Chances of the incidence of cancer continuing to rise: 100%.

98. The Incidence Of Bankruptcy Will Soar

Vast numbers of small companies will go bankrupt because of payments being made late by big companies. This is now one of the most serious problems, with big companies taking more than six months to pay their bills. Sadly, small companies get threatened and taken to court or made bankrupt if they go over 30 days. The biggest culprit for late paying is the government and a large number of official departments are regularly very late paying their bills.

The number of companies going bankrupt is increasing dramatically, many being pushed over the edge by the tax authorities who seem to delight in forcing people and companies into bankruptcy. Naturally, this destroys everyone's chances of getting any money but in these circumstances the tax people behave a bit like Mafia protection money gangsters who haven't been paid. Burning the place down doesn't bring in any money but it does help encourage the others.

So, we have the absurd situation where the government is almost deliberately pushing companies into bankruptcy. One department doesn't pay its bills on time and then another department (Her Majesty's Revenue and Customs) takes the company to court and forces it into bankruptcy. Utter madness.

There are now so many bankruptcies in Britain that the UK has become the bankruptcy centre of Europe. People are flooding into the country to declare themselves bankrupt. In Germany it can take nine years to be discharged from bankruptcy. In Britain, debts can be written off for a year. The immigrants go bankrupt and return home a year later debt free.

Moreover, new laws make it very easy these days for companies who are in financial trouble to use a clever form of administration which enables them to emerge from bankruptcy without any debts but with all the assets they had in the first place.

Britain may no longer have a manufacturing industry and its banks and bankers may be regarded with a mixture of contempt and loathing. But we're leading the world in bankruptcy. It is, I suspect, something at which we are going to keep getting better and better.

The chances of bankruptcy becoming commoner are 100%.

99. Tomorrow's Generation Will Have Little Imagination (as a result, imagination is going to be at a premium)

Modern children are growing up with stunted imaginations. They do not play imaginative games in the way that children used to play games a generation or two ago. Today's children rely entirely on electrically operated gadgets and devices for their entertainment and for the provision of fantasies and daydreams. The television, still a mainstay, has been joined by the computer, the mobile telephone and a vast array of hardware which operates games software.

None of this stuff requires much in the way of imagination. (And, from what I have seen of it, much of the software that is on sale also shows a distinct lack of imagination. In other words the people creating the software aren't much more imaginative than the people using it.)

Indeed, today's generation are so unimaginative that the manufacturers of cuddly toys (teddy bears and so on) sell their products already named. The bears actually have a name on a tag so that the child doesn't have to try and think of a name for its toy.

What next? It would not surprise me in the slightest to learn that young mothers were taking their babies home from hospital with names given to them by baby-naming bureaucrats using a computer operated name selecting programme.

Tomorrow's generation of children will have even less imagination than today's generation. Anyone who does have an imagination, and who can use it to create stories and scenarios, will find themselves in huge demand - though the theft of copyright will make it increasingly hard to make a living out of creative activities.

Chances of the next generation having powerful imaginations: 20%.

100. Big Government Will Get Ever Bigger

Our governments are getting bigger.

Since 1980 various British governments have created 25 new separate ministerial departments. This is far greater than any other country. In America, for example, only the departments sof Homeland Security and Veteran Affairs have been created.

And our governments have been extremely adept at redesigning its departments - invariably in such a way to ensure that there are more ministerial jobs available.

In Britain, the Department of Trade and Industry became the Department for Business, Enterprise and Regulatory Reform and then became the Department for Business, Innovation and Skills.

Every time a department changes its title staff are redeployed, paid off, given huge sums of money in redundancy payments and then promptly rehired - often at higher salaries so that they `harmonise' with their new colleagues. Money is wasted on stationery, signs and new offices. New logos are created (often at absurd expense) and new nameplates designed and manufactured.

When Gordon Brown became Prime Minister in 2007 he authorised the reorganisation of 10 government departments - at vast expense to the taxpayer.

None of this is going to change.

Our politicians are as much in love with important sounding titles, chauffeur driven ministerial cars and enhanced pension rights as they are with clean moats and new duck houses.

Our governments may now have very little to do (all the laws are created by bureaucrats in Brussels) so they will spend their days making themselves bigger and more expensive.

Until the EU gets rid of the House of Commons (and its trappings) this will not change.

Chances of our governments getting bigger (and more expensive): 100%.

101. More People Will Carry Guns (and use them)

The UK is the 2nd biggest arms dealer in the world. In a way this is not surprising since the British taxpayer subsidises the arms industry by around £900 million a year. The government doesn't like subsidising trains but it will happily use our money to subsidise the production of landmines designed to blow the legs off small children. Yippee. Makes you glad you pay your taxes doesn't it?

We sell arms to everyone. During the illegal invasion of Iraq (sorry, I just can't help mentioning the illegality) our troops were shot at by armies who were using weapons and ammunition we'd sold. Neat, eh.

Around 60% of the small arms which are manufactured end up in the hands of criminal gangs, rebel groups and civilians. Arms dealers, many of whom are British, don't much care who buys the stuff they sell as long as have the money. And since it's the gangs and the terrorists who have the most money they're the ones who get the ordnance.

Britain never used to have much of a gun culture. British crooks tended to use socks full of wet sand and bits of lead piping. Only the most villainous used sawn off shotguns.

But multiculturalism has changed all that and today if you live in london, Manchester or Nottingham you probably live no more than half a mile from the scene of a gun crime.

The arms industry will continue to get government support. And multiculturalism will continue to erode traditional British values and to replace them with new ones (usually involving knives and guns).

So, it doesn't take much intelligence to forecast a future in which gun crime continues to rise.

Naturally, the rise in the incidence of gun crime will give the police an excuse to start carrying guns more often. And using them more often too.

Chances of there being more guns in Britain by 2020: 70%.

Although we contribute billions every year to the European Union we cannot rely on being helped by the EU if (or should that be `when') our nation's financial state becomes critical. At some point in the next few years the International Monetary Fund (I.M.F.) will be called in to help sort out Britain's financial mess.

We are not members of the euro and so the EU will turn its back on us and force us to seek help from the International Monetary Fund.

If the IMF is called in the experience will not be a pleasant one. Prior to Greece asking for help in April 2010, Britain was the last country to call in the IMF, back in the 1970s, when a previous Labour Government destroyed the economy.

Although it sounds `international', the IMF is controlled by the Americans. And the Americans always put American interests first, second and third. The so called special relationship that British ministers think they have with American presidents will turn out to be worthless.

The IMF's charter requires an 85% majority vote for anything to happen. That seems fair enough until you realise that the USA has 17% of the votes. This means, of course, that nothing can be decided by the IMF unless it suits the Americans - undoubtedly the meanest nation in the world. (The Americans control the World Bank too.)

Once it is asked for help the IMF invariably imposes harsh conditions. These tend to make things worse. Most countries which have ever had any contact with the IMF would rather deal with the Mafia.

The IMF won't allow Britain to sort its problems out over time. It will demand instant action. The IMF's primary concern will be the American banks with interests involving Britain. The result will be massive cuts in public spending (including huge cuts in the money being spent on civil servants salaries, bonuses and pensions). In March 2010 the IMF suggested that central banks (including the Bank of England) could target an inflation rate of 4 per cent rather than 2 per cent. This tells us what the IMF will do if it takes over Britain. It will get rid of the debts through inflation. And managed inflation invariably leads to hyperinflation. There will be wage cuts of 10-15% in the public sector and hundreds of thousands of public sector jobs will be lost. Any public employee under the age of 40 who is relying on their public sector pension should think again. The government may have promised them a fat pension but governments do break promises.

There will, inevitably, be much rioting and many strikes as the head-in-the-sand unions encourage people not to accept cuts in their wages, expenses, bonuses or standard of living. The rioting and the strikes will make things worse.

Chances of Britain needing to call in the IMF: 70%.

103. Juries Will More Or Less Disappear

The EU doesn't much like juries. They are expensive, time consuming and terribly independent. They are sometimes so bloody minded that they will find a defendant not guilty when the police think he is guilty.

Both main political parties have proposed encouraging magistrates (unpaid, volunteer judges who are largely pompous, self-important prigs - an up market variety of the sort of people who volunteer to work as `special policemen' because they like being able to boss people around and wear a uniform) to take on more responsibility and try more crimes.

Now, where do they use magistrates and give them more power. Ah yes, France.

Magistrates courts already do most of the work in the British judicial system. If you go to court you have about a 14 to 1 chance of being sentenced by a magistrate. No judge. And certainly no jury. Just a bloody estate agent/window cleaner/doctor's wife with an overblown sense of his/her self importance.

When Labour got into power they obediently and repeatedly tried to get rid of juries altogether. And they've done their masters well. The country dispenses with juries when the case is very complex. (Guess who decides it is too complicated for a jury to understand). And juries are done away with if there si a fear of jury nobbling. (Guess who decides there is a danger of jury nobbling.)

By around 2015 you will, if you find yourself in court, have a 20 to 1 chance of having your fate being decided by a lone magistrate.

By 2020 juries will be as rare as honest politicians.

Chances of juries disappearing (or becoming rare) by 2020: 70%.

104. The NHS Will Continue To Deteriorate

The NHS will continue to deteriorate; infections will become commoner and more and more people will be killed by iatrogenesis because the service provided by the NHS will get worse. Despite the deterioration in the quality of service provided the NHS will introduce charges for patients in England.

All professionals now work under the supervision and control of lawyers, regulators, administrators and lobbyists. For every worker there are a host of parasites. Nowhere is this more apparent than in the NHS where there are more administrators than beds or nurses. Moreover, Gordon Brown politicised health care with pointless targets which endangered millions of patients.

No other country in the world has ever bothered to try and copy the British health care system. There are good reasons for that. The NHS costs £1,500 for every man, woman and child in Britain (we could all do a great deal better for ourselves if we had the £1,500 in our pockets and were free to spend it on medical insurance and private health care) and now has a total payroll of 1.5 million of whom less than half have any medical, clinical, nursing qualifications. The NHS is a bureaucratic monster which employs over 1,600,000 people. In the run up to the May 2010 election the government insisted that the country was growing and out of recession because unemployment was falling. Unemployment was falling because the NHS, the most bloated organisation in the world, was hiring people it didn't need as fast as it possibly could. Only two organisations on the planet employ more people: the Chinese People's Liberation Army and the Wal-Mart supermarket chain.

And yet despite its cost the NHS provides appalling health care and very poor value for money. For example, taken at random, I see that according to the latest available WHO figures, Singapore spends 3.4% of its GDP on health care (compared to 8.4% in the UK). And yet the infant mortality rate in Singapore is 3 per 1,000 whereas in the UK it is 5 per thousand. And life expectancy at birth is higher in Singapore than in the UK.

The WHO puts the UK in 18th place for health care provision. And that is truly appalling. In December 2009, North Somerset's public health director was quoted as `asking residents to choose wisely when they fall ill, to help the work load on staff'. It's no wonder that many immigrants go home if they fall ill and need medical treatment.

In February 2010 an independent inquiry found that there had been shocking and systematic failures of hospital care at Mid Staffordshire NHS Trust between 2005 and 2008, leaving patients routinely neglected humiliated and in pain. The inquiry was ordered after an investigation suggested that at least 400 people had died due to poor treatment. The investigation documented cases where patients had been left unwashed for up to a month and lacked food, drink and medical treatment. The conclusion was that managers had been `preoccupied with cost-cutting, targets and processes' and had lost sight of their basic responsibilities.

My first thought on reading about this was that Shipman didn't kill as many as 400 patients. But unless it has all happened very quietly none of these managers have been taken to court.

My second thought is that in order for this to have happened an enormous number of patients and relatives and hospital visitors (not to mention staff) must have ignored all these awful things and gone around believing that Mid Staffordshire NHS Trust was doing a wonderful job. It wouldn't surprise me in the slightest to hear that the managers have a thick file of letters from patients and relatives thanking them for the excellent care.

The sad truth is that today many patients spend their hard earned money buying private medical care rather than entrusting themselves to the NHS. Rude, uncaring consultants, often employed as full time NHS staff and frequently operating from the security of NHS premises, charge £400 to £600 an hour for a brusque and snarly service.

There will be NHS cut backs. They will affect the most vulnerable and least vocal. Funding will be cut from services for the mentally ill and the elderly. Areas which are surely less deserving will be protected through political correctness. For example, the number of sex change operations performed on the NHS has tripled in the last eight years. Each one costs around £10,000 and between the year 2000 and the end of 2009, 853 men and 12 women were given free operations. I have the greatest sympathy with and for people who genuinely believe that they were born the wrong sex. But although the Appeal Court decided some years ago that being born in the wrong sort of body is a legitimate illness I find it difficult to believe that transsexual operations should take precedence over operations being done to save lives from cancerous growths. And, as long as there are people dying from untreated cancer (which there are), that is exactly what is happening.

After due reflection (and having worked in it for a little more than a decade) I have decided that the NHS was really stupid idea. Bevan, the founding idiot, believed that if the state gave the people free health care everyone would be well all the time. It was one of the most stupid ideas of all time. He might as well have argued that it is possible to conquer poverty by giving everyone a sack of money.

The quality of care provided by the NHS has been deteriorating for years. And the quality of care will continue to deteriorate.

Chances of NHS care continuing to deteriorate: 100%.

105. The Number Of Regulations Will Soar (but will do nothing to protect the innocent)

More regulations will do nothing positive but will make life increasingly difficult for the small investor, the self employed, and the small business owner.

As investors who have lost money in such apparently `secure' investments as Bradford and Bingley, Northern Rock, zero dividend preference shares, Equitable Life and Railtrack will confirm, financial regulators have consistently failed small investors and pensioners (the very people they are paid to protect and who, indeed, pay them their huge salaries and thoroughly undeserved bonuses).

One of the reasons for the crisis of 2007-9 was the failure of the regulators to do their jobs properly (a failure for which they were rewarded with massive bonuses). The government's solution to this has not been to punish the incompetent regulators (firing a few zillion of them would have been a good start and might have encouraged the remaining ones to pull their fingers out and start thinking) but to announce that we need more regulations and more regulators.

Who else but politicians would have the audacity to announce that the solution to a huge problem is to increase the size of the problem? It would be like dealing with overcrowded roads (and (alleged) climate change caused by too much traffic) by providing car buyers with a cash incentive to buy another car. Oh, whoops, they did that too, didn't they.

The official thinking seems to be that regulations are worse than useless and the regulators are crap but that everything will be fine if we have more crappy regulators and let them carry on being crap. It tires me out just to think of it.

What's worse is that most of the regulations which are brought in seem designed to stop little old ladies taking money out of their accounts and to protect the bastards who have been stealing and cheating and generally losing other peoples' money by the skip-full. In the spring of 2010 Gordon Brown showed that he alone in Europe wanted to protect the interests of hedge funds and private equity groups. It was embarrassing and humiliating. The Germans and the French and quite probably the Latvians were desperate to see these blood sucking demons controlled by at least a few rules and regulations. Not Gordon. He fought for the hedge funds and the private equity groups. It was easy to see which side our then Prime Minister was on. This was, after all, the same Gordon who in 2008 invited the world's worst banker and fellow Scot Sir Fred Goodwin to enjoy drinkies and haggis at taxpayers' expense at Chequers, the Prime Minister's country residence.

When one looks at things generally, it is impossible to escape the conclusion that the main reason for most regulatory activity these days is to delay things, to tie entrepreneurs down (or up) in bureaucracy, so that they spend huge amounts of their time answering and arguing about small and insignificant issues. I'm serious. One of the UK's largest homebuilders recently admitted that it now spends more money on planning and planning related fees than it does on bricks. The EU, which is like all fascist states a merger of bureaucracy with big business, hates independent people and so does whatever it can to oppress and suppress.

Many EU regulations have been designed by big companies to stop small companies and individuals succeeding. For example, the cost of filing a patent in the UK and across the rest of Europe can now cost well in excess of £100,000. To the costs of establishing whether or not a product or process is patentable have to be added translation costs and, inevitably, registration fees. An inventor who wants to protect himself in America, or the rest of the world, has to find even more money. Naturally, what this means in practice is that individual inventors (men in garden sheds) are being forced out of business. And yet many of the greatest inventions have been the work of individual inventors, working by themselves or in tiny companies. The huge conglomerates have deliberately persuaded the regulators to make it difficult (and expensive) to patent a new invention because this suits them and protects them from the danger of one of their products being replaced by a new invention by a solitary inventor. As ever the regulators are on the side of big industry. It's another example of practical fascism: Mussolini's dream union of government, industry and bureaucracy.

There are now so many regulations governing companies that in order to continue to make profits companies need to cut quality. That's one of the reasons why I was able, some years ago, to forecast that everything is going to get worse.

Governments don't like the self employed. They consider them to be a messy, nuisance and something of a threat. They want to get rid of them with a mixture of official harassment and red tape. Endless regulations, vast varieties of rules, increasingly complex tax rules all make being self employed virtually unbearable. Governments will, therefore, continue to regulate hard-working, ordinary folk instead of the people who really need regulating. Bankers will survive unscathed (and well rewarded) while little old ladies find that without a passport and a driving licence they can't access their own money and entrepreneurs are strangled to death by pointless regulations applied with the full majesty of the law.

Chances of our lives being blighted by more regulations: 100%.

106. The Enduring And Expanding Myth of Mental Illness Will Endure And Continue To Expand

Back in the 1970s I helped introduced the concept of `stress' to the general public in a book which was called `Stress Control'. I argued that stress was, in whole or in part, responsible for 90% of all modern disease. And then a few years ago I wrote a book called `Toxic Stress' in which I argued that we now live in a world in which much of the stress which harms out bodies and minds is beyond our control. I have long believed that stress is an underestimated cause of physical and mental illness. I have also long believed that the effects of stress depend upon two things: the stress itself and the way we react to it. The human's response to stress is crucial and is, of course, the reason why some people fall ill when exposed to small amounts of stress while others seem able to cope with unending amounts of stress. (This may sound very obvious now but when I first suggested this in the 1970s I was attacked viciously by members of the medical establishment who laughed at the idea that stress could be responsible for illness.)

We can, of course, control some of the things that happen to us. We can avoid people who annoy us. We can resign from jobs which we find exhausting or too difficult.

But we live in a world where we are surrounded by stress. It comes at us from all sorts of directions. I called this unavoidable stress `toxic stress'.

After years of studying the effects of stress on the human body and mind I am now convinced that all mental illness that isn't caused by mal-development or physical damage (a bleed, a clot, an injury, a tumour etc) is caused by stress; all mental illness is a response to stress.

I repeat: all the diseases which we describe as types of mental illness are caused by one of two things: physical damage (as caused by poor development, injury, malformation, and the sort of damage produced by vaccination) and stress. This is true for schizophrenia, autism, compulsive obsessional disease and every other psychiatric disorder you can think of. The more sensitive you are the more vulnerable you are, and the more likely you are to become ill in some way - whether it be depression, a phobia or some other labelled disorder. All mental illness is, therefore, a result of a combination of unavoidable stress and an inborn, irreparable sensitivity. Paranoia is an extension of normality. Schizophrenia is a confusion created by an inability to cope with what is going on without and within. Depression is an inevitable consequence of a susceptible organism struggling to survive in an increasingly toxic world. The people who cope best with our toxic world are the individuals who are least sensitive: the people whom we usually describe as psychopaths. Because they have little or no emotional response to stress they are able to ignore moral and ethical issues and sail painlessly upwards to the very top of our society.

Our foibles and neuroticisms are what make us what we are. To dissect them and remove them (or to attempt to remove them) through pseudoscience such as psychotherapy is as wicked and as clumsy and as destructive, in its slower bloodless way, as psychosurgery. To blunder clumsily, and without direction, through the forest of half hidden fears and hopes which are our psyche leaves wreckage and confusion behind. To attempt to treat them with drugs is as irrational and counter-productive as it would to attempt to treat a malfunctioning motor car by pouring porridge or treacle into the petrol tank. Kurt Vonnegut saw a psychiatrist and was afraid that therapy might make him normal and well adjusted, and that would be the end of his writing. His son, a doctor and a wise man, assured the writer that psychiatrists weren't nearly that good.

Psychiatrists and general practitioners have become increasingly enthusiastic about drug therapy in recent decades. They claim that they can treat a wide range of disorders with psychotropic drugs and so a goodly portion of the nation now regularly gulps down happy tablets. Here's the evidence that psychiatry isn't a science at all. It isn't even an art. Its more of a confidence trick; a collegiate confidence trick with pretensions of grandeur. The simple fact is that there is no evidence that there is any such thing as `chemical imbalance'. Ask any psychiatrist about this and he will agree that I'm right: `chemical imbalance' is a still unproven theory. It's never even been properly tested so how could it ever be proven? So how can psychiatrists and drug companies possibly treat the problems which they claim are caused by `chemical imbalance'?

You may be surprised to learn that psychotropic drugs (widely promoted by doctors who have close links with the companies making them) have no provable, useful effects. They do, on the other hand, have massive and provable serious bad effects (such as death). How are these drugs supposed to work? That's not exactly known. It is, however, known that they flatten the emotions and cause a numbing and dullness of the mind which makes patients taking the drugs less aware of their problems. Patients become so numb that they don't notice the nasty world around them. These drugs don't cure mental symptoms; they simply cover them up. The best patients can hope for is that the side effects aren't too bad.

Psychiatrists do not, and will not, agree with any of this, of course. They have a rapidly growing dictionary of labels which they can apply to their patients. The big problem with their labels (I'm talking about diseases such as ADHD and schizophrenia) is that none of these diseases (none) actually exist. Not in the way that pneumonia and tuberculosis exist, with real signs and symptoms. Psychiatric disorders are created and agreed upon by groups of psychiatrists who meet together and think up new disorders. I'm not making this up. There is proof that diabetes exists. There is scientific evidence to show that heart disease is real. But there is no proof to show that any psychiatric disorders really exist. They are labels which are often created merely to find a market for a newly invented drug. Diagnoses are made, and treatment begun, without any evidence that a patient has anything wrong that can be treated. Drugs are prescribed in the vague hope that they will produce an improvement. Most of the time they produce a change - but the change is more likely to be a deterioration than an improvement.

A vast variety of entirely non existent diseases is becoming forever commoner, taking up a constantly increasing part of a constantly decreasing health service budget. Many psychiatrists claim (apparently meaning it) that we are all mentally ill and that we all need treatment. This is not a social comment so much as an excuse to hand out prescription drugs which do more harm than good. (My own experience of medical colleagues who are psychiatrists is that they are all barking. Psychiatrists are pretty screwed up people; deviants and neurotics. That's why they become psychiatrists. A few of the students I studied medicine with became psychiatrists. There were all barking. All the psychiatrists I knew at medical school were as mad as hatters. By anyone's standards they were potty. They became psychiatrists because they couldn't deal with the logical science of real medicine. They chose, instead, to drift into the world of psychiatry where nothing is written down in black and white, and where judgements are made subjectively rather than objectively.)

Many psychiatrists have such close links with drug companies that they promote drug therapy for all with missionary zeal. Whenever psychiatrists make a suggestion one only has to ask `Who benefits?' to see what is going on. In 2010 a proposal to screen the entire population of Britain for depression was abandoned, possibly because it was realised that a virtually bankrupt nation could not afford to conduct an inefficient but incredibly expensive survey into mental health, possibly because a civil servant somewhere realised that the cost of providing anti-depressants would push the nation further into bankruptcy and possibly because someone realised that the nation was so despairing that a survey would probably show that the whole country was depressed. (That, I am sure, was the plan. Just think of the profits to be made out of prescribing antidepressants for everyone in the country.

Drug companies concentrate on me-too drugs, the money makers, ignoring diseases that affect the third world and ignoring rare diseases. They want long term medications for long term problems and psychiatric drugs are the most profitable. Drug companies love mental illnesses. Patients don't die from them. They live long, healthy lives and so, once diagnosed, can be given drugs for decades. Patients never get better and so the drug therapy is eternal. These disorders are self reinforcing. When told they are `mentally ill' people tend to become anxious, introspective, less interested in the outside world and more self obsessed. Doctors talk about exogenous and endogenous depressions but the only real difference between the two is that in one the cause has been found and in the other it hasn't. The two varieties of depression are basically identical. Both are caused by stress.)

The sad truth is psychiatry is a nonsensical speciality. And all its treatments are unproven rubbish. Aversion therapy, behaviour therapy and hormonal rebalancing are nonsense. Drug therapy is as dangerous, in its way, as psychosurgery. Diagnoses are made without evidence existing. Treatment is prescribed in a purely subjective way. And the diagnostic symptomology is so vague and far reaching that I could, without much difficulty, find some definable mental illness in every person in the UK.

Some people make friends when they travel. I have an acquaintance who can't pop into the local supermarket without finding new chums to add to his formidable Christmas card mailing list. If he goes for a walk in a deserted park he will somehow come back with half a dozen new chums. I'm not good at making friends. Too shy, I suppose. But this means that I am suffering from quite a number of mental disorders. According to the official definitions and symptom lists I reckon I am suffering from autism, ADHD, ODD, obsessive compulsive disorder and several dozen other psychiatric disorders. And I don't mind betting that you are too. Today just about every human emotion or behavioural pattern is a psychiatric disease; an official medical diagnoses. Shyness, homesickness, suspicion, having ups and downs and distractibility are all diseases. Women who have small breasts are suffering from micromastia. There are special drugs for all these disorders. New diseases soon likely to be classified include: `apathy disorder', `compulsive shopping disorder and `internet addiction disorder'. If your doctor says you've got one of these then you're officially mentally ill. Lack of self control and impatience are now officially recognised as diseases. Welcome to the worldwide club. There's a drug with your name on it. And a long-term sick note just a scrawl away.   Many of the new diseases relate to children. There's a good reason for this. Once a child is started on a drug there are likely to be decades of prescribing (and profits) ahead.

How do psychiatrists define new diseases? Easy. A bunch of 27 of them (most of them with links to drug companies) simply decide what is officially a disease. Psychiatrists actually have meetings to vote on whether diseases exist or not. Homosexuality used to be a disease, but political correctness pressures resulted in a vote deciding it was not. That's what psychiatrists call `science'. Thanks to their efforts, everyone can be diagnosed as mentally ill and everyone diagnosed will be treated. Providing drugs for mental illness is an industry worth a third of a trillion dollars a year. It's hardly surprising that new mental diseases come thick and fast. There is no evidence that any of the drugs prescribed can `cure' anything (partly because none of the diseases being treated can be properly diagnosed or specifically identified) but there is plenty of evidence showing that the drugs being used produce a huge variety of known, and sometimes deadly, side effects.

There are now nearly 400 psychiatric medical diagnoses in the official lists. There are specialists and drugs for all these diagnoses. And not one of the 400 has been tested or proven to exist. If you ever have a dull moment in your life get yourself a copy of the latest edition of the `Diagnostic and Statistical Manual of Mental Disorders' and flick through it looking for the daftest diseases. It's hardly surprising that no one is now truly normal. These diseases aren't found in a laboratory or identified by epidemiological studies: they are created in marketing departments. And why not? Drug companies can make 500,000% profit on the drugs they sell.

Drug companies use marketing experts to persuade well people they are ill and need to take a pill, preferably permanently. Patients groups are set up and funded. In the UK, one of the big groups catering to autism sufferers takes drug company money. Journalists are bought and diseases created. In the business this is called disease mongering. It's big business. Research is funded by drug companies and not surprisingly, the research with embarrassing or inconvenient results never gets published. Medical journals (which rely on drug company advertising) are bent as are journalists. The medical community is corrupt and up to its eyes in drug company money. When TV programmes want to speak to a doctor about drugs they invariably contact one of the `hired hands' recommended by the drug companies. Doctors who tell the truth are banned and marginalised. Governments say they can't find any doctors without conflict of interest to sit on committees assessing drugs. (Well, I'm here. An acknowledged expert on drugs and iatrogenesis and a licensed, registered med practitioner. But, surprise, surprise, they never approach me.) Doctors go to conferences run and or paid for by drug companies. No doctor who is likely to oppose or question drug therapy will be invited to speak. (The last time I was invited to speak to NHS personnel I was quickly uninvited when drug companies found my name on the list.)

Many of the commonest problems are behavioural conditions

associated with children and which are diagnosed subjectively and increasingly diagnosed by nurses and teachers rather than by psychiatrists. The doctors are too busy signing the prescriptions to bother with actually seeing patients. ADHD, autism and Asperger's syndrome will all become default condition soon. Their incidence is increasing so absurdly fast that children without one of these conditions will be regarded as abnormal and will, of course, need treatment. Autism became popular because its a damned sight more convenient for drug companies to create a new disease than it is to accept that children can be brain damaged by vaccines (another drug company product). For drug companies it is a double whammy. They avoid the vaccine lawsuits. And the new diagnosis enables them to sell treatments for a newly created and non existent disease. Parents are often enthusiastic and don't seem to care that the evidence shows that a walk in park is better than drugs for children with ADHD. Pushy, expectant parents with not very bright children temper their disappointment by accepting that their children have a new and fashionable disorder. A doctors note showing that a child has add enables him and family to jump to the front of the queue at theme parks, and to jump the queue for school lunch. It's hardly surprising that one in 20 in Britain have ADHD. And yet the symptoms are so vague that I doubt if there is a child in Britain who doesn't have it. The more intelligent doctors who prescribe drugs for ADHD and other entirely imaginary diseases know damned well that the whole thing is a scam: useless products for imaginary disorders; non-existent solutions for non-existent problems. I suspect that many patients know its emperor's new clothes stuff; the intelligent ones anyway. They go along with the con because it is easier to accept (and to tell their friends and relatives) that their child is rude and badly behaved because he has got a brain disease, rather than because he is, well, rude and badly behaved. And poorly brought up. And they get extras too. Sympathy, care, even extra money. A disabled sticker for the care. No need ever to wait in queues. Only the stupidest doctors, together with social workers and school teachers of course, are unaware that it is all a scam; an expensive, dangerous but massively profitable scam.

New diseases are being invented almost daily. There's another exciting disease around now. It's ODD (Opposition Defiant Disorder). The symptoms are an absence of respect for authority and anger management issues. Those with ODD are surly, defiant, uncooperative and hostile towards authority figures. Psychiatrists believe that ODD affects between 1 and 16 per cent of all school age children (nice of them to be so precise).

I've no doubt that many of these children need help. But some need help to deal with real problems (deafness, low IQ etc) and most need help to deal with the overwhelming stress and pressure in their lives.

I can't prove my theory. But they can't prove any of theirs either. And I have two advantages. First, my theory is not based on commercial expediency. I profit not at all from it. The psychiatric profession cannot say the same. Second, I am prepared to match my track record at spotting dishonesties and medical trickery against that of any ten psychiatrists the medical profession wishes to offer.

So, what the hell is really going on? Is all this just about profits?

Well, here's an interesting quote from the National Association for Mental Health: `Principles of mental health cannot be successfully furthered in any society unless there is progressive acceptance of the concept of world citizenship. World citizenship can be widely extended among all peoples through applications of the principles of mental health.'

And here's a quote from Dr G Brock Chisholm, psychiatrist and co founder of the World Federation of Mental Health: `To achieve world government, it is necessary to remove from the minds of men their individualism, loyalty to family traditions, national patriotism and religious dogmas.'

Ah yes, of course.

The bottom line, of course, is that since the psychiatrists and the drug companies decide what mental illness is and is not, the incidence of mental illnesses will continue to soar. The lunatics have truly taken over the asylum.

Chances of mental illness becoming commoner (and the number of treatments available increasing): 100%.

107. Racism Will Increase

Immigration is the big problems all politicians deny. They don't like to talk about it. This is partly because in the rarefied circles in which they operate questioning immigration is regarded as `racist'. It isn't, of course. But it is mainly because it is the EU which insists that Britain's borders are open to immigrants. And no politician will criticise the EU. There is, of course, also the fact that the people who support unlimited immigration tend not to live in circumstances where they see immigrants taking jobs and homes which they would like. They live in comfortable upper-middle class ghettoes. Many have policemen stationed outside the door for 24 hours a day. (Most objections to unlimited immigration come from people who work and who want to raise families. Scroungers don't much care.)

Politicians may ignore the situation but immigration is creating problems everywhere. It is creating problems in schools (unassimilated immigrants are encouraged to retain their traditional culture rather than to adapt themselves to British cultures and they have different expectations and priorities), health care (immigrants often suffer from different diseases and sometimes bring new diseases with them) and everywhere they are the language problems. In 1,500 schools in England, English pupils are now in the minority. And things are getting much, much worse. There are schools in England were English is a second language. (You think I'm exaggerating? Already over half of inner London school pupils have a first language other than English.) On a recent trip to London my wife had been in the city for ninety minutes before we heard English spoken by a native speaker. Every single person we met was clearly speaking their second language. There are over 200 languages within the EU and Britain (which always bends over in a way other countries regard as contemptible) spends a fortune providing translators and interpreters and printing official leaflets in scores of languages.

Many of our leading politicians even encourage immigrants to retain their own law. In 2009 one Muslim leader speaking at a pro-sharia law demonstration predicted that within ten to fifteen years the queen, like all women, will be forced to wear a burka and Buckingham palace will be turned into a mosque. Some sharia law has already been accepted. Many politicians seem delighted by this. It is tempting to let the feminazis plough on if only because the prospect of seeing Harriet Harman wearing a burkha is undeniably an attractive one.

People are fed up because immigrants are coming into the country and being given free accommodation within weeks or days of their arrival. The indigenous population, the people who have lived here for generations, are made to wait. The politically correct, multiculturally minded idiots who promote this system simply don't understand how this enrages people - and turns sensible, good-hearted folk into racists. I wonder how they would like it if they arrived home for tea and found their wives serving their dinner to a complete stranger who'd turned up unannounced? They might not mind the first time. But what if it happened for years on end?

The majority of immigrants don't care about Britain (or its history or its culture). It isn't their country and it never will be. They didn't come here because they love it and admire it. They came here for money. So they don't care or fight for it. But if we go to their countries then we must abide by their laws and customs.

`Immigrants - whatever their colour - don't like us, don't like our culture, despise our history, resent us, are constantly ungrateful and want us to change all our habits. Why do they come here and stay?' asked one angry reader.

Government ministers allow and defend Muslim extremists in name of fairness but then they want to outlaw and ban Britain's fourth largest political party (the British National Party) which has support of large part of indigenous population.

Immigration results in damage to our culture and history. England is now full of ghettoes, not because immigrants have been rejected by the local population but because immigrants have chosen to congregate in communities which reject our way of life (including the role of women in society). To express concern about this is to be accused of being racist. I wonder how many of those who are female and who make this accusation will be content when they are ordered by law to cover their heads in public and to recognise that they are second class citizens.

There has never been any discussion of immigration.

Is immigration a right or a privilege? should we allow unlimited immigration? or do we have rules and limits? These are questions no one dare ask. There is no net economic benefit to the existing benefit from immigration. Indeed, if the cost of providing extra infrastructure is included immigrants are a huge cost which we simply cannot afford. Thanks to the

EU, England is already the most densely populated country in Europe (with the exception of tiny Malta). The British Government estimates that the population of the UK will be 70 million by 2030 and that immigration will account for 70% of the increase if the net inflow is 190,000 a year. Since the government has consistently and grossly underestimated the figures the likelihood is that the net inflow will be at least twice that (around 4 million immigrants have come into the country since labour came to power in 1997 and the number has been increasing dramatically as EU laws, and new EU countries, have made immigration easier). Immigration continues without our views being taken into account. Even to discuss the problems is dismissed as racist. The price for this will be a dramatic increase in the incidence of racism and a rise in the popularity of parties which disregard the law and are frankly racist (and much more so than any existing parties).

There is still much hypocrisy about immigration in Britain. It is a subject which polite politicians prefer to ignore. But it is, for the vast majority of the indigent population, a huge problem. Gordon Brown's political career ended the day he described a woman who had asked a perfectly reasonable question about immigration from Eastern Europe as a bigoted women. He might have got away with it if he hadn't apologised and pretended he misunderstood. The woman was asking a question which everyone in Britain understood. Brown was furious that he had been exposed to a real person with a real concern but his absurd response (both to the question and to the furore it inspired) showed just how out of touch he was. It was the end of his chances of winning the election.

One of the big problems today is that racism has been institutionalised and it has become legal to give preference in many ways to people who aren't white. The police have been told to give non-white callers preference. Many white citizens feel more than a little aggrieved that police forces have been told to give priority to black people over white people who have called 999. (A friend of mine insists that if she ever needs to dial 999 and is asked, as she will be, for her racial origin, she will say that she is a gypsy or a black African.) The police are given targets which are described as `positive discrimination' but which are, in reality, nothing more than pure old-fashioned racism. For example, the police are expected to solve 28% of the crimes in which a white woman is raped by a white man but they are expected to solve 40% of the crimes when black women are raped by white men. Even the law has got itself involved. According to the law if a black woman is raped by a white man then the crime is more serious than if a white woman is raped by a white man. Employers are so frightened of ending up in court that they fall over themselves to hire non-whites whenever they can and to promote non whites whenever possible. Councils make housing available to non-whites before it is available to whites. When an Englishman wanted to fly the English national flag he was told by his local council that he could not because it might annoy other people and be seen as racist. (The same local council flies a flag for the EU, the most fascist and offensive state the world has ever seen. A state that Hitler would have been proud to have led.) Immigrants (all of whom chose to live in our country) constantly put down England and Britain but none of this is regarded as `racist'. Black rappers sing of `white bitches'. Would a white rapper get away with singing about `black bitches'?

Not surprisingly, many white people (who were born in Britain, who are loyal to the country, who are proud of their heritage and their culture, who have lived here all their lives and whose work and taxes have created the infrastructure) get pissed off by all this. It seems crazy to many that we are at war with countries from which immigrants are pouring into our country. Did Britain encourage German immigrants during World War II?

You can call it reverse discrimination, affirmative action or positive discrimination or anything you like. But its racism, pure and simple. And people are noticing and they're getting angry.

Britain is a Christian country and many feel aggrieved that Muslim women are allowed to wear the burkha (even, or especially, in positions of authority) but that Christian women are not allowed to wear a simple crucifix around their necks lest their modest display prove offensive. There is growing resentment at the fact that bigots who attack a mosque or synagogue are likely to receive a harsh sentence whereas a bigot who attacks the Christian church is likely to be given a pat on the head, a pile of free CDs and an apology for any upset that has been caused.

Under these circumstances racism isn't a possibility, it is an inevitability.

National newspapers have shied away from reporting what is going on but I've been monitoring local newspapers from around the country and there is, believe me, an enormous amount of racial crime in Britain today. Here, almost at random, is a story from the Hereford Times. A teenager and two friends attacked two Lithuanians because they were foreigners. The two Lithuanians (both in their 20s) then collected a plank and, in a revenge attack, killed one of the teenage boys, who was 17, and attacked a 16 year old girl and broke her arm. This, let me remind you, occurred in the peaceful little country town of Hereford and not in some suburb of Birmingham or Manchester. And it wasn't in the slightest bit unusual. Racial attacks of this kind are no longer considered `news' by the national media.

Many white males now regard themselves (with some justification) as members of a persecuted ethnic minority. There is no doubt that multiculturalism threatens the integrity of a nation and the people who live in it. There is much confusion among the chattering classes who do not seem able to differentiate between racism and nationalism. The result is that (as I predicted in my book `England Our England' both racism and nationalism are bound to rise.

Indeed, EU policies are leading to racism all over Europe. Romanians, for example, are now unwanted in parts of the rest of Europe. Posters went up in SNCF trains in the Midi-Pyrenees in France stating: `A number of bag thefts have been noted. All sightings of Romanians must be reported.'

It was hyperinflation which led to Hitler's rise in Germany. We have the EU's absurd, unpleasant and unwelcome immigration policies to add to the hyperinflation.

So, what are the chances of a new Hitler appearing in whatever remains of Britain before 2020? Very high.

Chances of racism increasing: 100%.

108. Health Screening Will Become Compulsory

I have for nearly 40 years been arguing that health screening programmes do more harm than good. They miss symptoms of disease and they pick up non-existent symptoms. People with genuine illnesses are given false reassurance and people with nothing wrong with them are investigated at length and at great expense to the nation; often at great risk to their own health.

Back in the 1970s I argued that having a medical check up of any kind was having a bank statement: it provided a one-off view of your health on that day, in just the way that a bank statement provides a one-off view of your financial health on a given day. Both are equally useless and equally misleading but the medical check up is potentially far more dangerous than the bank statement.

Today a growing number of reviews and reports have substantiated my fears and encouraged more and more doctors to accept my view. It is now widely accepted that pointless screening programmes result in thousands of men and women having cancer misdiagnosed and being treated unnecessarily. The same screening programmes result in thousands of missed diagnoses, false reassurance and early deaths.

Despite the accumulating evidence the screening industry will continue to grow in strength and lobbyists will persuade politicians that the best way to protect health, and cut health service costs, is to do more expensive screening.

Screening will increase in many areas. There will, for example, be screening for many types of mental health problem. The drug companies will probably towards the screening programmes. Such programmes are, after all, a good way to find something wrong with everyone. And when people have a label then can be given a drug. Politicians like to have people labelled as `ill' because it keeps them frightened and under control.

And so, despite the enormous risks, health screening will become compulsory. And millions will be unnecessarily labelled and medicated.

If you don't accept your screening appointment you will be denied treatment if you subsequently fall ill.

And eventually you will be fined and sent to prison if you fail to turn up for screening.

It is as inevitable as compulsory vaccination.

Screening, like vaccination, is based on a myth. But it is a myth which makes a lot of people a lot of money.

And a profitable myth is always believed.

Chances of screening becoming compulsory: 90%.

109. Sex And Race Discrimination Will Continue To Get Worse

The current government policies which involve discrimination against males and against whites of both sexes will continue. (In Orwellian newspeak politically correct discrimination is described as `positive' but it's still discrimination, it's still unfair, and it's still racist and sexist.)

I suspect it's going to get worse.

Chances of sex and race discrimination increasing: 80%.

110. The Premium Rate Phone Scam Will Continue

As the depression deepens just about everyone who can will devise new ways to part you from your money.

It's already started.

For example, when you ring your bank, utility government or government agency to ask for advice or to complain or to reply to a letter or you telephone for customer support you pay more than the standard rate. Many GPs (despite being better paid - for less hours - than at any time in history) now greedily use premium rate numbers for patients ringing to ask for help or make an appointment. Why else do you think they keep you hanging on and on and on after the call has been answered? You are being charged at a high rate while you wait if you have telephoned 0845, 0844, 0870 and 0871.

I telephoned HMRC the other day (to request the extra forms I needed in order to complete my annual return). After what seemed like several hours of recorded piffle promoting the HMRC website, a voice told me that all their agents, employees, whatever, were busy. (I had this image of them all crowded into a porch outside the building, have a lengthy fag break.) `Ring back,' I was told.   So I had to ring back and listen to the piffle about the damned website again. And again. And again. Was it a premium rate number? Probably. If you or I run a premium rate telephone number we're supposed to tell callers. Government departments don't have to obey the law. They're above it all; bloated with self importance, floating aloof on clouds of indifference.

How long will it be before every call you make to a government or council department involves a premium rate telephone number?

Not long.

Chances of virtually all calls to government departments and utilities involving a premium rate charge: 90%.

111. Mortality Rates For Women And Men Are Going To Equalise

In my book `How To Live Longer' I pointed out that mortality rates for women are longer than those for men not because of any inherent physical advantage but because for years women their lives differently to men. Women who stayed at home to look after the household duties, didn't work with chemicals or in dangerous surroundings and they didn't spend their days sitting down at office desks They did physical work but it was varied. They walked to and around the shops. They swept the floors and hung out the washing and ironed it afterwards. There was stress, of course, but it was far less toxic than the sort of stress endured by men worrying about earning money to feed and clothe their family.

On top of all that women didn't smoke or drink as much as men.

Men had more stress in their lives, their work (and their commuting) was unhealthier and their lifestyles were unhealthier too.

It is hardly surprising that men died five or ten years earlier than women.

The women's liberation movement has changed all that. Women can now go to work and claw their way up the ladder of success. They can smoke. They can drink alcohol. And they can, and do, die earlier too.

Statistics show that my prediction, made some years ago, was accurate.

Women are no longer living longer than men.

There never was any basic difference between men and women that ensured that women lived longer.

It was all a question of lifestyle.

And now that women live as men, they are dying at the sort of age when men usually die.

Chances of life expectation rates for women to begin to match those for men: 100%.

112. Deflation Won't Happen. (Deflation is good thing - so we won't be getting much of it in the immediate future.)

Inflation occurs when the government prints more money and the value of the stuff in existence goes down. Deflation is a sort of opposite to inflation, though it doesn't usually occur because the government is burning up the notes.

During a period of deflation, the value of goods falls and the value of money rises. Wages may fall too, on the grounds that it now costs only £1 to buy a loaf of bread, instead of the £2 it used to cost. Deleveraging and debt repayment are deflationary. But governments in a mess hate deflation because it doesn't get rid of their debts.

Deflation is a good thing for savers who have money in the bank because it means that every pound that they have saved will buy them more than it would have done.

But deflation is a bad thing for people who have debts because it means that their debts effectively grown.

During bouts of deflation creditors win and debtors lose.

Many economic commentators have forecast that we are due for a long period of deflation. They claim that the economy is in a mess and so there will be deflation ahead as a shortage of money results in the value of goods rising and the amount paid in wages falling.

Poppycock.

I would be very happy to see several years of deflation.

But I don't believe it will happen.

Governments hate deflation with a vengeance because it pushes up the cost of their debt and delays the rate at which the debt is paid off.

No British government cannot afford a period of deflation at the moment and so the establishment will do everything possible to ensure that we have oodles of inflation instead.

It may be logical to expect deflation.

There may be good reasons for there to be deflation ahead.

But I wouldn't bet on it.

No British government can possibly allow us to live through a period of deflation.

So it won't happen.

Chances of there being an extended period of deflation: 0%.

113. Inflation, Hyperinflation and Superinflation

Great British Pounds have value only insofar as they represent value guaranteed by the British government. The problem we now face is that in order to bail out the incompetent (mainly Scottish) banks which would otherwise have gone bust, Gordon Brown's Government needed to give them lorry loads of Great British Pounds. (The money wasn't his to give, of course. It was given on behalf of the British taxpayers who weren't asked and who had in any case never voted for Gordon Brown as Prime Minister and who almost certainly would have preferred Basil Brush or Roland Rat or a dead but still missed Screaming Lord Sutch if they'd ever been given a choice.)

Now, I genuinely don't know whether anyone in the Labour Party knows enough about the real world to understand this but the value of something depends almost entirely on its rarity. If Leonardo da Vinci had painted a million identical copies of the Mona Lisa, just about anyone who wanted one would be able to afford one and the painting, instead of being beyond price, would be quite affordable.

Or, to put it in a way that politicians might understand, if three dozen former cabinet ministers make themselves available to lobby former colleagues and alter government policy then the price of hiring any one of these former ministers will fall. If there are just three former ministers prepared to sell themselves then their value will be higher.

It's true of almost everything.

If someone suddenly found a huge gold mine that contained a million tons of the stuff then the price of gold would crash. If an oil exploration company sank a well and found a trillion barrels of easily recoverable high grade oil then the cost of oil would fall.

The same thing happens with currency.

If you print tons of the stuff then the value goes down.

And during 2008 and 2009, the British government had the printing presses working overtime in order to produce pound notes that could be handed to the incompetent Scottish bankers so that they could stay in business and continue giving themselves huge bonuses.

So the value of the pound is going to fall and keep falling. It will take a year or two or possibly even three for the policy of `quantitative easing' to affect inflation but in the end it will.

Because, contrary to what a lot of people think, inflation isn't produced by the price of goods going up but by the value of the currency going down. And if you double the amount of something in existence then, as a rule of thumb, you have the value of what is left.

Inflation is a relatively new phenomenon and is a consequence of greed and debt. It's the easy way to make debts shrink. In 1914 prices were lower than 1870 and in 1939 prices were lower than 1922. Investors happily bought government gilts paying just a few per cent interest and were very happy with their income because there was no inflation.

Inflation first hit Europe in a big way in Germany in the periods between the two world wars. The Treaty of Versailles which was signed after the end of World War I stuffed Arabia and Africa by carving them both up according to the whims of the Americans and the British (and according to where there was or wasn't any oil). People who had been hostile to one another for longer than anyone could remember were put together in the same new, entirely artificial country and to everyone's feigned but enduring surprise endless wars were the result in both continents. The Treaty also put such huge financial burdens on Germany, for having started the war in the first place, that the Germans ended up with a devalued currency and massive hyperinflation which wrecked their economy and destroyed the savings of the middle classes (the rich never lose their savings - they move them long before the trouble really starts). It was, of course, the destruction of the currency and the economies which eventually led to the rise of Adolf Hitler and, eventually, World War II. In the 1930s Germany suffered massive hyperinflation because the government always took the soft option. It is always the same. Governments refuse to do the tough things because it is unpopular. (Do you think any British government will dare do all the things that need doing? I don't. Will hyperinflation in Britain produce a new Hitler? Given the encouragement being given to racists by the EU's immigration policies I would say that the chances are much better than even that it will.)

But that's in the medium term future - five or ten years down the line.

Before we get to that, we're still got to deal with the immediate future.

When it was printing money as fast as it could Brown's Government talked about getting rid of the extra currency when things got better. I never thought of Brown as a natural comedian but that was one of his funniest lines. No Government was or is ever going to get rid of all the extra cash that has been printed. The result would push up the value of sterling, destroy exports and produce massive deflation.

Commentators and economists have used up acres of newsprint and endless hours of airtime discussing whether or not we are going to see deflation in the next year or two. They were wasting their time. Britain is a natural candidate for inflation. The Government gives the Bank of England its inflation target and the Bank of England is expected to ensure that the economy is managed in such a way that the inflation target is met. The British Government has issued a lot of long-term bonds, the value of (and therefore cost of) would be dramatically reduced by inflation.

The fact is that Governments hate deflation more than they hate anything else. They actually hate deflation as much as they love inflation. And they love inflation.

Oh how they love inflation.

Here's why.

During the years 2007 to 2010 our Government debt has virtually doubled. As a nation we owe so much money that it's difficult to think about it without going giddy. We owe so much that it will be impossible to clear the debt simply by cutting expenditure and raising taxes.

The other way to get the debt under control is to make sure that the economy grows for quite a few years in a row. If the economy grows by 7 per cent a year then the debt to GDP ratio will, in ten years, halve.

The problem is that our economy is going to grow by 7 per cent a year. It isn't going to grow by anything like that. In fact it probably isn't going to grow at all.

So the only other option is inflation, the politician's dearest friend.

If inflation reaches 7 per cent per year then it will have the same effect as growth - it will reduce the effective size of the debt by half over ten years.

Inflation of just 6% a year over 10 years would get rid of most of the nation's debt. It is the easy solution and no British government will be able to resist it. A nice bit of inflation would also be the solution to the housing price problem; it would take some of the air out of the bubble. The trouble is that once you let inflation start it is very difficult to stop it. You think you'll stop it at 6% and then, before you know, inflation is running at 20%. Or 50%. Or 10,000%. Or 1,000,000%. And you think you're living in Zimbabwe.

Governments always pretend to loathe and fear inflation. But in reality it is, and always been, a solution to a nation's economic problems. Faster inflation makes it easier to reduce public and private debt levels because, quite simply, when you print more money you devalue the stuff. Faster inflation reduces the value of a nation's currency and helps restore cost competitiveness in depressed industries. Faster inflation helps disguise a whole range of financial problems associated with debt. Inflation transfers money from the prudent to the greedy and the reckless but it also saves politicians who have borrowed too much.

Brown, by printing money so fast that there will eventually be inflation, and lowering interest rates has destroyed the savings of the prudent. Anyone who had a positive net worth in 2007 will have had to work hard not to have lost a large proportion of their savings by 2015. It's already been happening since 2007. Money has been transferred from the prudent to the reckless. Savers who wonder where their money has gone need only look around at their neighbours who are still living in homes they could never afford and shouldn't have bought and at the bankers who are, despite all their mistakes, still enjoying multi-million pound salaries and bonuses.

No British government will allow deflation to take hold. A deflating economy will push up the value of money and make the government's debts even worse. So the one thing of which I am sure is that the deflation a lot of economists and commentators are expecting simply won't happen. The government will fit the printing presses with superchargers before they allow deflation to make the debts even worse than they are.

But once the inflation they so desperately want takes hold it will almost inevitably go out of control. Inflation is like a forest fire. You may think you can just burn a few dead trees, but before you know it the fire is out of control and four million acres of woodland are ablaze and whole towns have to be evacuated.

Governments always think they can control inflation, but they never can. The problem is that currency revaluations have a huge impact on inflation but are totally outside political control. And the strikes which are going to be a huge feature of British life for years to come will also result in more inflation as public service workers holding the nation to ransom demand, and receive, unreasonable pay rises. During the crisis cautious Britons built up their savings. The Government will use inflation to transfer debt from savers to debtors.

The seriously rich already know what is going to happen. That's why they are investing in farmland, Ming vases, gold coins, rare watches, first editions, classic art and bottles of exceptionally good wine. All of these items have one thing in common: their supply is limited and so they will hold their value better than the not so Great British Pound. Investors who want to hold currency are buying Australian dollars, Canadian dollars and Swiss francs. The first two have the advantage of belonging to countries which have huge quantities of minerals tucked safely away under their soil. The third has the advantage of being almost as good as gold.

The sad thing is that inflation forces ordinary investors to take risks. In the spring of 2010 interest rates were around 1% pre tax but the official inflation rate was 3.7% (that means at least double that). So a saver would need a pre tax income of considerably more than that just to stand still. So investors bought equities, bonds, property or commodities. And took risks.

The bottom line is that the alternative to inflation is default and confiscation, though just what Britain has got left that any creditors would want is difficult to imagine. Do the crown jewels belong to the nation or are the Queen's personal property? We've already sold London Bridge to the Americans. How much would they pay for the Houses of Parliament?

Chances of inflation being a major problem: 100%.

114. Obligations And Rights Are Going To Separate Still Further

Nearly 40 years ago I wrote an article for the Daily Telegraph magazine in which I argued that one of the big problems in our society was that responsibility and authority had been separated. I was, I seem to remember, working as a young doctor at the time and I was conscious of the fact that while I had an enormous amount of responsibility for my patients, all the authority lay with the new breed of bureaucrats who were, at that time, taking control of every aspect of medicine.

If things have changed since then it has simply been an even sharper separation of responsibility and authority.

But now something else has happened.

Obligations and rights have been separated too.

Those who work and pay tax are the ones who have all the obligations. And the individuals who rely on the state are the ones with all the rights.

Think about it and you'll see what I mean.

The more obligations an individual has, the fewer rights he seems to have.

But the individuals without obligations seem overly endowed with rights.

It's going to get worse.

Chances of obligations and rights continuing to separate: 90%.

115. The Number Of Street Beggars Will Soar

Begging used to be very much an amateur business in Britain. It was done in a very gentle sort of way. Today's beggars are professionals; far more `in your face' than their ancestors with their demands for `spare change' or their searing, shouted, personalised request that you buy a copy of the `Big Issue'. (The Big Issue is probably, incidentally, Britain's worst magazine; it makes Exchange and Mart seem riveting and imaginatively written. And the sellers are breeding. Two days ago I passed three of them within a single hundred yard stretch in a local High Street).

There are professional beggars in Britain now making £70,000 to £100,000 a year tax free and going home to much greater luxury than most of the people who subsidise their lifestyles could dream of emulating.

Begging has become an industry. Many of the professionals claim state benefits but still in the sunshine on a pleasant day, collecting coins (and notes) from commuters hurrying to and from work. (When it rains they can be spotted sitting a local cafe drinking expensive coffees and nibbling daintily on croissants and chocolate muffins.)

I know one Big Issue seller who has a nice caravan home, a job on a farm and an income from his columns (about being homeless), his television appearances (about being homeless), his lectures to schools (about being homeless) and his book (about being homeless). He moaned to me once about a generous passer-by who had bought him a steaming hot pasty. `It had carrots in it,' he complained. `I hate carrots. Didn't she know I hate carrots? It's in my book.' He is a successful, professional beggar. I've no doubt he will soon be appointed Professor of Begging at one of the newer universities.

Looking in the window of an expensive department store I overheard the following conversation between a female `Big Issue' seller and a man, presumably her husband who was laden with shopping bags.

`There's a lovely lampshade in the other window,' she said. `Pop in and get it would you? It would look perfect in our living room.'

I know another group of beggars who share a baby. There must have been an article about it in `Beggars Weekly' because it's not an uncommon trick these days. Or maybe they teach the trick in `A Level' Betting. A woman standing on a street corner with a baby in one arm and the other hand outstretched will receive far more money than a woman without a baby. If the baby is crying the take will be even better. So, to get the best financial return out of a baby a group of beggars will share one. They do the same thing with dogs.

The average British town and city has more beggars than Istanbul and indeed that is probably where a good chunk of them come from. There and Romania. We really don't need to import beggars.

Donna Antoinette dropped a note into the hand of a beggar. `He's poor,' she explained, when she caught up with me.

`So are the people working in Tesco's', I pointed out. `But if you go in and give them money they'll be offended. And they're working hard to try to help themselves.'

These days I don't give money to beggars unless they're busking (and making a real effort to be entertaining) or very old and probably drunk. I don't give money to any beggar under 50. They're usually receiving benefits for themselves and the dog (they get another £10 a week benefits for the dog). And when I see unconscious drunks I tuck money into their clothing so that they will have something to cheer them up when they wake.

The number of beggars is going to soar as more and more people struggle to make ends meet. Benefits are going to have to be cut as the nation tightens its belt. Unemployment levels are set to soar.

Begging is the one guaranteed growth industry in Britain. If you think there are a lot of beggars now just wait a year or two. You need to have a philosophy about what you will give, and to whom, or you're going to find a walk through your local shopping centre expensive and emotionally draining.

The chances of there being more beggars on our streets in 2020 are 100%.

116. The Government Plans To Steal Private Pensions

The Government has, for years, been filching money from private pension funds in order to pay out public sector worker pensions. Up until now they've been doing it fairly stealthily (by altering tax rates and so on) but have, nevertheless, managed to help themselves to many tens of billions of pounds. Changes Gordon Brown made to pension legislation have taken around £100 billion out of pension funds over the last twelve years. That's one hell of a stealth tax but it is not, however, anywhere near enough. And the Government will follow Robert Maxwell's example and help themselves to more money out of private pension funds - probably by forcing private pension holders to invest their money either directly in Government gilts or in annuities based on Government gilts.   The problem is that government pensioners want pensions and benefits costing far more than they have contributed and since the government's pension schemes are operated along the lines of a giant Ponzi scheme (the money you save is being put away to pay for your pension, it is being used to pay the pensions of today's pensioners, your pension will, if you are lucky, be paid by your children or their children). Since today's ex civil servants demand (and receive) huge pensions the nation is building up debts which the next generation, and the one after that, will have to pay in addition to paying your pension demands. The situation is now surreal. Each child born in America in 2010 came into the world owing $170,000. In the UK the figures are equally startling. And the debts get bigger every year. As long as the American dollar remains the world reserve currency the Americans can, to some extent, print their way out of trouble simply by making more dollars and reducing the value of the ones in existence. The British government does not have this facility and so we will be in serious trouble before the Americans.

The size of the unfunded liability for public sector workers pension schemes is something of a mystery but experts claim it is in the region of £1,200 billion. It's probably more. But £1,200 billion is a lot of cash for a country which is already horribly in debt. The real cost of public sector pensions is estimated at in excess of £30 billion a year and rising annually. Now that the number of civil servants (particularly highly paid ones) has soared the cost of providing them with pensions will also soar. How much will public sector pensions cost in ten years time? £100 billion a year does not seem an unreasonable estimate.

The members of public sector pension schemes have a greater claim on future taxpayer' earnings than have the holders of government gilts. The position is, in short, unsustainable and is a major cause of resentment among the rest of the nation.

(Many large British companies which were once owned by the government are now little more than pension funds with the stump of a business tacked on. British Airways (which has a pension deficit of between £3.7 billion and £7 billion depending upon who operates the calculator) and British Telecom are just two of the companies with big problems. Most businesses which have links to the government have given their employees far too generous pensions. It's the size of the pension deficit which makes Royal Mail an unappetising prospect for potential purchasers.)   As an aside it is worth asking just why companies should be expected to pay pensions to their workers. This does seem to be a Victorian and rather patronising thing to do. (`We are going to look after you in your old age because you will be too stupid to do it yourself.')

Something has to crack.

To begin with the government, and local authorities, will attempt to deal with the problem (which does, after all, affect senior employees as much as junior ones) by putting up taxes and cutting services. But the government's huge debts, and the cost of servicing those debts, means that they won't be able to find enough money that way.

State pensions for civil servants have created the worst form of inequality in the country. The average civil service employee will get a pension of £28,900 while the average private sector employee will be lucky to live on £11,600. The private sector worker will, of course, also be paying for the pension of his civil service pensioner living up the road in the bigger house. Tony Blair's taxpayer funded pension as a former PM is worth £3.5 million which is more than twice as much as any taxpayer who has earned his own pension is allowed to have without being hammered by massively punitive tax penalties. Blair has, of course, made himself exempt from these penalties. Vast armies of state employees retire in their 50s on absurdly generous inflation proofed pensions.

When a policeman had to resign in disgrace it was revealed that although he was less than 50 years old he would receive a pension of at least £110,000 a year. While private sector employees see their pensions shrinking or even disappearing, and self employed individuals see their pensions losing value, those individuals who have enjoyed public sector pensions paid by taxpayers have been safe, secure and laughing.

Even worse, many government employees retire in their 50s and take a little job to keep them occupied. This is, of course, destroying the jobs market for people who need to work to earn a living. It has always been a problem for writers and photographers (who found themselves competing with people who had a steady income and were prepared to write an article for £5 or sell a bunch of photographs for £20 and the fun of the thing) but now it is a problem for everyone looking for a job. The two worlds which have been created are causing much resentment.

The laughing civil servants may be about to stop laughing.

Public sector unions will fight hard to preserve those unaffordable pensions but the government cannot possibly afford to pay them.

And so public sector workers are going to have to lower their expectations. Many are going to be very disappointed. And they are not going to like it.

While private sector employees suffer ravaged pensions, part time work, redundancies and in many cases lower pay, public sector workers who have enjoyed 12 years of financial glory during the labour government, still refuse to contemplate cuts in their pensions or their pay. Maybe they and their unions do not realise that there has to be a cut in public expenditure and that if they don't join the rest of the community in accepting cuts then the result must be a cut in public sector and infrastructure services and everyone, particularly the poorest will suffer? Or maybe they and their unions just don't care about anyone except themselves.

The unavoidable truth is that since the greater part of public sector expenditure goes on salaries, bonuses and pensions a failure to cut in these areas will lead to massive cuts in services. There has to be a cap on public sector pensions and public sector workers have to start paying for their own pensions - in the way that most private sector workers and all self employed individuals have to pay for their own pensions. Any other solution will lead to national bankruptcy.

Since public sector workers are treated so generously it would obviously be unfair and stupid to remove tax relief on pension contributions. But the government is doing precisely this. They have started by removing tax relief for high earners and they will gradually extend the changes to cover most if not all pension contributions.

In the future, private sector workers and the self employed will have little or no chance of ever obtaining worthwhile pensions. The charges are so high and returns now so low that to obtain an inflation proofed income of £20,000 would require a fund of £600,000. The average worker in Britain has a pension pot of 30 to 40K - enough to provide an annual pension of around £1,000 a year. New rules being introduced by the EU will mean that even these paltry sums will be reduced quite dramatically within the next year or two. Pensions for those outside government and EU employment will be in future be vastly reduced. Anyone who has put money into a pension fund has a right to feel cheated and aggrieved. I used to be a strong supporter of private pensions. But in recent years I have become increasingly sceptical about their value. Today, in my view, there is no incentive for anyone to take out a private pension. The government wants people to do this (because it knows that it is the only way Britain's streets will not be filled with starving old people in another generations time) but it does everything to discourage saving. People who put money into a private pension fund a decade ago may consider themselves lucky if what they now have is the same as the amount they put in. The Government has snatched a good deal of it in taxes. Fund managers have taken loads in absurdly high fees and lost loads more through incompetence. And the rest has gone because the economy has been appallingly mismanaged. The whole pensions business is so complicated that not even professional advisers understand it. And the government discourages people from saving by ensuring that those who prefer to spend their money on holidays, cars and clothes will receive a state hand out in the form of a pension credit. And if you do take out a private pension, and there is anything left when everyone else has taken a chunk out of it, and the EU's latest rules have resulted in a terrible performance, you will when you come to retire, be allowed to take only a small portion of your savings and forced to take out an annuity with the rest because although you have proved yourself to be a prudent person the government and the EU don't trust you not to blow the lot on sweets.

New rules and regulations governing annuities mean that private sector pensioners will receive smaller and smaller annuity payments.

The EU has damaged private pensions. The big pension companies have, through huge fees and incompetence, failed to make money for investors. And the government has helped itself to billions from private pension funds.

But I believe that worse is to come.

The government will force those holding private pension funds to put their money into government bonds. The returns will be poor and so, even if public sector workers' pensions are cut savagely, the divide between public sector pensioners and private pensioners will grow ever wider.

Chances of the government stealing private pension funds to help pay its debts: 80%.

117. Consumerism Has Gone Mad (but is about to settle down).

In the early part of the 21st century there were whole industries making scented candles, entire shops devoted to selling them and real, live, breathing people spending large amounts of their time choosing and buying the damned things.

Half the world is starving to death (in large part, thanks to the European Union's Common Agricultural Policy) and the people of Europe are making and buying scented candles. The Financial Times interviewed six shoppers during the January sales in 2009. Four of the six said that they were buying goods they admitted they didn't need. They were buying them because they were cheap. This is consumerism gone barking mad.

When the recession first hit Britain, Gordon Brown and his ministers encouraged us all to keep spending. The theory was that if we continued to spend money we didn't have then the economy would boom and we would drive our way out of the coming depression.

It was a theory based on wet sand, of course.

And it isn't going to work.

The depression is coming anyway.

And then consumerism will begin to die.

There is no future for scented candles or any of the other rubbish that characterised the end of the 20th century and the start of the 21st century.

Chances of consumers continuing to buy scented candles (and other nonsenses) in 2020: 10%.

118. Photography Will Become Increasingly Illegal

It is illegal for parents to take photographs of any of their children who might be appearing in the school nativity play (a dangerous concept in these anti-Christian times) or taking part in the school sports day. Two reasons are usually given. The first is that taking photos might infringe the privacy rights of other children. That one always makes me laugh a lot. Every street corner, every stretch of road and every public building is now fitted with cameras recording our every movement. Britain has more closed circuit television cameras than any other country on the planet. We are spied on more than any other citizens. We have no privacy. The second reason for the ban on parents photographing their children is that allowing cameras into these areas would be a boon to those parents who are also paedophiles. Putting aside the fact that one might hope that there weren't too many parent-paedophiles in the average school these days, this is also clearly rubbish. The BBC merrily broadcasts live shots of tiny gymnasts parading around in skin tight leotards to satisfy the depraved yearnings of any number of paedophiles. Photographs of half a dozen kids dressed up as three wise men are unlikely to prove anywhere near as attractive.

It isn't just school events that are illegal hunting grounds for photographers. The police have, in the last year or two, been having a real clamp down on the photographing of public buildings and public places. On numerous occasions they have demanded that tourists, taking perfectly innocent pictures of landmark buildings, delete the pictures they have taken.

This is just bullying and the best way to deal with bullies is to stand up to them.

The last time I was stopped by the police while going about my perfect law abiding activities I was photographed by a police video camera operator. As soon as I saw what was happening I took out my own camera and started taking pictures of the policemen who were filming and interviewing me. I wandered over to a nearby police van and started taking pictures of the policemen inside it (they were so camera shy that one of them slammed the van door shut, though not before I'd got some good snaps of them all).

I don't know what happened to their photographs and film of me, but my photographs of them appeared in a national newspaper a few days later under the heading `Hand of Plod'.

The moral is that if we let them continue to take away our civil liberties and our freedom then they will.

But if we stand up to them, and refused to be cowed by their bureaucratic bullying, then we will win at least some of the battles.

Chances of photography become increasingly illegal: 70%.

119. Interest Rates Will Rise

Early in 2010 I telephoned the manager of my SIPP to ask how much interest I was getting on the money in my current account. I was, he said, receiving interest at the rate of 0.0001 %. There may have been one or two more noughts than that after the decimal point. I rather lost interest after the first two. A conversation with a bank manager showed that I was receiving a similar rate of interest on the money in my deposit account. I, like everyone else stupid enough to have saved money during the `splash-it-about' decades at the end of the 20th century and the start of the 21st century, was paying a heavy price so that the Government could support the bankers who had gone bust and the homebuyers who had purchased homes that were well above their pay grade. Things were being made worse by the fact that the retail banks were desperately trying to recoup their losses by charging quite high rates of interest when lending money to businesses but paying out absurdly low rates of interest to depositors.

And, of course, the absurdly low interest rates weren't the end of the problem. When tax was taken off the low interest being paid most depositors ended up with only just more than half of an absurdly low interest rate. And when inflation was taken into account (at a real rate of at least double the government's official rate of 3%) the money in the bank was shrinking week by week.

During the crisis it would, of course, have make real economic sense to let interest rates rise. This would have encouraged saving (which the country desperately needed), reward prudence and thrift and helped to control inflation.

But instead Brown's Government spent a fortune keeping interest rates down in order to prop up property prices. The policy was directly transferring wealth from savers and pensioners to overly indebted borrowers. Thousands of people living on their savings were mugged by the Government and found their incomes devastated by this policy. Many have chosen to take great risks with their capital by investing in shares or bonds in order to obtain some income.

Tight fiscal policy will keep interest rates low for a while and that could result in foreign traders borrowing sterling and turning our currency into the bottom end of the carry trade (whereby traders borrow one currency which is available at low interest rates and then invest it in something else). The problem with the carry trade is that it really only works as long as the currency you are borrowing doesn't rise in value. Indeed, it works best if the currency you are borrowing falls in value. And so the traders who borrow sterling will short it and make sure that it becomes worth less when compared against other currencies such as the dollar and the euro. That will reduce the amount the traders will have to pay back when they close out their carry trade.

Shorting sterling could well result in a big collapse in the currency. Since much of what we consume (food and oil to name but two) has to be imported, that will inevitably result in massive inflation.

Our economy is destroyed.

I wish I could think of a better way to put it. But I can't. Gordon Brown has destroyed the economy for years to come. And if the rest of the world decides that we, as a nation, are the national equivalent of an unemployed mechanic in Ohio with a half million dollar mortgage to service then we could, as a nation, easily end up paying 4 or 5 percentage points more than any other country in order to borrow the money we need to find in order to pay the interest on the money we've already borrowed and can't afford to pay back. That means we could, within a year or so, be paying 8 or 9% as a nation. And if that happens (which is no more likely than that it might rain a week on Tuesday and about as easy to forecast) then people with mortgages and loans will find themselves paying 12% or 15% or another number considerably higher and scarier than that.

The only good to come from this will be the fact that people with money in the bank will suddenly find that instead of receiving interest at the rate of 0.0001% they will be receiving interest at 10% or even more.

Sadly, however, inflation will be eating away at their savings at a considerably faster rate.

Chances of interest rates rising (and staying high): 90%.

120. There Will Continue To Be Too Many Managers

Under Margaret Thatcher it was entrepreneurs who ruled the world. Today it is managers, regulators and consultants. These are the people hired by Brown to set targets and ensure that they are met. These are the people who have put into practice Brown's destructive and damaging policies of social management and control.

In 1997, when Brown took over as Chancellor, the NHS had 12 hospital beds per manager. Today there are just four hospital beds per manager.

During the same period the number of council staff earning over £50,000 a year has risen from 3,300 to 38,000. The result has been damaging in many different ways. Highly paid council workers require staff of their own. And large offices and expense accounts. And the more administrators there are the more forms and rules and regulations there are. Most important of all, it is the pensions that are killing local authorities and will continue to do so for decades to come.

Management consultants and efficiency experts (too many of them 21 or 22 years old and equipped with a crisp diploma, more than fair share of arrogance and nothing else) have, over the years, helped destroy much of the world's industry. After management consultants told Railtrack to `sweat their assets' there was a series of accidents and the company duly collapsed. Management consultants advised Swiss to invest in other small, European airlines. Predictably, Swissair, which had been doing very nicely thank you, went bust.

The same sort of so-called `experts' (who are in reality usually young graduates who have never had a real job or earned any real money in their lives) are now destroying public life and organisations such as the NHS. Billions of pounds sof public money is paid to them by governments which have realised that a good way to avoid blame is to hire people to take decisions and give advice. `We acted on the best professional advice when making these decisions,' absolves politicians from all responsibility.

Sadly, the obsession with giving authority to managers (and taking it away from the people who have the responsibility) is, literally, killing people.

For example, in one recent year the number of mistakes in British hospitals rose by a quarter. In one London teaching hospital (allegedly staffed by the best doctors and nurses, and run by the best managers the nation could find) doctors and nurses recently made an average of 135 mistakes a week when giving drugs to patients. A quarter of the mistakes were serious ones.

The administrators and managers are quite good at working out how many mistakes are being made and I must congratulate them on this.

However, they are no good at all at finding ways to cut the number of mistakes being made.

Since it is management consultants and efficiency experts who decide how many management consultants and efficiency experts are employed I do not expect this trend to change within the next decade.

On the contrary, management consultants and efficiency experts will (aided and abetted by new laws introduced by management consultants and efficiency experts working for the European Union) continue to introduce changes and `improvements' which destroy all aspects of public life.

Getting rid of these unnecessary and expensive managers will be almost impossible. Very few government, council and quango employees are willing to speak out about waste. For one thing they themselves are usually enjoying an undemanding workstyle, a high salary of their own and pensions and perks far better than anything they could ever hope to enjoy in the private sector. And, they know that if they hang around for a while there's an excellent chance that they too will be promoted to the higher echelon of management.

Chances of the mass of unnecessary and unwanted managers keeping their jobs: 70%

121. Progress Will Be Limited

There will be very little progress in the next decade; and very few good new ideas introduced to improve our lives. The reason? Rules and regulations. Health and safety.

In medicine, for example, how many wonderful new drugs are thrown out because they fail preliminary tests? I have no idea, and nor does anyone else. But I can tell you that if modern drug testing methods were used (particularly experiments on animals) then most of the really important drugs we rely on (aspirin, digitalis, morphine, penicillin) would not be allowed. Toxicity tests on animals would have resulted in their being outlawed.

Similarly, I have no doubt that if someone today invented the aeroplane, the ship or the motor car, the health and safety idiots would have them banned. Can you see the guys in cheap suits allowing a couple of hundred people to travel high in the sky in a heavier than air machine at several hundred miles an hour? Exactly.

I knew that I was right about this when I saw a headline in The Economist which read `Modernisation is hard to argue with'. The Economist, more than any other publication I know, always gets things wrong. In fact it gets things wrong so often that it can be relied upon to get things wrong.

Chances of great inventions improving our lives before 2020: 20%.

122. The British Obsession With Property Ownership Will End

The British have, for many years, regarded property ownership as a basic human right. People have, for generations, bought property they could hardly afford and then spent years paying off huge mortgage bills in the happy expectation that at the end of the mortgage period they will own a property worth far more than they paid for it.

For generations the British have confused home ownership with investment and have used the mortgage system as a way of leveraging their wealth and making far more money than they could have hoped to make in any other way.

That is all about to end.

Property prices are not going to continue soaring ever higher. If things go very well for property then houses will, in five years' time, be worth approximately what they are worth today. In ten years' time they may have edged ahead a little. If things go badly then houses will, in five years' time, be worth considerably less, in real terms, than they are worth today.

Houses and flats in Britain are absurdly overpriced. Foreigners simply cannot understand how or why we have allowed this to happen. Property in Britain is so overpriced that even the Swiss, the wealthiest people on earth, marvel at the prices we pay for our homes.

The fact is that renting now makes far more sense than buying and the British (like the French and the Germans) are going to have to come to terms with this fact.

Look at the figures.

Assume, for example, that you buy a home for £500,000. (A huge sum of money that will buy you a very modest three bedroomed dwelling in the Home Counties). In addition to the cost of the house there will, of course, be other costs. There will be a one off stamp duty payment of £20,000 and the survey and legal charges will probably take up another £10,000. Maintenance and insurance costs will probably reach another £10,000 a year - every year. If you have a 100% mortgage you will probably pay £25,000 in interest charges and a chunky sum towards paying off the loan. The £25,000 will, of course, be lost forever.

As the owner of your own house you will, of course, have no rent to pay. You will have security. If you keep paying any mortgage costs you will be able to stay in your house (though if you fall behind with the payments you will be vulnerable). And, of course, if the value of your home rises you will have a tax-free capital gain. Many people have, over recent decades, become quite indecently rich by buying and selling houses. You start with a house that costs £100,000. You sell that one for £150,000 and take on a bigger mortgage and buy one for £200,000. You sell that one for £300,000 and buy another for £400,000. And so it goes. Soon you are living in a £1 million mansion.

Now, consider the rental costs.

If you rent a house that might cost £500,000 you will probably pay £20,000 a year. You will have a one off cost of, say £3000 for a lawyer to check your contract. And you will have to insure your belongings (though not the property) and probably pay the council tax (which you would, of course, have to pay if you were the owner.)

But you don't have to pay the interest on a loan of £500,000 and if you actually have the £500,000 you can put your money to work somewhere. Even with interest rates low it should be possible to have a tax free income of £25,000 a year from £500,000.

You don't stand to gain from any rise in the price but, on the upside, you don't have to pay for any repairs. If the house turns out to have dry out the owner has to pay the bills. If the roof blows off it is the owner who must worry.

And, of course, you aren't stuck in the house.

If the neighbours turn out to be noisy and nasty you can give notice and move easily and at little cost. If the council decides to build a road through your front garden you can just pack up your belongings and go somewhere else. You don't have to worry about estate agents, surveyors and stamp duty. You may be slightly less secure (but these days the laws protecting tenants are extensive) but you are free and you have none of the worries associated with property ownership. You have flexibility. If you work at home you may even be able to claim tax relief on some of the cost of your rental payments.

It will slowly become clear to many that without the huge advantage of a tax free capital gain there are very few advantages to owning your own house - and very big advantages to renting your home.

The problem, of course, is that the British regard home ownership as a sign of growing up. Renting seems rather uncertain. Buying a house suggests that you have become a member of the landed gentry. Your castle is your home. Renting suggests that you are merely passing through.

But the advantages of renting over ownership are clear and certain.

I strongly suspect that, as house prices stall and inflation eats away at the value of homes all over Britain, so an increasing number of people will realise that renting really does make sense.

And that, of course, will result in house prices declining still further. Buying a house in 2010 or 2011 will, I suspect, be a very good way to lose a good deal of money.

Chances of more and more people choosing to rent rather than buy their home: 70%.

123. Banks May Start Changing Interest Rates Retrospectively

If governments can change the law retrospectively (and the British government has, in recent years, got into the habit of doing this quite frequently) then why shouldn't other large organisations change their rules retrospectively?

Banks in other countries have already changed interest rates retrospectively and so it won't be long before British banks try this. Existing agreements will be unilaterally abandoned when they are found to be unprofitable. Savers will find that they suddenly receive far less interest on their account than they were promised and house buyers will discover that they are paying far more interest on their loan than they were promised they would have to pay.

All these may sound bizarre and slightly unbelievable but if, ten years ago, you had told me that the Government would change the law retrospectively I would have laughed at you.

Chances of banks changing interest rates retrospectively: 70%.

124. Digital Radio Will Take Over

We've all been forced to watch digital television (when the analogue signal was better and the analogue devices were often easier to operate).

The next step will be radio.

Despite the fact that the signal is often poor, and the radio sets themselves overpriced and not very good (we've had to throw away three expensive digital radios because they simply stopped working) it is clear that anyone who wants to listen to the wireless will soon have to do so on a digital radio set. This will enable the government to flog off the wavelengths used for broadcasting, and make some more money by flogging off something that belongs to us all and by inconveniencing us all.

Donna Antoinette and I possess old fashioned radios that are half a century old or more and which still work perfectly well. We will have to bin them. Car radios won't work and elderly folk who cannot afford expensive new digital radios will have to learn to live in silence. The radio industry is offering a miserable `scrappage' discount on old radios.

The government plans to switch over to digital radio in 2015. Theoretically, digital coverage must reach 90% of the population and all main roads by 2013. No one seems to care much about the fact that motorists will be deprived of their radios if they dare to wander off the motorway.

The whole scheme will be a disaster. It will be unpopular and will ruin life for millions who get pleasure, enlightenment and companionship from the radio. From the consumer's point of view digital radio is overhyped and without purpose. There are, however, undoubtedly advantages for the industry, the BBC and the government.

Chances of our being forced to buy digital radios if we want to listen to the radio: 100%.

125. Charities Will Become Ever More Crooked

Running a charity has become a career or many individuals and charities today are run like big businesses. There is a ruthlessness about charitable organisations which would have seemed quite alien just a few years ago.

Numerous medium sized charities now have staff on six figure salaries with expense accounts and pensions to match. It is by no means uncommon for a charity to spent 75% to 85% of its income on salaries and administration. That, of course, means that if you give a pound to a charity then the good cause you hope to help will receive just 15p to 25p.

Moreover, although the government department which controls charities (it may be known as the Charities Commission but it is a Government department) is supposed to exclude organisations which don't satisfy strict criteria there are grave suspicions that a good many charities are set up largely to benefit the people who set them up, rather than anyone else.

And it is not unknown (by which I mean it is far commoner than it ought to be) for charities to have subsidiary commercial companies which are responsible for fund raising. This means that there is another layer of administration to be paid for, and a whole new raft of expensive salaries, pensions and expense accounts to be dealt with out of the money coming in. Using a commercial company as a subsidiary is helpful because it enables the charity part of the charity to stand apart from whatever nastiness goes on and it also enables the charity to cream off much of the money coming in before it reaches the bit of the charity which hands the money out to worthy causes.

All this is going to get much, much worse.

The people who run charities today are, by and large, tough, commercially minded individuals whose primary loyalty is to the organisation which pays them rather than to the people they are supposed to be helping. People working for charities which campaign on behalf of specific groups have admitted to me that they don't actually want to change things. `If we solve the problem we exist to battle then we will put ourselves out of a job,' admitted one unusually honest charity worker.

Indeed, a surprising number of charities now readily accept money from surprising sources. For example, many charities set up to help patients with specific medical disabilities now accept funding from drug companies which make products designed to treat those disabilities. The charities claim that this enables them to provide their members with a better service and with plenty of glossy literature but, of course, it also compromises the charity. The drug company's aims are likely to coincide with the aims or the patients for whom the charity was set up.

Today, Donna Antoinette and I give money directly to people in need, rather than to charitable organisations.

The chances of charities becoming increasingly crooked: 90%.

126. The Unmarried Mother Boom Will Continue

There will be an increase in the number of unmarried mothers. When the best way for a 16 year old girl to get out of the family home and have a place of her own is to get pregnant then that's what she will do. There will be more than one child because the idiots who designed and run the benefits system will ensure that she won't be able to pay for the full service satellite television subscription unless she screws like a rabbit and regards contraception as interfering with her human right to a bigger flat. Her small army of snotty nosed brats will, of course, be brought up by a mixture of transient boyfriends and social workers to regard work as an offensive thought.

Chances of the unmarried mother boom continuing: 80%.

127. There Will Be A Powerful Grassroots Move Against Technology

I know at least two shops which have no website, no internet access, no email and no telephone (not even a mobile). The blokes running them do without any modern technology and seem to survive very well. They don't take credit cards or cheques. They have shelves full of books and a small metal cash box. Customers enter their shops and exchange cash for books. There is no simpler way to conduct a business.

And, despite the fact that the government is clearly determined to force us to do everything on the web, I believe that this way of doing business is going to thrive. Individuals with initiative will always find a way to make money and these days the cost and unreliability of machinery means that the easiest way to make a living is to manage without things that rely on electricity.

Everywhere I drive these days I see groups of men offering to hand wash my car. They are gathered at petrol stations and on pub forecourts. If you haven't seen them yet then you soon will. For £5 or so three or four men armed with buckets and sponges will wash your car in minutes. It's a cash business. One of them always speaks enough English to tell you where to park your car while they wash it and then give it a polish. They provide a faster and cheaper service than an automatic car wash. And they don't break your windscreen wipers or door mirrors. Are they officially part of the workforce? I doubt it. Do they pay tax, national insurance and insurance? I doubt it. Do they also claim benefits of various kinds? Probably. Will they survive the coming years of depression? Undoubtedly. It is the expensive automatic car washing machines which will disappear. Will Britons ever wash cars for a few pounds an hour? No.

Chances of there being a powerful grassroots movement against technology: 80%.

128. Entirely Healthy People Will Be Told To Take Drugs

The Government and the drug industry controlled medical profession are enormously enthusiastic about encouraging (or forcing) healthy people taking drugs.

A few years ago the authorities were very keen for all women to take a drug that was alleged to prevent breast cancer. The drug was called tamoxifen and the plan was to it to every woman in the world to prevent breast cancer. If millions of women had taken the drug on a daily basis the profits would have been massive.

I managed to put a stop to that by pointing out two things.

First, I pointed out that the drug caused cancer of the uterus and that although this side effect might be acceptable if the drug was being given to women fighting breast cancer, it was hardly acceptable for such a drug to be given to healthy women.

Second, I pointed out that the drug caused cancer in rats and mice. Now, I have long argued that animal experiments are pointless, misleading and irrelevant but the drug industry loves animal experiments because they offer a no win situation. If a drug is tested on animals and shown to cause no problems it will be passed as safe to give to people. On the other hand if a drug causes problems in animals it will be passed as safe to give to people on the grounds that animals are different to people. (I'm not making this up. This is how the system works. I have previously published a list of scores of drugs which cause cancer and other serious problems in animals but which are freely prescribed for human patients.) However, the problems caused by the drug being promoted as effective at preventing breast cancer were so horrendous that even the drug companies became embarrassed. (`You've rather got us this time,' admitted one pro industry, pro vivisection `expert'.)

And so I managed to stymie the plan to give the drug to every adult woman in Britain and, indeed, the rest of the known world. (And then I wonder why I am so disliked by the government and the industry owned medical profession.)

But the drug companies haven't given up on their plans to persuade perfectly healthy people to take potentially dangerous drugs.

For a while, healthy individuals were told to take aspirin to prevent heart attacks. I looked at the research and found that there was no convincing evidence that taking aspirin on a long term basis was either safe or effective. And now the medical profession seems to agree with me.

There are many millions of people in Britain now taking cholesterol-lowering `superdrugs'. In July 2008 it was revealed that these drugs might cause problems (readers of my book How To Stop Your Doctor Killing You had been aware of problems associated with these drugs since 1998) but they remain popular for the time being. And millions of healthy people around the world now risk their lives taking a drug when they could be helping themselves far more effectively by simply changing their diet.

The drug companies love it when they can persuade healthy people to take drugs. It increases the size of their market. And they always love drugs which have to be taken on a daily basis. The sales and the profits are so much higher.

And so more and more healthy people are going to be conned into taking drugs that are supposed to help them stay healthy, but which may kill them.

Chances of more entirely healthy people being told to take prescription drugs: 90%.

129. Party Politicians Will Become Indistinguishable And Interchangeable

At the end of the election debates in April 2010 the three leaders (I use the world loosely) shook hands and grasped arms like loving relatives at a wedding.

They seemed to be chatting away very merrily.

`I thought you did very well. How do you think I was?'

`I thought you looked good. Lovely tie. Did you pick it out yourself?'

`From the Burlington Arcade. Beautiful suit you had on.'

`My image consultant got me a dozen. Half price if I let the label show occasionally.'

`Your teeth look good. Have you had some more caps?'

I do not understand this.

In the distant days when I was allowed to debate with vivisectors and vaccinators and others of that ilk I would never shake hands with them. I despised them and what they stood for.

Chances of party politicians becoming increasing indistinguishable and increasingly interchangeable: 100%.

The country has been living beyond its means. Most of the citizens have too. However, incomes are now falling and will continue to do so. We're going to be poorer and feel poorer. Costs are already rising (have you tried travelling by train or aeroplane recently?) and incomes are going to fall. I just bought a train ticket for a journey I make quite often. The price of the ticket has gone up 20% in two months. A friend just emailed me to tell me that the price of an airline ticket has doubled in three months. I parked my car this morning and saw a notice warning me that prices will rise by 18% in a week's time.

Costs will rise because companies are struggling to maintain their profits in a world where red tape, an endless variety of new regulations and restricted borrowing from the banks mean that money is tight and it is increasingly difficult to make a profit and survive. Putting up prices when times are hard is the wrong thing to do. But large and small businesses alike will be forced to do it.

And just as prices go up, so wages will come down. Inflation will mean that people are poorer even if their wages and salaries stay the same. But a growing number of people will find that their incomes actually fall as hours are cut and bonuses disappear. Rising taxes and national insurance payments will ensure that incomes fall even faster.

The self employed are going to be hit particularly hard. The services and goods they sell are often discretionary (they don't provide banking facilities or electricity supplies) and so when the bread is eaten without jam their incomes will fall dramatically. (The government, which doesn't like the self-employed, will miss their work and the tax they used to pay.)

The UK is worse off than any country in the world. Our financial system is in a worse state than that of the USA - and we don't have a reserve currency to help bail us out. The UK needs to cut its consumption by 10%. Consumers and industry are going to suffer. As a nation, our standard of living will at best remain where it is and at worst fall in years to come.

People born after around 1980, and particularly more recently, the next generation (and the generations after that) will be far poorer than their parents and their grandparents. House prices are not going to make them rich, taxes are going to keep them poor, inflation is going to damage what savings they do have, and what they inherit, and thanks to high living costs for the elderly and inheritance taxes they aren't going to inherit very much money.

Chances of most people being (and feeling) poorer in 2020 than they felt in 2010: 90%.

131. Privacy Will Disappear

You should regard anything you tell the taxman, your doctor, your bank manager, your accountant, the council, the supermarket and any government department as being public property. As far as the authorities are concerned neither you nor I are entitled to privacy. If we have secrets then we must have something to hide. And if we have something to hide then we must be bad, bad people.

In the second half of 2009, Google, the American search engine received around 1,200 requests from British authorities for information about the internet activities of individuals and companies. The officials wanted to know how and where individuals logged on and wanted to see their emails. Britons are now officially among the most spied upon people on the planet. Only Brazilian and American authorities asked for similar amounts of information. The requests came from government departments, police forces and local authorities. Google is not legally obliged to provide information but usually complies with requests from official bodies.

My favourite headline from recent times concerned Google and appeared in the Financial Times. Here it is: `Google acts on privacy fears by giving users access to own data'. Which is, if you think about it, a bit like `Tesco acts on starvation fears by giving customers access to own food'. Bravos all round. In a television interview a spokesman for Google when asked if users of the search engine should share information with Google as if it were a trusted friend, replied `If you have something that you don't want anyone to know, maybe you shouldn't be doing it in the first place.'

The five year old misfits who run sites such as Facebook seem to have no respect for privacy but that is probably because they don't even understand the concept of freedom that goes with it.

I know of no other internet company that has generated as many complaints or protests as Google - one of my three most evil companies on the planet. (The others, since you're asking are the GM seed company Monsanto and the banking super-vampire company Goldman Sachs.) Authors, publishers, photographers and artists everywhere have complained and sued the company for stealing their copyright. When Google introduced its Buzz service, individuals who had email contacts found them turned into `followers', without their knowledge or approval. And, of course, there is the Street View service which was launched without consideration for privacy, protection laws or cultural acceptability. Google does blur the faces of people captured on its Street View cameras but people in many countries objected to being photographed without their permission and to having their photographs then published on the internet.

Google's mission is, apparently, to `organise the world's information and make it universally accessible and useful'. One can add the word `profitable' to that, though Google doesn't, of course. Are the people who work for this terrible company evil and malicious or just full of their own sense of importance and too stupid to realise how they are playing into the hands of Big Brother? I have no idea. But only an American company could show such extraordinary arrogance to assume that it has the right to manage the world's information - and to help itself to other people's work in the search for greater power and profits.

The internet has changed our lives for ever and only the dimmest nerd could claim that it has changed our lives for the better. Things are likely to continue to get worse. Anyone who wants to protect what is left of their privacy should understand what personal information they are giving, and how it is going to be used by other people.

Privacy is being eroded everywhere. The government will, for example, merrily sell details of your car to anyone who pays them. For example, you can put your car registration number into commercial websites and up will come a picture of your car. Do they have your name and address? Of course.

Supermarkets use a camera system which records the number plates of cars which enter and leave its supermarket car park. They then use this information to find out the owners name and address from the DVLA. Nothing you tell the government will be treated as confidential. They will either sell it or lose it. The authorities keep a record of which books you take out of the public library, they keep a record of which books you purchase online with your credit card and they, naturally, keep a comprehensive record of the websites you visit.

You should not consult an accountant, a financial adviser, a banker or a solicitor about your finances unless you want to find yourself investigated by the authorities. All must tell the authorities if they have any suspicions about your activities. And they must not tell you what they're doing. It is particularly important that you avoid this error if you are, and always have been, scrupulously honest in all your financial dealings. Honesty no longer offers adequate protection.

And the government has for years been working on a huge medical database, a £20 billion computer programme called Spine which will store 50 million medical records. The aim is to produce computerised records for every patient in the UK. (It doesn't sound like a particularly difficult task but the bill keeps soaring.)

A reader sent me a letter from the chief executive of his local branch of the NHS. The letter, apparently sent to all patients over 15 years and 9 months, tells people that they have the choice of having a Summary Care Record created for them. My reader is advised that if he wants to opt out he should let his GP practice know in person or in writing. Inertia compiling, which inevitably most people will ignore `If your GP practice does not hear from you by 12 June 2010 it will be assumed you are happy to have a Summary Care Record and the process of creating a record for you will begin.'

All hospitals and GPs and community care providers will cooperate in creating these damned things (which i thought they had forgotten about but which are, like ID cards, obviously EU drive). And then they can sell the information.

It is true that patients can opt out after viewing their proposed record online or asking their GP for a copy but this is inertia `selling' at its worst. If you don't opt out within a certain time limit you will deemed to have given consent and your records are stored automatically. Errors in your file will remain there indefinitely; they will be read by many and will stay there until you can finally persuade someone to make corrections.

The Government says we should shred bank statements and be very cautious about posting personal details online. The Government (in the guise of the tax people) say I must keep my bank statements. And the government makes my personal information (such as my date of birth) so readily available that a zillion strangers have already posted much of it on line without my permission.

And yet, although the government merrily loses our most confidential information without alarms or punishment, they introduce absurd legislation (allegedly designed to protect our privacy) which in reality causes mayhem. I discovered this letter in a financial magazine: `My eight year old daughter opened a savings account with the Halifax recently. The account is held in her name only...When I phoned with a query, I was told my daughter would have to phone and ask her own questions `without any promoting from an adult'., Is the bank correct?'

According to the magazine a Halifax spokesman replied that the Data Protection Act means that where children are the named account holders, their accounts are protected by the act and cannot be discussed with parents.

If you told me that this law had been made up by a bunch of retarded seven year olds I wouldn't believe you. No retarded seven year olds could be so damned stupid.

Britain has more CCTV cameras than any other country in the world. Britons are now the most spied upon people on earth. CCTV cameras were originally developed for military use. Now, police forces in Britain are acquiring drones - unmanned aeroplanes which were devised to help the military. The drones or spy planes are already being flown over British cities and towns so that the authorities can spy on anyone who might have been missed by the world's most comprehensive network of CCTV cameras. Remarkably, 8% of British homes are now equipped with private CCTV cameras.

When the government can't obtain information legally it obtains it illegally - buying it from bank employees who have stolen it from their employers. For example, the German government paid one thief £4.4 million for stolen bank data. The British government happily does this too. If you or I bought stolen bank information we would, rightly, find ourselves in court and, eventually, in prison. But when individuals working for the government buy stolen information they get salaries and bonuses and probably promotion. The world has turned upside down, inside out and back to front and morality is now confused.

In practical terms, there is no such thing as privacy any more. If you have a bank account or a credit card and use either or both in the normal way then the authorities (by which I mean the British Government, the EU, the American Government and anyone else to whom they decide to sell your information) will know how much money you have and what you do with it. Great Black Hope, American President Obama, has promised a crackdown on tax havens and has announced that `bank secrecy cannot be tolerated'. Nice of him to be so open about his objection to bank secrecy. Naturally, the British Government agree with him.

Secrecy is gone. Privacy is pretty well gone too. But there are things we can all do to retain some slivers of privacy. Pay with cash rather than a credit card, cash card (or cheque) whenever you can. Don't give copies of confidential documents to banks, solicitors etc to keep. They are entitled to look (in order to confirm your identity) but not to keep. And if you do need to send a copy of an important document through the post, write on it the date and a note making it clear that the document is offered only for the use of the person to whom it is being sent. Be careful when filling in forms. Don't fill in questionnaires unless you absolutely have to and don't give answers to questions that don't have to be answered. Once you have revealed private information you can never take it back. Don't give any information on the internet that you wouldn't want to see on a fifty foot high billboard opposite your home.

These precautions will help preserve a little of your privacy.

But the one guarantee I can give is that in the next ten years our privacy will continue to be eroded and we will have to be on watch to retain any privacy at all.

Chances of our privacy continuing to disappear: 100%.

132. Religious Intolerance Will Increase

Intolerance between religions is increasing. And religions are being polarised between the secular and the fundamentalists. This is true of Muslims, Christians and Jews. And it is happening world wide.

Religious wars are here to stay. And other religions, such as Hindus and Buddhists are being dragged into the conflicts. Everything is made more complex by a rise in the number of atheists.

Religious prejudice and bigotry are being so widely promoted (on the internet in particular) and aided and supported by laws designed to encourage religious tolerance and multiculturalism, that the number of extremists (whether they are Christian Fundamentalists, Muslims or Zionists) is increasing at a frightening rate.

Attempts to silence the most vocal bigots are stopped by laws protecting multiculturalism and religious diversity.

So we can expect more religious hatred in coming years.

Chances of religious intolerance increasing: 90%.

133. Breakdowns And Accidents On Our Roads Are Going To Increase.

Road traffic accidents are going to increase for two reasons.

First, it is now pretty well possible to take the driving test in the language of your choice. Our gold-plating of European laws means that we bend over backwards to enable people who choose to come and live in our country to continue to speak their own language. That makes the roads very hazardous because a large percentage of the motorists driving on them (including a lot of lorry drivers) don't speak a word of English and don't the faintest idea what any of the road signs mean.

Second, the failing economy and rising prices mean that many people can no longer afford to have their cars properly and regularly serviced. Despite the fact that there are 35 million cars on British roads, the number of car repair shops is falling by 1,000 a year. Many cars are being repaired at home by people who have to use a manual to enable them to open the bonnet.

There will, inevitably, be more breakdowns and more accidents. The only thing that will work against that happening will be the reduction in the amount of traffic on the roads - caused by high oil prices.

Chances of breakdowns and accidents increasing: 90%.

134. Mobility Scooters Will Make Our Pavements Ever More Dangerous

There are now over 250,000 mobility scooters in Britain and the damned things are breeding faster than rabbits.

Most of the people who use them don't need them, of course. They aren't really disabled. They're fat or lazy or both and a scooter you can ride on the pavement (and leave parked outside the shops) is a great way to get around.

For the rest of us, the innocent pedestrians, these wretched scooters are more of a menace than teenagers on bicycles were when teenagers rode bicycles. Mobility scooters will increase in numbers although many people who would like to buy one might find the cost prohibitive. Sadly, the people who cannot afford mobility scooters will probably be the frail elderly and the genuinely disabled; the people who need them most.

Chances of mobility scooters making pavements more dangerous for pedestrians: 90%.

135. We Will Continue To Live In The `Age Of The Scrounger' (despite the nation's economic malaise)

When Swine flu first struck the world it was quickly noticed that the infection was affecting more people in Britain than anywhere else in world. The Government set up a special enquiry team to try and find out why the incidence of Swine fly was at its highest on Mondays.

They just don't understand, do they?

The sad truth is that there are more malingerers and scroungers in Britain than anywhere else in the world. We started with a more than adequate supply and we have for years been importing more of them.

The problem was that once the Swine flu threat had been officially diagnosed, it was announced that anyone could phone the Government's special flu line, speak to a teenager (with no medical knowledge but a special interest in popular music and X factor contestants) and say that they had a cough and a fever. The Government's teenage representative would then issue a week off work and a free packet of Tamiflu.

Honest.

The Government (and it doesn't matter which party it represents) will always be kind to scroungers because they are loyal and enthusiastic voters - and there are a lot of them. (One in six children now grows up in a house where no one ever works and where, in many cases, people who work are regarded as stupid.)

The Government knows that if treats scroungers and malingerers kindly and generously then they will vote for it. And it also knows that if it attempts to cut their benefits they will riot in the streets and cause great unrest.

Until the workers make it clear that they have had enough of this, and that they want their interests to be represented, their taxes to mean something and their hard work to be recognised, the situation will continue to get worse.

Chances of our continuing to live in the `age of the scrounger': 90%

136. English Seaside Towns Are Due For A Revival

English seaside towns have been in steady decline for several decades. The main reason for their decline was, of course, the ease with which holiday-makers could fly to other countries for their holidays. For a number of years it has, for example, been cheaper to spend two weeks in Spain (where the weather is usually predictable and sunny) than to spend two weeks in Torquay or Bournemouth (where the weather is always unpredictable and only sometimes sunny).

Three things are going to change this.

First, the rising price of oil will make air travel increasingly expensive. The collapse of some airlines (such as British Airways) will add to the cost by enabling budget airlines to increase their prices. As airlines close and routes shrink so airports will close too.

Second, in an attempt to cut down the amount of fuel used by commercial aircraft, the authorities are going to continue to introduce laws will which make air travel increasingly complex and time consuming. It already takes longer to get through the airport than it takes to fly to Spain. The false threats of global warming and terrorism will be used to make air travel increasingly unpleasant.

Third, the economic collapse of Britain, and the collapse of the sterling currency, will mean that Britons will not be able to afford to travel abroad. Holidays in British resorts will be better value than they've been for decades.

And so resorts in Britain will enjoy a renaissance. Those resorts which have rail access, and a centrally situated railway station, will prove particularly successful. Resorts with no rail access will continue to suffer.

Chances of English seaside towns enjoying a revival: 80%.

137. Form Filling Will Take Up More And More Of Our Time

Routine bureaucracy is going to take more and more of our time. At a time when we all need to be working hard to pay off our debts (and our nation's debts) we will, instead, spend much of each week struggling to understand ever more complex forms.

Every time HMRC introduces a new, simpler tax form (something they seem to do annually) it takes much longer to understand it and fill it in. A few years ago I could fill in my annual tax return in a day. Today it takes a week. Seven working days lost to bureaucracy.

Chances of form filling becoming ever more onerous: 100%.

138. Bosses Are Going To Become Very, Very Unpopular

Bosses are going to continue to grab far more of the available wealth than they should. Just a few decades ago, the average boss earned around 40 times as much money as the average worker. So, if a worker earned £10,000 the boss would earn £400,000. And to most people that seemed quite enough. In Japan, the average big time executive earns about three times as much as an ordinary employee. (And, of course, around two and a half thousand years ago Plato suggested a four-fold maximum).

But today's UK bosses aren't satisfied with that sort of money. Today's bosses demand to be paid one thousand times as much as the average worker. Their pay has risen a hundred fold in the last year or two. So, if the average worker earns £10,000 the boss wants to be paid £10,000,000. I'm not exaggerating. Such salaries are no longer unusual. In april 2010 it was announced that the boss of a company called Reckitt and Benckiser which describes itself as a `genuinely global force' and makes the sort of things people keep under the kitchen sink (on its website its `latest and greatest' list includes Harpic, Vanish and Air Wick) had received remuneration totalling £93 million for going to work and being in charge though I believe he had to go in most days. At least eight chief executives of building societies had double figure pay rises in 2009, though interest rates were at an all time low and savers were suffering, and borrowers were hit by a increase in standard variable mortgage rates, refused mortgages an constantly at risk of having their homes repossessed.

Today's bosses find ways of rewarding themselves for their

performance whatever they do. They seem to spend a good deal of their time working out ways to reward themselves with extra money. If the company does badly and make a loss they will give themselves bonuses for looking after the company during difficult times and for copying with the stress created by such adverse circumstances.

It is staggering and appalling to realise that in 2007 the bosses of large public companies averaged 344 times the average pay of workers. In 2008, the combined revenue of 1,130 of the world's leading Chief Executive Officers was 2.224 trillion dollars. Would they do the work for less? Of course they would. (Would footballers kick a ball around for less than £150,000 a week? Of course they would if anyone had the guts to offer them less. What else are they going to do for a living? Wash cars? Cut lawns?)

And, since company bosses demand stratospheric salaries, senior civil servants also demand stratospheric salaries. The greed spread. They were, after all, times of apparently unending prosperity.

The excuse for all this greed was that if the boss isn't paid a telephone number salary he would quit and go somewhere else.

Really?

`I'll go somewhere else if you don't pay me a bonus.'

`I won't work hard unless you pay me an incentive.'

If the shareholders of big companies consistently refuse to pay such absurd sums, just where are these people going to find anyone prepared to pay their million pound salaries (complete, of course, with million pound pension, million pound bonus for turning up for work, million pound bonus to working on Fridays and million pound expense account)? These are, after all, a strange breed of men and women who spend most of their days hobnobbing with politicians and celebrities and arranging to give the shareholder's money away to political parties and charitable organisations (so that they can be philanthropists with other people's money and receive honours and awards) and who, if ever questioned about their former company's fraudulent activities, usually claim that they knew nothing about anything or didn't understand what was being done. They are certainly not people who create products, wealth or jobs. They are, quite simply, parasites. And they are parasites with very high opinions of themselves. In recent months a number of bosses have, for example, claimed that they have no loyalty to their shareholders. If they do have any loyalty to shareholders it comes after their loyalty to their employees and customers. This is, of course, arrant and arrogant nonsense. A boss's only primary loyalty is to the shareholders. They may be `little' people, pensioners and small investors with small stakes in investment trust funds and unit trusts, but the `little' people are the people who own the company. The boss works for them.

This obscene greed will eventually attract real anger. There will be a class war. But this won't be polite class war. Violence will be done.

But why shouldn't company bosses be exposed to market forces? Let shortlisted candidates for high executive office state the minimum salary they will accept if they are appointed. Then, as with most tenders, the lowest bidder wins the job.

In every factory, office or institution the pay of the highest paid worker should not be more than 25 or 30 times the pay of the lowest paid worker.

So, if the lowest paid worker in an office receives £5,000 a year the highest paid worker should not receive more than £125,000 to £150,000 a year.

If the fat cat at the top has a pay rise then the person at the bottom of the pile will have to receive a similar pay rise. This simple technique would help eradicate poverty, envy and greed in one swift move - while still rewarding initiative and effort.

A consultant surgeon takes on massive responsibilities and requires extensive skills (which take years to acquire) but he doesn't receive more than 25 times the salary of a porter. A judge doesn't receive more than 25 times the salary of a clerk. An orchestra conductor doesn't receive more than 25 times the salary of a violinist. Why should a company executive be paid 300 or 400 times as much as the lowest paid worker his company employs? These are the sort of salary differentials which exist in the world of show business where a rock star might expect to earn that much more than a roadie on the grounds that his talents and skills are not only unique and bringing in the customers but are also likely to have a relatively short career.

There are two reasons for this absurd state of affairs. One is that most company private shareholders are these days forced to hold their shares through nominee accounts. And that means that they cannot vote on company affairs. The second reason is that institutional shareholders (who hold shares on behalf of those who have private pensions or who hold shares in unit trusts or investment trusts or other investment funds) are too chummy with the people who run companies. They know that their own salaries and fees are absurdly high and so they don't do anything to rock the boat. We can get round this simply and easily by insisting that private shareholders be allowed to vote and that institutional shareholders be expected to consult their shareholders on issues such as corporate pay.

As the days ahead get darker and darker, and as most people find that they have to tighten their belts as we struggle to pay off the debts bequeathed to the nation by Gordon Brown and his idiot chums, so the anger and resentment against bosses will bubble and come to the boil.

Bosses may find that unless they are prepared to take huge pay cuts they and their families will have to enjoy their absurdly inflated pay packets behind locked gates if they are to remain alive.

The chances of bosses becoming very, very unpopular are 90%.

139. Big Bonuses Will Be Paid To The Undeserving Even As The Economy Struggles

Bonuses (or tips) used to be something that posh people gave to poor people. Taxi drivers, waiters and hotel doormen got tips because they were poorly paid and it was a way for their temporary employers to show their gratitude (and superiority). Factory workers making things on a production line were given bonuses if they made things faster than expected.

Just a decade or two ago no self-respecting banker, company director or civil servant would have accepted a tip (or a bonus) for doing their jobs. They would have been as unwilling to accept the idea that they needed fiscal encouragement as would a doctor or priest. (Try offering £50 to your surgeon as an incentive for him to make a neat scar and you'll see what I mean.)

But bankers and public sector workers have lowered their social vision of themselves. These days they are quite happy to be lumped in with cabbies and bellhops and very pleased indeed to be able to trouser extra cash for actually doing what they get paid to do anyway. In 2007, banks that were encouraging debt and taking risks with depositors' money, charged 41% of the profits of the corporate sector in fees and bonuses. More money for rich bankers. Less money for pensioners and shareholders.

If bank staff had pocketed just 10% less in pay and bonuses over the last decade the banks would have had £50 billion more in capital. If they'd taken just slightly less in undeserved bonuses the banks would have been awash with cash when the crisis hit. The £50 billion is about what the British Government claims it had to give the banks so that they could stay in business and keep paying out the bonuses. Was it any wonder that in Greece demonstrators set fire to a bank? The only wonder is that banks all over the world aren't all still smouldering.

There is, of course, a big myth about bonuses.

Today, it is widely believed that giving people bonuses encourages them to work harder and better. The system works for production line staff whose productivity can easily be measured but it doesn't work for most other people. It is, indeed, complete bollocks. Giving a doorman a tip may mean that he remembers your name. Giving a waiter a tip may mean that (if you visit often enough and he remembers you) you will get a smile when he hands you the menu. But the door won't be opened any more effectively. And the tea and crumpets won't taste any better.

In order to check the effect of bonuses on performance four North American professors conducted human experiments. In one they gave subjects tasks that demanded attention, memory, concentration and creativity. A third of the subjects were promised a day's pay if they performed well. A third were promised two weeks' pay. The final third were promised five months' pay. The result was that the low and medium bonus groups performed the same. The group offered the big bonus performed worst of the three.

In a second experiment graduate students were given an opportunity to earn either $600 or $60 by performing one four minute task. The result again showed that a big carrot led to poorer performance.

Bonuses clearly don't work. They cost employers (and when the people receiving the bonuses are public sector workers that means taxpayers) a good deal of money and they result in less effective work being done. Bonuses result in poorer performances than bosses would get without them.

Banks, big companies and the civil service will, without a shadow of doubt, ignore this evidence and continue to hand out big bonuses. Civil servants now expect bonuses for not having holidays all the time. They will protest vigorously if any government tries to take away their new perks. They won't want to enter the real world any more than bankers do. There will be strikes galore. Indeed, striking will be the new growth industry.

And the money for the bonuses will be provided by shareholders and taxpayers.

Today, the bonus culture is in full swing again. Bankers in London are involved in litigation against banks which didn't pay discretionary bonuses. (Can you believe it? The bankers succeeded in losing a ton of money and yet the banks still wouldn't pay out bonuses!) Bankers who had lost fortunes and paid themselves extravagantly well announced with extraordinary arrogance that if they were not given huge bonuses and retention payments and sweeteners and golden hellos, goodbyes and goodnights they would leave. Just where they would go, or what they would do, was never discussed because, in truth of course, it takes probably less skill, talent and training to be an investment banker than it does to be a bus driver. (This is the best kept secret in the banking industry. Indeed, it is probably the only secret.)

In America between 90% and 100% of the earnings achieved by the major banks are now being shared among employees as salaries, bonuses and benefits. Nothing is being put aside for a rainy day and nothing is left for shareholders. Bonuses were originally designed to encourage (they don't, as we have seen, but that was the thinking behind them) but today they are often paid to directors, civil servants and executives just for breathing and turning up occasionally. Bosses and civil servants who have, by any conceivable standard, failed miserably still get their bonuses. The venomous snakes at Goldman Sachs paid themselves £100 billion in bonuses for conning the taxpayers out of a great chunk of money. Or was it £1,000 billion. Or a £1000 trillion. In February 2010 it was reported that the Royal Bank of Scotland had lost £3.6 billion and paid out £1.3 billion in bonuses (which the government, on behalf of the taxpayers, owning the bank, approved). Two employees were due to get £7 million each in bonuses and more than 100 employees of this utterly useless bank got bonuses of a million each. I tried to get RBS to help with my business. They didn't even reply to letters. Too busy counting their bonuses I guess.

Nothing has been done about moral hazard.

The chances of bigger and bigger bonuses being paid to the rich, the very rich and the megarich: 90%.

140. Climate Change Myths Will Continue

The politicians claim that the scientists have proved that climate change exists and is man made. This is, to be polite, a damned lie. It might well transpire that climate is changing and caused by man but there is, at the moment, no scientific evidence to support this hypothesis. Politicians everywhere have leapt on the theory and now pretend its fact. It isn't. The theories are driven and promoted in order to provide an excuse for new controls and new money making legislation. There is a remarkable similarity to the official AIDS hoax that terrified millions (and even resulted in healthy people killing themselves). The AIDS scare was a confidence trick which was (and is) sustained by an international mixture of interested professionals. Exactly the same thing is happening with the climate change myth. The climate change proponents are abusive, hysterical fanatical and so convinced that they are right that they deliberately distort the truth in order to defend and promote their message; ignoring the fact that if their evidence were truly correct and convincing they wouldn't have to do any cheating.

Town councils all over the UK are now turning off street lights 'between midnight and dawn' in order 'to be kinder to the environment' and to protect us from global warming. There is no mention of the fact that this is really to comply with absurd and dangerous EU legislation. Nor is there much talk of the fact that the financial savings will be used to pay for council staff pensions. Citizens everywhere are forced to sort their rubbish into five different piles. This, too, is allegedly being done 'to save the planet'. Lies, lies and more lies.

The whole green 'save the planet' nonsense has even reached Formula 1 motor racing which is now desperately pretending to be green, spending billions on searching for new technology that might save a trillionth of what they spend on flying everyone around the world in private planes once a fortnight. It can't be green or environmentally friendly but it feels it has to be, or has to pretend to be, in order to survive. They put green ink marks on some tyres (to distinguish different types) and these were then known as 'green tyres'.

The last international climate change conference was held in Copenhagen in December 2009. (They never hold these things in Wolverhampton or Milton Keynes). Prince Charles and Gordon Brown both travelled in their own private planes. The United Nations Climate Conference in Copenhagen at the end of 2009 had 15,000 delegates, 98 world leaders and 5,000 reporters and, doubtless, a few pop singers who wanted to be seen, and to snuggle up to the usual gaggle of war criminals, who between them turned up in 12,000 limousines. They came in so many private jets that some of the aeroplanes had to be parked in Norway. An estimated 40,000 tons of carbon dioxide was put into the air by those attending the summit which is more than 60 of the world's smallest nations together put into the atmosphere in an entire year. This was the conference where everyone agreed to have the foie gras, the river trout, the venison and the 1948 claret but no one would agree to do anything about climate change. It was, entirely predictably, just another international beano for the army of useless bureaucrats, hangers on and general, mixed unemployables who live the high life on expenses. The word hypocrisy just won't go away. If all climate change meetings were cancelled the world would doubtless be a healthier and finer place.

The Copenhagen conference was a chaotic, ill coordinated and ultimately expensive and pointless; a shindig where smug, self-satisfied hypocrites with personal carbon footprints the size of China took great delight in attempting to tell us all what we must do to save the world from their extravagance (extravagance, it must be pointed out, which was largely paid for by taxpayers who had none of the fun but just paid all the bills). In the end they couldn't agree on what to say so they all piled into their limousines, drove to the airport, climbed into their private jets and flew home again.

In the same month the EU announced that it was paying £6.5 billion to help other countries deal with climate change. All EU countries were instructed to contribute and, naturally, our Prime Minister at the time, Gordon Brown, announced with great pride that Britain would contribute £1.5 billion to this fund (More than any other country in the EU. (France and Germany were each giving £400 million.) Gordon Brown loved making grand rich man gestures with other people's money. £1,500 million used to be serious money before Brown took over the nation's piggybank. This absurd generosity was announced in the same week that Institute for

Fiscal Studies said that for the next eight years each British family must pay £2,400 extra in tax (at the best guess of the chancellors) to pay for Brown's mistakes.

Whenever there is a conference someone from the British government is always there (flown in by private jet and met in a limousine of course) to promise that whatever else the rest of the world is going to do we will do more of it and whatever else anyone else is paying we will pay more.

Moreover, all three major political parties in Britain have agreed to give £18 billion to China and India in order to help those two countries deal with the non existent problem of climate change. Even if climate change was proven by scientific evidence (which it isn't) this would be extraordinary. Britain is fighting against bankruptcy but China and India are almost certainly the two richest countries in the world.

The truth, of course, is that the only people who still support the climate change theory are the ones who are making money out of it and the ones who haven't done any research or don't understand how science works. It was for a long while a convincing story. But you really do have to be a little slow-witted to still support the story.

There is a widespread assumption among journalists that if someone is a `scientist' then whatever he says must be taken seriously. If he is a `scientist' working for a university or some important sounding institution then his words must be given the sort of respect usually reserved for stuff carved on tablets of stone.

Sadly, this is bollocks.

The theory that man made carbon dioxide emissions were causing global temperatures to soar has never been proved. Indeed, on the contrary, global mean temperatures haven't risen for more than a decade. Computer generated predictions say that terrible things will happen. But in real life the terrible things don't actually happen.

The climate change theorists ignored the evidence, of course. They continued to shout (very loudly) at anyone who questioned their research and their predictions and they merrily manipulated the evidence to say what they wanted it to say.

The problem, of course, is that the vast majority of scientists long ago sold their objectivity and became hired hands prepared to propagate whatever theory seemed to offer the most profit. And today there are tons of money available to scientists who are prepared to say the right thing. Climate change scientists are no different to the ones who told us AIDS was going to kill us all or the ones who insist that genetic engineering is a good thing and who assure us (without any evidence) that genetically modified food is perfectly safe to eat. They are no different to the scientists who claim that vivisection is the only way to test new drugs (when the evidence proves conclusively that it is worse than worthless because it is dangerous) or the ones who claim that vaccination is an excellent way to prevent disease (when the evidence shows that it may be hugely profitable for doctors and drug companies but as far as patients are concerned it is obscenely dangerous).

Anyone who feels that scepticism is unreasonable should note that the UK Met Office has been leading the assessment of research into global warming and climate change. This is presumably the same UK Met Office that has given up on long range forecasts and seems to have difficulty in knowing what the weather is going to do in the afternoon.

Scientists have been accused of manipulating data on global warming and have refused to provide detailed information about the data allegedly supporting their claims. Requests for information under the Freedom of Information act have been turned down. Fake data, irrelevant data and manipulated data have all been used. There is a feeling among the public (promoted by the media) that scientists are an honourable bunch who can always be trusted. My experience, based on many years of assessing scientific information, is that scientists are, on the whole, a dishonest bunch who will fiddle their results whenever they think they can get away with it if there is some financial advantage to be had. It is remarkably easy to fiddle the way results are presented (inconvenient truths are simply suppressed) in order to please political masters (who may be handing out grants) and commercial masters (who are probably paying for the research). Fraud is so common in the world of medicine that it is safe to say that every medical paper must be regarded as fraudulent until proved otherwise. (This is nothing new. I have been exposing medical fraud since the mid 1970s in early books such as The Medicine Men and Paper Doctors.)

The scientists now admit that there has been no global warming since 1995. They made it all up. Just as the AIDS guys did. Al Gore's film was a terrific feature film, scarier than anything Hammer ever made. Coincidentally, Gore is now estimated to be worth over $100 million as a result of lectures and global warming businesses.

It is worth remembering that just a few years ago the climate change specialists, the same mythologists now spreading the myths about global warming, were warning us that the earth was getting colder and the ice caps over the poles were getting thicker. The fake scare stories just keep coming. (There is, of course, a commercial purpose. There is always a purpose.) The problem with the climate change argument is that it is built on political and commercial interests and lies by scientists. There is too much deceit and hypocrisy to take the whole thing seriously.

The latest figures show that 50% of British voters believe that politicians make a fuss about climate change in order to distract us from other issues while 47% think that climate change is just another excuse to raise taxes. It is comforting to know that so many people have the measure of our politicians and recognise another confidence trick when they meet one.

Climate change propagandists are either paid to do so or they are woefully ignorant and possibly more than a little stupid. Politicians claim to believe in climate change because it is convenient and profitable but although some journalists propagate the nonsense because their owners tell them to do so many swallow the story because they are surprisingly naive and actually believe it; these are, after all, the same vulnerable and susceptible idiots who believe that GM foods are safe and that vaccination saves lives and who, just a decade or two ago, believed that AIDS was going to kill us all.

It is difficult to avoid the feeling that the goal of the climate change advocates is not the reduction of global warming but the enactment of a world wide system of regulation which transfers wealth from private citizens to governments (though regulatory fines and so on) and to control individual behaviour through new `climate change' regulations.

The climate change advocates are mad environmentalists, self satisfied, hypocritical, pseudoscientific myth manipulators who want to bully other people into doing pointless things `to save the planet' while ignoring the big environmental and health issues (such as genetic engineering, carcinogens in food, polluted drinking water, overbuilt flood plains, noise and light pollution, diesel poisoning in cities, toxins in the environment etc) because these things are protected by their fascist paymaster overlords

Are governments promoting the climate change/global warming myth because they really believe it, or are they promoting the myth because they know the oil is running out and the policies promoted as part of a climate change/global warming policy enable them to force us to cut our oil consumption without actually causing a global panic by telling us about the coming oil crisis. (`I read part of your book Oil Apocalypse,' a reporter for The Independent newspaper told me. `But it frightened me so much I couldn't read the rest.'

Chances of climate change myths continuing: 90%.

141. The Incidence Of Diabetes Will Rise

The incidence of diabetes is rising. It is going to rise even faster.

Here are two quotes, relating to this forecast.

`There are twice as many cases of childhood diabetes now as there were 30 years ago. Nobody understands why.' - Financial Times (2009)

`By 2014 sixteen per cent of the population will be diabetic. It will be the genetic factor which will be primarily responsible.' - The Health Scandal, Vernon Coleman (1988)

Type 1 Diabetes (the type that affects children) is an inherited disorder. It can be treated but not cured. You don't need to be a genius to work out that as the years go by there will be more people suffering from it.

There is, of course, a corollary.

The incidence of obesity is rising rapidly.

And type II diabetes (aka maturity onset diabetes) is largely caused by obesity.

So Type II diabetes is going to rocket too.

And in 30 years times the Financial Times will, no doubt, wonder why.

The dramatic increase in diabetes has proved to be a tremendous cost for the NHS and the nation. A disease that can be treated but not cured must always cost a great deal of money. When that disease is inherited and is becoming commoner and commoner the cost will rise at an even faster rate.

Diabetes will continue to be an unrecognised economic problem for some years to come.

Chances of diabetes becoming much more common by 2020: 100%.

142. Vital Medicines Will Be Banned

Vitamins, supplements of many kinds, homoeopathic remedies and, herbal remedies are all likely to be banned in the next few years.

The EU (in this instance obeying the drug company lobbyists) is determined to make such products illegal. It has, of course, been trying to do this for years and has, so far, failed. But what the EU wants it gets and in the long term no amount of protesting, complaining, petition signing or letter writing will change this outcome.

The strange thing is that many people who strongly object to the idea of not being able to buy their favourite supplement are also keen supporters of the European Union.

Nothing will change until more people recognise that virtually every infringement of our rights and liberties comes from the European Union: the most oppressive organisation that has ever existed.

Chances of vitamins and other supplements being banned: 80%.

143. Roads Are Going To Get Worse (and toll roads are going to become commonplace)

Our roads started to deteriorate about thirty or forty years ago. I remember realising, at that time, that road surfaces were never again going to be as good as they had been. Potholes were becoming an increasing problem and roads were cracking and breaking up on a regular basis.

It is, of course, entirely possible that road building skills have been lost, or that, to save money, modern roads are not built robustly enough to stand up to the wear and tear they are bound to receive.

But I suspect that lorries are the main problem. First, the canal system was abandoned (though it provided an excellent and economical way to move goods around the country) and then the idiotic Beeching took an axe to large parts of the rail network. The only way for businesses to move goods around the country was by road. And, to make road transport more efficient, haulage companies started demanding, buying and using ever larger lorries.

Today's huge lorries are absurdly overweight and oversized and they cause massive amounts of damage to our roads. It is always the slow lane on motorways and dual carriages that breaks up first, and that isn't because of the little old ladies trundling along at 30 mph in Morris Minors.

The obvious answer would be massively to increase the tax on lorries and to make rail and canal travel more attractive. Subsidies on both those forms of transport would, in the long run, save the country money by reducing the need for road works and the associated traffic jams.

But none of this sensible stuff will happen.

Instead, we are about to see the return of toll roads on a huge scale. The government will sell more and more of the bridges, tunnels and roads that have been built with our money. The (mostly foreign owned) companies which buy our bridges, tunnels and roads will then charge us to use our own bridges, tunnels and roads. We paid to build them and maintain them and we will pay to use them.

Chances of our roads getting worse: 100%.

Chances of the number of toll roads increasing: 90%.

144. England's Best Way of Leaving The EU Is To Encourage Scottish Independence (and when the English realise this they will fight for Scottish independence)

Britain has been run by Scottish politicians ever since the Labour party came to power in 1997. And the Scottish politicians have been running Britain for Scotland. Look at the facts: First, Scotland has a population of around 5 million but of these only 163,000 are net taxpayers - an astonishing 4,837,000 are kept by English taxpayers. Second, the British Government currently spends £1,503 more per head on Scottish citizens than it spends on English citizens. This is why Scottish cancer patients are given life-saving drugs which are denied to English patients. It is why English university students must pay tuition fees while Scottish students get their education free. It is why the elderly in England must sell their homes to pay for nursing home care while the elderly in Scotland get free nursing home care.

Most Scots, being an ungrateful bunch, want independence for Scotland and believe that if the United Kingdom was broken up into its constituent parts, Scotland would be a richer and stronger country. The Scots are keen on the EU which, they believe, gave them their own Parliament and helped them take the first step towards independence. Most Scots, being poorly educated, do not realise that the EU merely gave them, the Welsh and the Irish EU regional parliaments. The Scots who do realise what is happening keep quiet about it. (And many of those who do realise what is happening are undoubtedly riding on the EU gravy train.) At times the cheek shown by the Scots is almost unbelievable. During the run up to the May 2010 election, vocal Scots were campaigning to protect Scotland from spending cuts caused by the crisis created by obscenely incompetent Scottish banks. The economic crisis threatening Britain with ruin and bankruptcy was almost entirely made in Scotland but the Scots don't want to have to pay any of the resulting cost.

If given the chance the English would vote to leave the European Union. England would once again be a strong and independent nation. England would be free of European red tape and richer by several billion pounds a year.

If the English can persuade the Scots to demand independence, and the break up of the United Kingdom, England will be able to break free of the EU. (Scotland can pretend to be independent but, of course, it will simply be a region of the European Union which is what it is now.)

Without Scotland and the EU to support the English will be much better off. England will have much better schools and hospitals. And lower taxes.

Once they realise all this the English will fight hard for Scottish independence. It is, quite probably, the only way that England will be able to leave the EU and retain its own history, culture and very existence.

Chances of the English fighting for Scottish independence: 70%.

145. The Scares Will Keep Coming

The scares will keep coming. AIDS, SARS, bird flu, swine flu. They were all obviously not the end of the world despite valiant attempts by politicians (anxious to terrify us into not noticing what is really going on in the world) by scientists (desperate for grant money to support their pet projects) and by lobbyists (with their own interests to promote - usually products to sell). The scares that do best are the ones that have the most powerful commercial interests behind them. Politicians and regulators lie and exaggerate and conceal and confuse with enormous enthusiasm as they attempt to meet the demands and requirements of their various benefactors.

The scares are then promoted by journalists who don't know the first thing about assessing scientific evidence (though they describe themselves as science journalists or medical journalists). All they really know is how to create a good scare story to help revive their sagging sales and drag a few more advertisers away from the internet. And the broadsheet newspapers (with an even less viable economic model) are as bad as (or worse than) the redtop tabloid newspapers at creating scares out of pseudo-scientific nonsense.

Swine flu turned out to be less deadly than ordinary flu. Officials and lobbyists distorted the figures by deciding to count every case of flu and every common cold as a case of swine flu. No one could understand why it was relatively rare in Wales compared to the rest of the country because no one in Whitehall had the brains to realise that there is no point in bothering to take your free Tamiflu and your seven days off work if you are unemployed. Bird flu turned out to be pretty bad for turkeys. I can't remember what SARS turned out to be. AIDS, of course, was the biggest confidence trick of the twentieth century. When it was clear that AIDS wasn't going to kill us all and the scientists making a good living out of it needed to boost the figures they started counting cases of tuberculosis, malaria and anything else they could find as AIDS. Such fraud suited everyone's purposes, though it did mean that tuberculosis (the real killer) was ignored and allowed to become a major threat again.

They have all, of course, missed the big one. The big cause of cancer. The one killer food that is responsible for millions of premature deaths every year. The big story for which I can provide bullet proof evidence.

The one thing I can guarantee is that there will be many more scare stories coming our way.

It's their way of keeping us worried, suppressing dissent and delaying revolution.

Chances of new scares continuing to frighten us half to death: 100%.

146. Politically Correct Nonsense Will Get Worse

Political correctness has become the law and it is legally (as well as morally) no longer possible to oppose the absurdities the politically correct come up with. In today's world racism, sexism and bullying are all in the eye of the beholder. If the alleged victim says that they have been bullied (or whatever) then the system agrees that they have been.

All you have to do is say it for it to be the truth. Protestations of innocence are ignored, overruled. If the `victim' says it is so then it is so and that's an end to it. That, believe it or not, is official policy in our mad, mad world.

(I believe that as a white, elderly male I am discriminated against for my colour, my age and my sex. I believe this to be true and so it is. I would not, however, put money on my chances of winning a case against the government. How can that be? Is that another example of discrimination?)

The people who claim to know about these things claim that one in three of us are officially disabled that one in three of us are gay and that bullying happens everywhere and is a major cause of physical and mental illness at school, at work and at home. Huge organisations, which spread across the wastelands occupied by private pressure groups, charities and quangos consume vast amounts of money and constantly expand their remits in order to expand their power and their money making capabilities. The problem, of course, is that by spreading the problem, and extending it beyond all good sense, they diminish it. If one in three of us are disabled then being disabled cannot be such a bad thing.

The money wasted by attempts to satisfy the politically correct is obscene. In London, hundreds of millions of pounds of public money is being spent so that the disabled in wheelchairs can have access to the London Tube. (They already have access to free taxi services.) Hundreds of millions are being spent to provide `step-free' access to wonderful Edwardian railway stations. It would be far, far cheaper to give every disabled person a free car for the rest of their lives. Or to give them free access to buses. Or to give them free travel passes entitling them to free travel by taxi. But that is not the point. The disabled must be given access to the underground platforms whether they want it or not because, well, because they must and that's an end to it. Of course, once they are on the platform the disabled in wheelchairs will not be able to board any of the trains because that involves stepping up from the platform. The truth is that hundreds of millions of pounds of public money is being spent so that disabled tube train spotters can have access to the underground platforms.

Our obsession with political correctness means that we are forced to bend over backwards to favour anyone who is disabled in any way. I do not believe for one second that in a reasonable world a sighted David Blunkett would have been given ministerial power. He was, in my view, a most dangerous Home Secretary (certainly the worst the country has ever had) and he has left us with some very damaging legislation. I believe he regarded his blindness as a voting ploy, and that as a politician he got away with a potent mixture of arrogance ignorance, stupidity, crookedness and Stalinism. When I dared to criticise his policies I was frequently attacked and told `leave him alone, he's blind'.

Similarly, on a radio programme some years ago I was viciously attacked by a vivisection supporter who claimed that I was not properly medically qualified. After I objected to this libellous remark and asked for an apology on air I was attacked in the press because the vivisection supporter was in a wheelchair. On another radio programme, a book of mine received the standard BBC sneering treatment from a presenter who was blind. When I ventured to defend myself and to ask how he'd managed to read the book (no braille edition was out at the time) the response was predictable. I was the `bad' person for daring to question his judgement - even though he could not have possibly read the book.

The truth is that the politically correct are destroying our world and even our history and our culture. (I have in recent years seen productions of Robin Hood and 39 Steps which had women in leading roles and there was, apparently, much talk of a female Dr Who. How long will it be before a black woman plays James Bond?)

Finally, if I tell you that there is news as I write that a blind, deaf and severely disabled man wants to join army and drive a tank, and that equality legislation from the EU means that the army has to make it possible for him to achieve his aim you will not, I feel sure, know whether or not to believe me.

The chances of politically correct nonsense increasing: 100%.

147. Prepare To Pay For Everything

The government will continue to fail and if you want to get things done you will (despite paying more taxes than ever before) have to pay for it.

If you want decent education for your children you will have to pay for it. If you want your children to go to university you will have to pay for it - and, quite possibly, send them to a university abroad. If you want medical treatment for an inconvenient or life threatening disease, and you want a decent chance of coming out alive, you will have to pay for it (unless you are prepared to risk your life in a bug ridden NHS hospital swamp). If you want a GP who will be available when you have an emergency you will have to pay extra. If you want decent dental treatment you will have to pay for it privately. If you want protection from vandals and hoodies with knives and dogs you will have to pay for private security. If you don't have time to spend a day a week sorting through your rubbish and putting it into the correct containers you will have to pay for a private collection service.

Chances of most of us having to pay for everything we want: 90%.

148. Infections Are Coming Back

I forecast that serious and deadly infections were coming back in my book Superbody.

Sadly, I was right.

It wasn't a difficult prediction to make.

Doctors overprescribe antibiotics. Farmers give the damned things to their animals. The bugs we thought we had conquered are getting stronger by the year. They are no longer sensitive to the antibiotics we have available. And so people die.

Our hospitals, instead of being havens of cleanliness and hygiene, are filthy dirty. Lazy staff and dirty wards are a breeding ground for new killer infections. Like bedsores, every case of MRSA or clostridium is a disgrace, a sign of inadequate, unprofessional and incompetent nursing. The incidence of deadly infections within the NHS should be a cause of shame and embarrassment among the nursing profession. But nurses, like everyone else in public life, take no responsibility for the deaths they cause.

Chances of infections becoming a major problem: 100%.

149. Shopping Is Going To Be An Increasingly Unpleasant Experience.

Small independent specialist shops will continue to disappear. Today, there are very few music, stationery, art, sport, toy, sweet shops around, for example. There is nowhere to buy a decent pen, a CD of a classical music piece, a DVD of a classic film, a decent toy, a book by Charles Dickens, or a box of decent paints. Even junk shops are disappearing (destroyed by charity shops). The number of good bookshops (as opposed to chains and newsagents that sell a few bestsellers) is disappearing at such a rate that the owners of the remaining bookshops will soon be able to hold their annual general meeting in the woodshed at the bottom of our garden (though, actually, why they would want to is beyond me).

The interesting, exciting, shops are being replaced by charity shops, estate agents, phone shops (please defend us from these soulless places) and strange shops selling novelty fridge magnets, models of fairies and pens that have a name printed on the side (though never the name of anyone you know, of course).

All these delightful little shops, sometimes run by slightly eccentric owners, are disappearing for several reasons. First, local councils are charging such absurd local taxes that shopkeepers cannot possibly pay them and make a profit. Second, insurance companies have increased their premiums by a trillion per cent in the last year or two. Third, the EU has introduced so many daft rules and regulations (all of which have been gold plated by the British authorities and which are now policed zealously by small-minded zealots who have no idea how difficult running a shop can be) that running a shop, employing one or two members of staff and trying to provide a service to the public has become a thankless task. I know shopkeepers who have closed down because their shops can only be entered via a step (not allowed) or who have had to give up because part of their store can only accessed via a staircase (not allowed). Fourth, EU rules about the employment of staff mean that shop owners dare not offer their staff any instruction or adverse comment. As a result staff are almost universally rude. It is as though surliness was considered sexy. Sixth, the number of commercial properties is shrinking because many owners are knocking them down to avoid the empty-rates liability legislation brought in by EU bureaucrats to punish property owners who cannot find tenants. (Only EU bureaucrats would think that punishing property owners for not finding tenants is a good idea or even a logical one.) And finally, of course, the internet has helped close down shops by offering cut price everything from mail order suppliers.

The next generation will probably never have the joy of entering a shop where the shopkeeper knows his subject, is an enthusiast and is prepared to help you find whatever it is you are looking for.

These days, shopping is a soulless and unsatisfactory experience.

In the new world there are new rules and the first and most important is that the customer is always wrong and probably stupid too. The staff in the ubiquitous shops selling telephones seem to me to take all the prizes for stupidity, arrogance and ignorance. In one shop, not long ago, I asked if they had a pay as you go device for collecting emails. Two young assistants sneered and agreed there was no such thing. I picked up a thin brochure from a pile they had on display and looked inside. In the centre there was a double page spread devoted to precisely such devices. `I was thinking of one of these,' I said. Not even a blush.

No one in shops ever knows anything about the products they sell. They pretend they do. But they don't. (Once again, this is especially true of shops selling telephones and electrical equipment.) If, when you get your product home, you need help there will be a premium rate number to call. When you ring the helpline you are likely to find yourself talking to someone in India, Pakistan or Scotland. Whichever it is they won't understand you and you won't understand them and they won't know where Birmingham is. If you have the temerity to argue with a client agent on the telephone they put the phone down and make you wait another 45 minutes to speak to another agent who then sees that you have a red mark next to your name and is consequently deliberately unhelpful. If you've bought a television set or something similar they and are prepared to pay more they may agree to send someone round to look at it for you. He will be described as an expert or a consultant. He will probably have no more idea than you do how to make it work. The last time we bought a DVD player we had three visits from the shop's experts. They managed to plug it in but that was about the limit of their skill.

It used to be that a test of character used to be in treating strangers decently - even when they were not obviously important. People in any sort of service industry used to be trained to please their customers - not by obsequiousness but by being aware of their needs and trying to satisfy them honourably, decently and fairly. Those principles have disappeared.

Customers are treated as though they are a nuisance. Respect has gone and been replaced with resentment and suspicion. The result is that customers are miserable or cross before they get to the pay desk. And they are miserable or cross before they enter the next shop.

So shop assistants are, in the end, paying the price. Instead of being greeted by happy customers, they spend their days greeting unhappy customers.

Chances of shopping becoming an increasingly unpleasant experience: 100%.

150. Sex Offences Committed By Children Are Going To Increase

In May 2010 special security precautions had to be taken at the Old Bailey in London where two boys, aged 10 and 11, were on trial for the rape of an 8 year old girl. After much stress and heartache the little girl admitted that she made up the allegation because she had been naughty and was worried that she might not get any sweets. The boys were subsequently found guilty.

Putting aside the question of how effective a 10 year old boy would be as a rapist I find myself wondering just why educationalists cannot see how closely this awful story must be connected with the absurd modern policy of giving sex education lessons to primary school children.

As sex education classes are become a part of our culture so vast numbers of young children will be determined to experiment and to try out the things they have been taught.

Real and imaginary sex crimes committed by young boys will increase dramatically. Thousands of male and female lives will be ruined as a result.

The real villains will be the educationalists who dreamt up the idea of teaching five and six year olds about sex. Sadly, they will probably claim that the answer is not less sex education but more. It's not impossible that pre-school infants and play school inmates will receive sex education along with the fingerpainting.

Chances of sex offences committed by children increasing: 80%.

151. Shareholders Will Increasingly Be Ignored (by the people they pay to run the companies they own)

It has been happening for some time. But now it's official. Companies are now being run in the interests of directors, employees and customers rather than in the interests of shareholders.

In April 2010, Paul Polman, chief executive of Unilver, announced that he did not regard shareholder value as the main driver of a company's business model.

The truth, of course, is that shareholders own companies. Directors and executives and everyone else, work for shareholders. It is shareholders who pay the salaries, the wages, the bonuses, the pensions and for the private planes. And it is shareholders who take the losses when things go wrong.

In my view company directors who do not run their company primarily in the interests of the shareholders are failing in their primary duty. I don't buy shares in companies where directors do not understand this.

Chances of shareholders being increasingly ignored by the people they pay to run the companies they own: 100%.

152. Home Owners Will Be Forced To Rent Spare Rooms To Immigrants

Immigrants are flooding into Britain. Many come from other EU countries. Others, encouraged by the EU, come from further afield. EU law means that there is nothing that Britain can do to prevent these people coming into the country.

The inevitable resultant shortage of accommodation (exacerbated by absurd Government policies which mean that existing homes which reach a certain age are being demolished on the grounds that they are not `energy efficient' while the application of planning rules means that it is difficult to get permission to build new homes) will mean that anyone who has an empty room in their home will be forced to rent it out (at some predetermined rate) to one or more lodgers. This will not be an option made available to willing home owners. Home owners will be required to take in lodgers if they have rooms they are themselves using. Home owners who refuse will find themselves in serious trouble - with their homes being confiscated.

The lodgers and room-owners will be put in contact with one another by an EU inspired bureaucracy which will take a percentage of the sum paid as its fee.

If you think this is unlikely you should know that the EU is already forcing house owners who have what is considered to be `spare land' to make it available to gypsies who are looking for somewhere to set up camp. The gypsies do not pay for the use of the land, even though the house owners will almost certainly find that the value of their home plummets. Indeed, the unfortunate home owner's home, with gypsy encampment adjoining it, will probably be unsaleable.

Chances of home owners being forced to rent out spare rooms: 70%.

153. Licences Galore

We are entering the era of the licence.

If your job requires training and a skill then, however long you have been doing it, and however good you may at it, the EU is insisting that you must pay for an annual licence. (The important word here is, of course, `pay'.). So, for example, the General Medical Council, which regulates doctors, now insists that in future I and all other registered doctors, must be licensed. I have to pay them hundreds of pounds a year for the equivalent of a driving licence.

Over thirty years ago I pointed out that it was absurd that whereas airline pilots should have to take refresher exams at regular intervals doctors should be able to practice until they were 80 or 90 years old without anyone ever checking to see whether they had caught up with new developments. (At the time I pointed out that there were doctors in practice who had qualified before the discovery of penicillin.)

But this new system of licensing is, like everything to do with the EU, flawed and open to corruption.

It is flawed because the fee the GMC is charging is so high that doctors who retire will stay retired. They won't be able to help out in times of crisis because they won't stay licensed. And it is open to corruption because I suspect the method of licensing will mean that doctors who don't follow the official party line on all aspects of medical care might find themselves struggling to obtain that all important annual licence. What, for example, will be the prospects of a doctor who opposes vaccination or vivisection being allowed to renew his or her licence? (The process is being called `revalidation'.) I intend to find out.

Thanks to the EU, we will soon all need licences for everything we do, every skill we possess, and every job we do.

But that's not all.

We will also need certificates to show that every piece of equipment we own has been checked by an EU approved, licensed technician. Our boilers, gas fires and fridges will need an annual certificate just as our motor cars need an annual MOT certificate. Our homes will have to be certified to show that they are energy efficient. And if we have pets they will all need licences too.

Every licence will involve an annual examination of some kind and, of course, a fee. Part of the fee will kept by the technician doing the testing and part will go to the Government (or, eventually, the European Union).

Chances of us having to buy more licences: 90%.

154. Intelligence And Productivity Will Both Continue To Fall

A recent study of 1000 adults by the University of London found that habitual emailing and text messaging reduces intelligence and intellectual productivity by 5-15 IQ points. That's more than the damage done by being a regular pot smoker.

Most office workers are seriously addicted to email and spend several hours of every working day sending one another pointless email messages. At nights and weekends and on holidays they remain glued to their Blackberrys and iPhones in case they miss some item of gossip that will, of course, become worthless if read an hour or two too late. Children are trained for this strange existence by sending one another text messages throughout every waking hour of every day.

Chances of intelligence and productivity continuing to fall: 100%.

Fascist politicians (and since the EU is an exclusively fascist organisation there are plenty of them around in Europe), union activists and others have enthusiastically blamed free enterprise for the financial crisis and have taken full advantage of the opportunity to attack free markets and to replace imagination and creativity with the dulling hand of authoritarianism. They want, and see this as their opportunity to obtain more state control, more regulation, a clampdown on any form of free enterprise and higher taxes. It is this attitude which will turn Gordon Brown's manufactured depression into a long, long slump which will segue effortlessly into the problems created by the Oil Apocalypse. The risk takers, the imaginative people who have ideas and who create new businesses will be assaulted on all sides; they will be attacked by armies of regulators and bureaucrats and smothered by red tape.

What the fascist politicians and the union activists and the statists fail to realise, of course, is that the wealth of any nation depends entirely upon the ingenuity, optimism, enthusiasm and capacity for hard work of its entrepreneurs. Without pioneering entrepreneurs there will be no new business, no private employment, no wealth creation, no exports and no taxes to pay for the massive, ever growing machinery of the state. Entrepreneurs are the growth engine of a nation. They employ most of the people. And without sole traders and small companies a country has no future. It is, after all, from those small beginnings that large multinationals will eventually develop.

Starting a new business is always difficult. Hope and ambition has to overcome fear of failure (and its consequences) as well as all the natural problems of starting something new and imaginative. But when would-be entrepreneurs spend much or most of their time fighting and worrying about bureaucratic demands, and the awesome complications of endless new legislation, then the downside simply becomes too much. Many of today's brightest young people are choosing to take employment in the public sector. And why not? The salaries are high, the perks tremendous, the pension guaranteed and the bonuses massive and not dependent on success or hard work.

The awful bottom line is that entrepreneurial activity will fall. Due to reduced risk taking, reduced incentives and laziness. And the fact that the brightest people now realise that the best career path is to work for the State.

Chances of entrepreneurial activity falling in Britain: 80%.

156. Town And City Centres Are Doomed (and will become gloomier, darker, less inviting places)

I assume that councillors spend their days sitting around trying to work out ways to destroy local businesses and to make the towns they control less pleasant places in which to live. Only if this is true can they be proud of themselves and claim that they have achieved their objectives. If they do not deliberately intend to destroy local businesses then they are clearly either incompetent or crooked or both.

Sometimes, indeed, I get the impression that local councillors, and local council employees, get real pleasure out of closing down small businesses. There is a vindictiveness about some of their actions which cannot be a result of anything other than spiteful intent. I do sometimes wonder to myself if these highly paid (and well-pensioned) individuals might not all be in the pay of the French or, more likely, the Poles. Or maybe councillors and council staff genuinely believe that our town centres will not be satisfactorily designed until they consist of charity shops and nothing else.

There is a twist to all this, of course.

Large, national chains are moving out of our derelict town and city centres and into special out of town shopping malls where there is heaps of free parking and where shoppers can be soothed with calming music as they wander from one huge store to another.

It's all going to end in tears.

As the oil price soars (and it will) so these out of town shopping centres will become huge white elephants. No one will go to them and no one will want them. The only good thing about them is that most of them are so badly built that within a few years they will blow down, or fall down, and within a few more years there will be nothing left to remind us of them other than a few piles of rubble, covered in weeds.

By then our town centres will also be derelict, unwanted and largely abandoned. The interesting buildings, the old ones, the curious ones, will have been knocked down by developers working hand-in-wallet with local planners, and turned into soon-to-be unwanted office blocks for banks and quangos.

Chances of town and city centres becoming gloomier, less appealing places: 90%.

157. Encouraging A Multilingual Society Is Going To Continue To Cost Us All Money And Make Our Country More Dangerous

A reader sent me a book called Welcome to Barnsley - New Arrivals

Handbook'. The book is available in the following languages: Farsi, Urdu, Arabic, French, Russian, Lithuanian, Latvian, Polish, Spanish and Albainian (sic). Oh, and you can also get a copy in English if you want one.

Our multicultural society is bankrupting us. Can you imagine how many small provincial towns in France or Spain produce literature in such a variety of languages?

Numerous government departments now produce all their literature in a mass of different languages. All these cost extra money to produce and to print. Wales has destroyed its economy by providing every form and road sign in two languages. Now the rest of Britain is doing the same thing but a dozen, two dozen, times worse. There are 230 languages in 27 nations in the EU and our government departments aim to cater for them all.

There are even some official phone lines now available in a variety of European languages. Press 17 if you want to hear this message in English.

Just before the May 2010 the government at last announced that all immigrants must learn English. But that was merely a sop to the Britons who object to their country, their history, their culture and their heritage being suppressed by the hordes of immigrants flooding into the country. The fact is that driving theory test centres still offer candidates the choice of taking their driving test in more than 20 languages.

The expense must be enormous and this is the sort of gold-plating of EU rules and multicultural philosophies that makes Britain a European laughing stock. No other country does this.

And has anyone in the Government realised that it really is rather dangerous to have millions of non-English speaking motorists on the road - especially since our road signs are, at the moment, still only available in

English.

Does anyone in the Government realise how dangerous it is to have hospitals staffed by people who don't speak English?

These are serious problems, created by the obsession with multiculturalism and the needs of creating a European superstate.

Chances of our multilingual society being more expensive and dangerous by 2020: 100%.

158. University Degrees Will Become Increasingly Common And Increasingly Worthless (but the proud graduates will spend much of their lives paying for them)

Today, around 43% of young people go to university. Most are not suited for further education. Most don't want to study and are not particularly well suited to academic study. They choose a college degree course as an alternative to unemployment. They go to university because it is now what everyone is doing. And they go because governments which want to disguise unemployment figures put pressure on them to go to university. Most students prefer to take `soft' degree courses. Instead of studying maths, engineering or something else that requires lectures and textbooks they study hairdressing, beauty studies, nail technology, brewing, media studies or tourism. The whole damned nation is awash with beauticians, hairdressers and girls qualified only to apply nail varnish. These are all service occupations which add nothing to a nation's wealth. In fact, of course, all `services' cost money. And, sadly, many of these new graduates are unemployable. The brewing industry only needs a small number of graduates with brewing degrees and high expectations. What it really needs is a lot of men who wear brown coats and are good with grease guns and spanners.

In an attempt to ensure that even more school leavers go university the last Labour government announced plans to enable students to get their first degree in two years. A third year's study would presumably provide doctorates for all. If the sole criteria is making sure that degrees are universal why not give them away free with petrol or cornflakes?

Naturally, the Labour government which pushed students into taking degree courses they really didn't want also makes them pay for the privilege of obtaining useless bits of paper. Most students now leave college encumbered with huge debts which will take them years to pay off. These debts are about to get much worse. Universities want to double their annual fees from £3,200 to £6,000. And there are plans to make middle class students pay more than other students to punish them for being better off. The result will be that the average student will leave university with a worthless degree and debts consisting of a loan of £20,000 and interest of £10,000. The interest rates will be way above mortgage rate and students will not be allowed to pay back their loan in one lump but will have to keep on paying the usurious interest rate. Welcome to the real world where even governments behave like Shylock and even students are treated as marks.

It would make excellent sense to persuade students to study genuinely useful subjects - such as engineering - by making such courses `free of charge'. This might encourage a few of those studying brewery and hairdressing to take a potentially useful course instead.

Better still, why not provide solid (instead of hollow) encouragement for students who want to take practical apprenticeships in useful subjects such as plumbing?

None of this is likely to happen.

Politicians have devalued education and created a whole army of teachers who are trained only to teach `artificial' subjects that are of no real value - but which are easy to learn and no challenge even to the intellectually challenged. Politicians use further education as a method of measuring their country's progress. But worthless degrees are no measure of success. Worse still, they use further education as a way of keeping young people out of the unemployment figures. Their policies raise false hopes and financial expectations and are creating millions of young unemployables - while at the same time the nation is crying out for skilled workers. And so that none of this costs the state money it cannot afford (since most of what is available is wasted on civil service pensions, quangos and duck houses) students must now pay for their own studies. The result is that poor students leave university with huge debts which will hang around their necks for decades to come.

Chances of university degrees becoming increasingly common and worthless: 100%.

159. Travel By Plane Is Going To Become Increasingly Unpleasant (and far more dangerous)

Because someone once allegedly tried to blow up a plane with a tiny bomb secreted in his shoe, millions of travellers now have to remove their shoes and have them X rayed before boarding the aeroplane for which they have bought a ticket. The cost of this utterly absurd exercise must now run into hundreds of millions of whatever currency you like to think in. No more bombs have been found and no tragedies prevented but a lot of feeble minded security guards have been given the opportunity to humiliate their betters, and the companies making shoe X-raying equipment have doubtless made a tidy bundle.

What will the authorities do when someone is arrested for having a bomb in their bra? It would surely be considerably easier to hide a bomb in a bra than in a shoe. A woman who normally wears a AA bra could pack enough Semtex into a GG garment to make even a Cuban heeled shoe bomber blanche with envy. And I doubt if it will be difficult to devise an explosive substance that looks like human tissue on an X- ray machine.

Will all women be forced to remove their bras before being allowed onto planes?

And what will the authorities do if someone is caught with a bomb in their knickers?

The latest security gimmick is, of course, the full body scanner. This device, which sounds like the sort of X-ray device dreamt up by lusty schoolboys, effectively sees through clothes and enables the guards to examine the `naked' bodies of travellers. To my astonishment and dismay, travellers seem to regard this invasion of their privacy with remarkable equanimity.

It will, of course, be years before we know for certain just how safe (or dangerous) it is to X-ray individuals in this way. How much damage will be done to regular travellers? How dangerous will the scanners be to airport employees? How long will it be before it becomes apparent that airport security is responsible for far more deaths than terrorists?

A few years ago iris scanners were promoted as the new and effective way of identifying individuals. My argument that such scanners might well prove to be harmful to the eyes was taken up and no one seems to talk about such devices any more. I'd like to think that my warning about whole body scanners might prove equally effective. But, sadly, I fear that these days the authorities are less sensitive to public opinion and more inclined to ignore it.

And so I predict that airport will become increasingly intrusive and dangerous.

Chances of air travel becoming more unpleasant and dangerous: 100%.

160. The Cost Of Utility Bills Will Rocket

The cost of all utility bills (water, sewage, gas and electricity will rocket in the next ten years.

Gas and electricity bills will soar because the price of energy will go up. (And because our infrastructure providing us with these things is old, falling apart and totally inadequate.)

Water and sewage bills will soar because our infrastructure in these areas was built in Victorian times and is rather in need of repair. A conservative estimate suggests that bringing the system up to date will cost around £100 billion. The real cost will, of course, be considerably higher. Until the improvements are made, huge amounts of money will have to be spent on keeping the systems working. Once the improvements have been made huge amounts of money will have to be spent on servicing and repaying the related debt. Global water shortages won't help the price problem, either.

Finally, costs will rise because new EU regulations require water to be treated in a more energy efficient manner in the future. (Sadly, the more energy efficient treatment programmes are less acceptable from an environmental point of view. But, hey, the EU will doubtless introduce a new system of fines to ensure that the industry pays extra for adopting the required new techniques.) These new treatment programmes will also result in more expense and, in the medium term and long term, much higher bills.

Chances of the cost of utility bills rocketing: 90%.

161. Service Will Get Worse

These days when I ring the bank or the tax office or the whoever I have frequently forgotten why I called by the time someone gets round to answering the phone. And it usually takes me a minute or two to realise that it's a real person and not the damned recorded voice that has been inviting me to hold on because my call is important and the agents are waiting to hear from me and all I have to do is shut up and listen to the music and they are very, very grateful for my call and if I press six they will give me the address of their website and if I hang on they will connect me with one of their agents and my call may well be recorded for training purposes, though what use my call is going to be for training and I can't help suspecting that it's more to make sure that when I eventually get through to a person I mind my manners and don't complain and when they can't answer my question I say nothing impolite.

Public servants became public sector workers because the word `servant' became unacceptable. But when the word servant disappeared the public sector workers forgot that they were employed by the public to serve the public and started to see themselves as superior to the public.

You can see it everywhere - police, hospitals, town halls and so on. (Sometimes there are practical manifestations of this sense of superiority. One council official with responsibility for helping the homeless and a salary of £52,000 a year, evicted frail and elderly tenants from their bungalows and then, paying a reduced rent, moved into one of the bungalows with her partner, also a senior housing official. No one seemed particularly surprised or shocked.)

Sadly, I fear that the deterioration in service that we have seen from public sector workers is now likely to contaminate the private sector.Already letters, phone calls, emails and faxes are ignored unless the object of the communication is something of specific concern to the company concerned.

Service is going to deteriorate. And more and more firms are going to trick and deceive their customers. The days when companies cared about their customers, and wanted to look after them and retain their loyalty, are long gone. In bad economic times companies start to think not about the long term but about being able to pay their bills this month and next month.

And we are going to be ripped off more and more, as increasing number of companies struggle to stay alive. Unable to avoid increasing taxes and unending (and expensive) new regulations they will cut costs by reducing the quality of the goods or services they provide and abandoning such unaffordable concepts as after-sales service completely. Here's what the Financial Times had to say about crappy products the other day: `The practice of selling sub-standard products is legitimate business, and always will be.' So, now you know.

Today, there is very little point in complaining about any public sector service or about any public sector employee. Within a year or two there will be equally little point in complaining about any private sector service or employee.

And things are just as bad on the other side of the counter. Shopping has become a quasi-military experience. Instead of being a pleasant experience shopping has evolved into a modern inferno; a place which would have startled Dante. Shoppers at `sales' exhibit the manners of starving wild dogs, snatching at items they perceive as bargains as though their lives depend upon it. Women link arms like ranks of soldiers to force their way through crowds. Mothers use push chairs as battering rams, blocking aisles and using them to build a cordon around items they want to cherry-pick. In America a Wal-Mart worker was trampled to death when he was caught between a crowd of shoppers and a pile of cut-price DVDs. It won't be long before the same thing happens in Britain. It is, perhaps, hardly surprising that store employees look and behave as though they are manning a fortress and repelling the enemy, rather than manning a sales desk and serving customers.

The future is bleak for every type of service. State and local services will fall for years to come. And, at the same time, taxes will rise so we will receive less for me. This is not conjecture. It is unavoidable.

Chances of service deteriorating: 100%.

162. Scientists Will Continue To Come Up With New Scares

Scientists have always claimed that they, and they alone, understand and can solve the world's problems. You can't blame them. Being able to identify the world's challenges, and to offer the appropriate solutions, is the quick way to fame, honour and fortune and a regular spot on prime time television quiz shows. The problem is, of course, that scientists are as likely as estate agents and politicians to succumb to evil temptations. And they do, oh how they do. Once they spot a good grant opportunity or a knighthood glimmering on the distant horizon, they forget all about scientific principles and boring things like facts and become just as capable of writing fiction as the Dr Who script writers.

And so it's a pretty safe bet that at regular intervals during the years ahead we are going to be terrified out of our mind by scientists who will have a new threat with which to scare us and who just happen to have found the solution. It won't just be politicians who will be inventing scares. (The ones who have found the solution first will, with great good fortune, always be able to find the problem to go with it.)

Chances of scientists coming up with more scares: 100%.

163. More Rubbish Rules About Rubbish Collecting

Local councils take the blame for the bizarre new rules on rubbish collecting which are being introduced. But the real culprit is, of course, the European Union and its EU Waste Framework Directive targets. Unelected and anonymous EU eurocrats in Brussels have arbitrarily decreed that 50% of household waste must be recycled (and that 70% of construction and demolition waste must be recycled by the year 2020). Many local councillors don't realise where their orders about recycling come from. The ones who realise that they come from Brussels say nothing because it is, of course, `not allowed' to blame the EU for anything.

The result is that many citizens in Britain now spend a huge chunk of their time sorting their rubbish and preparing it for five different collections on three different days of the week over a two week period. The collection dates (and the putting out times) all vary in an apparently random way according to bank holidays and the whims of some idiot in the local council offices. There are ironies everywhere. The government (in the form of the Royal Mail) dumps a vast quantity of unwanted, unaddressed junk mail through the letter box and then we have to pay the council to take it away. Councils constantly changing their bin collection days and then fine honest citizens if they put your bin out on the wrong day. Everyone looks out of the window and then rushes out to put bin out in time. At least one council insists that rubbish should not be placed on the pavement more than an hour before the collecting time. In practice this means that law abiding citizens must have regular days off work in order to deal with their rubbish.

Our local council puts expensively printed leaflets through our door from time to time to tell us the schedule for the coming months. These leaflets are incomprehensible and usually wrong and we are always phoning the council (on a premium rate telephone number) to find out when we should put out our plastic, our bottles or our waste paper. From time to time `they' send out expensively printed glossy charts telling us when we must put out which types of rubbish. The charts usually arrive several months late. Different days of the week are allocated for ordinary rubbish, garden rubbish, plastics, bottles, paper and kitchen food waste. It is just about a full time job keeping up with it. It is in the weeks after Christmas that chaos really reigns and rubbish collection days are never the same for weeks at a time. I have a huge chart pinned on the wall and alarms in my diary. If we put out the wrong sort of rubbish on the wrong sort of day we can be punished and fined. In the end the lorries take their separate loads to the same place, dump the stuff into one big pile. It is then shipped out to China on the ships which brought us television sets and refrigerators. In China the rubbish is used as landfill.

And there are a thousand anomalies. They won't take shredded paper in with the paper but we can't put it in with the plastic or the bottles or the food so what do we do with it? No one knows. We aren't allowed to have bonfires. Some packaging contains cardboard and plastic sealed together and separating the two takes knives, scissors, strength and sticking plaster for the inevitable cuts. Where do we put used sticking plasters? They count as medical dressings and have to be disposed of in a very special way. But we're not a hospital so we don't have access to that sort of facility. What do people do if they eat fish? The law, as I understand it, is that the remains can only be put into the container that the council will collect if it became rubbish the day before. This presumably means that people can only eat fish the day before their used fish rubbish is collected.

Do you put a tin still containing food (gone out of date and therefore not suitable for eating) into the container for tins or the container for food? Or do you open the tin and pour the contents into the food container and the empty tin into the container for tins. What if the tin is swollen through botulism? Should you separate the bacteria causing the problem from the food contents and if so does the council provide a special container for clostridium botulinum? I have asked my council these questions but, sadly, am still awaiting a reply, presumably because the 16 year old who is in charge of such matters is away on a course learning to read.

A council employee dumped on our door step a 400 page glossy A4 book explaining how we can avoid waste and containing a list of depots where we can deliver such assorted items as used yoghurt cartons, old beer cans and so on.

Do you know one person who wanted these changes? They aren't progress. They don't make our lives better in any way. Most of us have such ever-changing lives that they don't want more change unless it actually makes life better in some notable way. The changes in rubbish collecting clearly do not. Remember: those horrid plastic wheelie bins permanently decorating our streets are there thanks to the EU. Bureaucrats and councillors talk much nonsense about forcing us to sort our rubbish so that we can save the planet. This is, of course, fraudulent, an all excusing constant excuse, a damned lie and even the idiots who believe in the `climate change' nonsense must realise that. I remind you: the rubbish we spend our days sorting into five different varieties of plastic container is all taken away, thrown into a massive communal tip and shipped to China, not to be turned into electricity or cars or shopping catalogues but to be dumped into huge landfill sites. The endless rules about how we must sort and sift our rubbish are being introduced for much simpler reasons: to control us and keep us busy, enslaved by sorting our rubbish and too busy to protest; and to find an endless number of reasons to fine us. Put the wrong can into the wrong box? That'll be £500. Put a used yoghurt carton into an inappropriate box? That'll be £1,000. Credit card payments only. No cheques. No cash.

Recycling causes as much pollution as it is intended to save (there are far more lorries trundling around collecting separated rubbish, which is then dumped all together and taken to China). Recycling plastic uses up vast amounts of energy (more than it saves) and causes massive pollution. It is also a health hazard.

The rules will lead to stinking, dirty streets, to more infections, more accidents, a good deal of confusion, great resentment, fights in the street, and anger as residents are fined by their council. Fly tipping is going to soar. If you have a garden which fronts a lonely road you can expect to find a lot of rubbish dumped over your fence in coming years. And getting rid of it will, of course, be your responsibility. We sold a tree plantation partly because we were fed up with having to deal with the sacks full of rubbish dumped there.

The tiny front gardens of thousands of neat terraces in smart town and city centres will now forever be permanently scarred by wheelie bins and the absurd confusion of smelly plastic containers. Citizens spend hours sorting their yoghurt cartons from their fish bones from the beer cans and the council spends a small fortune collecting all the little containers, takes them separately to a single dump where they are thrown together onto a tip and then shipped, expensively and with no regard for the environment to China (travelling there in the ships that brought over flat screen television sets, motor cars and computers that might have been built in Britain if the citizens hadn't been too busy sorting their yoghurt cartons from their beer cans and their fish bones). For all this we can thank the EU.

There is, in all this, an enormous business opportunity for someone prepared to start a company offering to take away unsorted rubbish - and to deal with. There are, I suspect, a good many people who would happily pay an annual fee to have their rubbish collected in black plastic sacks - as it was collected before the EU started to interfere in something that is truly none of their damned business.

Is it all a plan to bewilder and confuse and wear us down so we don't notice the big stuff that is happening? Does that sound paranoid?

Do you really think they wouldn't? Couldn't? Haven't?

Chances of there being more rubbishy rules about rubbish collecting: 100%.

164. Dog Owners Will Have To Buy Insurance

Forcing every dog owner to buy a dog licence is a very EU way of doing things. Licensing systems enable the authorities to keep a close eye on everyone and the money they bring in is useful when there are a zillion overpaid bureaucrats to be kept in expense accounts, limousines and private aeroplanes.

But the EU surprised me with its plan to force dog-owners to buy insurance in case their dog attacked someone else. The scheme isn't intended to control dogs, of course. The people with dangerous dogs don't have car licences, car insurance, television licences or much else in the way of licences. Why would they buy dog licences? The scheme is designed to transfer money from middle class, law-abiding citizens to the new European state. When the EU bureaucrats think they can get away with it they will introduce cat licences, parrot licences and goldfish licences. You may laugh but you should know by now that the EU is not a laughing matter.

And, although there will be protests and pointless discussions, the dog licensing (and the subsequent cat, parrot and goldfish licensing) will come.

The result will be that our streets will be overrun with ownerless, uncontrolled, dangerous dogs, increasingly vicious and becoming feral.

The new legislation will, as always these days, make things worse rather than better.

Chances of dog owners having to buy special insurance by 2020: 70%.

165. The Word `British' Will Disappear

A good many companies which have `British' in their names are going to drop the `British' within the next few years.

Companies such as `British Airways', `British Petroleum' `British Telecom' and `British Gas' will, I believe, all find excuses to spend a small fortune changing their name to something else.

Why?

Simple.

Now that the European Union is a country, and Britain is just part of that new country, there is no Britain.

The continuing existence of these out of date names will be seen as an embarrassment.

Chances of the word `British' slowly disappearing: 90%.

166. Britain Plc Will Become Increasingly Foreign Owned

In the last few years numerous large British companies have been taken over by foreign companies. Mobile phone companies Orange and O2 were taken over by France Telecom and Telefonia respectively. BAA was taken over by a Spanish company very few people in Britain had ever heard of. British Energy was taken over by a French electricity company. Scottish power was taken over by a Spanish company. Scottish & Newcastle breweries was taken over by a Danish company. And so on and so on.

In the future, it seems certain that more and more British companies will be taken over by foreign companies. Unlike governments in other countries, the British Government does nothing to protect British companies against foreign predators. The result is that a great many British workers are now employed by foreign companies. Their allegiance is, naturally, neither to Britain nor to their British employees.One of the most shameful episodes in recent history was the takeover of the iconic British chocolate company `Cadbury' by an American cheese company called `Kraft'.

The House of Commons business select committee said that Kraft had acted `irresponsibly and unwisely' in its £11.7 billion hostile takeover of Cadbury. The committee lambasted Kraft for reneging on its pledge to keep open Cadbury's factory near Bristol, soon after it won the takeover battle. Production at the factory was moved almost immediately to Poland, despite the promise. MPs were disappointed that the boss of Kraft, someone called Ms Rosenfeld, chose not to give evidence to the committee but sent her deputy instead. (If Parliamentarians had any balls at all they would have the damned woman extradited, grilled her and then banned her from ever coming into the country again. But now that so many MPs are female, balls are in rare supply in either House.) Cadbury was born in England. Now the company is run by foreigners, living and working abroad and having no knowledge of or care for the company's heritage or responsibilities. Moreover, if they follow Ms Rosenfeld's example, and renege on promises, the company will soon lose its reputation and become just another piece of typical American corporate rubbish, grabbing a buck here and a buck there and ignoring the principles of English decency which Cadbury once espoused.

But the real sting in the takeover is surely the fact that it was the disgraced taxpayer owned Royal Bank of Scotland which provided the cash for an American cheese company (Kraft) to buy the iconic British company Cadbury. There seems little doubt that thanks to RBS, thousands more British jobs will now be lost as Kraft moves the manufacture of Cadbury products to less expensive, less regulated countries.

RBS, surely one of the most incompetently run banks in the history of banks, would have gone bust if it had not been rescued by the British Government (so that Scottish jobs would not be lost) and at the time when it provided the loan for the irresponsible American company to buy the iconic British company, RBS was owned by British taxpayers and was being accused of not doing enough to help British businessmen trying to raise loans.

As big businesses are taken over they put pressure on the Government to adapt its policies to suit them. And these will be policies which suit companies based in other countries (usually America) and they will not benefit Britain or the British. One of the obvious policies will, for example, be encouraging more immigration because this leads to lower staff costs.

Chances of more and more of Britain being owned by foreign companies and businessmen: 90%.

167. Statism Is Going To Grow And Grow.

You thought the state controlled too much now? Wait a few years. The state is going to control more and more of your life. We already have far too much government. We're going to get a good deal more.

It is almost comical to realise that the state is only there to provide the infrastructure so that we can live our lives without disruption or inconvenience. Governments have a role to play - but a role which is infinitely smaller and less intrusive than the role they have adopted. The job of the central authority known as `the state' is to provide services and regulation that cannot fairly be provided by another means. The proper function of government is to protect individual's rights; to protect citizens from physical violence. The police are there to protect citizens from criminals. The military are paid to protect the nation from foreign invaders. The law courts are there to protect property and contracts.

But we have gone far, far beyond that. The state is now to be worshipped. The state is all. Today's politicians believe they have a responsibility to lower unemployment, increase growth and improve the lives of the people. That's statism. In a free country all politicians have to do is to try and maintain conditions under which good things may happen.

During the last decade or so, the last Labour Governments, government spending has risen from 36% of GDP (what it was in 1999) to

48% (in 2009). In Scotland, government spending is well over 50% of GDP. Public sector employment rose by over a million while Blair and Brown were in charge. In 2009 alone, as the private sector lost 900,000 jobs the public sector added 300,000 new, and entirely unwanted, jobs. By 2013, public sector debt in the UK is expected to rise to over 80% of GDP. (If that is what the Treasury is expecting you can bet it will go much higher than that.)

England's traditional exports were law and free trade. When England ruled the seas any man of any nation could go anywhere in safety. But, as the repressive element became dominant and England turned to statism, the empire fell apart.

A statist society has very high costs. This is bad for the economy in a number of ways. In the real world mistakes must be paid for in some way. But the state never apologises or pays - and nor do its employees. When state employees make mistakes (and when they do, which is often, their mistakes tend to be huge and to have far reaching consequences) it is the taxpayer who picks up the bill.

The main trouble with statism, like the trouble with socialism, is that eventually the people spending run out of other people's money. And that is what has happened. The state will, however, continue to interfere. The state, as redefined by Blair and Brown, has acquired a life and purpose and needs of its own and today exists to collect and redistribute wealth. The state (managed by totalitarian dictators) decides what is in the public interest. The state has a monopoly on the use of physical force. And the state forces obedience on pain of imprisonment or death (or death by a thousand investigations - and strangulation by red tape).

Chances of statism continuing to grow: 100%.

168. More Patients Will Be Sectioned (and committed to hospital as involuntary patients)

Here's another little thing you should no. The Government is implementing changes which will allow anyone to be sectioned with the approval of one doctor instead of two.

They said, they were, making this change in case there was a shortage of doctors in the future.

Suspicious readers might wonder if the Government is planning to increase the number of people being certified insane. (A trick, you will remember, which was widely used in the former Soviet Union as a way of dealing with dissidents).

Personally, I'm not bothered. Indeed, I welcome the change. I'm gathering together some forms and if anyone comes from me I'll sign the relevant documents to ensure that they are all sectioned. In a variation on the old `fastest draw in the West' theme it will be a question of who can sign their forms first and since I always have a pen in my hand I'm happy to bet on myself.

Chances of an increase in the number of patients being sectioned: 80%.

169. Savers Will Pay Other Peoples Bills

The people who helped create the problem (by borrowing more money than they could reasonably afford to pay back) cannot get us out of this mess because they haven't got any money - they've only got debts.

So the people who are going to have to get us out of the mess are the people who have money: the prudent, cautious, careful people who have saved more than they've spent.

The very rich will not pay anything, of course. They never do. They don't pay taxes.

The people who will pay to get us out of the mess we are in will be middle class savers.

They have, of course, already been paying because for the last couple of years their cash savings have been earning them considerably less than the rate of inflation. Their money has been slowly disappearing.

The sad truth is that it is those who are self sufficient in money who are least selfish. By saving and investing wisely they have allowed the state to concentrate its effort on those who need or want help and who are, for whatever reason, incapable of looking after themselves or too greedy to satisfy their desires themselves.

Self sufficiency is the ultimate in selflessness but it is not one that attracts approval or respect.

Modern governments will punish the virtuous because they make an easier target.

Chances of the prudent paying the price for the imprudent: 100%.

170. The Number Of Professional Politicians Will Continue To Increase

In recent years there has been an explosion in the number of politicians. Running them costs the best part of a billion a year in salaries and expenses. Heaven knows what it costs in terms of pensions. Churchill presided over a war cabinet of nine people. Today there are 35 politicians in Browns cabinet. In 1980 there were 3,000 paid politicians in Britain. Today there are 30,000. A tenfold increase. Full time salaried councillors, political advisers everywhere, new EU regional Parliaments in Scotland and Wales. Britain now has more professional politicians than ambulance staff. In Victorian days, when Britain ruled a quarter of the world very effectively, MPs weren't paid at all. Today, MPs do nothing much at all except look after their moats and duck houses. The EU runs the country. The MPs just take expenses.

The chances of there being more professional politicians in 2020 than in 2010: 100%.

171. Litigation Will Continue To Be A Growth Industry

The rise of `no win-no fee' lawyers will continue to encourage vexatious and frivolous and opportunistic litigants. Libel, medical negligence, employment claims, personal injury, product liability - the world seems to be being remade in the interests of the morally deficient areas of the legal profession. Regulations (mostly derived from the EU of course) dovetail neatly with the new habit, imported from America, of finding someone to blame for everything that happens, and mean that everyone needs increasingly expensive specialist lawyers. Risk aversion is the name of the game. New health and safety regulations, spiced up by the no win no fee lawyer advertisements, mean that fear of litigation grips everyone: charities, schools, businesses, householders, councils, insurers. Costs soar everywhere as people struggle to pay ever rising insurance premiums. Honest people pay off litigants who have no honest case rather than risk years of time consuming litigation. Lawyers and faded female television presenters, past their view by date, are getting fat, fatter and fattest on the `Tripped over a shoe lace? Let us help you sue the shoe manufacturer' industry, imported from the good old US of A.

The law has become a joke, being abused and used for all sorts of bizarre and unreasonable circumstances. Schoolteachers dare not give a child an aspirin or stick a plaster on a playground graze without obtaining legal advice and consulting parents, doctors and lawyers. People buy a house near to a race track where motor racing has taken place for decades then, weeks later, complain about the noise and demand that something be done about it. Something usually is. Yesterday I read that the vicar of the St Mary the Virgin church in Greater Manchester was told to install sound proofing or be fined after residents from nearby flats complained about the noise the bells were making. The church's bell ringers have been ringing the bells for 400 years. The flats where the complainants live were built in 2006. Justice has never been a close friend of common sense but this sort of judgement shows that the two aren't even on speaking terms.   We are all of us drowning in information. And yet it you don't act in accordance with the rules you are in trouble. Ignorance is no excuse but we are all ignorant

The only driving force among lawyers these days is that of materialism. Lawyers earn large fortunes (their pay has outstripped inflation by a massive amount) and their assistants and associates earn vastly more than real professionals who have been educated and trained in other disciplines.

The number of lawyers continues to soar. In Britain the number of practising solicitors, too many of them amoral guns for hire, has increased by an average of 4% a year since 1979 - far more than the increase in the population. The total cost of litigation in the UK is measured in hundreds of billions when wasted time is included.

There are now over 120,000 lawyers in England and Wales. That's 0.23% of the population. One firm in London has 2,684 lawyers. Or did when I last looked. It's probably a lot more by now. They breed like cockroaches. America has more of course. There are well over a million lawyers in America. Only Israel and America have more lawyers per head than Britain.

In Japan in the 1980s there were 5000 lawyers for a population of 125 million but in the USA, at the same time, there were 750,000 lawyers for a population of 250 million. That's 75 times as many lawyers per head of population as in Japan. There was, at that time, very little crime, especially violent crime in Japan. The inverse relationship between the density of lawyers and national happiness is always clear to see. American lawyers now grab at every opportunity to start a lawsuit. After BP's disastrous oil leak in the Gulf of Mexico, around 200 lawyers announced that they were starting class action lawsuits against the company. One lawyer alone proudly announced the list of clients he had acquired and on whose behalf he intended to lodge claims against BP. The clients included a freelance journalist who had lost a magazine commission to write about big game fishing in the Gulf.

What a pity we can't sell our lawyers (and the growing number of ambulance chasers we seem to have acquired, thanks to America's bad example) or at least swap them for something useful. We could, say, give some poor country 10,000 assorted lawyers and get something useful in return: cotton, corn, coal, rice husks, anything.

Chances of there being more litigation in 2020 than there is in 2010: 100%.

172. Computer nerds Will Continue To Overpromote The Usefulness Of Computers

I believe (and have done so for some years) that the world would be a far happier, healthier, more peaceful and generally better place if computers had never been invented and if Mr Babbage had, instead, invented something socially useful such as a bicycle bell that works properly.

The nerds will, of course, continue to claim that computers are going to take over the world. This is tosh. Computers, like robots, are clumsy and will remain so.

Next time someone tells you that he has a chess computer that can beat you at chess, ask him if it can beat you at table tennis?

The computer won't even be able to understand the challenge.

Come to that, the nerd probably won't be able to understand it either.

Chances of people continuing to over promote (and over sell) computers: 80%.

173. A Tax On Emigrants Will Be Introduced

The Government has belatedly realised the problem being created by the fact that many of the nation's high earners are leaving the country. Discouraged by a failing infrastructure, unsafe streets and steadily rising taxes they are moving abroad in search of a better way of life.

Up until recently the government didn't give a stuff about this. Ministers sneered at emigrants and waved them goodbye with a loud `good riddance'.

But the nation's impending bankruptcy has changed things. The Government suddenly realised that the people leaving the country were the ones who had all the money and that without them the country's financial position was getting worse even faster than might otherwise have been the case.

And so they started tightening up the rules (a process which can also be described as changing them retrospectively).

The new rules meant that people who decided to leave the country really did have to leave. They couldn't keep a little house in England, they couldn't allow their children to stay at schools in England and they couldn't even retain their membership of their golf clubs. The tax authorities made it clear that if you weren't going to liable to UK tax then you had to have left properly, completely, finally and totally. Paying for the care of relatives, renting out a former home and even visiting relatives might, if you are rich enough and the tax authorities feeling nasty enough, mean that you become liable for tax on your past earnings. There is no limit to the amount of tax that can be claimed back. There is, it seems, no limit to the number of years back that the tax collectors can go in their quest to take money from emigrants. It is now even clear that even a permanent overseas work contract is not a guarantee that an individual will not be considered resident in the UK for tax purposes. The only rule is that the rules are made up by the authorities and they never favour the individual.

This was, of course, a huge change.

Up until 2010 emigrants had been allowed to leave the UK for tax purposes as long as they didn't spend more than a certain number of days in the country. Holders of British passports couldn't become non-domiciled simply by leaving the country, but they could officially become non-resident. Emigrants either then paid tax in their new country of residence or, if they became what Harry Schultz termed Permanent Travellers they moved about the world, never spending more than a few months of the year in any one country and never, therefore, becoming liable to pay tax in any one country.

There is going to be another big change which will, ironically, enable emigrants to re-establish their links with their old country.

The UK is now so short of money that I suspect that the government will soon follow the example set by the United States of America and start taxing its citizens wherever they might live.

So, if you are British and you move to France you will still have to pay British tax. If the French demand that you pay them tax too you will, thanks to tax agreements between the two countries, be able to claim relief from the French government. This utterly unfair system is exactly what the Americans have been doing for years. What it means, of course, is that the American Government receives tax income from Americans living in Britain but that Britain provides services, facilities and infrastructure for those Americans.

It's utterly unfair, unreasonable and disreputable. It is, therefore, typically American.

And it is something the British government, which is now realising that if the well-off and the middle classes continue to leave the country then the nation will never be able to pay off its huge debts, will doubtless introduce at some point in the near future.

They may even introduce a special tax on citizens who decide to leave; taking, perhaps, five or ten per cent of an individual's wealth if they choose to live in another country.

Britons will still leave the country, of course. The country will still be unsuitable for habitation.

But leaving the country will become increasingly expensive.

Just what happens (and when it happens) will depend upon when the European Union introduced standardised tax rates throughout the new European State.

When standardised tax rates are introduced the EU will, I suspect, follow the American example and charge citizens the standard EU rate even if they choose to live outside the EU state.

Chances of a tax on emigrants being introduced: 80%.

174. The Unrelenting March Of Technology Will Bring An Unceasing Storm Of New Products (mostly unwanted and useless)

We are going to be overwhelmed with pointless but heavily promoted new technology. Some of it will be marginally useful. A new improved device for trimming excess axillary hair would no doubt prove attractive to millions of women. But much of the new technology introduced, most of it indeed, will be as useless and as unwanted as whatever the latest DVD replacement gimmick is called; just more pointless variations on existing themes.

As companies try to make money in a diminishing market the number of useless new inventions being introduced will increase. But consumers won't have the money and are, in any case, increasingly wary. I've gone from LPs to cassette tapes to CDs and the quality has steadily deteriorated. I've been forced to go from videos to DVDs and, like most people, I find that DVDs are far inferior in almost every conceivable way. No more, thank you.

The future for technology will be about software not hardware. And the software that does well, in a world where `free' has been acknowledged to be the only sensible price, will either be given away free or sold for pennies.

Chances of technology continuing to bring endless new swathes of complex but often unwanted and useless products: 100%.

175. Drug Companies Will Continue To Use Animal Experiments (even though they are unreliable and produce dangerous results)

Vivisection has been proven not to work. It is a barbaric and fundamentally flawed way to acquire information. I can demolish all pro-vivisection arguments in less than one minute with two simple arguments.

First, vivisectors readily admit that over 50% of all vivisection experiments give misleading information. There is no question about this. It is generally accepted. But if they know that over half the results they get are worthless, but they don't know which results might be useful and which are worthless, how they can possibly rely on any of the results they obtain?

Second, here's another undisputed and easily proven fact. When experiments on animals show that a drug causes cancer or some other serious problem in the animal on which the drug is being tested, the drug company will dismiss the results as irrelevant on the grounds that `animals are different to humans'. I can give you the names of scores of drugs which are on the market today, and prescribed for millions of human patients, but which are known to cause serious problems when given to animals. On the other hand when experiments on animals produce no adverse effects the drug company involved will use those experiments as proof that the drug is safe to be given to human patients.

Years ago I used to debate with vivisectors on television and radio. They always lost. Whenever there was a public vote I won an overwhelming share of the public vote. Sadly, however, vivisectors have refused to debate with me for many years. They steadfastly refuse to enter any studio with me. When I was invited to debate vivisection at Oxford University debating society no vivisector would debate with me. The University responded by withdrawing my invitation and replacing me with someone the vivisectors would accept.

Moreover, the evidence clearly shows that the system of testing on animals simply doesn't work. According to a report in the British Medical Journal (dated 3.7.04) adverse drug reactions caused by drugs tested on animals kill 18,000 people a year and cause 600,000 hospital admissions in the UK every year.

There are, of course, much safer and more effective ways to test new drugs and other treatments. It has been known for years that testing new drugs on human stem cells, on human tissue and on computer programmes is much, much more effective than testing on animals. But drug companies don't like these tests because they tend to result in too many drugs not reaching the market. Tests on animals are perfect as far as the drug companies are concerned because they enable them to put new drugs onto the market whatever the results might show. And that's far more profitable. It may result in thousands of patients dying. But it is more profitable.

Vivisection is the most indefensible human practice since slavery. It is cruel to animals and it doesn't help human beings. But it is extremely useful to drug companies. And so it will continue to be used.

The Labour Party were sceptical about the value of vivisection until it came to power. They then realised that in order to keep the profitable drug industry in Britain (a major source of income for the State) they would have to allow vivisection (which is used to enable drug companies to introduce new drugs onto the market without testing them effectively).

In 1997, when they trying to win votes, the Labour Party talked to me of a ban on vivisection. (The documents are available in some of my earlier books.) But the moment they got into power all the promises turned out to be lies. Under Labour the number of animals used in laboratories in the UK has risen. In 1997 it was less than 3 million. Today it is 3.7 million and rising steadily. The most recent figures showed a 14% year on year increase.

The talk of a ban on animal experiments was a cold-blooded, deliberate vote catching ploy. They would have promised everyone a trip to the moon if they'd thought that would have won them votes. But once they were elected the Labour Party did nothing.

Animals are now considerably worse off than they were before 1997. Hunting continued because the police bleat that the Act brought in to ban hunting is unenforceable (though they managed well enough to persecute Hunt Saboteurs).

Vivisection has increased and massive new laws have been brought in to outlaw legal protests and campaigns against vivisection. Peaceful campaigners are constantly intimidated by the authorities. Those who campaigned against vivisection are officially classified as terrorists. Indeed, anyone who opposes cruelty to animals is now officially classified as a terrorist too. Factory farming has increased and government hired killers go around the country slaughtering badgers.

There is no doubt that anyone who supports animal experiments is either stupid or crooked, a liar or a fool. But it is illegal to tell the truth about vivisection. Why don't they arrest me? Well, perhaps they will. Or perhaps they won't because they know I'm right and since I've been researching the subject for decades I know more about vivisection than the vivisectors or the people who support what they do. If they take me to court a judge somewhere is going to have to listen to me and the whole pro vivisection movement is going to look about as well founded as the Equitable Life pension fund.

Meanwhile, scientists will continue to perform barbaric experiments on several million animals a year. And, as a direct result, hundreds of thousands of human patients will fall seriously ill, or die, as a result.

Chances of the number of animals used in experiments increasing by 2020: 90%.

176. We Are Still Going To Be At War In 2020

It sometimes seems difficult to realise it, but we are at war. We have been at war since Blair decided to boost his personal marketability in the USA by sending British troops to invade Iraq (a country which had not threatened us in any way). The only weapons of mass destruction in Iraq were the ones we and the Americans took there. Former Prime Minister Blair claims he thought that invading Iraq was `the right thing to do'. The Yorkshire ripper is alleged to have said the same thing after murdering a series of unfortunate women in Yorkshire.

It seems likely that we will remain at war for many years to come. Lawsuits and wars are easy to start and difficult to stop. The war in Afghanistan is likely to make the hundred years war look like a skirmish; it will not end unless we are prepared to walk away and admit defeat. History shows that we will not win in Afghanistan. No invader (and that is what we are) has ever won there. Even if our politicians wanted the war to end (which they don') they would find it difficult to find a face-saving solution. And the Americans are so desperate to keep fighting that they are increasing the size of their army by giving citizenship to recruits. There are now 30,000 non citizens on active duty and 11,000 non citizens in the reserves. (Some even speak Arabic.) Non citizens can now apply for expedited American citizenship after serving one day on active duty.

Every time we (and our allies) kill another wedding party and bomb another christening party we acquire more enemies. We and our allies have spread thousands of tons of depleted uranium over Iraq, Afghanistan and the Balkans. It is the weapon of choice. It's waste material that is otherwise difficult and expensive to get rid of. Its use is banned by the United Nations. The fact that the damned stuff is toxic to the soldiers who use it is of no consequence to the armchair generals back in London and Washington. We're creating generations of hatred and generations of people who will do whatever it takes to kill us. The average wage in Afghanistan is a little over £1 a day (though Taleban fighters receive around £10 a day). In the last year or two the UK has spent around £20 billion on the illegal, wicked and pointless wars in Iraq and Afghanistan. And that's £20 billion on top of the normal defence budget. If we gave the people of Afghanistan what we spent on bombs, bullets, landmines and depleted uranium we would win their hearts and minds and save a good many British lives. But then that wouldn't give us any of the oil or help in the pro-Zionist war on the Muslims.

The wars we are fighting were sold to us as part of the war on terrorism. That was a lie of course. They are oil wars. We are at war only with the terrorists we dislike. There are many terrorists who have been accepted into polite society (think of the IRA, Nelson Mandela and many historic figures in Israel). Our leaders enjoy a version of Christianity which allows them to pick and choose the dictators they attack. They go for the ones who have oil or who won't do business with us but remain on good terms with the ones (China, Zimbabwe) with whom profitable relationships have been established. Ethical bond funds now shun UK government gilts and American treasury bonds because of the warlike nature of the governments involved. Thanks to our `leaders', we live in an unethical country.

Terrorists are now defined as those who favour or use terror as way of governing or of coercing groups of people. Naturally, this means that the Israelis are terrorists just as much as the Palestinians. It means that Nelson Mandela, hero of the politically correct, was a terrorist. And it means that Blair and Brown and their supporters are terrorists too. They have not been punished, and probably won't be, because these days war criminals are only punished if they are not on the same side as the Americans. As an aside, I have long believed that politicians who vote for war should have to fight, or send their families to fight, on the front line. That's what leaders always used to do in the days when leadership meant something. If the war is worth fighting then it is worth dying for. Leaders should lead from the front. Would Blair have invaded Iraq if he or his sons had to go and fight there? Blair claims to be a religious man but I don't believe he will ever have any real convictions unless the international war crimes tribunal can get him (or the police can firmly tie him into one of the numerous little scandals with which he was associated). It is heart-warming to believe, and to cling to the hope, that the loathsome, grinning Tony Blair could end up on trial as a war criminal. (George W.Bush will, as an American, probably be immune.) As it becomes increasingly clear that the invasion of Iraq was never legal, and that Blair took Britain into the war in order to please his American friends and guarantee some well-paid jobs after he handed the keys to No 10 Downing Street to Gordon Brown, so the calls for Blair to stand trial will grow. Blair's government lied about the reasons for the Iraq war so much that I started referring to him as Tony Bliar. The sub-editors at the newspaper where I was writing a column kept telling me that I was spelling his name wrongly. It took an age to persuade them that I was right and they were wrong and by then it had become something of a cliche.

Our wars were sold to us as wars on terror, being fought to protect us, but were, as everyone knows oil-gathering wars which had the added, very significant advantage of enabling governments across the Atlantic to terrorise their populations and bring in oppressive new laws which would have never been accepted in peacetime. Anyone who opposes the absurd `war on terror' is officially classified as a terrorist. Clausewitz argued that war is merely an extension of politics. Hitler certainly knew that. And so did Napoleon. Our modern leaders certainly know it. Terrorism, a branch of war, is used for political ends and politicians use war to manipulate, frighten and control the voters.

The wars will go on because they serve two purposes. They enable America to grab as much as it can of the world's oil. And they enable politicians to keep us frightened and willing to accept virtually any oppressive new legislation they want to introduce.

You and I might be overwhelmed with shame and guilt as our country bombs the shit out of poor nations. We may weep and gnash our teeth as Afghan wedding parties die, as Iraqi children die and as young British soldiers are brought back home in coffins, after giving their lives to fight a war they don't understand for a reason they don't know.

Politicians are different. They aren't like you and I.

Madeleine Albright, a horrible American woman, gave it away on the Larry King television show some time ago. When she was reminded that 500,000 Iraqi children had died as a direct result of American (and EU) sanctions, preventing the Iraqi people having access to clean drinking water or medicines, Madeleine Albright, representing the American Government said: `we think the price is worth it.'

After a while, wars become self justifying. Thousands of people have been killed and so we must continue or it would be an insult to their memory and a waste of much money. And so wars, which started for no good reason, continue. The original reasons for the wars were excuses designed (like a magicians stagecraft) to distract attention from what was really going on (the chase for the oil).

In March 2010 Gordon Brown admitted that he bungled his statistics and misled the Iraq inquiry on the budgets for the armed forces. (You could have knocked me down with a feather.) He told the Commons that he was wrong to claim that the defence budget rose in real terms every year since 1997. Brown also said he couldn't remember seeing the all important paper that set out the legal barriers to going to war. When asked about it he said he didn't recall seeing it. It was the paper which said that a legal justification for war would require incontrovertible and large-scale proof of weapons of mass destruction, and that the intelligence did not show this.

The wars aren't going to end in a hurry.

They are too useful.

The politicians, owned by greedy people, don't care about the cost (unless the money actually runs out and Britain goes bankrupt).

I suspect that the wars abroad won't end until the rioting starts at home.

Chances of Britain still being at war in 2020: 90%.

177. The Number Of Women In Positions Of Power Will Increase Dramatically

In 2009, across the EU, just 10% of big company board directors were women.

That's about to change dramatically as legislation spreads across the EU forcing publicly traded companies to increase the number of women on their boards.

The legislation has already been introduced in Norway and the number of women on Norwegian boards has consequently risen from 7% to 44%. Spain and the Netherlands have also passed similar laws (though theirs are not due to take effect until 2015 and 2016 respectively) and

France is about to introduce this soon-to-be-EU-wide legislation.

As always when discriminatory legislation decides who gets what jobs, women will become company directors because they are women rather than because they are good at what they do. (Just as women have become MPs because they are women rather than for any other reason.) What effect will this have on company successes and failures? No one knows.

This legislation will be introduced in the UK very shortly.

Chances of the number of women in power increasing dramatically: 100%.

178. Global Violence Will Continue To Grow

Thomas Hobbes pointed out many years ago that, outside society, man is a naturally violent creature. He was probably right but society has broken down even further than he feared possible, and the violence is increasing. I doubt if any society has ever known more violence than ours. And the extent of the violence is increasingly at a frightening rate.

Many commentators complain about films such as those in the James Bond series. Others complain about cartoons such as Tom and Jerry. The truth is that the violence in these films is not real. I believe (and have argued since the mid 1980s) that it is the violence displayed in programmes such as the BBC's Eastenders that does the real harm. This sort of violence (often domestic in nature) does far more harm because it is portrayed in a realistic fashion.

When the BBC first started broadcasting Eastenders some years ago I wrote an article condemning the broadcaster (and the producers) for introducing a depressing programme that would create misery and violence. I see no reason to change my mind.

There is another cause of violence in our society: the killing methods used to turn animals into meat are crueller than they have ever been.

New rules and regulations (guess where they came from) mean that animals now have to be transported vast distances before they are killed. Animals are crammed into lorries and taken on enormously lengthy journeys without food or water. The animals on the lower tiers of the lorries are constantly drenched with urine and faeces coming from the animals on the upper tiers.   You may or may not care much about the animals themselves, but the adrenalin surge in these animals is enormous. And when the animals are eventually killed the process is even more terrifying. The result is that there is a vast amount of adrenalin in their bodies when they die.

How much effect does all this adrenalin have on the people who eat the meat taken from those dead animals?

I don't know.

And I doubt if anyone else does either - though we do know that eating meat does makes people more aggressive. The meat sold for consumption these days is drenched in adrenalin because the animals who are killed to provide us with meat are terrified for hours before they die and their adrenalin levels, when are finally killed, are astronomical.

My guess is that increasing meat consumption around the world (particularly in China and the rest of Asia) will lead to much more aggression.

As meat eating becomes commoner in places such as China so the epidemic of violence will spread around the world.

Chances of violence continuing to grow around the world: 100%.

179. Smoking Bans Will Be Extended

The EU forced pubs to ban smoking. The result is that millions of people who used to enjoy a quiet drink and a fag at their local pub (where they doubtless had a chat with their mates and maybe got a little gentle exercise throwing darts) now stay at home. Because they are miserable and lonely they take booze and fags home from their local supermarket. And because both are much cheaper in the supermarket than they are in the pub they drink more and smoke more than they ever did before. And, whereas in the pub the only people who were exposed to their second hand smoke were other smokers at home it's the family and the children who get to breathe it in. So, once again, the EU has screwed up and caused far more harm than they've avoided. I've been opposed to smoking, and trying to persuade people not to do it, for longer than the EU has been the Common Market, but there are ways to do things that work and there are ways to do things that make things worse. The EU always picks to do things the way that makes things worse. They always mess up.

What I find particularly hypocritical about all this is that money from the EU has helped create the tobacco growing industries in EU countries. For years the EU supported smoking; subsidising European tobacco farmers with billions extorted from English taxpayers, and then encouraging the tobacco farmers to flog the stuff to natives in Africa. Don't anyone ever, ever try to tell me that the EU is a moral organisation that cares too hoots about people or peace. The EU's bizarre and irrational anti-smoking policies result in thousands of workers and diners shivering as they puff away on freezing cold pavements, catching their death of cold. It probably makes economic sense for smokers to die early without troubling hospitals. Much of the tobacco grown in the EU is considered pretty second rate and is, therefore, sold to African countries where poor people who have managed to avoid malnutrition (generated by the EU's agricultural policies) smoke it and get cancer and die.)

The ban on smoking in pubs (even among consenting adults) has meant that thousands of employees have lost their jobs. No one from the EU has bothered to find out whether the loss of 100,000 jobs in the UK in the last five years has resulted in more deaths from stress etc than the number `saved' by not allowing smoking in pubs among consenting adults. A report in the British Medical Journal showed that a 1% drop in income results in 21 deaths per year. It's fair to bet that on average most of the 100,000 have lost at least 50% of their income. Those working in country pubs probably find no replacement work. That translates into 1,000 deaths. The EU smoking ban is killing people. It is killing children and it is killing pub employees and since smokers who smoke alone probably smoke more and probably suffer from loneliness and stress as well it probably kills them too.

Now that the tobacco grown within the EU is sold outside the continent, I have no doubt that the EU, the modern home of hypocrisy, will strengthen the home grown ban on smoking.

My guess is that smoking in private cars will be banned next. Then smokers will be banned from smoking outside pubs and offices. Smoking in the street will be banned completely. And then they'll stop people smoking at home. And then they'll introduce special licences. Buy a special licence and you'll be allowed to sell the stuff. Buy another special licence and you'll be allowed to smoke it. And at some point they'll introduce huge fines for people who buy and sell the stuff. They won't put people in prison, of course. That costs money. They'll just keep fining people and charging them a fee to sell it or smoke it.

Chances of bans on smoking being extended: 100%.

181. The Scots (And The Welsh) Will Come Out Of The Depression Much Better Than England

In the run up to the May 2010 election the Scottish nationalists insisted that Scotland should be exempt from the cuts needed to pay off Britain's debts.

You can't blame them for trying.

But, for two reasons, this does show a considerable amount of cheek.

First, the financial crisis that has almost bankrupted Britain (and which might yet do so) originated in Scotland. It was two huge and badly run Scottish banks which caused the real problems. And it was Brown's determination to protect the Scottish electors from the pain of unemployment that resulted in those two banks being rescued with English taxpayers' money.

Second, Scotland has, for years, been receiving an unfair proportion of Britain's wealth. Why should it now be protected from the coming pain? Why should Scottish civil servants avoid the danger of redundancy or pay rise freezes? Why should the services in Scotland (already much better than the services in England) not be cut back?

If Scotland really is part of Britain then surely it would be fair for it to help deal with Britain's problems when things are black?

Of course it would.

But Scotland is different.

First, many of the politicians who rule Britain are Scottish, and have taken an oath to put Scottish interests above all else.

Second, the Scottish politicians sitting at Westminster, and representing Scottish constituencies have an entirely unreasonable influence over the whole country. Their votes are crucial. And yet they always put Scotland first.

Third, Scotland is determinedly loyal to the European Union. Many Scots still believe that their incredibly expensive Parliament is a first step towards independence. (It is, of course, merely a regional parliament of the EU.) They believe that the EU will enable them to free themselves of their link to England. This loyalty to the EU is constantly rewarded.

My prediction is that Scotland will suffer far less than England during the coming decade.

Chances of the Scots coming out of the depression better than the English: 100%.

182. Hospital Infections Will Become An Increasing Problem Within The NHS

Hospital infections cause more deaths, and more serious illness, among patients in NHS hospitals than among patients in any other hospitals anywhere in the world.

The authorities don't know why.

I do.

The problem is that the NHS is awash with people giving orders and short of people actually doing things. The NHS employs 1,500,000 people. Over a million of those are administrators and clerks who spend their days sitting in offices having meetings. They are very good at choosing biscuits and writing memoranda but they are absolutely useless at organising things. And, of course, they don't know how to run hospitals.

There are lots of people in the NHS with authority, but no one prepared to take responsibility for anything. NHS employees are trained to avoid blame. No one will ever accept that anything is their fault. And they always prefer to blame `nature', or `bad luck' or `circumstances' rather than bad management or poor work. The truth is that most NHS wards are filthy dirty. Nurses have given up nursing and no one on the wards understands how infections are spread. When a patient has a dangerous, infectious disease a notice will be put up on their bed warning everyone that they are contaminated. But no one working in the hospital behaves any differently. Time and time again I have watched clerks and auxiliaries walking in and out of rooms where infectious patients are being treated without any effort to prevent cross-infection. I have repeatedly spoken to NHS staff (some of them with specific responsibility for preventing infection) who have absolutely no understanding of how bugs move between patients.

And so I suspect that infections are going to continue to be a major problem in the NHS for the foreseeable future.

There will be lots of committee meetings held to discuss the problem.

But nothing useful will be done about it.

Chances of hospital infections being a greater problem within the NHS: 70%.

183. Killer Hospital Bugs Will Spread Outside Hospitals

British hospitals are the most dangerous in the world. And they are likely to retain this reputation for some time to come. Infections such as those caused by methicillin resistant staphylococcus aureus (MRSA) and clostridium difficile and necrotising fasciitis (aka the flesh-eating bug) mean that hospitals are dangerous places. A complete lack of understanding of the basic principles of hygiene among hospital staff mean that hospitals are going to continue to remain dangerous. Hospital staff either don't understand or don't care how infections are transmitted. Whether its ignorance or incompetence the problem is getting worse.

And there is a new, inevitable, horrible twist.

Some of the killer bugs that were previously known only inside NHS hospitals have got out and have been found in all sorts of other public places. They are not yet a problem. They could become a problem. To protect ourselves my wife and I now put plasters on even small cuts when leaving home. And, of course, we wash our hands with alcohol wipes before eating outside our home.

The chances of hospital bugs becoming a big problem outside hospitals: 50%.

184. Snitches Will Continue To Thrive (some are volunteers, some are pressganged)

We are in the age of the snitch, and the number of people who will report you to the authorities is increasing daily.

Bankers, accountants and even solicitors are now forced to tell the authorities if do anything that might be considered not to be in the interests of the state and state control. So, for example, these people whom you are paying for their services will snitch on you and tell the authorities if you move money offshore or onshore (for example because you have a holiday home in Spain); they will tell the authorities if you pay into the bank what they consider to be a large amount of cash; they will tell the authorities if you take out a large amount of cash; they will tell the authorities if you conduct any (for you) unusual financial transactions; they will tell the authorities if you buy gold. And so on, and so on.

They will tell the authorities about your business affairs because if they don't then they will get into trouble.

Oh, and they won't tell you that they are telling the authorities because if they do then they will get into more trouble.

The adviser whom you have regarded as your friend for thirty or forty years is now a snitch.

Like any bunch of fascists, the Government likes using snitches. They recruit them by using threats and bribery. Your neighbours are encouraged to snitch on you if you put your rubbish out on the wrong day or if you put an empty beer bottle in with your empty yoghurt containers. Your neighbours are encouraged to ring the authorities if they suspect that you are breaking the law in any way. They will be rewarded for their loyalty to the state with cash rewards.

For the State and its functionaries there is a triple benefit.

First, of course, there is information they obtain. The information about your private affairs enables them to bully you and threaten you. Information is power. When they have all the information, they have all the power.

Second, if you have done anything against the law (and since the laws are complex and constantly changing that is quite likely) they can fine you, punish you and confiscate your goods and money. The State and its functionaries (who are given bonuses according to what they confiscate) will get richer.

Third, and this is probably the biggest advantage, the authorities benefit by making us live in fear.

All this is, of course, already happening. It has been happening for several years.

But it will get worse. A good deal worse.

Whom can you trust?

Probably far fewer people than you think.

Your garage mechanic? I don't think so.

Your hairdresser? I suspect not.

Your doctor? Certainly not.

Your friends? Your relatives?

You alone can make that judgement.

And, sadly, it is a judgement we are now forced to make. The snitches are all around us. And, every day that comes, there will be more of them.

Even motor cars have become snitches – now that they are being equipped with computers which record everything the driver does.

Chances of snitches thriving: 100%.

185. Selfishness Is On The Increase

When Labour came to power in 1997 well over two thirds of the population said that they believed that looking after the community's interests rather than their own was the best way to improve the quality of their lives.

Today, after 13 years of Labour misrule, the number of people who believe that has fallen to well below half. More than half of all people believe that looking after themselves is more important. Most people are no longer interested in what they can offer to their community or their employer. They are interested only in what they can get for themselves.

Sadly, we are, as a nation, more selfish than we have ever been.

When you look at the example set by MPs, company directors, bankers, celebrities and reality television performers it is difficult to be surprised.

Selfishness is the new way of life and I suspect that things are going to stay that way for some considerable time.

Most people are going to realise that in order to survive the coming hard years they have to learn to look after themselves. Society is going to get tougher and rougher.

It's an awful thought.

But it is the society we are going to have to live in (unless we are prepared to emigrate).

Chances of selfishness increasing: 100%.

186. Children Will Continue To Be Abused (and social workers will continue to do nothing to prevent it)

Britain is awash with social workers. And yet there are more social problems today than ever before. What went wrong?

The answer is simple and can be summed up in two words: social workers.

Highly paid and full of self-regard, social workers would be acceptable if they existed and didn't make things worse. But they have and do make things far worse.

They have helped destroy the structures which previously existed to help the needy and they have replaced them with a professional, uncaring bureaucracy which removes children from caring and thoughtful middle-class parents (who, for example, make the `mistake' of questioning the value of vaccination) while allowing children to remain with cruel and wicked parents (who are suitably multicultural).

The result is that there will be lots more examples of children being abused and of social workers failing to protect them.

Social workers have always been an arrogant, humourless, patronising, self important and utterly useless bunch. They're good only at organising meetings. They serve no practical purpose whatsoever.

Here's a story which explains precisely why social workers are so useless.

One Friday evening, when I was a young GP I was called to see a young woman who had abdominal pain. She had advanced bowel cancer and needed to be admitted to hospital as an emergency. I telephoned the local hospital and the ambulance service and made the arrangements and then I hit a snag: the woman had two young children but she had no husband, no boyfriend, no relatives and no neighbours. What on earth could I do with the children?

I telephoned the emergency number of the local social services department.

After I had explained the problem the duty social worker said that he would leave a note on someone's desk and ask them to contact me on Monday morning.

`You don't understand,' I said rather impatiently. `I need help now. The two young children have nowhere to go. In about three minutes time their mother is going into hospital.'

`Can't you do something with them?' asked the social worker.

`I live alone in a small one room flat,' I replied. `And for the next 72 hours I'm on emergency call for about fifteen thousand patients.'

`Well I can't help,' said the social worker irritably.

`But the social services department runs all sort of homes for children,' I explained. `Can't you take them into care for a few days while we sort something out?'

`I can't do that,' said the social worker. `I'm on emergency call.'

`I know you're on emergency call,' I said. `That's why I called you.'

`I can't leave the office,' said the social worker. `If I leave the office there will be no one here to answer the phone if there's an emergency.'

I put the phone down and gave up.

When the ambulance had come and taken their mother to hospital I put the two small children into my car and drove round to a nearby nunnery. The nuns, who were my patients, agreed to look after the children for a few days.

I spent ten years as a GP. That was the only time I ever asked a social worker to do anything. It was the only time when social workers could have been useful. And yet several times a week I was invited to attend meetings and conferences which the local social workers had organised.

Social workers talk a lot. And they're good at meetings. But they're good for nothing else. The only thing that has changed since that Friday evening nearly forty years ago is that today's social workers are vastly better paid - with many of them `earning' £100,000 a year or more. (Naturally they enjoy short working weeks, long holidays and massively generous pension schemes.)

The social services sector has become a huge self-serving, ever-expanding business. The needs of the poor have been forgotten. That is why babies are killed by brutal parents despite the existence of huge bureaucracy designed to protect the innocent from the lethal. Huge amounts of money are poured into social services. None of it does any good. The main benefactors of the multi billion pound social services system are the middle class `liberal' professionals who earn huge salaries for attending meetings and writing reports.

Several decades ago I suggested that we would be better off sacking all the social workers and putting the money we saved into dustbins on street corners, together with a sign saying simply `Help Yourself'.

Chances of children continuing to be abused: 100%.

187. Television Programmes Are Going To Get Worse (much, much worse)

In the last three years there has been a 25% reduction in expenditure on programming content for British television. If you watch much television you probably noticed. There are far more channels than ever, but the money spent is falling at a spectacular rate. Money spent doesn't always mean quality, but it has an impact. We will never again see such wonderful programmes as `A Perfect Spy' or `Brideshead Revisited'.

All sorts of terrible things are coming. Product placement is coming. Actors and actresses will be talking a great deal about their favourite soaps/cornflakes/cars/perfumes in coming years. (How will the BBC cope with product placement in programmes it buys in? Maybe they will put little fuzzy patches over the products and bleep out the endorsements.) Commercial companies will be allowed to put far more advertisements into their most successful programmes, as they struggle to cope with the loss of advertising which has migrated to the internet. The BBC alone is drowning in money, suffering under an ever-flowing waterfall of the stuff.

As the number of channels goes up, as advertising revenue falls (and is fought for ever more keenly) and as there is less money available so reality television programmes will take over the schedules even more than they have done already. And the participants will become ever more exhibitionistic.

There will, have no doubt about it, be more reality television programmes (they are extraordinarily cheap to make) and the millions who spend their days and evenings watching television will suffer as they struggle to survive on a regular diet of intellectual rubbish. It's as unhealthy as trying to survive on a diet of nothing but cows' milk. We are already awash with celebrity chefs, cleaners, decorators, handymen, gardeners, estate agents. What madness this is. Celebrity cleaners? Who would have believed it. People watch this crap. Reality television summaries all that is nasty in Britain today. It's going to get worse. You probably cannot imagine how bad it is going to get. They have to shock more and more to gain attention, viewers and revenue.

Television, which offered such hope, such prospects, destroys children's imaginations and sense of wonder and fills them with a constant and bewildering mixture of superiority, invulnerability, inadequacy, anxiety and fear. Only a complete idiot would argue that violence on television hasn't encouraged violence behaviour in the streets or that sex education programmes haven't encouraged sexual experimentation by children with the resultant spread of sexually transmitted diseases and the epidemic of teenage pregnancies. The BBC, drunken with licence fee payers money, regularly produces and airs programme that revels in violence, abuse and antisocial behaviour.

Sadly, however, Britain who is now full of people who deny these obvious truths. These people are all members of a bizarre cult. We call them social workers or teachers.

We have become a country of bullies and people aware of their rights but ignorant of their responsibilities. Cowell, Robinson and Ramsey are perhaps the three best known, best paid performers on television. All are bullies. But no one seems to notice or care. People who watch too much British television lose their moral compass and get accustomed to nastiness.

Freak shows such as Big Brother are worse than those Victorian circuses which celebrated tattooed sailors and fat women. Today we glorify the woman who doesn't know where Wales is and revel in and laugh at her woeful ignorance. Television is a rich and rewarding playground for human riff raff. The alleged comedian who crudely boasts of his sexual conquests. The talentless woman who is famous for having huge plastic breasts, children by several men and living a train crash life in public.

I don't watch soaps on television but I bought a random sample copy of `TV Choice' at the end of March 2010. There was a section in the magazine headed `Soap Choice: The hottest stories this week'. This is what I found:

* Eastenders: Jack is shot

Kylie turns up at Lauren's birthday party, produces a gun and shoots Jack (intending to shoot Billie). Jack is rushed to hospital and Max collapses in shock.

* Coronation Street: Becky's agony

Becky has a miscarriage. An examination shows that she is unlikely ever to be able to carry a child to full term. A heartbroken Beck blames herself for shattering her baby dream. Plus, in self-destruct mode after Joe's death, Tina admits to Jason that she kissed Nick. Jason attacks Nick. David also slaps Nick. Jason gets drunk and has an accident at work. Rita books a date with a gigolo.

* Emmerdale

Ashley is traumatised after being assaulted by Sally, a crazed stalker. Laurel bursts into Sally's flat and, out of control, pushes Sally close to the edge of her balcony where she pleads for her life. Rumours circulate about Aaron's attack on Paddy. A frustrated Chas reports her son to the police.

* Doctors

Karen falsely accuses Sapphire of stealing. Sapphire collapses in the toilets and is diagnosed with Crohn's disease. Simon tells Will that he loves him. When they part one of the homosexual men goes home to a wife and child.

* Hollyoaks

Jake is arrested on suspicion of abducting a little girl called Holly.

* Neighbours

Donna's night of passion with Andrew is broadcast to everyone at Charlie's.

* Home and Away

Marily returns and runs over Aden's brother. Xavier leaves after seeing Gina in a compromising position with John.

All of these programmes are broadcast at times when young children can watch. A week or so later I noticed that three of the most popular soaps were running strong homosexual story lines. (Running homosexual story lines is a way for writers and producers to appear to be `dangerous' and `cutting edge' without any risk of there being complaints. No one in public life would ever dare about there being too many `homosexual' stories on television.)

The average child in the UK will have watched an entire year's worth of television by the time they are six. More than half of three year olds have television sets in their bedrooms. A 1999 study by the American Academy of Paediatrics linked early exposure to television during critical periods of synaptic development' to `attentional problems' and numerous doctors and psychologists now agree with me that too much television causes enormous damage to children's development (when I first argued this now fairly mainstream viewpoint, over 30 years ago I was, of course, dismissed as a nutter).

Attempts to compete with free American internet services providing stolen video (you and they know who they are) mean that British television is going to get crappier and more packed with advertising because as stations suffer more and more so advertising restrictions will have to be lifted

The medium will, increasingly, take priority over the message.

Actually, the message was lost years ago.

It's all about the medium.

Chances of television programmes deteriorating in quality: 100%.

188. They Are Going To Deliberately Make Us Feel Unsettled

We all like routine; it provides security, comfort and a basis for the other things we do; routine gives us strength, like a skeleton gives a body strength.

But they want us unsettled, nervous and wary. They know that when people are unsettled, nervous and wary they are unlikely to complain or rebel or make any sort of a fuss. Unsettled people are compliant people.

So they keep changing the rules and changing our routines. Just as we have got used to one set of rules they're thrown away and another lot are introduced. Best of all are the retrospective changes. Those really do unsettle folk. When you don't know whether what you did last year will or will not prove to be illegal next year it's difficult to think of revolution.

Chances of our lives being ever more unsettled: 100%.

189. VAT Will Rise And Rise Again

VAT is going to go up above 17.5%.

It might well not go up in 2010 or even 2011.

But it will go up to at least 20%, and probably higher.

I am sure about this for two main reasons.

First, raising VAT is the quickest way for the government to raise some of the money it needs, fairly and without completely screwing up the economy. Raising VAT cuts spending but doesn't discourage people from working. On the contrary, raising VAT rates actually encourages people to work harder because the things they want to buy cost more money. Taxes on spending, rather than income, are healthier and better in that they encourage productivity and economic growth.

Second, Britain has the fourth lowest rate of VAT in the European Union. (Only Spain, Cyprus and Luxembourg have lower VAT rates.)

The average rate of VAT within the European Union is over 20%.

And the European Union wants tax rates standardised throughout Europe.

Standardising VAT rates is the easiest and most obvious place to start.

There is also the point that VAT is a popular tax with fraudsters. (Fraud involving VAT costs an estimated 12% of VAT revenues across Europe.) The EU loves fraud. The whole damned organisation is built on fraud and thieving and trickery.

Since the EU now owns Britain, what the EU wants it gets.

So I feel pretty secure in saying that within a year or two VAT in Britain will hit 20%. And, over the next year or two after that, go even higher. The higher VAT rate will help raise money for the government and for the EU and for all those white collar fraudsters the EU loves to molly coddle.

Chances of VAT being higher in 2020 than it was in 2010: 90%.

190. The Number Of Rules Will Increase Dramatically (and many of them

will be just plain stupid)

On January 10th 2005 my father took his Skoda motor car to Pollits Devon Diahatsu Centre in Exeter for an MOT. The car failed and my father had to drive the car back home, make a fresh appointment and then take the car back to be tested again. Naturally, there was another fee to pay. The garage gave just one reason for refusing a Test Certificate. Here it is: `Offside lower windscreen has a sticker or other obstruction encroaching into the swept area by more than 40 mm outside zone A (8.3.1e).' The refusal form was signed by P.J.Spencer. The `sticker or other obstruction' was actually my father's cardboard disabled parking badge which he had left visible, propped up against the windscreen. My father was 84 years old at the time. I keep the form by my desk as a constant reminder of the world in which we now live. This is the sort of bizarre mentality which the system allows and expects. We all see examples of it everyday. It is the world they have given us and too many people are prepared to do their bidding.

I've fought for years about all sorts of things I believe in and where the evidence convinces me that I'm right - and it has been exhausting and largely pointless. The red tape becomes ever more impenetrable. There are several reasons for this. Most people have been brainwashed into believing that the system is right and that the politicians are doing their best and the bureaucrats are just doing their jobs. The people who still care simply don't have any fight left.

There are too many people with too much time on their hands now working as councillors and making rules for the rest of us to obey. Many of these professional second-class politicians are unemployed or on benefits. They pay no taxes. They are therefore protected from, and disinterested in, the consequences of their rule making. They make their rules not to improve the world but out of a sense of vindictiveness and to show that they can. We, being too busy earning money to pay the taxes to keep them in style, moan but do nothing about it.

Whole armies of people are employed solely to castigate, admonish, reprove, berate and scold. Adults are treated like children who need to be constantly ordered about, controlled and punished. Anyone who allows the authorities to know that they are sensitive or delicate will be exposed; once they smell weakness, they are like dogs: they go for the jugular.

The rules have become so absurd that a friend of mine (who, having sold his house abroad and returning to the UK was awash with cash) was refused permission by an estate agent to look at houses for sale because he was not on the electoral roll. Contradictory legislation means that another friend was told by one government employee that he must keep full records of all his customers indefinitely while another government employee told him, equally sternly, that it was an offence to keep any records of his customers and that to do so would be a breach of several pieces of legislation. The intrusive, absurd legislation never seems to stop coming. Employers are supposed to see (and keep copies of) their employees passports and birth certificates. It is against the law to pay more than £100 for something in cash. It's institutional madness. The people who devise the rules may have a row of Mont Blanc pens in the breast pockets of their Yves St Laurent suits but they're still men with pens displayed in their breast pockets.

A straightforward house application would have taken 8-12 weeks 25 years ago, today the bureaucracy has increased so much that a similarly straightforward application can take 18 months. A shopkeeper who wants to put a display table on a wide pavement outside their shop will face months or even years or expense and delays. An application to put an A frame sign outside a shop can entail lawyers, architects, surveyors and endless visits from council employees with pens in their breast pockets. Every form that has to be completed must be submitted with a cheque. Why do things take so long? It is because bureaucrats always make things last as long as possible. It is their way of making themselves appear important. And the whole system is geared around their professional needs (making them feel important) rather than the needs of the community (approving good building projects and rejecting bad ones).

Most people put up with all this crap because it is what they are used to. People will accept all sorts of nonsense if it becomes commonplace. Experiments have shown that five out of ten people will give complete strangers lethal shocks if they are told to do so by a man in a white coat and a firm, officious manner.

In our wonderful new world criminals get better treatment than victims and law abiding citizens. The people who survive most successfully are the ones who `know their rights' and have learned how to whine loudest; who expect endless support, who have no sense of shame and who are prepared to milk every ounce of sympathy you can.

A Government Minister recently said that all employees should have the right to demand to work part time. (The parents of children under 6, or disabled children under 18 can already demand flexible working - that's 3.6 million people plus 2.8 million who care for sick or elderly relatives who are entitled to work when and how they want to work) Fathers and mothers are to be given the right to 13 weeks of paid parental leave at any time before their children reach the age of five and paid paternity leave for new fathers of a month. These absurd `rights' are fine for government employees (no one will notice whether they are at their desks or on the golf course) but it isn't possible to run profitable businesses this way. The rules governing the workplace are now so complex, and cover so many aspects of life, that life is becoming intolerable for small businessmen and women. One reader employs ten members of staff and discovered recently that no less than six of them will be on maternity leave at the same time. He cannot find full time replacements but has to find interim replacements, who need to be trained. The original holders of the jobs can wait until later before deciding whether or not to return to work. About half do and half don't. Who knows? It is illegal to find a permanent replacement until you know for sure.

The system keeps creating rules and regulations, because it has to create new jobs for officials, inspectors and regulators and establish an ever growing and permanent need for more legislators and a bigger judiciary. Anyone who tries to run a business will find themselves forced into breaking the law or giving up. And the penalties are quite out of proportion to the sins. I received a document earlier this week telling me that if I fail to do something - I can't remember what it was - I will be liable to a £500,000 fine. It is as though politicians and administrators hated all small businesses and wanted their owners out of work and out of the way. Everyone with a little money has seen the system in action. The solicitor you've known for decades has to see your passport and your birth certificate and two gas bills before he can act for you. A solicitor I know told me that he knew the system was absurd when he found himself asking his own father (also a customer) if he had any identification. We all have to prove we are who we say we are whenever we want to do anything - however trivial. It is done in the name of security and saving the planet and preventing money laundering. But all this is smoke. It is, in truth, done to oppress us and keep us busy, quiet and frightened. A friend of ours who runs a shop nearly gave up his business when a council employee told him that he had to provide wheelchair access to his shop.

He did give up when council workmen suddenly, and for no reason, painted yellow lines outside his shop and a man from the council told him that neither he, nor his customers, not delivery drivers could park outside his shop but had to park in the nearest public car park a mile and a half away. He closed the shop and went abroad. The shop is now occupied by a council operated facility providing advice for drug addicts. It is hardly surprising that nearly everyone we know has now moved abroad - either to retire or to run businesses in countries where the bureaucrats do not live their lives with such obvious determination to close down every small business. A dentist friend of ours nearly went bankrupt putting in a lift so that patients in wheelchairs could visit him. (He didn't have any patients in wheelchairs because his practice was on the first floor of a small building, but that didn't worry the bureaucrats.)

We are attacked on all sides. Would be soldiers are told that it is good strategy to attack your enemy from all sides. It keeps them unnerved and uncertain and fearful. The bureaucrats have clearly been to military college. Their aims are also clear.

The rules are going to become dafter. More and more time is going to be wasted. As people try to drag themselves, their businesses and their country out of the huge mess it has been put into by Brown and his greedy and incompetent Scottish banking friends so the bureaucrats will continue to erect one obstacle after another.

Chances that we will be besieged by more rules (most of them daft): 100%.

191. People In Poor Countries Will Continue To Starve

People in poorer countries will continue to starve. Indeed, things will get much worse.

There has been much talk in recent years of globalisation, with the implication that as the world becomes a smaller place so the poorer countries will benefit from increasing international trade.

In reality the playing field upon which rich and poor countries play has been more uneven than ever.

Poor countries suffer because large companies (mostly American) are patenting their seeds, their plants and their heritage. If farmers want to plant seeds their ancestors have been planting for centuries they are now obliged by international law to buy them from an American company. Everything is being made worse because American companies have encouraged Indian farmers to plant genetically modified seeds. The farmers are told that the seeds will produce bigger crops and more profits. Sadly, this hasn't worked out quite as promised. According to the last count I saw around 125,000 Indian farmers had committed suicide because their had harvests failed, leaving them ruined and penniless.

Poor countries suffer because big countries (such as America and the UK) have decided that using biofuels will help keep vehicles on the road for longer, and delay the consequences of the coming oil shortage. The problem is that using crops as a source of oil means that there is even less food to go around in poor countries. And so people starve and die.

Poor countries suffer because rich countries (particularly the European Union and America) dump their unwanted crops in places like Africa. They sometimes do this for profit (selling their surpluses) and they sometimes do it as part of their `aid' plan (it enables them to pretend to be doing good things without actually having to give away anything worthwhile). When unwanted crops are dumped, local farmers (who often have to struggle with poor growing conditions) are unable to sell their own meagre crops and so they go bust.

Poor countries aren't financially strong enough to bail out their banks and so their bankers cannot take the sort of taxpayer funded risks that British and American bankers can take. The result is that poor countries lose any decent home-grown bankers (who rush off to Scotland or America to make their fortunes out of taxpayer funded banks) and cannot compete in the international market place.

The sanctimonious pop singers who love to pretend that they are players on the world stage and who so much enjoy rubbing shoulders with political leaders might one day acquire enough understanding of the way the modern world works to feel ashamed of themselves and their friendships. But I doubt it.

Chances of people in poor countries continuing to starve: 90%.

192. Public Sector Workers Will Continue To Waste Public Money

Public sector workers waste money all the time. Here's a small, personal example. Every year I receive a payment for when books of mine are photocopied. The sums can be quite substantial because a separate payment for each page that is copied. So, for example, if 6 copies of a 200 page book are made then there will be a total of 600 separate payments.

I'm not complaining about the money. It's mine. I earned it by writing the books. But what does worry me is that most of the photocopying is done by schools and other public sector buildings (I realise that this may well because only public sector employees actually pay the photocopying fees, because it isn't their money, but that doesn't alter the point of my concern) and most of the books they are copying are still in print and easily available.

That, for me is the killer.

Instead of spending a few pounds buying the books they need, these public sector workers spend vastly greater sums photocopying the one book they already have.

Now, however you look at it, that is egregious waste. It's a waste of paper, it's a waste of electricity and it's a waste of public money.

Just before the May 2010 election, Browns Government commissioned a report on government spending which found that the government was wasting £70 billion a year. Nothing happened. The government just carried on wasting £70 billion a year but now they knew about it.

That £70 billion that they have uncovered is, of course, merely the tip of the proverbial iceberg. Just about every Government department was wasting money as though it was going out of fashion and they were trying to get rid of it.

Take the Defence department.

In early 2010, current defence projects were an admitted £35 billion over budget and five years late. Moreover, it was clear that the equipment that had been ordered wasn't `appropriate' for the military's needs. The MoD was buying aircraft carriers and something new and zappy to replace the Trident missile system but what the army actually needed was more decent boots, more armoured vehicles and more helicopters.

As the three parties lied and promised and lied and promised their way through the 2010 election campaign they all promised to cut billions from government spending by eliminating identified waste. They could, they said, get rid of the massive trillion pound deficit (or however much it really is) simply by eliminating waste.

Why, in the name of everything, didn't they just cut out the waste as soon as it was identified?

And how did they come to waste so much in the first place?

I can tell you why and how they waste so much money.

It's because idiot school teachers and idiot bureaucrats are allowed to photocopy books that are still in print and leave taxpayers to pay their enormous bills.

No one cares because it isn't their bloody money.

And government workers aren't going to stop wasting money until a few thousand public sector wasters are fired.

They don't do that, of course.

Public sector workers don't get fired for wasting any more than get fired for being incompetent.

So, the wasting of public money isn't going to be stopped.

And we won't clear the national deficit by cutting out waste.

In fact, the wasting is going to get worse.

Because as soon as auditors stop one wasteful practice the people wasting money will find another way to waste money.

Chances of public sector workers continuing to waste public money: 100%.

193. The Rise And Rise Of Fascism Will Continue

Here are some of the things all fascist regimes have in common:

1. Enthusiasm for the state (for the EU, not individual former countries)

2. obsession with national security

3. Fraudulent elections with candidates being imposed on the electorate and questions being asked about results

4. A need for and identification of a lot of recognised enemies.

5. Huge military spending.

6. A contempt for the rights of ordinary citizens

7. Control of mass media and silencing of critics

8. The use of public money to protect corporate power eg banks

9. The transfer of money to large organisations (eg the banks)

10. An obsession with creating new laws

11. Giving the police unlimited powers

12. Cronyism and corruption

Many writers laughed at my book `Living In A Fascist Country' but I don't think quite so many of them are laughing now.

Chances of our country become increasingly fascist: 100%.

194. Food Is Going To Be Scarce, More Expensive And Less Nutritious

The Americans are burning food to keep their cars going so the global food shortage is going to get worse. The EU approves of, and is a keen supporter of, biofuels too. This obsession with burning food in cars and lorries means that a lot of people will starve to death, but bureaucrats don't want to be the ones to stop people using their cars. So food will become increasingly scarce and expensive.

In order to try and keep up with demand, farmers are encouraged to use genetically modified seeds. There is no evidence to show that these are safe but, hey, what does safety matter when there are big profits to be made? Farmers are also encouraged to use vast amounts of fertiliser and pesticides. Many even use hormones. Millions of animals are given antibiotics because it makes them grow more muscle. Some of the chemicals given to animals are carcinogenic. (That means they cause cancer in the people who eat them.) But no one much cares about that either.

Food in Britain is deteriorating in quality faster than food anywhere else because the food market in Britain is dominated by just four large supermarket chains. In no other country in the world is the provision of food in the hands of such a small number of people. The result is that the big supermarkets have the power to drive down prices and that inevitably forces suppliers (both manufacturers and farmers) to cut costs and provide poorer and poorer quality food. It is partly because of the fact that their margins are constantly being squeezed, that farmers give their animals antibiotics (to make them grow bigger muscles) and use vast quantities of carcinogenic pesticides and insecticides and other nasties on their farms.

It would, of course, help if consumers could understand what they were buying by looking at the labels. But the food companies don't approve of that sort of nonsense. So it doesn't happen. Indeed, anyone who still imagines that the European Union exists to protect individuals should consider this. When in March 2010 efforts were made to introduce colour-coded warnings on food labels they were defeated in a committee vote at the European parliament. Consumer groups, acting on behalf of citizens throughout Europe, had pushed hard for the so-called `traffic light system' because it is acknowledged to be the simplest way to inform Europe's increasingly obese citizens about the real nutritional value of food. Food companies would, if the legislation had gone through, been required to label the front of their packages with red, amber or green icons to denote the amounts of fat, saturated fat, salt and sugar they contain. A trade group representing food companies such as Coca-Cola and Nestle opposed the scheme, arguing that it would hurt them commercially and would demonise foods that contained a good deal of fat. They proposed instead a scheme keeping most nutritional information on the back of packets, in tiny type and far less comprehensible. The EU's environment committee sided with the industry. `We're very pleased with the outcome,' said a spokesperson for the trade group. I bet they were.

The result of all this is that you need a degree in mathematics to know what you're buying. For example, the label on a food item may appear say that it contains 2% fat per so many grams or meat balls or cheese biscuits, but when you look closely you realise that it says that the stuff it contains 2% of your daily allowance per little bit so you can get through a week's daily total fat allowance in the time it takes to turn on the digital television set and wait for it to warm up. (Why do digital televisions take longer to warm up than the old ones with valves?)

And what about the messages they put on food? The best before dates? The use before dates? According to the Food Standards Agency `best before' usually refers to quality rather than safety. Eat it after the date given and the food might not taste as good, might lose flavour or texture, but will still be edible. `Use by dates' appear on foods that go off and even if they look and smell ok could be dangerous. But `use by' doesn't necessarily always mean `eat by' because you can freeze it and maybe use it later. All this confusing, bewildering nonsense is, of course, the reason why the British throw away almost as much of the food they buy as they actually manage to eat. People don't throw away food because they want to, or because they suddenly decide they've changed their minds about it. They throw away food because they are worried that if they eat it they might die or vomit for a week or both.

None of this is going to get any better.

And if the food manufacturers, and their chums at the EU, have anything to do with it, things are probably going to get a good deal worse.

Just to add to the fun, eating out will be increasingly dangerous. This applies whether you have a five course meal for £200 at some overpriced restaurant run by a megalomaniac with a shiny teeth and a TV show or you buy a sandwich. Health and safety regulations and compliance officials will ensure that things will get not-so steadily worse. There's a hardly a sandwich or a salad served in the UK that doesn't come supplied with an extra portion of escherichia coli bacteria. If my princess and I eat out these days we take our own food with us. When restaurants allow customers to bring their own food (as well as their own wine) we'll patronise them.

Chances of food becoming scarcer, more expensive, less nutritious and more hazardous for your health: 100%

195. There Will Be A Big War In The Middle East (and there is a chance that Israel may disappear completely)

Israel was created at end of World War II when everyone was feeling guilty about what had happened in Germany. The Jews were given a big chunk of Palestine and allowed to call it theirs. If was as if the Tamil Tigers had been given most of Wales and all the Welsh had been pushed into a tiny bit of their country around Port Talbot. The Welsh would have been very pissed off. And if the Tamils had then repeatedly nicked more and more of Wales the Welsh would have become very, very pissed off.

Since its birth Israel has systematically and illegally colonised occupied land and seems to be doing so in order to make any deal with the Palestinians quite impossible. The killing of Palestinians has resulted in the bizarre fact that the median age in the Gaza Strip is now just under 16 years. Israel has put itself into a position where its future must inevitably be a bloody one. Israel's supporters in America are powerful, rich and vociferous but how long will America continue to defend and support (financially and militarily) a country which causes so much offence among countries which still control much of the world's oil? The Israeli habit of killing its enemies may be no worse than America's assassination policy but it still doesn't fit well with a nation which wants to be accepted. Cold blooded murder may be acceptable in a James Bond film but in real life it's morally repugnant and bad strategy. Israel's lack of ethics and disregard for international law is causing major problems. The activities of Mossad (retitled by some as `Murder incorporated' are increasingly regarded as unacceptable. Some Israelis seem to give the impression that they believe in racial supremacy and apartheid (where have we heard of those before) but others are embarrassed by much of what is said and written. The real battle in Israel is, perhaps, between the orthodox and the seculars, the Zionists and the pragmatists.

It is true that the Americans still object to any criticism of Israel for example - and inaccurately describe it as anti semitic. Anyone who criticises the Zionist lobby or the brutal methods used by the Israelis is automatically reviled as a fascist, anti semitic, racist and all the other popular politically correct abuse. But America's wealth and influence are declining fast and Israel now threatens to go it alone.

I suspect that Israel will continue to drag the world to the edge of destruction because Israelis believe (probably accurately) that their country's very survival is at stake and that they have rights denied to others. There is talk of `chosen people'. But why would God have a chosen people? And who would want to be the chosen people of a god who chooses?

For years now Zionists have been pushing America into starting a war with Iran. (`Go on Dad, beat him up.') but senior American politicians have already talked about the very real chance that the state of Israel may not see its 75th birthday.

The Israelis are going to do something even more stupid than all the stupid and selfish things they have done so far (and that is a list long enough to have embarrassed any bunch of thugs). With or without American approval, they are probably going to attack Iran. They'll apologise afterwards for the embarrassment. If there is anyone left to listen to them.

Some Israelis suspect that the threat to their country's survival may well come from the EU which is increasingly becoming a Muslim rather than a Christian country. The anger about Israel's behaviour isn't, however, confined to Muslims. Here, for example, is an anonymous letter I received from a British reader who certainly didn't sound as if his anger was based on religion. `Instead of blaming the world's financial crisis on greedy Jewish bankers governments are blaming people who borrowed money to buy houses. And they are demonising savers. All this is a distraction. It's like a magician using a pretty half dressed girl to keep people's eyes from his sleeves. The fact is that most of the bankers who caused the financial crisis were Jews. They are the ones who should be punished. But no one dares to say this because they are Jewish and no one is allowed to criticise Jews.'

It may not be acceptable but it has not escaped the public notice that a disproportionate number of the banks and bankers who were and are involved in the bonus-grabbing and sharp practices which have sent us all to penury seem to be American and of those the majority appear to be Jewish. This perception may be unjustified. It doesn't matter. It is an unspoken perception which is spreading wider through the global community, helped on its way by the obscene and unforgivable tactics of the Israelis. On a train journey recently I overheard two businessmen talking about the Madoff scandal. One pointed out that most of the people responsible for the financial crisis - the leading bankers etc - seemed to be Jewish. His companion agreed with him and then lowered his voice and, not realising that he could still be overheard, whispered that it wasn't a view he would dare to utter in public.

Presumably aware of this, in March 2010, an Israeli professor said that Israel had the capability of hitting most European capitals with nuclear weapons. `We possess several hundred atomic warheads and rockets and can launch them at targets in all directions, perhaps even at Rome. Most European capitals are targets of our air force.'

When he was asked if he was worried that Israel might be considered a rogue state he quoted former Israeli Defence Minister Moshe Dayan who said `Israel must be like a mad dog, too dangerous to bother' and added that `Our armed forces are not the thirtieth strongest in the world but rather the second or the third. We have the capability to take the world down with us. And I can assure you that this will happen before Israel goes under.'

The UK has put itself into an impossible position. Support for Israel's behaviour has exposed us to the justifiable fury of Muslims at the same time as our government (led by the EU) has been encouraging Muslims to pour into the country at such a rate that there is little doubt that within a generation or two the nation will be Muslim not Christian. (This is a perfect example of the mess we get into through trying to please America and the EU at the same time.)

The chances of a major war in the Middle East before 2020 must be 50%. The chances of Israel disappearing are 20%

196. Our Society Will Continue To Break Down

We live in an extraordinarily complex society.

A century or two ago most people, particularly those who lived outside the cities, lived astonishing independent lives. A family would draw its own water from a nearby well, cut its own firewood, collect its own kindling, grow its own food and rely for very little on the outside world. Clothes would be made in the home, or by neighbours. Furniture would be made and repaired locally. Rubbish, such as it was, would be burned or turned into compost. Medical aid was provided by a grandmother or neighbouring `midwife' or `wise-woman'. Citizens relied on themselves (and a big stick) for security. If there was a fire they carried water from the well and relied on their immediate neighbours for help. Societies were small. We knew the people upon whom we relied.

Today, our complex society require us to rely heavily on one another. We trust that the postmen will deliver the mail, the dustmen will take away the rubbish and the doctors will look after us when we are ill. We trust the railway workers to move us around the country efficiently and safely. We rely on supermarkets for our food. We rely on the electricity and gas companies for our heat and light. We rely on water piped to our homes and we rely on the sewage company to take away our liquid waste. We pay for these services as we use them.

And we have to trust the Government. We trust the Government to provide us with decent roads and to keep them cleaned and repaired. We pay taxes for these services.

But the whole system is hanging by a thread.

We cannot trust the postmen, the dustmen, the doctors or the railway workers to do what we pay them for. They do not take their responsibilities to us seriously. They consider only their side of the equation - what they get out of it. And they forget, or ignore the fact, that they too are dependent on others.

A delicately structured society, which has been built on trust and shared responsibility, is now dependent for its success upon millions of individuals who trust no one and who feel a sense of responsibility only to themselves and, possibly, their immediate families.

People who aren't getting what they want, and think they deserve, will go on strike at the drop of a hat. Moreover, people will go on strike if they think they aren't getting what someone else thinks they deserve. Greed is infectious and everyone expects to earn more next year than they did last year and to have a better standard of living than their parents enjoyed.

Society is now built upon entirely false premises and it is going to continue to crumble.

As Britain struggles to pay the huge debts built up by Brown so the distrust, fear, resentment and disappointment will spread and turn into anger and violence.

We cannot prevent this happening.

But we can be prepared.

Chances of our society continuing to break down: 100%.

The Author

Vernon Coleman was an angry young man for as long as it was decently possible. He then turned into an angry middle-aged man. And now, with no effort whatsoever, he has matured into being an angry old man. He is, he confesses, just as angry as he ever was. Indeed, he may be even angrier because, he says, the more he learns about life the more things he finds to be angry about.

Cruelty, prejudice and injustice are the three things most likely to arouse his well developed sense of ire but he admits that, at a pinch, inefficiency, incompetence and greed will do almost as well. He does not cope well with bossy people, particularly when they are dressed in uniform and attempting to confiscate his Swiss Army penknife. `Being told I can't do something has always seemed to me sufficient reason to do it,' he says. `And being told that I must do something has always seemed to me a very good reason not to do it.'

The author has an innate dislike of taking orders, a pathological contempt for pomposity, hypocrisy and the sort of unthinking political correctness which attracts support from Guardian reading pseudo-intellectuals. He also has a passionate loathing for those in authority who do not understand that unless their authority is tempered with compassion and a sense of responsibility the end result must always be an extremely unpleasant brand of totalitarianism. He believes that multiculturalism on a global scale is perfectly appropriate but that individual countries are best left to be individual. He regards the European Union as the most fascist organisation ever invented and looks forward to its early demise.

Vernon Coleman has written for The Guardian (he was a teenager at the time and knew no better), Daily Telegraph, Sunday Telegraph, Observer, Sunday Times, Daily Mail, Mail on Sunday, Daily Express, Sunday Express, Daily Star, The Sun, News of the World, Daily Mirror, Sunday Mirror, The People, Woman, Womans Own, Spectator, Punch, The Lady and hundreds of other leading publications in Britain and around the world. His books have been published by Thames and Hudson, Sidgwick and Jackson, Hamlyn, Macmillan, Robert Hale, Pan, Penguin, Corgi, Arrow and several dozen other publishers in the UK and reproduced by scores of discerning publishers around the world. His novel `Mrs Caldicot's Cabbage War' was made into a film and a number of his other books have been turned into radio or television programmes. Today he publishes his books himself as this allows him to avoid contact with marketing men in silk suits and 19 year old editorial directors called Fiona. In an earlier life he was the breakfast television doctor and in the now long-gone days when producers and editors were less wary of annoying the establishment he was a regular broadcaster on radio and television.

He has never had a proper job (in the sense of working for someone else in regular, paid employment, with a cheque or pay packet at the end of the week or month) but he has had freelance and temporary employment in many forms. He has, for example, had paid employment as: magician's assistant, postman, fish delivery van driver, production line worker, chemical laboratory assistant, author, publisher, draughtsman, meals on wheels driver, feature writer, drama critic, book reviewer, columnist, surgeon, police surgeon, industrial medical officer, social worker, night club operator, property developer, magazine editor, general practitioner, private doctor, television presenter, radio presenter, agony aunt, university lecturer, casualty doctor and care home assistant. Much to his (and probably also to their) surprise, he has given evidence to committees in the House of Commons and the House of Lords. Whether they took any notice of what he had to say is doubtful. They did not fall asleep.

Today, he likes books, films, cafes and writing. He writes, reads and collects books and has a larger library than most towns. A list of his favourite authors would require another book. He has never been much of an athlete, though he once won a certificate for swimming a width of the public baths in Walsall (which was, at the time, in Staffordshire but has now, apparently, been moved elsewhere). He no longer cherishes hopes of being called upon to play cricket for England and is resigned to the fact that he will now never drive a Formula 1 racing car in anger.

He doesn't like yappy dogs, big snarly dogs with saliva dripping from their fangs or people who think that wearing a uniform automatically gives them status and rights over everyone else. He likes trains, dislikes planes and used to like cars until idiots invented speed cameras, bus lanes and car parks where the spaces are so narrow that only the slimmest, and tinniest of vehicles will fit in.

He is inordinately fond of cats, likes pens and notebooks and used to enjoy watching cricket until the authorities sold out and allowed people to paint slogans on the grass. His interests and hobbies include animals, books, photography, drawing, chess, backgammon, cinema, philately, billiards, sitting in cafes and on benches and collecting Napoleana and old books that were written and published before dust wrappers were invented. He likes log fires and bonfires, motor racing and music by Beethoven, Mozart and Mahler and dislikes politicians, bureaucrats and cauliflower cheese. He likes videos but loathes DVDs. His favourite 12 people in history include (in no particular order): Daniel Defoe, Che Guevera, Napoleon Bonaparte, W.G.Grace, William Cobbett, Thomas Paine, John Lilburne, Aphra Behn, P.G.Wodehouse, Jerome K.Jerome, Francis Drake and Walter Ralegh all of whom had more than it takes and most of whom were English. What an unbeatable team they would have made. Grace and Bonaparte opening the batting and Drake and Ralegh opening the bowling. Gilles Villeneuve would bring on the drinks, though would probably spill more than he delivered.

Vernon Coleman lives in the delightful if isolated village of Bilbury in Devon and enjoys malt whisky, toasted muffins and old films. He is devoted to Donna Antoinette who is the kindest, sweetest, most sensitive woman a man could hope to meet and who, as an undeserved but welcome bonus, makes the very best roast parsnips on the planet. He says that gourmands and gourmets would come from far and wide if they knew what they were missing but admits that since he and his pal Thumper Robinson took down the road signs (in order to discourage tourists travelling to Bilbury on coaches) the village where he lives has become exceedingly difficult to find.

If you found this book entertaining I would be grateful if you would find a moment to write a review on Amazon.

For information about my books please visit www.vernoncoleman.com or see my author page on Amazon.

Thank you

Vernon Coleman

23480122R00300